NORDIC ARCHITECTS WRITE

"In sampling a broad spectrum of critical writing over the last eighty years, this anthology fills a major gap in our understanding of Nordic architecture. There is a refreshingly unspoilt quality about all of these texts returning us, all but incidentally, to the original socio-cultural tenets of the modern movement in its prime."

Kenneth Frampton, Columbia University

"Architects are usually known for their buildings, not for their appearance or personality. This book offers a selection of original texts by Nordic architects that enables us to become acquainted with the humans behind the buildings – to see their interests and how they expressed them. We can form our own opinion of them, as we are not dependent on third-party interpretation. Thus the texts can help to blow the dust off the old masters and free us from prejudices against the younger ones."

Simo Paavilainen, Helsinki University of Technology

This anthology gathers together for the first time the most influential architectural texts from the four Nordic countries: Denmark, Finland, Norway and Sweden. Many of the texts appear for the first time in English, making them available to a worldwide readership.

The texts were written by some of the most significant architects who lived and practised in the Nordic countries, who have both designed projects and expressed their thoughts about architecture. This book thus contains the architects' own views on architecture in all its scope and diversity. The texts were written between 1925 and today and cover the most important architectural discourses in the Nordic countries during this period.

Anthology with texts from Denmark, Finland, Norway and Sweden by Alvar Aalto, Nils Ahrbom, Uno Åhrén, Stefan Alenius, Jan Angbjär, Erik Gunnar Asplund, Aulis Blomstedt, Johan Celsing, Peter Celsing, Johan Ellefsen, ELLT, Ralph Erskine, Kay Fisker, Poul Henningsen, Arne Jacobsen, Jan Olav Jensen, Knut Knutsen, Markku Komonen, Osmo Lappo, Henning Larsen, Kjell Lund, Boje Lundgaard, Kirmo Mikkola, Christian Norberg-Schulz, PAGON, Juhani Pallasmaa, Reima Pietilä, PLAN, Steen Eiler Rasmussen, Leif Reinius, Eliel Saarinen, Wenche Selmer, Magnus Silfverhielm, Erik Christian Sørensen, Jørn Utzon, Tegnestuen Vandkunsten, Håkon Vigsnæs and Nils Erik Wickberg.

NORDIC ARCHITECTS WRITE

A DOCUMENTARY ANTHOLOGY

EDITED BY
Michael Asgaard Andersen

First published 2008
by Routledge
2 Park Square, Milton Park, Abingdon, Oxon OX14 4RN

Simultaneously published in the USA and Canada
by Routledge
270 Madison Ave, New York, NY 10016

Routledge is an imprint of the Taylor & Francis Group, an informa business

Typeset in MetaNormal and Joanna MT by Wearset Ltd, Boldon, Tyne and Wear
Printed and bound in Great Britain by The Cromwell Press, Trowbridge, Wiltshire

British Library Cataloguing in Publication Data
A catalogue record for this book is available from the British Library

Library of Congress Cataloging in Publication Data
Nordic architects write: a documentary anthology/edited by Michael Asgaard Andersen.
p.cm.
Includes bibliographical references and index.
1. Architecture–Philosophy. 2. Architectural criticism–Scandinavia. I. Andersen, Michael Asgaard, 1973–
NA2000.N68 2008
720.948–dc22
2008014902

ISBN10: 0-415-46351-3 (hbk)
ISBN10: 0-415-46352-1 (pbk)

ISBN13: 978-0-415-46351-5 (hbk)
ISBN13: 978-0-415-46352-2 (pbk)

Contents

l

Library

Acknowledgements

The editor and the publisher would like to address special thanks to all the people and institutions that have generously supported and contributed to this book.

The book was made possible by grants from:
Queen Margrethe's and Prince Henrik's Foundation
Bergia Foundation
BoligfondenKuben
The Danish Ministry of Culture
Margot and Thorvald Dreyer's Foundation
The Nordic Culture Fund
Realdania

Foreword

Steven Holl (written with David van der Leer)

Northern Lights

In Northern countries curtains of light; electrons from the solar wind rain down along the Earth's magnetic field lines. Their colour depends on the type of atom or molecule struck by the charged particles. Today these northern lights — the aurora borealis, historically poetic and mythical — are full of new meanings.

In this first decade of the twenty-first century thoughts go beyond the horizon and "beneath the skin". Where science remains essentially mysterious, daily phenomenal experiences shape our lives and set a new frame from which we interpret what we perceive. Throughout our world consumer goods propelled by hyperbolic advertising techniques serve to supplant our consciousness and diffuse our reflective capacity. Many things seem to work against architecture as a creative endeavour. Instead of an architecture of fresh visions for this new century, a business-driven, conformist-marketing-of-culture approach prevails. What appears are risqué skins, cover over generic plans and sections; while the pathetic words of blasé critics in major publications give us no inspiration. A fetishism of analysis is profusely illustrated but is disappointingly followed by banal constructions. Today the "depth of our being" stands on thin ice, and in the spirit of possible architectures at the beginning of the twenty-first century, reflection is urgent. It is such a reflection that this volume of writings by Nordic architects can induce in us.

We architects have several ways to generate and present thought. Each time I design a project, I hope to discover another dimension that I could not have foreseen when I began and although that differs greatly from project to project one constant factor is the relation between architecture and its site. In 1989 I wrote *Anchoring*; and all the work I have done since then relates directly to the thinking and the short philosophical texts in that book. Anchoring is conditional for beginning a work of architecture. Each site, each culture, each circumstance is an individualized beginning and must be considered in itself – a kind of limit. If an original architectural concept can get deepened, rather than broadened, it projects significance onto the site. It fortifies a locus of thoughts and a set of philosophical hopes, or even humour and stories, which are oblivious to whatever style it may manifest. It is not Postmodernism, it is not Late Modernism. Its meaning is deeply rooted in the conditions of its inception that it's unfazed by fashion.

When you visit certain regions of Norway there is almost nothing there. The landscape is incredibly beautiful. It is all wild with a magnificent quality of light. You come across the green grass and white wooden farm buildings, and all of a sudden there is a black thing, a church covered with tar. Inside the scent of old tar is

Knut Hamsun Center in Hamarøy

so strong that you almost smell the darkness of the church. It is the combination of this tar, the wood, and the darkness that creates an amazing feeling that is unique to these old Norwegian structures. When we designed the Knut Hamsun Center in Hamarøy in 1994 it was essential that the site – this desolate region north of the Arctic Circle, far from Oslo, far from urbanization – would play a very important role. Although the Knut Hamsun Center might resemble these churches when it is completed in a few years, it is not a church just because it is sheathed in black wood: it is a new and very modern insulated building. It is incredibly intense in every element, from its conception to the details; everything has a meaning in relationship to the problem. The center will keep an archive of everything that Hamsun ever wrote, digitized and accessible. Now that we have this digital capacity to hold huge amounts of information, the problem is that there is so much of it. There's such a lot thrown at you, that it is very hard to connect things that have plausible likenesses and tenuous connections. You need a certain solitude and silence and coalescence. It can happen in the authentic place . . . the unique site on earth, as I hope that the Knut Hamsun Center will become.

A consideration of the above, the careful deliberation of "anchoring", is not simply contextualism. I always thought that many in the modern movement worked this way but could not say that they did so because of adherence to an ideological credo which was "the common truth". I have been suspicious of any strict obedience to a past architectural framework: from the general postmodern dialogue to the characterization of the city as a typology, to the diffusion of various modernisms, to unduly positivist stands on the issue of structural expression. All the way down the line, I remained sceptical of these kinds of ideological constraints and have always felt that site and circumstance were far more important than any overarching "-ism".

Kiasma, The Museum of Contemporary Art in Helsinki

It is my view that we are faced with the charge of making an architecture for our time and I remain convinced that theory, such as the texts collected in this volume, can teach us something. Where theory is driven by some hope for meaning that is extra-architectural, it may also enable us to further the development of architecture itself. The texts in this book can be seen as a parallax of architectural theory. The flux of perspectives – the changing position of the narrators – allows us to define transformative thought into oblique planes of movement. It is almost as with a building: when you move, the space moves and everything repositions itself in a distance. Although the texts in this book are organized by country, the structure does invite us to choose and read the writings in an *ad hoc* manner. This selection of different critical perspectives may reveal changes in time that surpass location. Since it is impossible to discuss all texts from this book, however inspiring they each may be, I have chosen to cut a small section as it were through Nordic time and place. The anthology runs a full gamut between form and hope on one side, to a socially engaged and experiential architecture on the other. I would like to begin at the end of this section and criss-cross my way back through a voyage in space and time: after all that is a way to perceive history. From Juhani Pallasmaa to Uno Åhrén to Steen Eiler Rasmussen criss-crossing through Nordic architectural thought.

The temporal fragmentation of modern life; the destructive effects of increasing levels of mediatic saturation leading to exacerbated levels of stress and anxiety, might be countered in part by the distension of time through the experience of architectural space. To Juhani Pallasmaa, in "Space, Place, Memory and Imagination", our spectacular time, polluted with background noise, demands that we find the space in which to register and contemplate the past. The key to all this is collective memory: something that Pallasmaa taught me personally in 1993 on the occasion of our winning competition for Kiasma, the Museum of Contemporary Art in Helsinki. I was completely unaware as to the subtleties in the Finnish culture and history. Our building would deface the site of a Marshall Mannerheim statue. In my naïveté I had not realized that Mannerheim was the Abraham Lincoln of Finnish history until I was confronted with 10,000 signatures opposing our scheme. It was Pallasmaa, kindly collaborating with us on this project, who introduced me to the collective memory of the State. As he recounts here in his essay, he showed me that memory is more than merely remembering an event; he insists on the physicality of memory; to that we speak of our senses and organs as being a sensor susceptible to the passage of time. And while I never defined it as clearly as he does, I began to realize how important Mannerheim was to the formation of the nation. When I started to read about him I decided to go to his house and study the paintings he had collected. I went to his favourite restaurants; I ate his food, as it were, and drank his Schnapps. I tried to become Marshall Mannerheim so I could understand who he was and how we from the outside relate to this. This physical knowledge and phenomenal memory, enabled me to imagine how complicated the situation was from a local point of view and enabled me to address the local populace in their own terms.

The hope, expressed by Pallasmaa can be traced back to the humanized and experiential architecture of the mid-century, as described by Christian Norberg-Schulz, Knut Knutsen, Leif Reinius, and Steen Eiler Rasmussen. It was around 1950 that the latter two set the standard for an architecture based on direct experiences and tied closely to its site. In *Experiencing Architecture*, a seminal book that still makes it to the reading list for my graduate students, Rasmussen writes:

> When in a modern city you build a modern office building with a façade that is a faithful copy of a Venetian palace, it becomes quite meaningless even though its prototype is charming, charming that is, in Venice on the right site and in the right surroundings.

Architecture needs to be activated by human beings: without that human form it is meaningless. A few years earlier Leif Reinius had already drawn a line under high-modernism when he stated in his article "Architectural Experiments" that:

> we are attempting to crush the dogma of the straight lines, right angle and level surface. Buildings must not be restricted by any kind of formal system at all but should be shaped as integral parts of their surroundings and society. And this setting – this society – must be a living context. The main object of study is mankind: human studies, with psychology and physiology should be the main subject at schools of architecture.

It is through the writings of Norberg-Schulz and Knut Knutsen that the discussion is lifted from the single building to the constitution of the city. Christian Norberg-Schulz writes in "Order and Variation in the Environment":

> this is true, of course, not only for the building, but for settlements and also for the city in its entirety. It is the task of the architect to create a suitable frame around our way of life, not only a practical frame, but a frame that helps the individual and the group to obtain a psychological foothold.

This contrasts sharply with Uno Åhrén's "Turning Points" in which sociological aspirations are the primary point of departure although they rarely come to the surface. His focus as with many of his contemporaries remains on space and form:

> Our very attitude to life is in the process of occupying a new position. Our once over-whelmingly static perception now tends to be more dynamic. Increasingly we see the world as movement, work, change.

Knut Knutsen is one of the architects liberating architecture from this stylistic quest. In "People in Focus" he aims for an architecture that is built for the public and not for systems. Looking back on history he realizes that it is the freshness of his time that allows an architecture for ordinary people, and surprisingly ahead of his generation he already calls for a green architecture: "It is necessary to build in harmony with natural habitats and not follow pre-arranged programmes that are supposed to cover all eventualities. One should build tall and compactly, low and spread or protectively sheltered – everything based on the natural environment." Today this quote is a distressing inspiration, when the twenty-first century presents us with one third of the earth already developed – much of it in sprawling waste. I feel that whether at the scale of dense city fragments, or the rural landscape with the solitary house, a deeper, more comprehensive vision of us humans and the earth we inhabit is an urgent issue for architecture to address itself to. More urgent in fact than it was in Knutsen's time. A fundamental change of attitude, a re-visioning of values, must take place.

"In the society of the spectacle we can only marvel, not remember", writes Pallasmaa as he characterizes modernity as dominated by futuristic tendencies. He continues: "The appreciation of newness has probably never been as obsessive as in today's cult of spectacular architectural imagery; in today's accelerated life, we can finally only perceive, not remember." Pallasmaa makes me realize that today the absolute is displaced by the relative and the interactive. Instead of stable systems, we work with dynamic systems. Instead of simple and clear programmes, we engage diverse and contingent programmes. Instead of precision and exactness we work with intermittent crossbred methods and combinative systems. My principle these days is that of uncertainty with regards to the necessary relationship between traditional wisdom and our cult of the new. The power of "working with doubt" or suspending disbelief is fundamental for creative thought in science and in architecture. The dynamic and interactive are qualities of contemporary architecture that set it apart from the clarity of the classic and of the functional purity of the modern. We desire an architecture that is integral rather than empirical, that has depth rather than breadth; we desire an architecture that will inspire the soul. Working with doubt can yield an intrinsic affirmation of human choice that gives presence to an idea. A reflective architecture and reflective thinking can bring us an architecture of its time and place. Thus the selection of Nordic thoughts exported throughout this book can inspire us to reconceive received functions so that they come to fuse and flow within the open volume of an emphatic testimony; so that architecture today can in and of itself shape and inspire new feelings and meanings.

Steven Holl would like thank Kenneth Frampton, Erik Fenstad Langdalen, Juhani Pallasmaa and Per Olaf Fjeld.

Introduction

Michael Asgaard Andersen

Considering Architectural Writings

This book brings together a broad selection of texts, whose previous publication has largely been limited to the Nordic languages and a wide range of different sources. The texts were written by some of the most significant architects who lived and practised in the four Nordic countries: Denmark, Finland, Norway and Sweden. They are architects who have both designed projects and expressed their thoughts about architecture in writing. This book thus contains the architects' own views on architecture in all its scope and diversity. The texts were written between 1925 and today and cover the most important architectural discourses in the Nordic countries during this period,[1] from Uno Åhrén's "Turning Points" to Jan Olav Jensen's "Affinity".

It can seem both self-evident and conflicting to gather texts from Denmark, Finland, Norway and Sweden. Self-evident because these countries have much in common and often are considered a unified whole.[2] And conflicting, because the four Nordic countries each consider themselves to be distinct from the others. But regardless of how one looks at it, seen as a whole, there are many current and historical relations between these countries, also in the field of architecture.

Through its selection of texts, this book focuses on what leading architects have expressed to a broader forum about architecture and hence what they considered to be vital. Together the writings draw up the contours of Nordic architectural discourses, and more generally add to those of Nordic building culture. Drawing up these contours should not be confused with Christian Norberg-Schulz's desire "to examine what Nordic building truly is".[3] Since, as the texts clearly demonstrate, one can hardly speak of a *true* or just *one* way of building and writing in the Nordic countries. In that sense the aim of the book is clearly not to determine, but rather to contribute to numerous new discussions on building culture and architectural theory with reference to or based on Nordic writings. Evidently, only a few of the many texts that have been written in these countries are included, however the expectation is that this book can also serve as a gateway for one to delve further into the field.

With the advent of magazines especially for architects around the beginning of last century, a new forum for architectural discourse arose in the Nordic countries.[4] These new magazines were mainly targeted at the members of the architectural associations and dealt with everything from building instructions and product information to architectural criticism and debate. In a professional sense, the magazines embraced a wide spectrum with everything from crafts to architecture and city planning. The growth of these magazines in the decades that followed meant that architects to a greater degree had the possibility of expressing themselves in writing to their colleagues. As a forum for the professional exchange of views and knowledge, they had a great importance. Therefore, many of the texts in this book were originally published in their native language as articles in these magazines. Some of them were first presented as lectures and their verbal origins are evident in the way the arguments are built up and put forward. Other texts were chapters in books, previously unpublished lectures or articles in interdisciplinary magazines, representing alternative forums for discussions between laymen and architects. Several of the authors have also served on the editorial board of the magazine that they wrote the article for and thus have participated frequently in the debate over a number of years.

The selected texts convey significant positions taken by the authors, even if these positions were not always the most prevalent or popular. In addition to expressing their professional stand, the authors frequently attempt to point out tendencies for future architectural development. They do this through a number of different kinds of argumentation, from which one can discuss to what degree Nordic architects have particular ways of arguing and expressing themselves. Like most architectural writers, they discuss buildings from the distant past up until our time in both prescriptive and descriptive fashions, and the contemporary buildings are both theirs and others' projects. Some of the texts have the character of manifestos, where the authors with overconfident and dogmatic terms explicitly attempt to convince the reader about a particular architectural direction. But in most of the texts, the positions are communicated in more balanced and underplayed ways. Here the points can be implicit, but that does not mean that they are less significant. Despite the different modes of expression, each text is written with the clear purpose of marking a position, with all the qualities and shortcomings that entails. In a historical perspective, these positions reflect not only the authors' own views but also pivotal aspects of the debate of which they were part. In this way the writings give an invaluable insight into the architectural discourses of the time. As the positions in the texts are far from being unequivocal or indisputable, they invite continued study and discussions.

All the texts deal with questions that attract a great deal of attention in current discussions on architectural design, theory and history. Most often they are questions that the authors have been confronted with in their daily work, whether that was in an office, architecture school or both. Only in a few cases are they decidedly utopian. The authors express thoughts and beliefs that lie in the vicinity of existing academic and social currents, making them more likely to be implemented in the architectural practice. In this way the texts indirectly convey a hope for a gradual development, rather than a radical change in society. But also a conviction that architecture plays a role in this development and that a text can make a difference!

The Danish architect Nils-Ole Lund (1930–) wrote that aside from the Nordic countries there are:

> no other places where one can so easily couple architectural expressions with the developments in society ... The marriage between social engagement and professional quality awareness is probably the most important feature in the Nordic tradition. Our political and cultural history makes it natural for us to see a connection between form and content, between ideology and society ... Architecture is just as much about ethics as it is about aesthetics. [5]

He argues in other words that Nordic architects have a great awareness and engagement in society.[6] The book's texts invite a deeper discussion of this proposition –
and more generally of the tensions between society and architecture – as they display
nuances and oppositions to the common perception of a so-called humanistic architecture and social welfare model in the Nordic countries.

The differences between the texts are evident not only in the way they are
written but also, to a greater degree, in the architectural positions they represent.
Seen chronologically, several of them refer directly or indirectly to earlier writings,
theories and discourses that prevailed in the architectural milieus. This can be seen
most clearly within each country, where the texts from one period often are reac-
tions against earlier ones. Through pertinent critique of former currents, they
become part of the tradition and development of the country. Between the countries
there are similar references, including those to architects, buildings and magazines,
as it is the case in PLAN's discussion of the latter in "Our Agenda". The references
point to some of the connections that have existed between the Nordic countries at
the time the texts were written.

The texts cope with many different aspects of architecture, which are woven
into one another and together open toward new areas of study and insights. These
aspects are examined from various angles and can be organised in many different
ways, as their uneven reappearances indicate numerous breaks and shifts between
positions, milieus and periods. By first organising the book's texts according to
countries (alphabetically) and therein chronologically, it has been the intention to
provide an easily comprehensible overview from which multiple new readings
can emerge, not privileging one over others. Hence, the hope is that all or parts of
the book will be read across time periods and countries, according to one's own
interests.

However, if analysed in terms of where the texts are from, they are of course
not just related to the country of origin and other Nordic countries. Several of the
texts are undoubtedly inspired by, or assimilations of, foreign currents and movements, as is among others evident in the recurring references to Le Corbusier's work.
The currents which have been completely or partially rejected were not usually
subject to much discussion and are therefore only to a lesser degree mentioned in
the book's texts. The selected texts indicate how foreign tendencies were encountered and how receptive each country was for the argument in question, that is to
say, if there were a readiness to observe and interpret them. Although today some of
the arguments are best known from their originating source, the interpretations can
be reviewed with regard to the varying degrees of treatment of content by the
Nordic authors. As Johan Mårtelius notes, Stefan Alenius, Jan Angbjär and Magnus
Silfverhielm thus introduce the architectural theory of Robert Venturi and others as
well as show its parallel in the works of their country's own architects. In this and
other texts, the treatment reveals not only the authors' interpretation of contemporaneous currents, but also aspects of the building culture that they were registered in
and become a part of.

It is too often seen how the architecture profession is roughly divided in two,
namely those who are internationally oriented versus those who are occupied with
tradition, innovators versus preservationists, avant-gardists versus reactionaries. This

is a division that some of the authors share, mediate or react against. Despite the fact that it might be an easy way of organising the profession and its discourses, such division is both oversimplified and misleading, since it hinders deeper and manifold understandings of vital questions and challenges. Rather, it seems to be far more productive to consider multiple and heterogeneous correlations, whether it be in each text, between the book's texts or in reference to other (con-)texts.

In the correlations between the Nordic countries and the surrounding world, there obviously have been influences in both directions and in a number of cases this book's authors have put forth significant agendas on the international scene in their own time. Hence, Steen Eiler Rasmussen, Christian Norberg-Schulz and Juhani Pallasmaa have contributed successively over nearly half a century to the discourse on spatial perception and experience, which is also a theme running through their texts in this book. Norberg-Schulz's "Order and Variation in the Environment",[7] which is translated into English here for the first time, is furthermore indicative of a decisive but often overlooked transition in his thinking from *Intentions in Architecture* (1963) to his ensuing books in the 1970s.[8]

More than just offering an opportunity for studies on the correlations between various writings, the texts also open for considerations on many other pivotal aspects of architecture, such as their influence on design processes and the built environment.

A part of almost every architect's work, to one degree or another, is to write. In the offices this is often limited to writing building specifications, corresponding with collaborators and keeping the minutes of a meeting. In addition to this, there is an increasing use of computer scripting in connection with three-dimensional project work, parametric design and interactive building components. At the architecture schools there is a quite different form of writing among the teachers. As a natural extension of lecturing and drawing-board tutoring, writing is a way to present the acquired experiences and insights. Most of the book's authors have been part of an academic environment and thereby to varying degrees have developed as architectural writers or lecturers. However, it has not necessarily been an obvious call for them to write and lecture about architecture.

One of the reasons that it has not been so – aside from the fact that it was not their primary activity as architects – is related to the question of so-called tacit knowledge. There have been countless connections between offices and architecture schools in the Nordic countries. This has meant that there have been close ties and consequently a great exchange between designing and teaching. Notwithstanding the considerable difference between the countries' schools, it has been common that the educations have to a greater degree been oriented toward the technical and artistic sides of the profession rather than the decidedly theoretical. For while there have been talented architectural writers, a broad and established tradition in the Nordic countries to theorise about architecture has not developed, at least not until recent years. Rather, there seems to have been a general confidence in tacit knowledge among architects and only a relatively small number have deliberately tried to challenge that in writing. The authors represented in this book are among these few architects, who have not been satisfied with unexplored tacit knowledge and therefore counteracted the general confidence.

While there may not have been a broad theoretical tradition, there has certainly been a great degree of continuity within the faculty of each school, which is partially because of the small number of schools and the limited exchange of teachers. Thus, one generation has taught the next, who has then taken over and so on. By comparing texts of writers at the same school incremental transitions rather than actual oppositions in their standpoints are prevalent. In spite of this continuity there are of course breaks and confrontations, even though they are usually more understated than what is common in many other countries. This is yet another reason that the texts in this book as a whole display different contours than those characterising countries with other academic environments and traditions.

However, due in part to the linguistic, cultural and geographical proximities between the Nordic countries, there are exchanges in the field of architecture on many other levels, of which the following are some brief examples. One example, which counteracts the conditions described above, is in the area of education where Nordic citizens in recent decades have had the opportunity of studying free of charge at universities (including schools of architecture) in the other Nordic countries. Another example is the exchange within and between political, cultural and commercial organisations associated with architecture, such as the Nordic Building Forum that through conferences and publications for many decades provided a place for the interchange of knowledge and products for the building trade.[9] A third example is the joint buildings, which include Sverre Fehn's Nordic exhibition pavilion in Venice, Berger and Parkkinen's master plan for the Nordic embassies in Berlin and James Stewart Polshek's Scandinavia House in New York.[10] But these are just a fraction of what constitute the formal public and private networks within architecture in the Nordic countries.

In addition there are the many informal collaborations and networks among the architects. These are being established in many different fashions; one way is in the offices where personal acquaintances are made. Such acquaintances were to a great extent made in the architecture milieus that during the Second World War arose in Stockholm. Here architects from all over Sweden and the other Nordic countries went to work.[11] At the office of Paul Hedqvist (1895–1977) – who had collaborated with Erik Gunnar Asplund, Uno Åhrén and several other architects on the Stockholm Exhibition in 1930 – worked Arne Korsmo from Norway,[12] Haldor Gunnløgsson and Jørn Utzon from Denmark, as well as Folke Björk, Peter Celsing and Carl Nyrén from Sweden.[13] After the war they all made important contributions in the formulation of the coming decade's architecture in their home countries. The personal acquaintances obviously reach far beyond the Nordic countries to academic and professional milieus around the world. Together the informal and formal networks point to exchanges between traditions and through generations, as it can be traced in the texts.

The authors' and others' buildings have not only influenced their writing, but in return these texts have also influenced their own and others' buildings. To express oneself in writing, has provided each author an additional way of developing and working with architecture. Furthermore, publishing the texts has allowed them to advance their viewpoints in a public realm. By giving words to their thoughts, the authors have been able to critically reconsider the profession and their own practice. Or put differently, writing has been a tool to reflect on designing and hence to progress with both. With a combined knowledge from many different areas of the profession, the texts give rise to questions about the different kinds of practice as well as the relationships between drawing and writing.

The act of drawing is usually considered to be the architect's primary mode of expression, whereas writing has often been reduced to just theory. This notion separates design and theory, which results in an insufficient degree of mutual discussion and thereby a lack of influence on each other. A way to overcome this separation conceptually is to argue that "theory itself is a practice: that is to say, a set of activities and procedures with a specific language and a known set of protocols"[14] as Stan Allen has expressed it. Thus one can say that drawing and writing are simply different kinds of practice in the field of architecture. While recognising differences and similarities between them, this approach offers better opportunities for these and other kinds of practice to form productive interrelationships.

With both drawing and writing, architects have the possibility of transforming expressed and tacit knowledge to new visions, i.e. to allow creative processes to emerge by thinking and doing through the work, regardless whether making sketches, models, notes or (manu-)scripts. In many of the book's texts, one can sense that such a process has taken place. Here known and accepted notions are shifted, developed and renewed. The authors thus contribute to change the tradition and construct new visions.

The authors' visions fan out in many different directions within the field of architecture, often starting with the questions at hand and in the scale of the building. Many of the visions are aimed at political and social goals, technological and environmental goals as well as artistic goals. In most cases, selected aspects of these and other goals are all included in the authors' overall visions. Despite the fact that it can be expedient to separate these aspects in order to study them closer, they are interdependent and often tightly woven together in the texts, just as they should be in buildings.

The matters that are discussed in each text are suggestive of what is important to the author's architectural practice as a whole. That enables one to consider what the connections are between the various parts of the practice as well as how and why these connections occur – or do not occur. The commonly accepted notion that in many architects' work there can be quite a distance between the different parts of the practice is thus challenged. Although the relations between for example a building (or a photograph of one) and a book (or a text from one) are not necessarily as straightforward as a visual juxtaposition could imply, it could be one of several ways to think about the tensions between them.

While some of the texts by themselves are attempts to formulate answers and solutions, the aim of collecting them in this book is to provide the opportunity of raising new questions and reformulate known questions in new ways. A few of the authors' texts stand out as manifestos, but as earlier noted most of them express their visions in a subtle fashion with undemonstrative terms and phrases, which hold potentials for rich and copious explications. These latent opportunities should be allowed to emerge in new contexts. And even if they are contexts that they were not meant to be a part of, there is nothing to prohibit them for being so. By setting them into new and unexpected relationships, the texts remain not just historical testimonies, but open for new possibilities in the creative processes.

The questions and relations that are raised in this introduction provide some suggestions to ways of reading and working with the texts. Many of them are further discussed and elaborated in the other introductory essays. These essays put the subsequent writings in perspective and offer a condensed account of the predominant architectural discourses in each country. In addition hereto, the introductory essays bring up a number of more specific questions regarding various aspects of the countries' writing and building culture. They thus set forth paths for further studies of Nordic architecture.

As stated initially, the aim of the book has been to make Nordic architectural writings more accessible by collecting and translating a broad selection of texts. Hence, it does not represent an attempt to determine a specific reading of Nordic discourses or buildings, nor to establish a complete canon. On the contrary, the book is an invitation to further critical and creative work with the questions brought forward in the texts. Or as one might have written if it had been a manifesto: Use it or lose it! It is an invitation to relate these texts to aspects of our physical environment and everyday life. An invitation to unfold potentials and latencies therein. To read and sense, as well as to draw, model and write; in other words, to learn and to make.

NOTES

1   On the decades leading up to this period, see for example Steen Eiler Rasmussen, *Nordische Baukunst*, Berlin: Verlag Ernst Wasmuth, 1940; Simo Paavilainen (ed.), *Nordic Classicism 1910–1930*, Helsinki: Museum of Finnish Architecture, 1982; and Lucy Creagh, Helena Kåberg and Barbara Miller Lane (eds), *Modern Swedish Design: Three Founding Texts*, New York: Museum of Modern Art, forthcoming, 2008.

2   Together they are often termed "Scandinavia", which narrowly speaking refers only to Denmark, Norway and Sweden. In other contexts, different definitions are used of both Scandinavia and Nordic, as can be seen in Ralph Erskine's text in this book.

3   Christian Norberg-Schulz, *Nightlands*, first published in Norwegian in 1993, Cambridge, MA: MIT Press, 1996, p. vii.

4   The Danish *Arkitekten* was established in 1898, the Swedish *Teknisk Tidskrift. Arkitektur och dekorativ konst* in 1901, the Finnish *Arkitekten* in 1903 and a bit later, the Norwegian *Byggekunst* in 1919. For an analysis of the development of these magazines, see the issues published in connection with their 100-year anniversaries: *Arkitekten* 23 and 24, 1998; *Arkitektur* 4, 2001; and *Arkkitehti* 2, 2003.

5   Nils-Ole Lund, *Nordisk Arkitektur*, Copenhagen: Arkitektens Forlag, 1991, p. 17.

6   For a more general introduction to Nils-Ole Lund's literary works see Kim Dircknick-Holmfeld *et al.* (eds), *At Fortælle Arkitektur. Et festskrift til Nils-Ole Lund*, Copenhagen: Arkitektens Forlag, 2000.

7   For an account of Norberg-Schulz's authorship, see Guttorm Fløistad *et al.* (eds), *Christian Norberg-Schulz. Et festskrift til 70-årsdagen*, Oslo: Norsk Arkitekturforlag, 1996.

8   Christian Norberg-Schulz, *Intentions in Architecture*, Oslo: Universitetsforlaget, 1963; *Existence, Space and Architecture*, London: Studio Vista, 1971; *Meaning in Western Architecture*, London: Studio Vista, 1975; and *Genius Loci*, first published in Italian in 1979, London: Academy Editions, 1980.

9   On the Nordic Building Forum see www.nordicbuilding.org.

10 There are several publications about each of these buildings, for the latter two see also www.nordicembassies.org and www.scandinaviahouse.org.

11 Finn Monies and Karen Zahle, *Tiden i Stockholm*, Copenhagen: Arkitektens Forlag, 1999.

12 Arne Korsmo was the leader of PAGON, see Christian Norberg-Schulz, *The Functionalist Arne Korsmo*, Oslo: Universitetsforlaget, 1986, pp. 70-2.

13 Carl Nyrén, . . . *som krokigt skall bli*, Haderslev: Anders Nyborg Privattryck, 1990, p. 15.

14 Stan Allen, *Practice. Architecture, technique and representation*, Amsterdam: G+B Arts, 2000, p. xvi.

Danish Introduction

Christoffer Harlang

Negotiating with the Surrounding Society

Is everybody who works with architecture fascinated by tales about its genesis? Has everybody experienced the sensation of being utterly captivated by descriptions of all the wonderful mechanics lying behind the creative processes involved in bringing forth the work? Even the slightest veil that is drawn aside for purposes of revealing the mental and physical processes propelling the architectural work toward its realization is alluring to the gaze. Because many designers surround their creative work with a certain element of secrecy, its mystique is heightened and the sense of curiosity is intensified. When these few and sporadic flashes of insight take hold of you, it is presumably because while in the midst of the solitude of the process of Gestalting, it can be very encouraging and very inspiring to know something about other artists' ruminations. What kinds of difficulties might they have been facing? What inroads, shortcuts and detours were they familiar with in the demanding process that is involved in getting the intention and the materiality to *work* in architecture? How in the world did the master architect accomplish that? What could have been going through the creator's head as the work was coming into being?

Despite a certain consensus about the premise which has for centuries established the basis of our work as architects, we often run up against an element of mysticism or the supernatural when we move more specifically into the formulations that are attached, often in the form of intellectual rationalizations-after-the-fact, to the process and the powers that have borne forth a particular creation. When it comes to international architecture of the twentieth century, what we see is that this manifests itself sporadically in the form of proper poetics, that is to say, in the form of accounts of an artistic method, describing architecture's *modus operandi*. And in asking the architects about what might have conceptually and mentally been taking place while sketching out the project or in statements they might have left behind regarding intention and process, we come upon the problem that it is more the exception than the rule that the architect expresses him/herself through anything other than his/her work. It is a situation that characterizes twentieth-century Nordic architecture as well as being generally true – with exceptions, of course – of the twentieth century's international architecture that architects are considerably more restrained when it comes to making statements about their work's own genesis than, for example, the same epoch's visual artists, musicians or writers. Accordingly, it is no accident that in the discourse surrounding Danish architecture, examples of architecture's objectives and formal manifestations are only given here and there. On the other hand, as we will come to see, the discussion about architecture as a negotiation with the surrounding society and especially with its social and technical development, occupies a considerable portion of what the most prominent Danish architects have been writing in the twentieth century.

The Finnish architect Juhani Pallasmaa, who has turned his attention on several occasions toward the conceptual and the instinctive in architecture has written somewhere about the artist's suspicious attitude about intellectual analysis. He quotes the renowned sculptor Henry Moore as saying that it can quite simply be counterproductive for an artist to speak or to write about how his/her own work has come into being since this releases certain tensions that are necessary to his/her work:

> In trying to express his objectives with coherent logical precision, he can easily become a theoretician, whose concrete works merely amount to a confined exhibition of the complex of ideas that are being developed solely by virtue of logic and words.[1]

According to Juhani Pallasmaa, the architect profession is split in the present day between, on the one side, the pragmatists' almost hostile attitude to theories and reflections and, on the other, the theoreticians' blind faith in the notion that theories and reflections are necessary conditions for being able to create any meaningful architecture at all. "As a consequence of this fissure, architecture has come to evolve in the manner of an instrumentalised construction that is devoid of poetic content or a pure medium for reflective philosophical and conceptual proposals."[2] However, even though Pallasmaa's characterization is highly applicable to a great part of international architectural production, it can hardly be termed symptomatic for all of Danish architecture that extends from the modern breakthrough at the end of the 1920s to the present day.

Moreover, in Pallasmaa's line of thinking, theory and design inform each other mutually and just as all outstanding architecture is a product of serious and precise thinking, the intellectual approach in many of the texts has come about by and large *through* the medium of architecture. This is well worth remembering at a time in history when our architecture schools in Denmark are letting themselves be seduced – out of blind faith in the universities' scientific research traditions – into relinquishing a specifically architectural kind of research, which has been based on our own culture and methodology and which has played a part in carrying Danish architecture into a position of great prominence.

As a matter of fact, the education of architects in Denmark has not historically been a part of the university-like educational milieu but has been more closely affiliated with a part of the Beaux Arts tradition – in its origins, an artistically based institution of continuing education for craftsmen – and accordingly it is, then, an education that is based more on *skill* than on *knowledge*. The educational background and especially the self-awareness with which Danish architects have met the craft during the twentieth century is, among other things, consequently more akin to the culture they are connected with through the craftsmen's taciturn knowledge than the polytechnic educational and research tradition in which their Nordic colleagues in Sweden, Norway and Finland are steeped.

In our conception of us as Danes it is precisely the mastery of substance and form that stands as a distinctive and salient characteristic. Nowhere else can this mastery

be seen unfurled with greater empathy and precision than in Carl Petersen's works –
those that he built as well as those that he penned. His background as a ceramist provided him with insights and experiences that he succeeded in putting into words in
the two legendary articles, "Textures" and "Contrasts", dating respectively from
1919 and 1920.[3] Still today, these articles stand as shining examples of how the
reciprocity between the hand's intelligence and the eye's formative activity can be
charted out as subtle insights – and charted out, we must note, with extensive
relevance to contemporary design proposals.

The young architect Poul Henningsen reached out and grabbed hold of these
insights. As a matter of fact, it was Carl Petersen's sense about the connection
between light and substance on which Henningsen based his groundbreaking work
with exposing the illumination of the incandescent lamp in graduated intensities.[4]
Poul Henningsen, or "PH" as he started to call himself – under the influence of the
modern era – was the new day's architect. He directed all his attention toward his
own time's currents and he remained focused on confronting problem complexes
related to the society of his day – a perfectly devised and modern way of thinking. In
the middle of the 1920s, PH set his mind to the task of solving – once and for all –
the design of the modern filament-bulb lamp. In addition, PH threw himself with a
great deal of eagerness, and with somewhat fluctuating degrees of success, into a
number of building projects. But above and beyond being the progenitor of the
ingenious and world-renowned PH-lamp, Henningsen is known primarily as a
culture critic and strong voice in the society. He left behind an extensive body of
written work, with society-related critical texts taking on topics that span the gamut
of aesthetic, social, psychological and political conditions. He was especially passionate about freedom of expression and about the emancipation of the modern secular-
ized human being, a topic that has renewed relevance when we come to think about
the current political situation in Denmark.

PH was caught up in the debate about society early on and seeing that the PH-
lamp quickly became a commercial success, he himself, already in 1926, came to be
independently wealthy to such an extent that he was able to publish his own culture-
critical periodical, *Kritisk Revy*, which he edited until 1928. To help with editing the
Kritisk Revy, Henningsen enlisted the aid of a select élite of cultural luminaries in
the fields of visual art, music and literature. The periodical with the modest format
had great ambitions and even carried on international contacts with people like Alvar
Aalto, who dispatched articles from Finland to PH's magazine. The greater part of
the articles, however, were authored by PH himself and accordingly, the piece that
ushers in the present anthology's Danish section, "Tradition and Modernism",
offers an accurate representation of the urgent questions that were being raised by
the architecture- and culture-critique in Denmark as we move toward the end of the
1920s. How are we going to address ourselves to the modern architecture and, along
with this question, what are we going to do with respect to our own tradition? In
Denmark, two years earlier, reporters had been sent to Paris by the periodical,
Arkitekten, to review Le Corbusier's contribution to the world exposition and these
critics had called his work a "pure bluff". Basically, the prevailing attitude among
Danish architects when it came to evaluating the new architecture that was being
launched on foreign soil was, to put it mildly, sceptical. This was aggravated further

by the fact that many of the people who were players in the Central European avant-garde were busy clearing the slate of what they regarded as being tradition's hopelessly outdated set of values. What they were advocating was *tabula rasa*.

In Denmark, the younger generation of architects had been searching during the years leading up to this time for a more constructive and delicately shaded critique and they had been busy drawing distinctions between what could be used and what would have to be left by the wayside in the process of what was rapidly becoming modernism's assimilation into the Danish tradition. PH's article can thus be read as an expression for what was a generally widespread attitude in Denmark, namely that the strongest position to assume was that of addressing oneself critically to the new epoch's architecture as well as to one's own tradition. When we compare this piece with the rest of PH's body of writings, what is extraordinary is that it is especially the *aesthetic* challenges in the new architecture to which PH turns his gaze. What PH is chiefly concerned with is that the new day's social and technical problems are going to call for a new aesthetic culture. He thus aligns himself with a large number of his contemporaries who were participants in the Central European avant-garde, ranging from De Stijl in the Netherlands through Le Corbusier in France to the Bauhaus in Germany. Completely in synch with PH, Oskar Schlemmer, who was a teacher at the Bauhaus, stated in 1922 that it was the architect's task to be a "pioneer of simplicity" and that the important matter was to find one's way forward toward "simple forms for all of life's necessities, forms that were both respectable and genuine".

Steen Eiler Rasmussen's manner of communicating ideas about architecture is legendary, first and foremost in the form of his widely disseminated book, *Experiencing Architecture*, which has been translated into several languages, but also through a lifelong and very extensive body of books and articles about aesthetic and culture-political questions within the architect's entire domain of activity. Although he was the driving force behind the construction – especially in the 1950s and 1960s – of an extensive number of residences and schools, Steen Eiler Rasmussen's influence on Danish architecture after the Second World War did not manifest itself, not to a visible extent at least, so much in his own building constructions as it coined itself in his tremendous commitment to teaching and even more especially in the wide dissemination of his ideas about architecture.

Another one of Danish architecture's most important figures, Kay Fisker, wrote about and was himself the champion of a kind of architecture that, on the background of principles of form with a national character, took its point of departure in what was given, especially in the potentials of the long single-story house with a low roofline which, through a sensitive placement in the landscape, would be erected with an implicit understanding about the local materials' limitations.[5] During his period of tenure as professor at the Academy (1936–63), Fisker supervised a systematic development of apartment house buildings that was based on methodical investigations of the new technology's possibilities. Fisker was, as we saw that PH had also been, interested in advancing "beyond style" and, in essence, working to gain a more logical and more honest accordance between content and expression. In a speech that he presented on the occasion of the Royal Academy's annual celebration in 1947, which was subsequently edited and rewritten in the form of the article that is included in the present anthology, Fisker characterizes functionalism as an upheaval of building construction's presuppositions and expressions, an upheaval that is more thorough than any other change in style since the time of the Gothic. Fisker refers to an interesting difference between the form principles in early industrialized architecture and those in the Renaissance and the Baroque periods: while industrialism's buildings were assembled from pre-fabricated parts that were mounted to form a whole, the buildings of the Renaissance and the Baroque were, on the contrary, built up or modelled up as wholes.

While Fisker was making his speech before the Danish Academy in 1947, it is quite conceivable that two young men were sitting among the audience in the Royal Academy of Fine Art's Festival Hall, two young architects, each of whom would come to set his own special stamp on the development of Danish architecture in the second half of the twentieth century: Jørn Utzon and Erik Christian Sørensen.

And, of course, it is not entirely a coincidence that Utzon's architecture often appears to be stretched out between the two form principles to which his teacher, Kay Fisker, constantly referred; the *modulated* and the *mounted*. By way of example, consider Bagsværd Church, where these two essentially different form principles operate in conjunction: the stacking of the pre-fabricated façade elements around the nave's modulated ceiling construction. Utzon has not written many texts about his vision of architecture, but what can be sensed none the less in the few texts he has left for us to read is a hushed modesty which, with a vibrating courageousness, is akin to that which emanates from his architecture. Louis Kahn's texts about the material's inherent essence and about the relationship between form and design also appear to bear a relation to Utzon's approach, but in the latter's writings there is absolutely none of that pathos that is part and parcel of Kahn's metaphysical way of thinking.

In what is perhaps Utzon's most seminal article, "Platforms and Plateaus", he employs his fascination with the Mayan pyramids scattered around the Yucatan peninsula to describe one of the recurrent fundamental features of his architectural vision: every building, you could say, through its own manner of Gestalting, has necessarily to secure its connection with the surrounding terrain and landscape. The plateau or the platform is just as much a social meeting place as it is a preparatory *a priori* that renders the establishment of the tectonic construction possible.

In the wake of the German occupation of Denmark during the Second World War, Danish architects on the whole had a great appetite to resume their overseas connections. A number of the most prominent architects had spent some years during the war in Stockholm, where first-hand impressions of Lewerentz's and Asplund's architecture would prove to be of inestimable and lasting significance.

Among them was Arne Jacobsen.[6] Jacobsen is certainly one of the most important figures in Danish architecture in the twentieth century, notwithstanding the fact that he was not especially talkative about his architectural visions and it was only seldom that he wrote down his thoughts about architecture for publication. In the lecture reprinted here, entitled "Contemporary Form and Design", it is Jacobsen's apprehension about the conditions surrounding architecture that serves as the theme, expressing both the sense of apprehension he feels in response to the politicians' involvement in future residential policy and his concern about the marginalization of the architect's role, which he regards as a grave problem. Jacobsen is entirely in agreement with Aalto, who had already underlined, back in the 1930s, his perception of the architect as the person who can humanize technology. As we can read as we near the end of Jacobsen's article:

> The greater part of my observations are small nudges, reflecting my worries about the devaluation of the coming generation of architects. A devaluation, which I believe, we can avoid when we add an absolutely necessary touch of humanity to the inhumane nature of industrialization, and raise building to an art form called architecture.

It would hardly be possible to overstate the significance of Jacobsen's generous contribution to modern Danish architecture and design. As could also be said about the renowned Danish furniture architect Kaare Klint, Arne Jacobsen was not a *renewer* as such but more of an *improver* who, through a sharp eye trained on whatever was stirring on the international scene, managed to transform foreign form ideals and incorporate them into a Danish building culture. His works were carried out internationally, but with a special hallmark of informal elegance that is generally regarded as being a patently Danish quality.[7]

The same thing can be said about another architect, Erik Christian Sørensen, who turned his gaze towards the United States at the end of the 1940s to absorb new kinds of impulses. Sørensen became one of the most distinguished professors at the Academy and in the 1950s he assisted Arne Jacobsen with his teaching duties there. In Sørensen's article, "On Form, In Space", it is the relationship between spirit and matter that is being examined, somehow similar to what we saw in Utzon's texts. In Sørensen's thinking, the *spiritual* is that which has its source in our understanding of the world while the *actual material* is regarded as that which is contingent upon our attitude to substance, which serves as the point of origin for the process involved in building or forming. About the way the material is handled, that is to say, quite simply about the process of designing, Sørensen's statements are based on his thesis that the visual constructive order is "a vital instrument for an existence of integrated culture".

In point of fact, Sørensen regards his own day as a time of transformation: "We are in an age of rapid changes from the past that formed earlier ideas: Changed technology and scientific progress bring along new potentials for the human society and open up the field for new realities to be interpreted by the artist."

The twentieth century was a century of great changes and in the different discourses we have encountered here, one of the recurrent themes has been the architectonic relationship to the dynamic society's rapid changes. This theme also comes to light in a contribution that the office Tegnestuen Vandkunsten made to the debate in 1974 with the polemical but optimistic title, "It Can Be Done!" "It is not just a question of understanding the building process, it is also about achieving a decent way of life", it says in the beginning of the article. Vandkunsten is settling its accounts with the notion of what is so beneficial or serviceable about entrusting all the determinations about the design of our physical surroundings into the hands of the omniscient architect who, as it is unfurled in the writings of Steen Eiler Rasmussen, fills out the role of synthesizing the social, technical and aesthetic conditions into a whole. In Vandkunsten's ideology, the control of the residential building lies in the hands of the *dwellers*. Although it can be said that, to a great extent, both the ideology and rhetoric of the article – with its progressive expressions of solidarity with residential housing's users and its anti-authoritarian critique of residential housing's political and aesthetic monopolies – are children of both PH and even more especially of the youth uprising of the 1960s, several of Vandkunsten's demands are still relevant today. The continued presence of the "free city" of Christiania, which was founded in 1971 in the Christianshavn section of Copenhagen as a social experiment, has contributed to the result that we are now making greater and greater utility of user-involvement and of user-guided decision-making processes. And in recent years, we have, in fact, been moving far along the road that Vandkunsten has been pointing towards.[8] Moreover, Vandkunsten has been blazing a trail through their contribution to the development of Danish residential housing.

Henning Larsen's prolific contribution to Danish architecture gathered momentum at the same time as that of Vandkunsten, that is to say, at the end of the 1970s and the beginning of the 1980s. Although it is important to avoid underestimating Vandkunsten's artistic ambitions, Henning Larsen's orientation is certainly far more explicitly aesthetic than Vandkunsten's will ever be. With his international orientation, Larsen moved his way – in the middle of the 1980s – into the world's absolute élite class of highly profiled architects and his very central position in Danish architecture was further reinforced not so much by his engagement and the instruction he offered at The Royal Danish Academy, where he served as a professor from 1969 until 1994, but more by virtue of his highly esteemed architectural firm and by the role he played behind the architectural gallery, Skala, and behind the architecture review of the same name.[9] Larsen conjoined the Danish architects' milieu with, especially, the more experimental parts of the international milieu, including the one that sprang up around the Architectural Association in London. During this period, his firm designed a number of excellent public buildings in Denmark and in places in the Middle East, often manifest as a kind of architecture that appears to have evolved as a sophisticated fusion among themes gathered from the modernist tradition and the Islamic world of forms. Thus, it is quite precisely Islamic architecture that inspires Larsen to discover how the light's meeting with the building's inner spaces can dissolve any sense about the building's constructive weight.[10] The space, the material and the light put us into motion. Music is immaterial and transitory while architecture is lasting and concrete. Nevertheless, it is precisely through the mastery of architecture's specific dimensions that it manages to catalyze abstract feelings that we recognize in the experience of listening to music, according to Larsen.

In Boje Lundgaard's article, "The Crisis in Building Technics", what can be intuited already in the title is a sense of apprehension about whether that mastery of architecture's technical reality which Larsen celebrates is actually in the process of slipping through the fingers of the Danish architectural profession. Is the utterly fundamental understanding of the connection between a building's technical Gestalt and the mental energy that it releases about to turn to dust in the hands of a group of architects that so willingly submit to more and more cumbersome circumstances? It is that segment of Danish architecture that lets its own expressions be based on borrowed images without remaining connected to any understanding of the material and technical bonds that worries Lundgaard. Since the time that Lundgaard authored the article, Danish architects' attention to tectonics and to material aesthetics has sharpened considerably, especially as a consequence of the highly esteemed examples with which, most especially, architecture from Switzerland and Austria has enriched the world. However, perhaps as a sufficiently sensible reaction to Dutch architecture's technical permissiveness and material-aesthetic poverty, we can witness a greater and greater interest in the points that Lundgaard – and Carl Petersen – are putting forth.

If we view these various discourses in relation to one another and consider their mutual coherence, we find that it is, by turns, architecture's *external* and *internal* conditions that are being weighed. While it is so that, in a number of the articles, the reader can spot certain reservations about enveloping the artistic method conceptually in a way that is too hermetic, what appears to be being unfurled in almost all the discourses is a more straightforward and simple way of taking hold of architecture's external relations. Accordingly, a connection can be seen between architects as different as Poul Henningsen and Arne Jacobsen, both of whom were apparently absorbed by how professionalism in the architecture craft can be secured in the meeting with the building industry's current relations of production. And many years later, Boje Lundgaard comments that this kind of concern among Danish architecture students seems to be dwindling. And the reciprocity between that which is *given* by the material's inherent qualities and the form's possibilities, which are released by a mental content, appears to conjoin architecture temperaments as widely divergent as Steen Eiler Rasmussen, Jørn Utzon and Erik Christian Sørensen.

But how are the discourses taking shape in today's current architectural productions? It is first and foremost a discussion about how architecture as an artistic expression can survive in the midst of a society that seems to be ever increasingly influenced by the forces of the market. At the present time the Danish architecture milieu is split into different camps with very different conceptions, including one which expresses no qualms whatsoever about bidding a short and unsentimental farewell to architecture as a branch of art, never failing to acknowledge Rem Koolhaas as an inspiration. As a matter of fact, Bjarke Ingels actually went so far as to say in the context of a 2005 newspaper interview that there was no longer any foundation for perceiving architecture as an independent branch of art.

Another kind of discourse seems to be pointed in the opposite direction inasmuch as it aspires to restore architecture's credibility as both an aesthetic and ethical matter. One common feature in these efforts is the wish to move into investigations of the formal in relation to the real, often with markedly subdued but original and characterful results, as can be seen in the work of architects like Mads Bjørn Hansen, Erik Brandt Dam and Nicolai Bo Andersen. Here the architect is being considered in a classical optics, that is to say as a *bound* artist who, through his/her encounter with diverse practical, formal and cultural factors that are binding and stabilizing, invests an emotional content during the process of Gestalting a work. For the time being, the works that are being realized within this particular discourse are few and far between and one can easily arrive at the conclusion that the architecture profession in Denmark is currently divided between those who are thinking about and developing architecture and those who are building it – or that a significant group of very large architectural offices is creating a kind of architecture that is split between these two discourses. Consider, for example, the work of firms like Schmidt Hammer & Lassen, 3xNielsen, Arkitema and Henning Larsen Architects.

For this very reason, Danish architecture is now standing at the crossroads. The one way leads across smooth and facile recapitulations of foreign models, accompanied by simplified rhetoric. The other seeks to generate its own meanings through *reciprocity* with the cultures that our forefathers have left behind. The texts selected for the present volume will contribute to qualifying this choice.

NOTES

1   Juhani Pallasmaa, "Begrebslig viden, indlevelse og tavs visdom i arkitekturen" in Kim Dirckinck-Holmfeld *et al.*, eds., *At fortælle arkitektur*, Copenhagen: Arkitektens Forlag, 2000, p. 84.

2   Pallasmaa, "Begrebslig viden, indlevelse og tavs visdom i arkitekturen", p. 85.

3   Published in Simo Paavilainen (ed.), *Nordic Classicism 1910–1930*, Helsinki: Museum of Finnish Architecture, 1982, pp. 35–38, 45–48. On Carl Petersen's sensibility, see Christoffer Harlang, *Nordic Space*, Barcelona: Elisava, 2000.

4   For a comprehensive account of Poul Henningsen's work, see T. Jørstian (ed.), *Light Years Ahead*, Copenhagen: Louis Poulsen, 1994.

5   For a collective study of Kay Fisker, see Stanford Anderson *et al.*, *Kay Fisker*, Copenhagen: The Danish Architectural Press, 1995.

6   On the work of Arne Jacobsen, see Carsten Thau and Kjeld Vindum, *Arne Jacobsen*, Copenhagen: Danish Architectural Press, 2001.

7   A cognate sensibility is evident in the work of Knud Holscher, see Christoffer Harlang, *Knud Holscher Designer*, Copenhagen: Aschehoug, 2005.

8   The architectural history of Christiania is recounted in a special issue of *Arkitektur DK* entitled "Learning from Christiania", *Arkitektur DK 7*, 2004.

9   Selected texts from the magazine, *Skala*, appeared in Ken Rivad, ed., *Skala*, Copenhagen: Arkitekturtidskrift B, 1999.

10 See Henning Larsen, "On Architecture" in *Living Architecture 4*, 1984, p. 101.

Dehn's Laundry by Poul Henningsen

Poul Henningsen

Tradition and Modernism

International trends

The ongoing conflict in the area of applied arts (including architecture) throughout the world seems to concern new form expressions. Modern artists in all countries struggle to ensure that the objects we surround ourselves with as well as the buildings we live in should look completely different than before the revolution brought on by social problems and new technology. The modern attitude seems to be that most new problems quite naturally demand new forms. The telephone, the radio, the car and the aeroplane cannot be designed successfully using traditional styles. These new products will nurture a new aesthetic culture, and we must allow the more decorative and indifferent objects, such as chairs, graphic design, lighting fixtures and so on, to be influenced by this new concept of beauty, which will thus result in a new style.

At the same time as we experience the new international currents, we are seeing new materials that are being made available to artists by inventors, technicians and manufacturers. These new materials will have an influence on applied arts in the sense that they will offer new opportunities. However, the question is how profound this influence will and should be. A characteristic feature of some of the modernism in Russia, Germany and France is that it attributes the materials an extremely great influence on the final artistic results. One does not argue that when a design problem such as a department store or an auto garage, requires a great span and fire precautions, then reinforced concrete is an excellent solution. Instead, the argument is the opposite in that reinforced concrete is a modern material and corresponds with contemporary artistic attitudes; it should not only be used for everything, but also be given its strongest expression in the form. Earlier one was forced to work with smaller spans and meticulous supports, whereas now, reinforced concrete can be used for great cantilever solutions. This must be expressed by always employing cantilevered reinforced-concrete decks. The new material requires new aesthetic statics.

The other two popular modern materials are steel and plate glass. Properly speaking, the question of the correct daylight area for a living room or a classroom should depend on if one employs plate glass with steel frames or ordinary glass in mullioned, wooden frames. But the façade opening in the latter case should be larger, in other words, the room would be colder with a wooden window than with a steel window. In terms of the façades, steel windows will appear decidedly smaller than wood windows with the same glass area.

As the daylight area in a room can be both too large and too small due to the interval in which the correct daylight area lies, then the steel window must lead to *smaller* window openings than wood windows.

However, the "modernists" do not agree with this. They feel the opposite, that because steel and plate glass offer the opportunity of employing much larger windows than ordinary glass in wooden frames, we should employ much larger windows in order to express these new materials.

While ordinary glass only permits a few per cent of the healthy ultraviolet rays to pass through, work is underway to produce glass at an affordable cost that is transparent for this radiation and will allow about 80 per cent to pass through. This will imply a revolution for indoor hygiene. For people and animals, it will be similar to artificial light treatment. One claims that in the area of farming, where more and more animals are kept indoors, this will imply an increase in vitamin A in meat and milk. It will also be a decisive factor in the disinfection of rooms. While at the moment, the glass area is only a question of lighting, which one can vary greatly without doing harm, and that modern architects and doctors have a tendency to demand too much light in schools and hospitals, so it will be a quite different situation if the glass employed allows the passage of ultraviolet rays.

It is not without reason that there is here an attempt for a perspective view of the enormous amount of work being done all over Europe to give plate glass an aesthetic expression, and the change of the entire dwelling's hygienic standard, which is being quietly and intensely prepared by the engineers and manufacturers of reasonably low-cost ultraviolet transparent glass.

At the moment the price is still so high, that one should consider reducing the size of the glass area in schools and hospitals to one half or one third of what it is now and employing ultraviolet transparent glass, and still provide the patients and students with far more healthy lighting. But in any case, where there is a risk of breakage one must definitely employ the old fashion, small mullioned windows. What do the modernists say to this interesting dilemma between form and content, aesthetics and hygiene?

The unattainable goal of criticism is not to be right, but to be read, to write well. The art is: *not to be misunderstood.*

In the letters, magazines and books we receive, it appears that many kindly consider us to be a Danish expression for the world movement "New Form". However, we are as far from that movement as we are from the circle of artists, "who work best with retrospective feelings". We do not stand in between. We feel we stand above.

No one has misunderstood our position about the superficial imitation of old forms on new problems. Now our task must be to clarify the idea that we do not want new forms on old, already solved, problems. *We do not want any new forms unless they are dictated by the problem.* The entire question of tradition and modernism needs the most careful critical evaluation. How can one demand that the public should understand the intention? On one hand, they are presented with a triangular or square "modern" chair, even though they believe that we were created primarily the same as our ancestors, and on the other hand they are presented with a classicist post office or a viaduct with Ionic columns, even though they ought to expect that a new project would result in another form than that of the Greeks.

But also the relation to the social side of the debate can confuse the public. We erect monuments to a known social democrat in an international-traditional style (empire style), N.F.S. Grundtvig and C. F. Hansen shake hands over the fallen soldiers in south Jutland. The international traditionalists (the circle of Academic Architects) ridicule the national traditionalists (Jens Møller-Jensen), the bourgeoisie live in empire style in the city and farm houses in the country and watch in surprise as Europe carries on with a modern prison style at exorbitant prices.

The judgment of this phenomenon, throughout the world in the area of art, demands a precise evaluation of what is important as opposed to what is not. It demands that each party rises above the contradicting viewpoints and instead become two sides of the same story. In other words, the question of old and new form, if modernism and traditionalism will prove to be understandable and clear with a critical evaluation.

The substance of the artistic problem

The definition of substance is an intellectual process, which in terms of the intuitive world is considered artistic. With the word substance, we must consider the posed problem such as a chair or a spoon with the liabilities and obligations that are inherent in the substance or content: that one should be able to sit on the chair with a given degree of comfort, that it should be made of a certain material and harmonize with a certain environment.

When music deals with sound, the main limitations for the substance of music, the content, are given, but that these sounds should also lie within the accepted musical scale is not something that is relevant in the final artistic expression. It is a further limitation, given in advance, of the content of the problem, a traditional prerequisite to which one can ask whether or not it is justifiable, but this discussion lies before the final artistic result, the creation of the art work. Thus, tradition is part of the posed problem as a more or less inescapable advance responsibility. With responsibilities like this, the artist's material is limited, or he limits it himself.

In a similar fashion applied art includes the demand for an object's usability as a prerequisite, one that limits and commits in terms of the number of possibilities that the artist has to choose between in the final solving of the problem. For the architect, the building codes represent limitations for the posed problem. It is within this limited framework that he shall and must solve his problem.

If the outer practical requirements assume an especially serious character, if one can say that the welfare of people and society are dependent on their being followed, then these become social demands. It can be said that at any time there is a hidden social moment in any reasonable practical requirement for applied art, but it can be hidden deep in the background, for example in the design of a chair for a wealthy man, or brought clearly forward, for example in the design of typical worker housing where economy and order, hygiene and culture become decisive factors and the significance of a mistake is seriously multiplied in its execution.

In the previously mentioned, where I describe the content of the posed problem, there are, in the case of applied art, requirements for suitability and the social aspects. For art in general, tradition is an inherent factor (providing that the current trends require that it be respected and that is to say, if it exists). Tradition can in some cases concern quite associative conditions, such as the class characteristics of an object – if it is fine or cheap. This is not necessarily dependent on its price or luxurious execution: the bourgeoisie has ennobled the peasant style by employing it in their summerhouses. In a similar way, a tradition has arisen with churches and public buildings concerning associations from earlier periods. However, this is a superficial tradition. The serious side of a tradition concerns it forming a type. When generation after generation have solved the same problem (with the same content), the result will naturally become more and more harmonious and admirable: a type will arise. It is obvious that the artists who are involved in the gradual creation of this type, each time have referred to their predecessor's work, which is itself in a tradition, and they work further based on this tradition.

In a similar fashion, it is inherent in a current trend as a prerequisite to the artist. The question if one worked in the Empire style around 1800 or not, is not as relevant as how and how well one solved the problems at hand within the framework determined by the Empire style.

Every time a Greek column was improved in form, it was naturally also an artistic event. But for the artists who follow, who must continue to improve the form towards greater perfection, the predecessor's work was given in advance, in other words it represented the substance, the content that he based his work on. To him, it was not a question of a work of art, but a known substance. The column is, when we imagine the time when it was created, naturally a work of art of great quality, but as soon as we use and reproduce it, it is no longer a work of art, but a completely known content that was formed once and for all as perfect as possible. Within this content, it is no longer possible to create art, only to reproduce. The columns on C.F. Hansen's Vor Frue Kirke thus do not make the church a work of art. What was once form, art, becomes substance, content.

Consequently, the existing historical art is merely art considered in regard to the conditions of its time – not from ours. The fact that historical art still provides us with a great aesthetic pleasure is due to several conditions. First, we involuntarily submit ourselves to the assumptions of that time, and in this way justifiably experience the great solution of the problem, which is always a pleasure. But the artists of the past can have dealt with problems that are still contemporary, so that we rediscover a great deal of today's efforts in historical art. What does this imply? That the artists of the past were so great that they were far ahead of their time, or that the problems they worked with have not been subject to any great development: in both cases, that the tradition in this area is not exhausted.

These aspects are also true in terms of the modern artist's perception of historical art. In terms of the art lover, it is a different question. In the acquisition of any work of art, he makes the same discoveries as the artist, when he created the piece. He has a better basis to understand the historical art than the modern, where the content is new to him. The enjoyment for him lies in the intellectual reproduction of the artistic process and he will thus prefer to understand, demand to understand and become angry if he cannot understand.

Free art, applied art

A major aspect of the artist's work is the evaluation of the content. After having found the content reasonable as a whole, the problem becomes one of evaluating the value of the content's individual elements. A primary division of the content must be the separation of the free in art from the obligations of function.

One could easily imagine producing an artistic window and a healthy window for a pigpen. The healthy window will function, although it is perhaps not so beautiful. The beautiful window perhaps, as free art, will be a work of art, but it will not be a pigpen window, in other words, not applied art.

This circumstance must be analogous with the question of free or applied science. Free science is free to find ways of expanding our knowledge, while applied science is more directly dependent on the welfare of people. This is not to say that one is more valuable than the other, but the relationship must be understood. If a sick person seeks a doctor who does not try to cure him but instead applies free science, then the doctor is deceiving the patient. If the public or a private person seeks an artist-craftsman or an architect, it is not enough that the resulting spoon is beautiful or the building is famous throughout Europe as free art. It cannot even be a consolation.

In applied art there also exists a number of freedoms, where the artist, without violating the problem, can exercise his artistic expression. But in applied art, the artist does not have the freedom to limit the content at will. The painter must decide with himself if he will attempt to create unity in a rich composition or settle for a simpler problem that he can make monumental. The artist who works with applied art cannot cut out the part of the problem's content that deals with usage. This is a moral requirement and the artist who has difficulty accepting this must thus go over to the other side of the profession, which is more free. The architect can design triumphal arches, monuments, churches, museums and such, where the requirements for usage are quite simple. The artist-craftsman can produce frames and vases but not chairs, eating utensils, and so on.

This is not a question of function being more important than beauty, but only that some things must be dealt with before beauty, just as the temporal comes before the spiritual. It is thus not a question of a false view similar to the historical "rationalism", which is just as unreasonable as aestheticism. But it must be the case, that the healthy person goes to the theatre, while the sick person goes to the doctor.

In a society where there is a balance between the citizens' demands and the life that society offers, the free side of art will flourish. During a peaceful epoch like this, the process of developing a type will approach its artistic completion. In a society where the conflict between the citizen's demands and what they are being offered is obvious, then efforts should be directed at the temporal necessities: food, hygiene, the welfare of children. The actual artistic demands must have a lesser priority. We find ourselves at the beginning of a type-establishment period, the first rough draft of the problem's content.

In a harmonious society (whose harmony in this imperfect world must always exist in a state of lethargy in the suppressed levels of society), the issue of function, practically speaking, will be solved. People are satisfied with homes and objects. To only consider the functional aspects would be to reproduce, while work with the finest artistic design of the known content would be to produce. Artists become free artists. The great artists will be found in the actual formal work.

In a time wrought with social conflicts the new challenge is to find a new content, to begin the creation of a new type that is in keeping with a new and more harmonious society. This work will be so extensive and so serious that the great artists of the time will be found in this area, and those who find the moment appropriate to busy themselves with secondary problems such as churches, monuments, photograph frames and so on, in short, the tradition, will no doubt be overseen, while they, if they had lived in another time, perhaps would have been the great leaders of art. It is conceivable that perhaps they would have become posthumously famous like those that have held the fires of art burning in less prosperous times. One must not believe this. In the times of upheaval the very few areas where tradition has not been lost during the upheaval will be of no interest. There will be no spiritual social life behind these areas. Monuments, churches, museums and so on, are really quite unimportant objects in the present, and objects like this, which our few aesthetes produce, will no doubt be influenced by total indifference of the time so that they become inconsequent and poor works of art or at best, reproductions of art from a time when the interest and culture were quite different.

Without a doubt, cultural life is marred and hampered by these stragglers, who have much in common. The fact that the dream of immortality still lives in the art world and blocks the way for useful productive work cannot be explained in any other way.

It is quite correct that the great names in history are most common in the harmonious periods where a great deal of strong, anonymous work has already been done to define the new problems, but this anonymous work is just as important as that which brings fame. The work in solving the completely new problems posed to us is just as important as when a later generation is to be fed with what we have struggled to achieve, and pluck the fruit of our works. We must achieve a perception of efforts and immortality that suits our time. But we must be aware of the fact that immortality is not synonymous with positive valuable efforts. Both in art, philosophy and science, names have remained because they narrow-mindedly worked from a point of view that later from a greater, more extensive standpoint proved to be wrong. In the naïve periods of culture, one had a naïve conception of intellectual creations; one stole them from each other and concealed them from each other. This situation seems to still be prevalent in the area of art.

It is absurd to dream the dream of immortality at a time when we live for our children, and where the efforts for social, unselfish work are a reality. How can one believe that this generation can create anything that can measure up to the next as a whole? If one should arise, he will be surpassed by the next – and for this is what he works. Our work is to seek the content that the next generation can form, and even better the generation after that. We, of course, form the first rough form alone by seeking the substance and trying to recognize it, but to create artistic values like those of the Baroque and Antiquity in their time, is an extremely insane thought. We have not even created a society that could support art like that. Actually, we have not created much more than that which brought down the old, as far back as the Renaissance society: the French Revolution, technology, industrialization, the proletariat – and the *new* society – are only inklings. Our culture is so young and barbaric, that we in our attempts to create a spiritual and artistic life that corresponds with the present society have not even reached the level of the Eskimos in their efforts to achieve something similar.

We must acquire a new perception of the artist as a worker for society, who has the right to a moderate livelihood, but whose work in itself is rewarding. It is of no great benefit for the modern artist to wait for the future and life after death.

The considerations about how art oscillates between free work and the formal, compulsory work with social and practical aspects leads further to the view that in a period of harmony, it will be the free arts, music, poetry, painting and sculpture that are the most prominent and the applied arts are only bearers and servants. In a period of unrest the applied artists will be in vogue supported by the social, technological and hygienic sciences, providing the upheaval deals with these areas. Therefore it is quite natural that *Kritisk Revy* was started by architects, and that the other arts find their place within the basic views suggested here. The chaos, which is prevalent in literature, poetry, dramatics, painting and sculpture in Denmark, must necessarily be replaced by just as clear a struggle for and against, as that being exercised at the moment in the area of applied arts. But in addition, the art forms that first regain consciousness and deeply established work with the artistic aspects, must be those that are furthest in the control of the content. Therefore, at the moment it is the art of engineering that has a good overview of its content, that is leading the battle for an artistic form, while architecture, which has not even begun to recognize its new areas of work, must therefore be behind and split in the circles that primarily but correctly work with the content as opposed to the circles that haphazardly work with "art".

The freedom of choice

As long as the posed problem only allows a single solution, will this solution hardly be considered artistic, but, more likely, if it was new, scientific. Theoretically, one could well imagine a problem like this being posed, that is, defined problems that only have one solution. If the outer demands (from society or the client or other conditions) are imposed in such a way that there is only one solution to the problem, then the artistic work, practically speaking, is already carried out in the already imposed demands, and the creation of a form from a so clearly defined problem can never be considered an artistic effort.

Furthermore, one could imagine that sufficient demands had not been made, so that the problem was vague as several different solutions could be characterized as socially and practically equally good. The artist has thus the freedom to make a choice, and that choice will affect the resulting work being art or not.

Finally, one could imagine that the demands contradict each other, so that if one of the demands is to be satisfied, the other must be neglected and so on. The artist's work becomes far more serious: a question of judgement, where the most essential aspects are more important than the nonessential and where the grand, economic, hygienic and cultural responsibilities rest with the artist.

If one includes everything; the practical, tradition, trends and so on, to the prerequisites, it becomes obvious that the unspecified problem is most characteristic for the free artists in a time where tradition is rejected and new trends have a greater influence. The specified problem most often arises in the most harmonious phase of a cultural period, where things almost solve themselves with effortless ease. The overly specified problem usually occurs in the applied arts in a period where tradition has been seriously exhausted and where new strong demands conflict with the old and with contemporary imprudence.

At the moment, the situation must be that the problems in applied art are overly determined. The economical demands on one side and hygiene and culture on the other contradict each other. However, in the case of free art, it does not really matter today how it defines its problems. No one in society makes serious demands to paintings, sculpture, music and so on. The practitioners of these art forms can, therefore, freely form their ideas according to their own needs and inner amusement. For society, their work becomes a quite irrelevant play with nothing, a dream of happier times.

This is of course only to place these tendencies in a glaring contrast to each other. In reality, no artistic problems are undefined, defined or overly defined, but consist of a complex of undefined, defined and overly defined problems. Therefore, we dare claim that in every problem there exist free conditions that are independent of the outside demands placed on the solution of the problem. Of course, these conditions are only free in the sense that we know of freedom. They are determined by intellectual thought, the state of culture, development and many other factors. But in general they are free as they depend on the character and inner life of the artist, his dependence or independence, his respect for tradition or ability to disengage himself and so on.

In the free arts, tradition will often assume a position equivalent to that of the applied arts in terms of the practical demands. In a similar way as a break with the practical aspects is justifiably considered immoral in the applied arts, a break with tradition is unjustifiably considered immoral in the free arts. Ordinarily a break is just an indication of a failing ability on the behalf of the artist to find a new artistic production within the traditional framework.

A specific conception gradually develops as to what music is, and when this conception is explored in depth by the creative artists, they break free and expand the area of music to the ire of the establishment. In a similar fashion Beethoven departed from the accepted music principles of his time and freed music from some of the traditional rules and could thus create new and interesting works without constantly having his compositional abilities paralysed by associations with what previous artists had created. At the moment, something similar is taking place in the area of light music in the case of the jazz bands.

Principally speaking, one must recognize the artist's free right in terms of the freedom of choice. In other words, free art should be open to determining which subjects it wants to treat, and the determined arts free in terms of a freedom of choice. If tradition exists in this area, or it is broken, is often an inner intellectual question in artistic circles. One must just not perceive a departure with tradition as decided artistic progress. One should not consider the new area, for example such as the one that music enters in a departure from tradition, as greater or more interesting in itself than the area that existed before the departure. The interesting element in this case is that it is new and thus seems to have a wider range. In reality it is a much greater art to create something new within the traditional framework, because it requires an extraordinarily fresh point of view, while it is far more difficult to create elegance within the new framework, because this requires an extensive knowledge of the content to create something that is impeccable. Therefore, in most cases, a break with tradition will lead to the new area that is introduced to art becoming quite small as it is otherwise impossible to create anything impeccable with the new materials.

This is characteristic of all revolutions in the area of free art. One must immediately create a quite limited framework in the new area in order to produce at all. Painting has always had the naturalistic depiction as a goal (aside from "Naturalism", the short period when reproduction was the *goal*, that is, the misguided artistic intent). When the painters, for a period of time, have escaped this condition in Cubism and Expressionism, it has been due to a completely understandable and justifiable exhaustion with the traditional, and via a new point of view to be inspired to create a new art. However the framework that Cubism determined in reality was far more restrictive than before, and the area that was cultivated was quite limited.

We are led by these considerations to differentiate between two kinds of tradition: one which deals with the outward demands in applied art, the requirements and obligations. If these demands are based on tradition or if this tradition has been broken is not something that the artist decides, but something that society decides. The artist cannot even as an artist influence this, but naturally by obstruction and lack of talent, delay the fulfilment of these *social conditions*. The peaceful development of society or its upheavals is directly reflected in art's social conditions.

The other kind of tradition is that of the free art: *style.* This is naturally also dependent on social conditions, on the intellectual movements and culture, but in principle, we must maintain the artist's freedom to follow or depart from style according to his own conscious. The result can only be that he ends up as a good or bad artist. In addition to that there is nothing in terms of society at stake.

As a result of this, a break in style will often occur in the area of applied arts, primarily in the long development periods where society is not subject to revolutions. The design solution of the same problems (a castle, a military barrack, a palace, a church and so on, as they were known from the Renaissance to Empiricism) will inevitably be dry like a hackneyed minuet, unless the times and the artist take over in terms of freedom of choice, the style. This changes as fashions change, and even though there can be the most serious intellectual reason for this change in style, it is given, that it is stimulating for art even if it is just an intentional change for the sake of novelty. In most cases, the historical styles were just a fashion storm that ravaged Europe with the same intensity as plus fours are at the moment.

The extent of the content

But to now make a critical judgement of an art object's value we must be familiar with the extent of the posed problem and evaluate the harmony of the final form. It is not possible to solve a problem of unlimited content. A problem must have its limitations. If one simply asks an artist to create a beautiful thing, he must establish his own limitations for the problem. The greater the content the more difficult it is to achieve a harmonious solution. If one says: create a cube, then there is only one solution and it is no doubt beautiful, but empty. Originally, the circle was also a work of art and the pyramids were works of art based on the level of mathematics and technology at that time. This is no longer true seen with modern eyes. If America will build them eight times bigger, the simple pyramid form cannot say anything more to modern man other than: expensive, large and triangular. To speak of the pyramids as a great aesthetic experience is pure nonsense. A tetrahedron can never be art no matter how big one makes it. It *has* been. In other words we see that content, which in a given cultural period was almost impossibly large and whose disposition occupied the greatest minds of the time and represented its greatest work of art, in posterity is reduced and reduced until the content approaches nothing, so that only a child can find a content. When the content is recognizably nonexistent, it can be freely formed. When most people can draw a circle or shape a pyramid, then it is no longer a question of an artistic creation for the benefit of mankind, but of a reproduction for those who find it amusing.

It is in this relationship, that a once given content shrinks and shrinks in size, that the explanation lies, that one must necessarily make changes in the content in order to create art at all.

A critical evaluation of art in the past must be based on the knowledge of how one was faced with the content treated at that time. If many others with just as great or better fortune treated it, then it was a question of a poor reproduction. However if it was new territory for art and an excellent form was achieved, than the work of art must be characterized as great in an artistic sense regardless if posterity could easily solve the same problem and consider the content to be known and very small. In this way and only in this way does the pyramid become a work of art.

In this way one can also define the great work of art: the clarified form with a rich content. The wealth of the content and the clarity of the form are both equally important factors for the judgement. The artist, who only manages to deal with a small content, is not better than those who strain themselves with a rich content and submit chaos. None of them are artists. The first is an empty formalist, an aesthetic, where the latter has honourably failed. However, the latter has no doubt made the right endeavour.

Again in this situation, the applied arts have a special position as one does not have the freedom to choose the extent of the content. Any condition made from the outside is without a doubt a relief as it thus limits the content. The number of solutions will in this way be limited. But because it is easier to find a solution, is not to say that the solution can be considered to be art. The outer conditions, even if they contradict each other, cannot prevent a solution – the problem must be solved – but they can hinder the solution becoming a work of art. Naturally, in a period of upheaval many interesting attempts to solve the problems posed by society will arise, architecture problems, worker housing, city plans, and so on, but there is no probability that the results will be impeccable, that they will be works of art. Among the problem's conditions are also of course the common understand-ing, the political conditions, the insight of those in power, the will of the people to achieve a better life, and the artist (the architect) can treat and influence these con-ditions, but he cannot disregard them; he must allow for the more or less poor final results that he can achieve. It is of no help to him at all if he is a socialist. He must base his work on the capitalistic society. It is of no help that he is an idealist. He must build on realities.

It is possible that the outer conditions spoil the possibility of creating art, but the artist cannot create without them. If he receives his material freely provided, he immediately starts to reduce it. Tradition is a relief for the artist, both when it exists in its serious form (society's conditions) and when it exists as a style, that is to say, as traditional limitations in the form of expression. If society's conditions are new the material appears chaotic to the artist – insurmountable. He can consider the freedom of choice as being immediately irrelevant: it is not the time for artistic experiments. He can use his time to organize the material in clarity. When he is confronted with defined problems, he is happy, when he is confronted with unde-fined problems, he allows chance to decide instead of using his right to freedom of choice. It is not the time for artistic considerations. The material is so great that he cannot give it any form anyway or even achieve an artistic result. If he runs into overly determined problems, he must judge on the basis of what he honestly believes to be the best benefit for society between the contradicting conditions.

But he can also use his precious time to create a set of conditions of artistic character, for example that the solution should lie within a recognized style, such as classicism, without too much disregard for the social conditions. It will then always be the case that he does more violence to the problem than is morally acceptable. Style toys will possess him, and he will have to defend his bad and socially unde-fendable dispositions with arguments that he has created something harmonious instead – a work of art. But even if he succeeds in solving the problem in a style, without doing violence to the content, that is to say that he really only employs his *right to freedom* of choice, he will waste time in styling instead of going more in depth with the posed content and perhaps finding an even better solution in terms of content. All those who have designed multi-storey buildings in empire style with uniform façade grids will claim that the apartments in these buildings are really not worse than in others, perhaps even better. But they could have been even much better if time was not wasted in efforts to create works of art that will make our time barbaric and ridiculous for posterity. It is no doubt possible in many situations to organize a plan symmetrically without doing violence to the problem, but why bother? Symmetry does not answer any intellectual needs in modern society. As an organizational concept, it is rated so low that we cannot defend it in a period of enlightenment. Why waste the artist's time with this kind of thing? Either the problem is naturally symmetrical (an automobile, an aeroplane, a church and so on) and it would do violence to the problem to make it asymmetrical – or otherwise the problem is inherently asymmetrical (a row house, the front or rear façade of a building and so on) and it would thus do violence to the problem to make it symmetrical. Finally, it can be irrelevant if it is organized symmetrically or asymmetrically (a police headquarters, a post office and so on). Why waste time with grand symmetries that emphasize an irrelevant side of the problem as being important?

After an upheaval, when the conditions in society are new, the freedom of choice in the applied arts is reduced to nothing or almost nothing. There is no time to work with anything other than the organization of the new matter. Works of art will not arise. In terms of the free arts, the situation is quite different. The intellectual demands of society will be practically nonexistent. There will be no interest in the free arts. The artist has complete freedom, which he cannot use and he creates arbitrary limitations of his new, immeasurable matter. A number of fashion trends arise. Gradually as the applied arts delve deeper into their given matter and can begin a forming, the connection and collaboration will re-emerge with the free arts, which have been homeless and uninteresting. The areas that the free arts cultivate will be quite narrow and arbitrarily limited in a period of waiting like this. The connection between the different art forms will thus fail.

In the applied arts, free artists will also appear who will attempt to create a new style or maintain the old style – the tradition. In both cases, they will do violence to the problem. The modernists will expand the area of freedom of choice beyond all reasonable borders. They will not place greater demands on a chair other than that one can crawl up and sit on it. Moreover, it will be built up of triangular planes and other elements and effects borrowed from technology. The traditionalists will imagine that there has been no revolution: we live as we always have, and an empire style building is still an excellent building for modern man. Typical of all these attempts to create art in the present is that these movements only pose very small formal problems. As an example, one can look at the systematists, who attempt to create a style by only treating the mathematical aspects of form. By demanding the employment of the Golden Section, they achieve a quite small, limited world, in which they cannot even create useful objects, but where they achieve a kind of harmony. At one time in the magazine *Klingen* I showed where this kind of effort led, however it all falls apart if one tries to introduce the physical world, gravity, and if one considers the social demands, there is nothing left at all.

In other words it is not possible to start with aesthetics and then gradually try to solve the practical aspects within the framework surrounding aesthetics. This is because aesthetics, *as such*, do not exist in reality. All rules of beauty (if any exist) and all rules of style are prerequisites that are part of the content, and they are there arbitrarily and wrongly. There is no other way to create art than to dig deeper and deeper into the matter. In the total control of the matter one can find the form hidden. In itself, form does not exist. But in the matter, one should understand the social conditions, which gradually through our awareness of them create types, and also the contemporary intellectual currents, unsnobbishness, clarity, economy, solidarity, which at one point will be reflected in the freedom of choice and allow works of art to arise.

The traditional and the modern problem

Modernists love to claim that all problems are modern – or should be treated as such. The traditionalists close their eyes and believe that most problems actually are the same as a century ago. None of this is true. In modern society there exist both problems with the same content as they have had for centuries and problems that have yet to be solved.

The chair is an old problem in terms of the fact that we are built much the same as our ancestors. Based on this fact, chair design can no longer be considered an art form, but as reproductive, and we cannot seriously consider the chair question as a meaningful one. But aside from the basic demands that one sits comfortably and correctly depending if it is an office, dining or living room chair, one can find a number of freedoms of choice in the design of a chair, which in the different style periods are considered to be naïvely decorative, in that one has attached contemporaneous fashion to the well-designed chair. We too must employ this freedom of choice in keeping with the philosophy of our time. We must in keeping with the cultural level that we find ourselves on, and which we no longer dare to call naïve (philosophically speaking), attempt to ensure that the freedom of choice is in keeping with the current needs for economy, unsnobbishness, precision and clarity.

When the modernists throughout the world design constructivist, Dadaist, surrealist and Cubist chairs, they reveal a need to ensure that the freedom of choice in designing a chair is in keeping with the times – often so drastically that it has a negative effect on the basic requirements and becomes uncomfortable to sit on. However on closer inspection, the judgement of what is in keeping with time depends on just as naïve and superficial a basis as the historical styles. It is only a question of superficial, technical basic forms, borrowed from the aeroplane and the sharp-edged technical objects, just like the rich and sweeping forms created an outer congruency in rococo objects. While the depth of this congruency was satisfying for its time as it was in keeping with the absolutist lifestyle, form of government, belief in a certain god and a good portion of philosophical naïveté, it is completely unsatisfactory in our critical century where we see things not as absolutes, but in a functional context and where the principal factors are more important to us.

Thus it must be said, that even though the chair is a solved and familiar problem, in its solution there still lies a great freedom of choice, which calls on the artist. It is a misuse of this freedom of choice and thus bad art to express a naïve and unnecessary congruency with the technological world, but it is no less reprehensible to continue to maintain the styles of the past on the chair, because they do not agree with our current mode of thought and because our current mode of thought is more correct and in depth than that of the past.

But in seeing the chair as an historical problem, aside from comfort and suitability, there is also the demand for a certain social character in response to the existing divisions in social classes. The middle class did not sit on the nobleman's chair and the nobleman did not sit on the farmer's. A copying results in the introduction of a false sense of class about objects. This false social character of things should today be reserved for the dying bourgeoisie and is of no interest to a modern, socially aware artist.

With the word unsnobbish as a current demand, I want to imply that one of the modern artist's greatest tasks is to erase the sense of class from objects. The fact that a chair is suitable as an office, dining or living room chair is sufficient in itself. It should be suited for these purposes for anyone and its cost should not be increased by the attachment of attributes to make it classier for the upper levels of society.

There are also other things about the traditional problem of the chair that point in the direction that certain parts of it are new. We are perhaps not completely the same as our ancestors, namely in terms of the demands for intensive rest arising from the intense lives we live. The very comfortable chair is already a new but quite resolved type, which obviously does not resemble an aeroplane or a car, but almost a crossbreed of a comforter and a sofa. This type is created and completed by those who do not consider themselves artists.

It is also given that modern production methods must affect the chair much more than they do. This does not mean that steel tubing is the only material that a modern artist can accept working with – probably wood is preferable. But mechanical production must not only lead to a simplification – it must also lead to the secondary forms of the chair expressing it. The bentwood chair, which is admired by modern architects but considered too common by the public, is actually a very beautiful chair, a work of art, where the treatment of materials, its use, production and price, work together as a synthesis in what we call a type. It is completely absent of a social characteristic, only in its price does it reveal its ordinariness and thus it is not a property of the chair itself but of the snob who looks at it.

If we then consider the problem of housing, the traditionalist will claim that it can be designed as it always has. The familiar Danish tradition needs only a careful modernisation. The urban architecture of the classicists, the cottages of the state smallholders and the rural housing of "Bedre Byggeskik" are characteristic examples. The modernists will claim that the modern materials have completely altered the house so that it must be terraced and built of concrete, steel and plate glass.

Confronted with this, we must say that all the prerequisites for housing have been abandoned, without our being able to define the new that shall replace them. The bourgeois way of life is faced with a collapse caused by the difficulty of finding domestic help, an insecurity in taste and lack of respect for this social class as a whole. The real problem, worker housing, has yet to be solved, not only because in itself it is an unsolvable, hopeless conflict between merit and requirement, but also because social ambitions are a reality, the worker will imitate the rootless bourgeoisie. Perhaps it is possible that it is the bourgeoisie that will lead the way, despite everything, to a more simplified way of life. Perhaps it will become fine to live in a simple fashion.

But far more important is the fact that mankind as such, will not be able to survive life in the big city. Most cities have only existed fifty years as big cities. The actual hygienic and moral effects cannot yet be judged at full strength, but already the need and the flow away from the city centre reveals that the generations that grow up, will place greater and greater demands. There is hardly any doubt that low-rise housing is the solution. Therefore it is a social event of high importance that through the efforts of many different instances it has been possible to build the row house and make it popular. The question however cannot be solved without incorporating the media with a social viewpoint and leadership, and this implies that one of the conditions for the dream of modern architecture being realized is that Mayor Pedersen (as a symbol) must understand the problem. The work involved at the moment in terms of propaganda, agitation, derision and struggle, before leading social democrats realize that it is their duty, is simply immeasurable.

On this chaotic basis rests today's most important architectural problem: *the worker's housing*. How can one expect the simple house, the simple apartment or the simple row house to become impeccable art, when the entire foundation, contemporary understanding, the city plan, the media, the worker's own wishes, fail? Seen in this light, we have come no further than getting the average bourgeoisie to move out into row houses and provide an example to be imitated.

But also the task of designing a row house offers a freedom of choice. The modernists will ask why don't they have flat roofs and be built of reinforced concrete. The traditionalist's will ask, why are they not symmetrical, and why the ugly exterior verandas. *Because they are propaganda*. This is how they should be seen. People shall primarily feel at ease with themselves. The freedom of choice in solving a problem can be employed in many ways. It can be employed in a pedagogical sense for the education and understanding of the later problems that must be solved.

In short, the problem is so overwhelming that we must give up all talk of art. The creation of a work of art is a process that takes generations. We are well aware of how the artistic process takes place. First, the outer demands and conditions must be present and be a valid expression of the best in society. This is far from the case. Society is not yet aware that it must provide its citizens with humane conditions – not even the social democratic municipalities seriously feel this. But when this requirement is not placed on the artist, how can he create a work of art? It will take generations before this situation, known as the big city and the proletariat, rise above their latent state to full awareness. Then the artist will also have mastered the matter, and the first acts of design can begin. Then the freedom of choice will be employed, not as now for pedagogics on how to swallow the pill (at best, or for desperate, rootless artificialities at worst), but to give society a final and strong expression in the form of the solution – to create a contemporary work of art.

This is not a pessimistic but a critical view of things. Perhaps great art will come into being before we know it. But it will not emerge unless we become like children and begin from the beginning. We can only facilitate the moment for the emergence of great art by working in a social context, and by turning, with equal strength, against the traditionalists' European decadence and against the modernists' American barbarism. The modern culture is neither the dream of a future America nor that of the Europe of the past, but a reality: the world of today.

Only art of its own time lasts forever.

Voldparken Housing by Kay Fisker

1947

Kay Fisker

The Moral of Functionalism

During these post-war years, eager attempts are being made to wind up the estate of functionalism. The logical conclusion of this is that functionalism must be dead, and this is no doubt correct so long as we look upon functionalism as a style. Its programme, nevertheless, includes more than the short-lived period characterized by functionalist ideals of form. Functionalism holds a moral that is eternal: the demand for functional architecture. Lately there seems to be a tendency towards a slackening of this demand; but it is important that it should be maintained and fulfilled during the years to come.

The victory of functionalism put an end to the prevailing eclecticism. During the nineteenth century, the historical approach to architecture had become so firmly anchored that it was maintained for the greater part of a century, in spite of changes in cultural pattern, the progress of democracy and liberalism, the emergence of strong and independent artistic personalities among the architects and the extensive technical and industrial development that had taken place.

Eclectic architecture is formal: concern with form supersedes all other demands. Custom, technique and social conditions are considered only in the light of a previously fixed ideal of form. No correspondence is demanded between contents and expression; the outer shell becomes a garment, a mask, without connection with the interior. "Architecture is decoration of constructions", said Sir Gilbert Scott, the main figure within the English gothic revival. A striking feature of the period was that completely new production methods, due to the development of industrialism, arose without immediately being given outward expression. Industrialization brought about standardization of the various parts of a building and eventually produced architectural innovations of a revolutionary nature. The architects of the Renaissance and baroque had worked on a principle of form whereby the house was constructed, almost *modelled*, as a whole; but industrialism entailed the building of a house out of fabricated parts which were then *fitted* into a whole. In the childhood of industrialism, these standard parts were made without reference to the nature of materials or to their effect on construction. Carried away by the new technical possibilities, people tended to forget that there were essential differences between plaster and cast iron. The material existed only to be painted, not for any intrinsic merit, and forms were taken from architectural history. But while apparently the form was borrowed, in fact a wholly new principle of form was created.

Functionalism was to carry this principle of form to its logical conclusion. New technical methods and new possibilities of construction, though often romanticized beyond their importance, were the most important influence in this evolution. The products of machine production – the ship, the automobile and the aeroplane – became the models, and steel and reinforced concrete served to create the new forms. In the nineteenth century, iron had made its appearance as a quite new element in architecture; but only a few men like Labrouste and Sullivan permitted it to become an artistic part of their construction. In the twentieth century reinforced concrete introduced an architectural factor that combined the massive qualities of masonry with the tensile strength of iron or steel. Sometimes design was dictated wholly by construction, as in Russian architecture of the early days of the Soviet Republic. Construction then became an end in itself, as well as the means: Tatlin's design (1920) for a monument for the Third International in Moscow is a large iron-grille structure with no content or expression other than its construction.

The space principles presented by functionalism as radically new also had their roots in the preceding century. Let us consider one development of the 1850s having to do with the formation of the house plan. In England, eclecticism brought about a special cultivation of the gothic tradition which led to a break with the established forms of classicism, at least so far as the dwelling was concerned. The English house plan of the 1850s broke completely with the French equivalent of the "railroad flat" type of plan that had formerly prevailed. Large suites disappeared; efforts were made to avoid the necessity of passing through one room in order to reach another, and to make each room as self-contained and private as possible. Convenience, spaciousness, division of the plan according to the use of the rooms, orientation for sunlight, ventilation and the best view – all these were considered more important than symmetry, regularity and monumentality, indeed even more important than the architectural proportions of the rooms, window bays and building elements. Thus the plan became free and irregular, with rooms grouped around a large, often two-storied, central room.

The shape and disposition of our rooms today is based on logical adaptations of this point of view. In the modern house, *exterior* and *interior* are no longer separate conceptions but merge into each other. As early as the 1890s, Frank Lloyd Wright had made use of this principle, and Le Corbusier has varied the theme in many ways. His architecture has often been described as a composition of cubical and cylindrical blocks. This is a misconception: his architecture is composed of flat surfaces and an interaction between exterior and interior; its constituents are not volumes, but wall-diaphragms enclosing space within which the rooms flow into one another. Often a large central room occupies several stories and ramifies into secondary rooms, while the whole interior is separated from the surrounding greenery only by a glass wall. The connection with English house design of the past century is here evident, and the development has proceeded with convincing logic.

The same thing may be said of that even more popular side of functionalism: its social aspect. This, too, represents an advance in a development originating in England. Principles employed first in houses of the rich were soon applied to houses for the population at large, and functionalism found itself concerned with the plain standard dwelling that constitutes 80 per cent of all house building. While functionalism's aesthetic language of form often aroused violent resistance, its social programmes almost from the outset met with general sympathy. Even those who were irritated by flat roofs and large windows found the social endeavours of the young architects praiseworthy and approved of their preoccupation with the solution of the problem of the house rather than with monumental building. This duty of the architect to serve the community was a convincing argument in any discussion. Yet even this aspect had begun with liberalism, a generation or two before.

Thus although functionalism was set forth as a violently revolutionary movement, so far as its basic tenets were concerned it would have been more natural had its course been continuous and evolutionary. In social and technical forces as well as in planning, the origins of functionalism had all been present in the nineteenth century. Only the language of form had lagged behind. By the end of the century, however, a few architects in widely separated parts of the world had made scattered and independent attempts to advance beyond style to a logical, more honest architecture, with accord between form and purpose. They were fighting for reason and humanity. "Form follows function", was Louis Sullivan's doctrine in the 1880s; "houses for people to live in", was Baillie Scott's programme; in 1902, Henry van de Velde lectured on *Vernunftgemäße Schönheit* (logical beauty); in 1906, C.F.A. Voysey wrote of "reason as a basis of art"; *Stilarchitektur oder Baukunst* (traditional architecture or the art of building) was the choice with which Hermann Muthesius confronted his age in a propaganda publication of 1912.

Many of the solutions arrived at by these men, under the influence of their own times, are misunderstood now, but the foundation on which they built was surely the right one, and the one on which the men of the 1920s were to build further. Of these pioneers, seventy-five-year-old Auguste Perret and eighty-year-old Frank Lloyd Wright are still active and are still faced with great tasks. Perret is rebuilding Le Havre, and Wright still confronts us with new and strange solutions. But both are the children of their own generation. In spite of his pioneer constructions, Perret is firmly anchored in Beaux-Arts classicism, and Wright has never discarded the ornamental principles of Louis Sullivan and Otto Wagner. Wright's field, however, is wider than those of his teachers: he loves and cultivates the raw materials of nature. He is the reformer of the community, who still believes in Ruskin and Morris and who works towards decentralization and a close connection with the soil. His ideas of town planning, by which every man is to own his own land, are the realization of Thomas Jefferson's first democratic manifestos of 1776 and have their roots deep in the philosophy of the American colonists.

Unlike Perret and Wright, Le Corbusier and Gropius speak the language of our time. They are as different from one another as each is different from Wright. Functionalism has been greatly enriched by the interaction of these three: Wright, the Anglo-Saxon nature-romantic; Le Corbusier, the Latin machine-romantic; and the Germanic and socially minded Walter Gropius, impelled by the romance of logic.

Le Corbusier is the artist, and his accent is ever on the aesthetic. He says:

Man has forged a new tool . . . Nothing in nature approaches the perfection with which the machine is able to create. Instead of the but imperfectly round orange, the machine produces balls, cones and cylinders cut with a precision never shown us by nature. The work is so wonderful as to . . . awaken new senses within us . . . The house should be regarded as a machine to live in . . .

All his writings are characterized by a lyric tone; the heart of his point of view lies in its aesthetic nature. But his genius is indisputable.

The Bauhaus school of Gropius fought for social understanding and for rationalism in the creation of forms: the so-called *neue Sachlichkeit*. It regarded as romantic nonsense all values except those dictated by considerations of technique, economy, analysis of function and use, easy maintenance and durability; artistic content was forced into the background. The designation *Baukunst* was replaced by *Bauen*; the architectural schools were renamed the Building Schools; and the architect would have preferred to exchange his title for that of engineer. Naturally, appreciation for architecture of the past faded, and architecture as an art could be mentioned only in cautious circumlocutions. Admittedly the study of the art of building in previous ages is our best guide for the teaching of form, but it must be seen against the social and cultural background of its time and not, as in periods of eclecticism, be regarded as a basis for imitation. The architecture of the past should be studied as the classical scholar studies Latin: not in order to speak the language but to understand its structure and coherence.

Functionalism was a cleansing agent which swept over the nations like a storm, liberating and stimulating. It was necessary, but it destroyed too much. Architecture became skeletal, sterile and antiseptic. At times the whole movement seemed inhuman. Reaction grew: not the reaction that called forth politically influenced styles of architecture, such as the dilettante classicism of Nazism and the monumentalized Cubism of fascism, but a spontaneous reaction throughout the world against the penurious, the puristic and the over-simplified. Undoubtedly this was caused by functionalism's apparently arbitrary creation of form, even though this may have been based on an honest accord between exterior and interior. A need was felt for richness, for artistic imagination, for *order* in architecture. Symmetry and monumentality are not necessary, but architecture must have as well a rhythm of orderly arrangement, corresponding to the joints of the body, the acts of a drama, the movements of a symphony or the chapters of a book.

During the post-war years we have been groping towards an answer. The war has shaken many of us so fundamentally that it seems impossible to pick up the thread from the remote prehistoric days of 1939. Catastrophe has left us uncertain and suspicious; we no longer know in what to believe. In some places architects have reverted to historic forms. In Holland and Warsaw former leaders of extreme functionalism are now designing large structures influenced by the baroque, and in France Beaux-Arts classicism has again come to the fore. The immediate direction of this development is unimportant, for reactionary tendencies have been present in every age. What should alarm us is the fact that those very architects who formerly helped to promote functionalism are now searching for other ideals.

Less alarming, but no more positive, are the attempts to make functionalism more palatable through decoration and other camouflage. "Ornament is always placed to conceal a misconstruction", says Le Corbusier. Evidently this point of view is not that of the present time. Young architects are writing articles about the coldness of functionalism which must be mitigated through ornamentation. A desire is spreading for decoration, sometimes of a purely external nature, groping and helpless. Often the actual decorative elements spring from the 1880s or from some other period, yet none of them has anything to do with architecture.

Now, after the first victory of the early raw functionalism, we should be concerned with the development of the more vigorous and human side of functional architecture: a clear and functional frame around modern existence, created with new means; further development of tradition, perhaps, but not a return to forms past and gone. The barren qualities of functionalism came not from the relinquishment of the old, but rather from the failure to utilize in a sufficiently imaginative manner the possibilities of the new – new materials and construction, new social conditions.

Many factors will influence the architecture of the future. We must expect further technical development, perhaps encompassing possibilities as yet dimly perceived. Sociological conditions have changed in many countries and will continue to do so, producing strong repercussions even in those countries where such changes have not yet occurred.

A building should be a shell around the life to be lived within it, a shell that will satisfy material as well as intellectual demands. The architect creates not life, but conditions of life. Raymond Unwin once said: "We cannot create life, but we can form the channels of life in such a way that the sources of life will flow into them of their own accord."

Definitions are fluid and ideals vague in these post-war years. But, in view of the tactical position on the architectural front today, it is impolitic to emphasize the errors of functionalism. It is easy to retrogress; to retain and apply a new idea demands endurance. Today the building of houses is an intricate and troublesome business. Ever increasing demands for comfort and mechanical equipment challenge the architect; new modes of living complicate construction; ever growing official intervention and restrictions limit planning; and everything is dominated by economy. Under these conditions, administration is assuming great importance; there will not be much room for free thought and for the idea that must be maintained. It is not enough to be receptive to outside influences; inner conviction must be allowed to grow and to lead the way.

Student Housing by Steen Eiler Rasmussen

1957

Steen Eiler Rasmussen

Basic Observations

For centuries architecture, painting and sculpture have been called the Fine Arts, that is to say the arts which are concerned with "the beautiful" and appeal to the eye, just as music appeals to the ear. And indeed most people judge architecture by its external appearance, just as books on the subject are usually illustrated with pictures of building exteriors.

When an architect judges a building its appearance is only one of several factors which interest him. He studies plans, sections and elevations and maintains that, if it is to be a good building, these must harmonize with each other. Just what he means by this is not easy to explain. At any rate, not everyone can understand it any more than everyone can visualize a building merely by looking at the plans. A man to whom I was explaining a project for a house he wanted to build said deprecatingly: "I really *don't like* sections." He was a rather delicate person and I got the impression that the mere idea of cutting into anything was repulsive to him. But his reluctance may have arisen from the correct idea of architecture as something indivisible, something you cannot separate into a number of elements. Architecture is not produced simply by adding plans and sections to elevations. It is something else and something more. It is impossible to explain precisely what it is – its limits are by no means well-defined. On the whole, art should not be explained; it must be experienced. But by means of words it is possible to help others to experience it, and that is what I shall attempt to do here.

The architect works with form and mass just as the sculptor does, and like the painter he works with colour. But alone of the three, his is a functional art. It solves practical problems. It creates tools or implements for human beings and utility plays a decisive role in judging it.

Architecture is a very special functional art; it confines space so we can dwell in it, it creates the framework around our lives. In other words, the difference between sculpture and architecture is not that the former is concerned with more organic forms, the latter with more abstract. Even the most abstract piece of sculpture, limited to purely geometric shapes, does not become architecture. It lacks a decisive factor: utility.

The master photographer Andreas Feininger has taken a picture showing a cemetery in the Brooklyn-Queens area of New York. The tombstones stand crowded together exactly like skyscrapers in an American city, the very skyscrapers which form the distant background of the photograph.

Seen from an aeroplane high in the air, even the most gigantic skyscraper is only a tall stone block, a mere sculptural form, not a real building in which people can live. But as the plane descends from the great heights there will be one moment when the buildings change character completely. Suddenly they take on human scale, become houses for human beings like ourselves, not the tiny dolls observed from the heights. This strange transformation takes place at the instant when the contours of the buildings begin to rise above the horizon so that we get a side view of them instead of looking down on them. The buildings pass into a new stage of existence, become architecture in place of neat toys – for architecture means shapes formed around man, formed to be lived in, not merely to be seen from the outside.

The architect is a sort of theatrical producer, the man who plans the setting for our lives. Innumerable circumstances are dependent on the way he arranges this setting for us. When his intentions succeed, he is like the perfect host who provides every comfort for his guests so that living with him is a happy experience. But his producer job is difficult for several reasons. First of all, the actors are quite ordinary people. He must be aware of their natural way of acting; otherwise the whole thing will be a fiasco. That which may be quite right and natural in one cultural environment can easily be wrong in another; what is fitting and proper in one generation becomes ridiculous in the next when people have acquired new tastes and habits. This is clearly demonstrated by a picture of the Danish Renaissance king, Christian IV – as interpreted by a popular Danish actor – riding a bicycle. The costume, of its kind, is undoubtedly a handsome one, and the bicycle too is of the best. But they simply do not go together. In the same way, it is impossible to take over the beautiful architecture of a past era; it becomes false and pretentious when people can no longer live up to it.

The nineteenth century had the very ill-advised idea that to obtain the best results it was necessary only to copy fine old buildings that were universally admired. But when in a modern city you build a modern office building with a façade that is a faithful copy of a Venetian palace, it becomes quite meaningless even though its prototype is charming – charming, that is, in Venice on the right site and in the right surroundings.

Another great difficulty is that the architect's work is intended to live on into a distant future. He sets the stage for a long, slow-moving performance which must be adaptable enough to accommodate unforeseen improvisations. His building should preferably be ahead of its time when planned so that it will be in keeping with the times as long as it stands.

The architect also has something in common with the landscape gardener. Everyone can grasp the fact that the gardener's success depends on whether or not the plants he selects for the garden thrive there. No matter how beautiful his conception of a garden may be it will, nevertheless, be a failure if it is not the right environment for the plants, if they cannot flourish in it. The architect, too, works with living things – with human beings, who are much more incalculable than plants. If they cannot thrive in his house its apparent beauty will be of no avail – without life it becomes a monstrosity. It will be neglected, fall into disrepair and change into something quite different from what he intended. Indeed, one of the proofs of good architecture is that it is being utilized as the architect had planned.

Finally, there is a very important feature which must not be overlooked in any attempt to define the true nature of architecture. That is the creative process, how the building comes into existence. Architecture is not produced by the artist himself as, for instance, paintings are.

A painter's sketch is a purely personal document; his brush stroke is as individual as his hand-writing; an imitation of it is a forgery. This is not true of architecture. The architect remains anonymously in the background. Here again he resembles the theatrical producer. His drawings are not an end in themselves, a work of art, but simply a set of instructions, an aid to the craftsmen who construct his buildings. He delivers a number of completely impersonal plan drawings and typewritten specifications. They must be so unequivocal that there will be no doubt about the construction. He composes the music which others will play. Furthermore, in order to understand architecture fully, it must be remembered that the people who play it are not sensitive musicians interpreting another's score – giving it special phrasing, accentuating one thing or another in the work. On the contrary, they are a multitude of ordinary people who, like ants toiling together to build an ant hill, quite impersonally contribute their particular skills to the whole, often without understanding that which they are helping to create. Behind them is the architect who organizes the work, and architecture might well be called an art of organization. The building is produced like a motion picture without star performers, a sort of documentary film with ordinary people playing all the parts.

Compared with other branches of art, all this may seem quite negative; architecture is incapable of communicating an intimate, personal message from one person to another; it entirely lacks emotional sensitivity. But this very fact leads to something positive. The architect is forced to seek a form which is more explicit and finished than a sketch or personal study. Therefore, architecture has a special quality of its own and great clarity. The fact that rhythm and harmony have appeared at all in architecture – whether a medieval cathedral or the most modern steel-frame building – must be attributed to the organization which is the underlying idea of the art.

No other art employs a colder, more abstract form, but at the same time no other art is so intimately connected with man's daily life from the cradle to the grave.

Architecture is produced by ordinary people, for ordinary people; therefore it should be easily comprehensible to all. It is based on a number of human instincts, on discoveries and experiences common to all of us at a very early stage in our lives – above all, our relation to inanimate things. This can perhaps best be illustrated by comparison with animals.

Certain natural capacities with which many animals are born, man acquires only by patient endeavour. It takes years for a small child to learn to stand, to walk, to jump, to swim. On the other hand, the human being very soon extends his mastery to include things which are apart from himself. With the help of all kinds of implements he develops his efficiency and enlarges his scope of action in a way no animal can emulate.

In his helplessness, the baby begins by tasting things, touching them, handling them, crawling on them, toddling over them, to find out what they are like, whether friendly or hostile. But he quickly learns to use all sorts of contrivances and thereby avoids some of the more unpleasant experiences.

Soon the child becomes quite adept in the employment of these things. He seems to project his nerves, all his senses, deep into the lifeless objects. Confronted by a wall which is so high that he cannot reach up to feel the top, he nevertheless obtains an impression of what it is like by throwing his ball against it. In this way he discovers that it is entirely different from a tautly stretched piece of canvas or paper. With the help of the ball he receives an impression of the hardness and solidity of the wall.

The enormous church of St Maria Maggiore stands on one of Rome's seven famous hills. Originally the site was very unkempt, as can be seen in an old fresco painting in the Vatican. Later, the slopes were smoothed and articulated with a flight of steps up to the apse of the basilica. The many tourists who are brought to the church on sight-seeing tours hardly notice the unique character of the surroundings. They simply check off one of the starred numbers in their guide-books and hasten on to the next one. But they do not experience the place in the way some boys I saw there a few years ago did. I imagine they were pupils from a nearby monastery school. They had a recess at eleven o'clock and employed the time playing a very special kind of ball game on the broad terrace at the top of the stairs. It was apparently a kind of football but they also utilized the wall in the game, as in squash – a curved wall, which they played against with great virtuosity. When the ball was *out*, it was most decidedly out, bouncing down all the steps and rolling several hundred feet further on with an eager boy rushing after it, in and out among motor cars and Vespas down near the great obelisk.

I do not claim that these Italian youngsters learned more about architecture than the tourists did. But quite unconsciously they experienced certain basic elements of architecture: the horizontal planes and the vertical walls above the slopes. And they learned to play on these elements. As I sat in the shade watching them, I sensed the whole three-dimensional composition as never before. At a quarter past eleven the boys dashed off, shouting and laughing. The great basilica stood once more in silent grandeur. In similar fashion the child familiarizes himself with all sorts of playthings which increase his opportunities to experience his surroundings. If he sucks his finger and sticks it in the air, he discovers what the wind is like in the low strata of air in which he moves about. But with a kite he has an aerial feeler out high up in the atmosphere. He is one with his hoop, his scooter, his bicycle. By a variety of experiences he quite instinctively learns to judge things according to weight, solidity, texture, heat-conducting ability.

Before throwing a stone he first gets the feel of it, turning it over and over until he has the right grip on it, and then weighing it in his hand. After doing this often enough, he is able to tell what a stone is like without touching it at all; a mere glance is sufficient.

When we see a spherical object we do not simply note its spherical shape. While observing it we seem to pass our hands over it in order to experience its various characteristics.

Though the many kinds of balls and marbles that are used in various games have the same geometric shape, we recognize them as objects of extremely different character. Their size alone, in relation to the human hand, not only gives them different quantities but different qualities. Colour plays a part, but weight and strength are much more important. The large football, made to be kicked, is essentially different from the little white tennis ball that is struck by the hand, or by the racquet which is simply an extension of the hand.

At an early age the child discovers that some things are hard, others soft, and some so plastic that they can be kneaded and moulded by hand. He learns that the hard ones can be ground by still harder materials so that they become sharp and pointed, and therefore objects cut like a diamond are perceived as hard. Quite the reverse, pliable stuffs, like bread dough, can be given rounded forms, and no matter how you cut them up, the section will always show an unbroken curve. From such observations we learn that there are certain forms which are called hard and others soft, regardless of whether the materials they are made of are actually soft or hard.

As an example of a "soft" form in a hard material we can take a so-called pear-shaped cup from the English firm Wedgwood. It is an old model but it is impossible to say when the form first appeared. It is very alien to the classical shapes which the founder of the firm, Josiah Wedgwood, preferred to all others. It may be that it is of Persian ancestry and was permitted to live on in English guise because it suits the potter's craft so well. You feel that you can actually see how it was drawn up on the potter's wheel, how the soft clay humbly submitted to the hands of the potter, suffering itself to be pressed in below so that it could swell out above. The handle is not cast in a mould, as on most cups today, but formed with the fingers. To avoid rims, the plastic clay is squeezed out like toothpaste from a tube, shaped over the potter's fingers and then fixed to the cup in a slender curve which is pleasant to grasp. A man at the Wedgwood works, who sat making these handles, said to me that it was lovely work and that he enjoyed curving the handle in towards the pear-shaped cup. He knew no words for more complicated sensations; otherwise he might have said that he liked the rhythm in cup and handle. But though he could not express this, he had experienced it. When we say that such a cup has a "soft" form, it is entirely due to a series of experiences we gathered in childhood, which taught us how soft and hard materials respond to manipulation. Though the cup, after firing, is hard, we are nevertheless aware that it was soft at the time it was shaped.

In this instance we have a soft thing that was hardened by a special process, namely firing, and it is easy to understand why we continue to think of it as soft. But even in cases where the material used was hard from the very beginning, we can speak of soft forms. And this conception of soft and hard forms, acquired from objects small enough to handle, is applied even to the largest structures.

As a typical example of a structure with soft forms we can take an English bridge built at the beginning of the nineteenth century. It is obviously made of brick, that is of a material that was hard at the time the bridge was constructed. Nevertheless it is impossible to rid yourself of the impression of something that was kneaded and moulded, something that responded to pressure in the same way the banks of streams and rivers do, acquiring the form of winding curves as the rushing water carries off masses of clay and gravel from one bank and deposits it on the other. The bridge has a double function: it is a raised roadway and a navigation portal that seems to have been hollowed out by the pressure of running water.

As an example of the opposite quality, that is, a structure whose form is manifestly "hard", we select the Roman Palazzo Punta di Diamanti. Not only is the entire building mass a clear-cut prism, but the lower part is made of stone with faceted rustications like projecting pyramids – so-called diamond-shaped ashlar. Here, the detail has been directly taken over from a tiny object and employed on a much larger scale.

Certain periods have preferred hard effects of this kind while others have endeavoured to make their buildings "soft", and there is much architecture which sets the soft against the hard for the sake of contrast.

Form can also give an impression of heaviness or lightness. A wall built of large stones, which we realize must have required great effort to bring to the site and put in place, appears heavy to us. A smooth wall seems light, even though it may have necessitated much harder work and actually weighs more than the stone wall. We intuitively feel that granite walls are heavier than brick ones without having any idea of their respective weights. Ashlar masonry with deep joints is often imitated in brick, not to produce a deception but simply as a means of artistic expression.

Impressions of hardness and softness, of heaviness and lightness, are connected with the surface character of materials. There are innumerable kinds of surfaces from the coarsest to the finest. If building materials were graded according to degrees of roughness, there would be a great number of them with almost imperceptible differences. At one end of the scale would be undressed timber and pebble-dash, at the other polished stone and smoothly varnished surfaces.

It may not be surprising that we can see such differences with the naked eye but it is certainly remarkable that, without touching the materials, we are aware of the essential difference between such things as fired clay, crystalline stone, and concrete.

In Denmark today sidewalks are often paved with several rows of concrete slabs separated by rows of granite cobblestones. When it is necessary to lift a slab of concrete, it is undoubtedly practical to be able to rest the crowbar against the hard granite, which is less likely to crumble. But the combination gives a singularly inharmonious surface. Granite and concrete do not mix well; you can almost feel how unpleasant it is right through the soles of your shoes – the two materials are of such different grades of smoothness. And when, as sometimes happens, this pavement is flanked by broad strips of asphalt or gravel and edged with kerbstone, the modern Danish sidewalk becomes a veritable sample collection of paving materials, not to be compared with the pavements of more civilized eras, which are pleasing to the eye and comfortable under foot. The Londoner calls his sidewalk the "pavement", and a more cultivated example of paving can hardly be found.

In Switzerland the cobblestone paving is exceedingly handsome, as can be seen in a tranquil little square in Fribourg where the beautifully laid pavement gives aesthetic pleasure to the eye and has its perfect foil in the uniform pale yellow limestone of the surrounding walls and the fountain. A great variety of materials can be used for paving with very satisfactory results, but they cannot be combined or used arbitrarily. In Holland they use clinkers in the streets and on the highways and secure a neat and pleasant surface. But when the same material is used as a foundation for granite pillars, as in Stormgade in Copenhagen, the effect is far from good. Not only do the clinkers become chipped, but you have the uncomfortable feeling that the heavy pillars are sinking into the softer material.

At about the time when the child becomes aware of the textures of various materials he also forms an idea of tautness as opposed to slackness. The boy who makes a bow and draws the string so tightly that it hums, enjoys its tautness and receives an impression for life of a tense curve and when he sees a fishing net hung up to dry, he experiences how reposeful its slack and heavy lines are.

There are monumental structures of the greatest simplicity which produce only a single effect, such as hardness or softness. But most buildings consist of a combination of hard and soft, light and heavy, taut and slack, and of many kinds of surfaces. These are all elements of architecture, some of the things the architect can call into play. And to experience architecture, you must be aware of all of these elements.

From these individual qualities let us now turn to the things themselves.

When we regard the tools produced by man – using the term tools in the broad sense which includes buildings and their rooms – we find that by means of material, form, colour and other perceptive qualities, man has been able to give each tool its individual character. Each one seems to have its own personality which fairly speaks to us like a helpful friend, a good comrade. And each implement has its own particular effect upon our minds.

In this way, man first puts his stamp on the implements he makes and thereafter the implements exert their influence on man. They become more than purely useful articles. Besides expanding our field of action, they increase our vitality. A tennis racquet can help us to strike a ball better than we can do with the hand alone. This, however, is not the most important thing about it. As a matter of fact, striking balls is in itself of no particular value to anyone. But using the racquet gives us a feeling of being alive, fills us with energy and exuberance. The sight of it alone stimulates the tennis player in a way that is difficult to describe. But if we turn to another piece of sports equipment – the riding boot, for example – we will immediately realize what different sensations the various things arouse. There is something aristocratic about an English riding boot. It is a rather odd-looking leather sheath, only faintly reminiscent of the shape of the human leg. It awakens sensations of elegance and luxury – calls to mind prancing thoroughbreds and pink coats. Or take the umbrella. It is an ingenious, thoroughly functional device, neat and practical. But you simply cannot imagine it in company with the racquet or the riding boot. They do not speak the same language. There seems to be something finicky about an umbrella, something rather cold and reserved – an air of dignity which the racquet utterly lacks.

We get to the point where we cannot describe our impressions of an object without treating it as a living thing with its own physiognomy. For even the most precise description, enumerating all visible characteristics, will not give an inkling of what we feel is the essence of the thing itself. Just as we do not notice the individual letters in a word but receive a total impression of the idea the word conveys, we generally are not aware of what it is that we perceive but only of the conception created in our minds when we perceive it.

Not only the tennis racquet but everything connected with the game – the court, the tennis player's clothes – arouses the same sensations. The garb is loose and comfortable, the shoes are soft – in keeping with the relaxed condition in which the player moves about the court idly picking up balls, reserving his energy for the speed and concentration which will be demanded of him the instant the ball is in play. If, later in the day, the same man appears at an official function in uniform or formal attire, not only his appearance will have changed but his entire being. His posture and gait are influenced by his clothes; restraint and dignity are now the keynote.

Turning from these examples from daily life to architecture, we find that the best buildings have been produced when the architect has been inspired by something in the problem which will give the building a distinctive stamp. Such buildings are created in a special spirit and they convey that spirit to others.

External features become a means of communicating feelings and moods from one person to another. Often, however, the only message conveyed is one of conformity. Man is less lonely when he feels that he is part of a general movement. People who get together for a common purpose try to appear as much alike as possible. If one of them finds himself a bit conspicuous, he is likely to feel miserable; the entire occasion is spoiled for him.

In pictures from a particular period people seem to look very much alike. It is not only a question of clothes and the style of hair-dress, but of posture and movement and the entire manner in which the people conduct themselves. In memoirs of the same period you find that the mode of living harmonizes with the external picture, and you will also find that the buildings, streets and towns were attuned to the rhythm of the era.

When it had passed historians discovered that a definite style had dominated the period and they gave it a name. But those who lived in that style were not aware of it. Whatever they did, however they dressed, seemed natural to them. We speak of a "Gothic" period or a "Baroque" period, and dealers in antiques and those who make their living manufacturing fake antiques are familiar with all the small details that are characteristic of each style in all its phases. *But details tell nothing essential about architecture, simply because the object of all good architecture is to create integrated wholes.*

Understanding architecture, therefore, is not the same as being able to determine the style of a building by certain external features. It is not enough to *see* architecture; you must experience it. You must observe how it was designed for a special purpose and how it was attuned to the entire concept and rhythm of a specific era. You must dwell in the rooms, feel how they close about you, observe how you are naturally led from one to the other. You must be aware of the textural effects, discover why just those colours were used, how the choice depended on the orientation of the rooms in relation to windows and the sun. Two apartments, one above the other, with rooms of exactly the same dimensions and with the same openings, can be entirely different simply because of curtains, wallpaper and furniture. You must experience the great difference acoustics make in your conception of space: the way sound acts in an enormous cathedral, with its echoes and long-toned reverberations, as compared to a small panelled room well-padded with hangings, rugs and cushions.

Man's relation to implements can be broadly described thus: children begin by playing with blocks, balls and other things which they can grasp in their hands. As time goes on they demand better and better tools. At a certain stage most children have the desire to build some sort of shelter. It may be a real cave dug into a bank, or a primitive hut of rough boards. But often it is no more than a secret nook hidden among bushes, or a tent made with a rug draped over two chairs. This "cave game" can be varied in a thousand ways but common to them all is the enclosing of space for the child's own use. Many animals are also able to create a shelter for themselves, by digging a hole in the ground or building some sort of habitation above it. But the same species always does it in the same way. Man alone forms dwellings which vary according to requirements, climate and cultural pattern. The child's play is continued in the grown-up's creation, and just as man progresses from simple blocks to the most refined implements, he progresses from the cave game to more and more refined methods of enclosing space. Little by little he strives to give form to his entire surroundings.

And this – to bring order and relation into human surroundings – is the task of the architect.

Own House by Erik Christian Sørensen

1957

Erik Christian Sørensen

On Form, In Space

On form

Building is, in our time, looked upon passively. It is a growing area – an evolution that is technological in origin and in a way apart from our feelings.

Buildings of today do not appeal to us in the same way as the constructions of the past. The art of building (design) is classified as a necessity, technical and economical in nature and of minor interest if not considered in conjunction with the functional background.

Once design and engineering were the same thing, architecture the end result. The complexity of the contemporary society has developed specialization. This is not to be regretted nor can it be otherwise. The single individual cannot master all the details of a building problem, and we have to engage in teamwork. But this does not alter the conception of architecture as an art, and its importance is not less. The fact is that building is one of the most influential tools of civilization.

And the art of building is the manifestation of the cultural level of its time, architecture is one of the subtle expressions of the human mind.

We can look at the buildings of history, and not only look for the style, that of course is also only a label of our own. We can see the houses as a synthesis of the level of technology, order of society, the spirit of man, and the development of art. The cultural pattern of a time – as far as we are concerned – is derivative from the work of artists. Not forced individually, but extracted from the plural. The work of the single is probably of brief value if it is not rooted in the existing, and if it does not try to interpret the new, the original, into an intelligible context with the contemporaneous.

To try to create a style, as we have seen at the beginning of this century with Jugend or Art Nouveau, must fail. The departure of design was taken in visual impressions from organic nature, but there was no correspondence to the means of production nor science. It was hardly based on an understanding of the structural principle of the forms which gave the inspiration. Though as a style it can tell us about a time of confusion, of a dissipated art symptomatic of its age.

What conditions make the premise for creative work, form the framework for a style? Style understood as more than a formalist scheme, explained as the common denominator of the art of an epoch. This is a general question, a part of which we shall deal with here when we ask: what can be our point of departure studying architecture, what can be our fundamentals as architects?

First of all, when we attend a school it must primarily be the tradition. The living tradition shall be understood and developed if we shall not form a new eclecticism but work for an art, which shall not become stale. Our sources must be the same that always have nourished the human artistic sense (human sensitiveness) and in aims of education we must intellectually make these unobstructed.

It can be believed that there are two things basic to the growth of art, they are Art and Nature. The space-phenomena of nature are, broadly speaking, the primary surroundings of man, and our senses, which experiences life in time and space, are complementary tied to nature.

A point of view on the establishment of an understanding of art like this is in conformity to the evolution of our philosophy.

Put in another way the same can be viewed as such: architecture is essentially tied in its expression to the human senses and orientation.

Nature is to be understood as the surrounding world. Nature with its forms, colours and spaces is the place where our knowledge comes from, and therefore also what we first have to pay attention to for a training of our eye and a development of our record of mental impressions and our emotional response. We will try to look at the outer world anew as if we have no direction of the movement of our evolution.

Not looking for any stylistic expression, we shall see the thing that originally has made an impression and been able to nourish our sense of architecture.

The first thing noted when watching nature is probably extension. The horizontal plane is the image of this, contrasted with objects erected from it. An example is how the boats floating in a little harbour tell us about the size of the landscape and make the space into a unity.

These approximately congruent shapes form together a spatial continuity (or a picture of space-time), which the eye can follow and we can perceive an intense experience of space. Everyone who wanders in nature has seen how different forms take shapes which can be understood. Volumes which accentuate, perhaps demarcate a space, can tell about order of spaces, and give an impulse to orientation in and understanding of the landscape. (I want here to refer to the European landscape painting which operates within foreground to background, like on a stage to describe the depth of space.)

A lake with mist illustrates that the continuity of objects can delineate a space. We look at the reeds side by side over the surface, we know what they are and how big they are, and so through them we can read distance at a glance. We see the stone and the point, and they give us an explanation to the background we can only see indistinctly but these things together give us an understanding of this particular piece of landscape. We saw the reeds (we can see objects) as an indicator of scale in a space because we know them, have had them singled out, have had knowledge of them, not only by looking at them, but also by touching. And in this way we can study the components of our surroundings.

We find that the external world is composed of distinctive qualities characteristic in growth, colour, texture, odour, manner of breaking or how they feel and so on. But as a picture it is the light that makes it possible for the eye to perceive the form, and it is through further study that we come to a perception which adds to and enlarges the visual experience. Our capability of seeing is so great that we observe new forms, new textures, and comprehend what the play of light tells us and easily distinguish different materials only by their particular texture.

From form and colour we identify the things. But an object observed alone is different than seen in relation to others. We discover that the information from the single item change in character when seen together with others. It then has not only texture and form but also scale and space, and, I think, is the first example of something that has an architectural importance.

If we look at a stone, we know it is all of its qualities we sense. It is our knowledge of stone which we have in mind, the specific gravity and structure as we know from the treatment of stones. It is the nature of the stone that determines its aptitude as a component in building. Our first lesson of links joined we get from the stone in the wall, a basic element of construction. When we see the stones as a base in the wooden house we feel an intrinsic accordance, and we understand at what level we can study our inheritance, not mixed up with stylistic considerations. (We try to investigate as if it were the first time we interpreted the phenomenon.)

In the same way we can also trace from the woodpiles how the wood, having been through the sawmill and cut into boards, is piled up to form a shape which can be examined as a man-made thing. The form has a functional background, the boards are separated with small sticks to make airspaces in between in order to dry them, they are lifted above ground to prevent decay, they are disposed length-wise, for easy survey and later transport.

It is altogether an order resembling the coherence we rediscover where man treats materials. Our knowledge of the wood guides our use of it. We recall from timber-frame construction, how it acts as the framework for the architectural expression, giving the bays and rhythm. We know the beauty that can rise when the innate rules are respected. It is so that buildings as well as woodpiles have an imperative set of rules, given by the materials.

If we look at some barrels, we see how the shape of the barrel is underlying two different ways of stacking them, each with its own visual feature. We see barrels put together into a volume, visible in the sunlight one by one and in their entirety as an orderly whole. It can be viewed as if it were a building principle expressed and as a carrier of an architectural order. We see the material, in this case the barrel, serve in accordance to its own character to function in the stack.

We cannot have a more direct illustration than the one we have in the suspension-bridge of the relation between material and static principle, that can be grasped in an instant. It can also serve to point out another fact of importance to me. We have in the bridge an elegant expression of a construction, in which the materials are used sincerely, and we can make a comparison to the house standing next to the abutment.

We do not think that houses necessarily must be built in accordance with the forms that the houses of history have been limited to by means of materials, technology and architectural expressions.

We have more or less nothing to guide us, and we have to search for rules and new ways. The formal idiom has, through the architectural revolution in the last generation, been substituted by a more simple mode of expression based on

Cubist form. It can be considered as having cleared the way for new values. It gave us wonderful clean-cut building forms, but also these were influenced by an ideal geometry which was not always in agreement with the structure. Later development has shown to us how one can build, as disciplined as in the 1930s, with the same simple guiding stereometric figures but it has also been possible to express a differentiation in the use of the component materials.

We like to see the bearing columns, the carried deck and the enclosing wall separated from each other to make an individual statement. It is a way of design with higher demands than the one working with preconceived forms. It is a method in which the involved objects are expressed according to function and material quality, and the architectural skill is to see how they form space in relation to each other and to the entirety.

We can see our new spatial possibilities not limited by formalist geometry, at the same time we presuppose a stern discipline, using the materials in a fashion true to their character.

We are in an age of rapid changes from the past that formed earlier ideas: changed technology and scientific progress brings along new potential for human society, and open up the field for new realities to be interpreted by the artist. And though it is true that no civilization can raise a cultural harmony without art, it has to be a true art not remote from life, an art genuinely interpreting its own time, reflecting all aspects of its time. This is to us an architecture that does not disavow its inheritance only to be novel, because history is one of our realities. An architecture that is not secluded in a tradition or eclectic form, but is open for permanent revaluations. An act of appreciation that always – and only – takes the human sense and knowledge as measurement.

We know that we live in an age of transformation. The human perception is changed, our understanding of nature and of our self is altered from previous time.

We are placed in new situations and so an individual as well as a society will seek for someone or something to guide the direction of action. Lacking a cultural pattern for adaptation of the new potentiality, it is natural to search the experience of history in order to, in the collective learnings, find values appropriate to the new circumstances. It also often happens that a technical progress does imply a retrogression. It can be so when the new is not understood and it is dressed in a historical form, but usually it is implicit of better technic that the untrue form becomes obsolete in a short time.

When we have an extension of knowledge we are compelled to find the relation of the new to the existing and try to evaluate the new and make a comparison with the known which the new eventually substitutes.

In periods of great changes it can also be of positive value to investigate other cultures, as done by us in the beginning of this century, when European art and architecture received much from both primitive and oriental art.

We have ourselves looked into antiquity, the gothic period, oriental buildings and primitive art from Africa or the South Pacific, and everywhere seen things and qualities for consideration and made comparisons between the objects in question and the society that produced them. That is a search for a lever in our own attempt to accomplish a cultural pattern balancing our technological advantages. In a fundamental revaluation it is a matter of course to try to determine primary things, thus we try to define architecture. We have seen that the art of building is closely related to its contemporary knowledge of man (the part not resumed here). We have seen it is not only the material that can confine architectural expression; at the same time we know that architectural forms are intimately tied to and dependent on the nature of materials. I will as a point of departure use the definition of architecture as being the order expressed when man forms his material surroundings.

For the conviction we want to assure that we have two fundamentals. First, *the spiritual*, the innate of architecture, the offspring of common knowledge of its age and, second, *the skilful* handling of the material, coherent with the technology and sensitive treatment of matter, which is the basis of the process of building and form.

The first, the connection between art and our present knowledge I will return to. The latter, the material transformed by man, and the rules for the process I will point out here. One can assume the thesis, that the visual structural order and the intelligible is not only a decorative possibility of civilization but a vital instrument for an existence of integrated culture. The intention in using these words is to bring our explanations closer to modern science.

Science has produced a definition of civilization, stating that it is the contrary of the entropic tendency of nature.

This we can explain: a branch of physics is called thermodynamic. Here it is confirmed that all matter tends to move towards the simplest state, the "thermodynamic equilibrium" or what we call disorder. This recorded alteration of the matter, this movement of thermal energy is measured by entropy. Or it could be said, entropy is the degree of thermal energy not transformed into mechanical work. To us it looks like the absolute formless, the amorphous homogeneous is what everything in nature drifts towards. And the human will to form is counteracting nature as such. Our design, handling of stuff, is form-giving.

It is a resultant of directed ideas which are anti-entropic, the polarization of these forces is called civilization, and form-giving, engineering and design is the canalization of, or determination of, the means and efforts we have for control of nature. Viewed in another way it can be said we cannot survive without precautions, as we are physically poorly equipped compared to the animals. In order to support life and to compensate for our naked hands we have invented tools. It is in these implements that the will to form is manifested. And a tool can be any physical apparatus extending our abilities.

Elementarily there is no difference between a spade and a bulldozer. An axe or a knife is our claw. A house is our protection against the climate. A wheel or a gear is augmentative to the motion paramount to our endeavours.

A fire and an electromotor are both tools important in the rise of our present civilization. In the same way bridges and roads, houses and towns and communication systems are means created by art and science. In buildings the faculty of forming is stated most evidently. The visual and the structural order in the process of civilization is the pronunciation of culture.

Fine architecture is an expression coherent with the presuppositions. The idea of how to create in space is inherent in the learning of our surrounding world, the medium is the materials of constructions.

We can cultivate our relation to the materials. There are some we like, some we think are beautiful. They appeal to our senses through their colour, form, texture for an aesthetic response.

The materials we work with create their own laws. The wooden house takes its shape from the peculiarities of wood. There are many forms we superficially classify as stylistic traditional (classic), for example the division of a door into frame and panel can be seen as a result of something formal but at the same time it is a merit of necessity, designed this way in order to guide the shrinkage of the wood.

Today our knowledge of the materials is not only empiric, since the research in the microscopic structure, chemical analysis and so on, are giving us further information necessary for intelligent procedure in the design process.

As much as we can find samples where the matter ascribes a form we can also see cases where we can use arbitrary shapes. There can be many reasons but naturally the form is bound to the structure of the material but not in the same way as we know it from the wooden house.

If we look at a Mexican stow-base we can see it has a volume-form as if it has been moulded by a sculptor. It has a surface that is our domination over the stone. It might be explained as a wish to give it a form that is stronger and bigger in scale than the decay in ageing. It can also be the pleasure of decoration, but usually the patterns derive from methods of joining the stones, as we know from weaving, basket making and so on. We can explain it in this way, when the form given by the function can vary and we have to choose, to design, our choice is derived from our architectural ideas. The curbed edge of a basin is the carrier of a form-idea, being the chosen one of many, whereas the curved roadside is one grown out of the local topography. The organic form we discover so many times in primitive building where materials and forms merge into a unity.

We can as a contrast see the pompous use of materials. When we look at the stone façade of a Renaissance palazzo, we find it is a big and strong house, it impresses us in the same way as the big Mexican stone monuments.

Another modus of European shaping, I will mention, is the one that explains the motif.

We can see it in a corner of Loggia dei Lanzi in front of the town hall in Florence. It is common to introduce forms that will guide our eyes to the intellectual understanding the designer wants the spectator to have of the composition of the whole building or façade. There are still other forms, forms derived purely from a function, for example we could take the millstone, or the more complex industrial design products. It could be a mixer or an automobile, we can only find them beautiful if we can trace the dominance of the human spirit over substantial matter.

We can learn from glassmaking, basket weaving, from the potters' turntable as well as from traditional house construction. Each has its pattern, its methods based on the material, and these have to be respected if the result shall be of genuine value.

We have seen the material organized and have had an understanding of it, but in our new buildings we are often without any prototypes or precedent of the problem we deal with because, perhaps, we use new materials or use the well-known in a new way. No matter what, it is mandatory for us to widen our understanding of the materials.

When we investigate the forms we find in nature it is as though there are two different kinds, we can experience. The one kind is where organic growth is manifested as in the seashell. The second is the kind where the form emerges from a physical-mechanical action in, on, or of a material. Both can be of interest to study and give beautiful experiences of forms.

We know the nautilus, the ingenious spiral or the beautiful leaf in which the idea of vegetation comes forth. And look at the sand dune, see how it has got the specific form from the wind setting the sand in movement into waves. From this we can learn something of the second kind of forms. We can see forms as a resultant of a motion.

From such forms we can learn lessons if we can comprehend the parallel of what happens when we use machines for production.

We might discuss more varied forms. But proceeding we shall look for the thing made in a genuine way formed to describe space, the most important step for the architect. Most simply this can be depicted in the rope. Close to this idea also comes the wood. It appears to us that we can perceive the one tree as the manifested form-idea but the many trees, the wood, as the space.

When we are building ourselves we try to find the organic order and with the system in mind design, organize in space. We see the great beauty when materials are handled in accordance to their character and their appearance in light, hence describing forms truly in space.

In space

It is evident that architectural forms are dependent on the nature of the material they are made from, and that the treatment of materials is guided by the processing technique. Construction is a direct indicator of civilization, but the understanding of form problems does not explain the relation between the architectural expression and its functional motivations. Few shapes are unvaryingly given by technique or material. To design calls for the creative faculty which in vision must be associated with the human conception. The work of an architect has a material and rational basis, but it is not prescribed by this in its expression as an art.

The art of building is dependent on the materials, the technique and the construction methods of its time. It would be of low quality if it is in conflict with these, but pertaining to space it is subscribing only to the spirit of man.

Architecture can be viewed as an expression of its contemporary knowledge, it is an offspring of the creative ability to render the ideas of the society in which it is reared.

For an understanding of our own time it would be easy if logical points of departure for design could be singled out – but that is impossible. Even if the progress of one branch of our activities could be described, a specific knowledge does not have the same validity for all parts of society. Our situation has to be viewed as a whole and be regarded in relation to the historic evolution. This means, that in education we must study the tradition with an eye open for conditions that are able to produce a change of, or a break away from, the accepted.

Most influential on our civilization is technology – for better or worse. Not considering the present second industrial revolution, we can see that the technical development has been continuously growing for a couple of centuries, but only in the last generation the architectural possibilities of the machine age has been realized.

The great buildings of the nineteenth century – harbours, bridges, warehouses, railroads and so on – were not inspired by architects. Architecture of that time was out of contact with everyday life, secluded in a revival of historic form, acting merely as an art of decoration. Nevertheless, the downright functional forms of the industrial age were what excited a new consciousness and aroused the new architectural tradition, which grew out of an international movement.

In many countries academic styles were overturned, and many obstacles, both social and professional, were removed. This does not mean however that we have an architectural revolution behind us. If we remember that architecture though dependent of technique and material is basically an expression of vision, we have to deny that the future can be framed by a functional tradition.

If we look upon architecture as an art, we know that the wider knowledge of today has to be interpreted in forms different from those which sufficed in the past.

I think it is right to say that we use the functional basis as a lever for a new concept, but it is not the reason for it. What brings it forward is the altered conception based on the new thinking of art and science, and again that is a development started back in the eighteenth century.

Before that time we saw art and science in collaboration, often mastered by the same person, today we hardly find any understanding from one to the other. After the declarations of Galileo and Newton, art and science have been separated. It was commonly believed, that they were excluding each other in method of working and in result. It was found that nature could be measured and described in mathematical forms and the knowledge gained led to a still greater control of our surroundings.

What could be measured precisely became important in our civilization – but the quantity was not the medium of the arts, and art consequently was regarded as less useful, that is to say of lesser value in society.

The necessary distinction for science to make was a disadvantage for the arts as long as it was not realized that science made research into a new nature and that the humanities had no new vision, working principally in the tradition inherited from the Greeks. In art since the Renaissance we are witness to a growing away from social and technical needs, and in the last century to a degeneration where new experiments did not concentrate on the essentials of the artistic medium.

We have seen that architecture was not in accordance with the technological progress of science. It was alien to the new technical demands and was so remote from the activities of the society that finally it did not have anything positive to offer. Art and science have in the great periods been in interaction, and I think one of the promising possibilities we now have, is that in modern science there is a trend toward the humanist, and at the same time art has given up its isolation. We know now that science and art are faculties of the human consciousness, and both inform us about relations, and give us images to work with. They both elaborate our perception, give us orders of meaning, and enlarge our knowledge of the environment.

What this signifies for the architect is that his preposition is to unite knowledge. A scientific insight and a technical principle can be directly translated from the innate concrete values, and this should be done from the primary impulses they have on his artistic perception, and not be fused into preconceived forms as we have become accustomed to since the Renaissance. This means that architecture derives not only from an able form-giving, or is an expression of a sense of colour or of pattern, but also as a true belonging of space. The essentials of architecture belong to the articulation of the material in space-time. And as we know that space and time are the exclusive dimensions of life, we know they are also the true dimension of art, if it shall be a living art. Therefore architecture, associated with the basic activities of human existence, providing the necessary shelter and frames for the life of society, also at the same time becomes of vital stylistic interest. Not every solution to a practical problem is of vital stylistic interest; it is only the one that moves us, inspires us or encourages us, only the one that satisfies all our needs.

It is in order to cope with the new demands of the technical civilization that our architectural vocabulary has to be enlarged. In our search for the fulfilment, we now know that architecture cannot be framed only by technical or functional requirements, for the utilitarian is of another world than the spiritual.

In classic Greek architecture we saw that it was not new functional needs which elevated the art of building. It was a perfection in order to meet the demand for an ideal house, a spiritual requirement for the acropole. The Greeks invented nothing in their architecture, they just developed what they had inherited from a more primitive building tradition. But they did it purposefully, not by producing anything according to a practical demand, and hardly in respect of the material or constructive technic, only by making an image. The Greek temple gives a pure expression of form, a monument which consecrated the ideal beauty and nothing else. In a different world and in a later period we find it in another way: the Gothic cathedrals. In a sense it was the practical demands which supplied the inspiration. The buttress is developed from a technique, but the result again is of an unexplainable beauty expressed in space. A higher unity of material and form is articulated based not on a constructive necessity but on a vision. A vision that is in accordance with the aspiration of society.

We think it is the total knowledge of a given time that creates the space concept and that determines the architecture. However we cannot expect new values if the builders are only schematically recording new trends; the real progress comes through the interpretations of those we call the creative. We have heard about Phidias, sculptor and architect in one person and we have seen works by Renaissance artists like Michelangelo who painted, sculpted and built. We do not know the names of the men who conceived the Gothic cathedrals, but we do know it is not right to share the romantic belief that they originated from an ideal of teamwork.

In the same way it is not unreasonable to think that the architect of today who would accomplish genuine results must have a broad foundation. We cannot think that a specialist training is right for an architect, but he should be one who can govern the many tendencies and possibilities of the present, and if we have this outlook in our contemporary architectural situation it is easier to come to a new understanding.

What I am saying does not indicate a condemnation of the functional in building. I do not mean that the analysis of plan-circulation, economical programming considerations and research in building technique can be reduced. On the contrary – but they alone cannot be a foundation for architecture.

In the strict functional buildings of today we find great beauty, taking as one example a bridge. The analysis of the function of the bridge brings us more than one design, and we have to select the one which most simply states one idea, the most beautiful bridge. We find here that the material carrying out the function becomes subordinated to an idea, in the same way as the stones of a pyramid are condensed into the idea of the pyramidal shape, the architecture of the pyramid.

I think this bears a relation to us and we shall proceed with this in mind when we look at the architectural progress and statements from our time.

We know we cannot associate ourselves with a formalist architecture because just as well as the classicist it removes the idea away from the concrete problem of handling material over to allusions and illusions, and it works with abstracts as space, form and plan which are composed. It is, so to speak, an intellectual play, and an academic training is required to get the full understanding.

Thus architecture placed itself among the other arts in a manner where it had not only the same medium but also the same goal. The functional, often in conflict with the ideal or the classic, has been a stronghold in the reaction against academic architecture, and contemporary architects have also – perhaps instinctively – tried to reach back to the Gothic period, where constructions were in true accordance with materials, and where painting, sculpture and architecture joined in a spiritual union.

Without speaking about the forms, it can now be said that the foundation of the working process is the analysis of the function in a broad sense and the means are the materials, but the unfolding is in the dimension of space-time.

The first condition for construction and form comes from the material. The relation to the other arts is explained, as we know that architecture cannot be an art in the same medium as painting and sculpture. It is denied that volume can be the only expression of space. Space cannot be registered by a cubic form just as water cannot be measured by a string. Architecture is an art in space and it is expressed in space-time. With the knowledge we have gained from science and the experiences from painting (the two-dimensional art), and from sculpture (the three-dimensional art), the architect's task is to shape material with divisions and precision into spaces, in which we move and which frame the life of man and give us rooms to live in.

As in all true art, it has to be able to mirror spiritually our contemporary knowledge. We know that it is not right as was done in the 1930s to overthrow the old space concept. It will exist always as it is a part of our cultural inheritance, it is a part of our knowledge, even if that alone does not satisfy all our needs. We will work from the tradition, but in addition to the static principle of the classic art we will introduce a dynamic principle as we have experienced it. This is understood only by few.

That we live in an age of transitions, however, is most evident. But a common belief is that a broadening of the progress of the 1920s and 1930s, backed up with a philosophy based on the human or the functional, is only what is needed. It is not understood that what is called human has become the self-grown, the picturesque, the denial of the will to form, and that the functional has not much innate for the artistic idea. The real progress of the past decades has been that we have become aware of the possibilities of the machine and found means to cope with it. The dark age was over, the architect could extend his field, plan on a broader basis but in the human scale. Unfortunately, architecture and design have not, in the same way as modern painting and sculpture, been freed from the past, nor have they been extended to respond to our new experiences in science and society.

Consequently the art of building has either been formalist or confused. Formalist with Cubism as a vocabulary, or it has been indulging in empiricist translation of the traditional.

It must be understood that the new architecture we strive for is not to be expressed only in the use of new materials or through a new technique with the consequently changed form-giving. Neither is it to be expressed as an idealization of the utilitarian. On the contrary, our materials are too often the same, and used in the same way as before, and the utilitarian which would produce a functionalism does not enter when we talk about the prepositions of our art. It belongs to the answering of practical demands.

What we seek is an architecture able to encompass the frame of life – to reflect all our experiences in the true order of art. This is basically different from the architecture which since the Renaissance has been the expression of western civilization.

It is our intention – today – to accentuate the dynamic construction and place it together with the formerly one and only static-symbolic principle of architecture. This is not only to work with materials in formal volume relations, but to accept the nature of the materials and use them only as the carrier of forces according to an idea, which comes to life in the constructions of space-time.

Sydney Opera House (during contruction) by Jørn Utzon

1962

Jørn Utzon

Platforms and Plateaus: Ideas of a Danish Architect

The platform as an architectural element is a fascinating feature. I first fell in love with it in Mexico on a study trip in 1949, where I found many variations, both in size and idea, of the platform, and where many of the platforms are alone without anything but the surrounding nature.

All the platforms in Mexico were positioned and formed with great sensitivity to the natural surroundings and always with a deep idea behind. A great strength radiates from them. The feeling under your feet is the same as the firmness you experience when standing on a large rock.

Let me give you two examples of the brilliance of the idea behind it. In Yucatan, in Uxmal and Chichén Itzá, the same principle is followed, based on identical natural surroundings. Yucatan is a flat lowland covered with an inaccessible jungle, which grows to a certain uniform defined height. In this jungle the Mayans lived in their villages with small pieces of land cleared for cultivation, and their surrounding, background as well as roof, was the hot, damp, green jungle. No large views, no up and down movements.

By introducing the platform with its level at the same height as the jungle top, these people had suddenly obtained a new dimension of life, worthy of their devotion to their gods. On these high platforms – many of them as long as 100 meters – they built their temples. They had from here the sky, the clouds and the breeze, and suddenly the jungle roof had been converted into a great open plain. By this architectural trick they had completely changed the landscape and supplied their visual life with greatness, corresponding to the greatness of their gods.

Today you can still experience this wonderful variation in feeling from the closeness in the jungle to the vast openness on the platform top. It is parallel to the relief you feel here in Scandinavia when after weeks of rain, clouds and darkness, you suddenly come through all this, out into the sunshine again.

In India and the East, not forgetting the Acropolis and the Middle East, many wonderful platforms of various kinds are the backbone of architectural compositions and all of them based on a great concept. A few examples follow.

The big mosque in Old Delhi is an outstanding one. It is surrounded by the markets and the bazaar buildings, placed in a pell-mell of traffic, people, animals, noise and nervous buildings. Here, raised approximately three to five meters above this is an enormous red sandstone platform surrounded by arcades on the outer contours of the platform. These arcades are closed by walls on three sides of the platform, so that you can look through only at the fourth side, and here, from above, have contact with the life and disorder of the town. On this square or platform, you have a strong feeling of remoteness and complete calmness. An effect, no client or architect would have dreamed possible in advance, has been achieved by so very few means.

Chinese houses and temples owe much of their feeling of firmness and security to the fact that they stand on a platform with the same outline as that of the roof or sometimes even of larger size, depending upon the importance of the building. There is magic in the play between roof and platform.

The floor in a traditional Japanese house is a delicate bridge-like platform. This Japanese platform is like a tabletop and you do not walk on a tabletop. It is a piece of furniture. The floor here attracts you as the wall does in a European house. You want to sit close to the wall in a European house, and here in Japan, you want to sit on the floor and not walk on it. All life in Japanese houses is expressed in sitting, lying or trawling movements. Contrary to the Mexican rock-like feeling of the platform, here you have a feeling similar to the one you have when standing on a small wooden bridge, dimensioned to take just your weight and nothing more. A refined addition to the expression of the platform in the Japanese house is the horizontal emphasis provided by the movements of the sliding doors and screens, and the black pattern made by the edges of the floor mats accentuate the surface.

An almost violent, but highly effective and wonderful contrast to this calm, linear, natural coloured architecture is created by the Japanese women moving noiselessly around like exotic butterflies in their gaily coloured silk kimonos.

The second example from Mexico is Monte Alban, an ingeniously chosen site for devotion to the gods. The human regulation or adaptation of the site has resulted in something even stronger than nature and has given it spiritual content.

The little mountain, Monte Alban, almost a pyramid, dominates three valleys outside the town, Oaxaca, in Southern Mexico. The top of the pyramid is lacking and leaves a great flat part, approximately 500 by 300 meters. By the introduction of the staircase arrangements and step-like buildings on the edge of the platform and keeping the central part at a lower level, the mountain top has been converted into a completely independent thing floating in the air, separated from the earth, and from up there you see actually nothing but the sky and the passing clouds – a new planet.

Some of my projects from recent years are based on this architectural element, the platform. Besides its architectural force, the platform gives a good answer to today's traffic problems. The simple thing that cars can pass underneath a surface, which is reserved for pedestrian traffic, can be developed in many ways.

Most of our beautiful European squares suffer from cars. Buildings, that "spoke with each other" across a square, either in axis systems or in balanced composition, are not corresponding any more because of the traffic flow. The height of the cars, their speed and surprisingly noisy behaviour make us seek away from squares, which used to be restful places for walking.

In some of my schemes, there are various traffic layers under the platform – for covered pedestrian intercommunication, for car traffic and for parking. The buildings stand on top of the platform supporting each other in an undisturbed composition.

In the Sydney Opera House scheme, the idea has been to let the platform cut through like a knife and separate primary and secondary functions completely. On top of the platform the spectators receive the completed work of art and beneath the platform every preparation for it takes place.

To express the platform and avoid destroying it is a very important thing, when you start building on top of it. A flat roof does not express the flatness of the platform.

In the schemes for the Sydney Opera House and the Danish Confederation of Trade Unions School, you can see roofs, curved forms, hanging higher or lower over the plateau. The contrast of forms and the constantly changing heights between these two elements result in spaces of great architectural force made possible by the modern structural approach to concrete construction, which has given so many beautiful tools into the hands of the architect.

SAS Royal Hotel by Arne Jacobsen

1963

Arne Jacobsen

Contemporary Form and Design

As a young and enthusiastic architecture student I used every opportunity to travel, as often as my small financial resources allowed, to Germany. I was excited by German culture, and a great admirer of the Bauhaus movement in Dessau. At that time, I never dreamt that I would be of any importance here, in Germany. Unfortunately, however, the first time this took place was during the Third Reich, when I was forced to leave my home country. This second time, however, is an occasion about which I am very happy, and which touches me deeply. Yes, times change, all too quickly. Trust has to be rebuilt between peoples and, it can never be too often repeated, not through insularity and resentment, but by working together and exchanging ideas.

The possibility for nations to work together has never been so great as it is today. Modern technology helps us to strive for a better insight, and therefore a greater understanding, of mutual problems. The aim is a world community, which we all look forward to, and it is to be hoped that, over the coming generations, man's egoism will play a lesser role. International trade helps by overcoming the reluctance to open barriers between nations. I do not mean that regional and national cultural identities should be destroyed, exactly the opposite. We should help each other to preserve them. It will surely not be so difficult to do this, as we already appreciate foreign things, and (as the Germans say) the cherries in the neighbour's garden . . .

These reflections are optimistic, but today there are many indications that they are not too optimistic. We must believe in positive future developments because, particularly in our profession, it is only on this foundation that we can continue to build.

Many people think that to be a real architect one must have a philosophy. I do not believe it is necessary, but I know how easily a "zealous" journalist can be "helpful" in forcing an architect to adopt a personal philosophy. I have, myself, very often experienced this pressure. If you were to ask me today, I would still answer that I do not carry around a ready-made philosophy. Such a thing is dangerous, a straitjacket for a natural architectural understanding, an alienation from reality, an idealistic construction, that all too quickly ages, and can lose touch with our lives now. An architectural philosophy can easily become something to which one clings, to support one's standpoint, a pillow on which one can sleep, undisturbed.

Today, the 35-year-old Bauhaus way of thinking is still relevant. Thankfully, functionalism still exists. If we were to abandon this tenet it would be very easy to stray along a dangerous path, leading to a futile architecture. Dangerous, because architecture is an applied art, and must remain so. Few great talents have been able to produce real art, by transforming functions into abstractions – and, anyway, does this not go too far in crossing the border between architecture and sculpture? Perhaps, it is not quite right, what I said at the beginning, that I have no professional philosophy, but Bauhaus thinking; the relationship between function, technology and aesthetics, has so deeply stamped our attitudes, that it is accepted as a matter of course by every honest working architect.

We are living at a time in which sober functionalism is even more influential than in the 1920s. I am referring to industrialized building. The question is, whether these systems, as yet in their infancy, will be directed by architects or engineers. I believe it falls to us, as architects. We must find an attitude and then work hard on mastering this problem. To ignore it would be to fail in an area of great importance, and would have severe consequences. There would remain for us only a few commissions for landmark monuments, those unable to be made economical through prefabrication. Residential, administrative and industrial buildings are falling out of the sphere of artistic design influence. In Denmark they already build hospitals, schools, and universities with pre-cast unit systems. Architects plan them but the use of the new building methods are, in part, dictated by building economy politics. Our efficient manufacturers export a mass of technically good, prefabricated, buildings, the majority of which are without spirit or design fantasy. So far, they cannot compete in price with the conventional building methods within Denmark although, apparently, they can do so abroad, which is due, in no small measure, to our bad exchange rates.

On broaching this subject I would like to warn my German colleagues and strongly recommend that they do not miss the opportunity to include this subject in the curriculum, so that our young men, *together* with the engineers, are fully prepared to solve this important problem, and can also, perhaps, win back already lost ground.

Before, one was justified in criticizing city planning failures. Today, in general, that is no longer necessary, but one can still find examples of planning which have fallen victim to prefabrication methods, because construction cranes run most economically on straight tracks – so, in the end, do they. Why though, at a time when there is so much money available, should principals of saving be so overestimated as to damage quality, especially the hard to define non-materialistic aspects?

For prefabrication it is important that, as much as possible, the number of different units be kept to a minimum. Two to three are "ideal". The architect's task is then only one of intelligent "combination". Now, imagine, if one deprives a child of all his building blocks, apart from two or three, how quickly he will lose interest in playing. Nevertheless, despite these grim future possibilities, we must not turn away from the problem, or be prejudiced against new building methods, as some architects have become; then we would be reactionaries. Our task must be to concentrate all our knowledge and strengths on the most important aspect of architecture, proportional relationships. Here, where we are dealing with a multitude of similar elements, proportions become even more decisive. The present rush of prefabricated construction is aesthetically unsatisfying and, I believe, it suffers from the fact that good architects are not being given any opportunity to be involved.

While I have criticized the occasional monotony of particular city plans, I would like now to mention the positive work done in relevant areas of landscaping for recreation. One opens up the countryside through nationalization, or by relying on the generosity of private landowners, to give the population the possibility of recuperating within nature. But, is enough being done to awaken social awareness, so that this populating of the countryside does not become a "plague in the landscape"? The hectic pace of life in our cities gathers speed from day to day. To relax, one escapes into the woods and fields, only to be confronted, not with the nightingale, but the portable radio. Organized camping sites blanket the landscape's beauty spots. The colours of the tents are without modesty, shrill red, orange or blue, none of which match their surroundings. In the freedom of personal choice, and with ever louder colours, one demonstrates one's independent good taste. The already ugly picture is made even worse by the colours of plastic camping equipment. It is a mystery why the beautiful, silent, grey and brown shades, subordinate to nature, which the military discovered and used, have so quickly been forgotten. The oversupply of primary, and contrasting, hues on offer today, threatens to blunt our natural sensitivity to colour.

Think about the transparent slides that we use. The four elements are presented for our eyes only in colours, which the film manufacturers are able to produce. Take for instance an Agfa, a Ferrania or a Kodak sky, each one more beautiful than the other, but totally different. One of the most uncanny and common colours is piglet-marzipan, used for faces, arms and legs. Here one has picked precisely the healthy, "sex colour", which the public expects. Have you ever taken colour photographs of a slum quarter in a large city, to give the loved ones at home an impression of the inhumane conditions under which people live? I tried to do so in Pakistan. The dirty, rag-clad children, the stinking gutters, all appear unbelievably romantic. The false, synthetic colours create exactly the opposite of reality.

Nevertheless, that is not the most dangerous aspect of colour photography. I believe that, slowly but surely, we will develop a false and unreal colour concept, which will make nature's purity and reality more difficult for us to experience. We will no longer be able to discover its inestimable values, which will appear washed-out when we, unconsciously, compare them to our pictures at home. In other words, we will become colour addicted.

When I have spoken of the preservation of our landscape and cities I have concerned myself with the most meaningful area of city planning. In the future, the majority of this work should be entrusted to architects. Unfortunately, in recent times, it appears that politicians prefer engineers to architects. I think that is wrong. Aesthetics, which for us architects are, and must remain, of primary concern, cannot be eliminated from city and landscape planning. Sensitivity for a milieu is of decisive importance, a discipline for which the city planning architect has a high regard. For example, the planner must involve himself with the difficult problem of traffic, and here I have the feeling that while concentrating on creating parking places the overall streetscape is forgotten. Where previously squares lay between the buildings there are now just undefined and unexciting spaces lined with buildings. Apparently, pedestrianized streets, which have recently started appearing, should replace the old street milieu but I believe these are no compensation.

Today, the question as to who should be the coordinator of the necessary city planning teamwork is passionately discussed. We are living in times greatly influenced by technology, in which, unfortunately, aesthetics have not been recognized as having a function. People feel at ease, are happier in their work, and feel more cheerful, within aesthetically resolved conditions rather than those which are purely technically perfect. Politicians, however, still believe this is a luxury that we cannot afford. I believe, that when it is finally discovered what a grave mistake has been made, politicians will recognize that the coordinator of such planning work must be an architect.

In talking about planning in the big dimension one must not neglect the building and its details. When we look at the buildings with which we have filled our cities after the war, we must acknowledge that we have not progressed much beyond where we were during the Bauhaus era. Nevertheless, I believe, that the high-quality materials, which are the result of enormous technical development, give us possibilities to greatly improve building results. This is obvious in the appearance, and has resulted in an architecture aesthetically dominated by the structural expression. Sometimes we are angry when we cannot clearly show columns and beams and, instead, must dress everything in a curtain-like shirt, a curtain wall. The many, more or less, well-proportioned office blocks are examples of a building type, which appears most often, perhaps too often, in our cities. The public has become a little tired of them, and we architects, too. I believe, the well-proportioned and thoroughly detailed curtain wall type of building still serves a purpose but, it appears to me, it does not bring us any further. Certainly, one has learnt much and will, in many places in the future, still need this building type. By separating out sections of the long curtain wall façade, and by using new construction forms, this somewhat stiff, hard architecture, could be more interestingly designed.

We have seen how Brutalism, which for example in England has been strongly influenced by Le Corbusier, has shown us new ways. I am no great admirer of this so-called style, although in some places beautiful examples have been built. It appears to me, paradoxically, both brutal and romantic at the same time. I continue to stand for clear Functionalism, and must say that I think Mies van der Rohe is the most important living architect, an excellent example for us everyday working architects of how one can achieve clear, sound, easily understandable architecture, without fashionable ingredients.

The building methods of which I have spoken do not include residential buildings, which represent the most meaningful task with which we are entrusted. Housing architecture is in the course of becoming totally influenced by commercial demands and, what is worse, by politicians. This is the case at least in Denmark. Meanwhile the housing problem has become the most abused political weapon, which virtually all parties know how to deploy. The politicians decree a building stop, reverse their decision, and then enforce it again. In this way they disrupt the building rhythm, necessary for a quantity of good housing to be constructed in the shortest possible time.

The greater part of my observations is small nudges, reflecting my worries about the devaluation of the coming generation of architects. A devaluation, which

I believe, we can avoid when we add an absolutely necessary touch of humanity to the inhumane nature of industrialization, and raise building to an art form called architecture. I want to say here that, as an everyday working architect, I believe it is now, more than ever, necessary to be an architect, if one has the calling, and possesses 10 per cent talent and 90 per cent diligence – I know, today one has to talk in percentages – and in this way, I believe, we can achieve responsible results, more one cannot expect.

Tinggården Housing in Køge by Tegnestuen Vandkunsten

1974

Tegnestuen Vandkunsten

It Can Be Done!

It is not just a question of understanding the building process, it is also about achieving a decent way of life, one could say, if one were to look further than just the building.

Density, growth, variation, basis dwelling and building tradition are well-known expressions. And one can well imagine that our thoughts about this can contribute to influencing the coming mass-building of dense/low-rise housing that is already part of many municipal disposition plans, on one hand. On the other hand, we also work with the shortcomings of technocratic awareness, which knows that 1,000 is more than 100, but has no idea what is better than the misery it has quantitatively forced on us. And which can also plan dense/low-rise housing into the heads of the users.

The ideas and notions that arise in this context, with no direct relation to building, are an expression of a "vision": a coherent notion of a better way to live, or in any case to inhabit, than that which we are asked to do in our grey, ordinary lives. In other words, a consideration of a quality of life – and the requirements that we feel are necessary. What does this have to do with dense/low-rise building? Nothing, other than we believe that one can live "dense/low" on the eighth floor, and that "the residents' collective assumption of control of their homes within the framework of a local society" is in any case, the most important issue, on one hand.

On the other hand, we would like to argue that the new buildings to be built in the next decade, should be dense/low-rise schemes with increased opportunities for communal living and a maximum degree of sovereignty. We would also like to argue that the planning of these schemes, to as great a degree as possible, is done in collaboration with those who will live there, as it is our experience up until now, that the resulting projects will benefit from this. We would also like to argue that the renovation and urban renewal are planned at a neighbourhood level together with the local residents who are forced to remain in their homes. And finally, we would like to argue that the mobilization of residents, which this and other things assume and imply, results in the formation and recognition of local societies, and a new municipal reform that ensures the residents' understanding and competence. The existing municipalities allow a certain degree of community spirit. The upcoming mega-municipalities will be too large for this.

In the last two years, we have sailed with SBI, the National Building Research Institute, as our mother ship.

We have had to define that, which for us, were natural and urgent actions, such as "experiments, action research and alternative professional praxis", and for the increasingly sparse appropriations, we had to produce more and more project programmes, process analyses and research profiles to the powerful administrators, who otherwise had a general understanding that "the traditional decision makers . . . should yield a certain degree of competence", as was stated in the first project programme.

We used time and money to bring the Køge project up to the level that is described on the following pages, and to prepare an Ålborg experiment, which aside from a new resident planned and governed housing project, also includes resident participation in the planning and managing of urban renewal in the quarters where we will try to find participants for the new housing project. We have worked at transforming that which we and others have called visions, to operational planning concepts. For whom, we often ask ourselves, when we discover that our concepts cannot immediately be adapted to the before-mentioned rationality, which automatically considers any notions of a better way to live and any attempts to realize them as utopian. For us and the residents. For the residents who are tired of living in the 1,000 apartment housing complexes, and who have the courage to live in a shared housing project, which primarily consists of people who have had the possibility to want to do something together and therefore can do something together.

The redirection of the group's interest – from new building toward renovation and urban renewal – is based on the pursuit of a social and political goal: that the experiment should be realized together with the economically and educationally less privileged members of society – based on the reasoning that the more privileged can take care of themselves. However, the problem is that the low-income groups cannot pay the rent that a new apartment costs today, and that they have a very precise awareness of this problem. If the goal is to be maintained, it must be redirected away from new buildings towards redevelopment and the renewal of the existing housing areas, where the majority of the low income groups are still obliged to live. This problem is not just ours. The public housing associations must have a similar one, as their goal is primarily the same as ours.

We feel that much of the experience and results from the Køge project can be applied to the urban renewal and redevelopment situation. And that this must be accomplished if redevelopment and urban renewal are to cease evicting entire city blocks. This concerns the need for a practical communal activity and it concerns the organizational principles from the stair councils to the local society. And this ought to be the idea. The idea must be that communal living and self-government are human values, which should be practised – and not only when it is a matter of new buildings, product development and profit.

The Køge project – for the moment

The Køge project in the town of Herfølge should be seen as the tenants' and project group's conclusion after a year's programming efforts. This should not be considered a sketch or preliminary project in an ordinary sense, even though the material contains the same components. The project is more an illustration of the problems, which the experiment group wants to discuss with the implicated parties: the building owner, the municipal and ministerial authorities and the financial institutions.

In order to even begin substantial negotiations, it has proved to be necessary to bring the programming phase up to an unusually detailed level – and also much further than we originally imagined. It is primarily the residents' planning process that has determined the level of detailing. At each step of the process it has proven to be beneficial to employ illustrated examples of the actual, and in many cases highly complex, problems. This has been true in the work with the master plan, where we have sketched and discussed a number of principle proposals, in the organization of the site plan for the neighbourhood and the housing group itself, in the context of building methods and construction costs, and last but not least, in connection with the economical and organizational structure in the area.

The project's final form will depend on to how high a degree the housing associations and authorities can satisfy the wishes expressed in the programme material, and to how high a degree the principles for the building scheme and the building methods prove to be viable during the final project work. At the moment, negotiations are going on in several areas concerning the realization of the project: Efforts are underway to ensure the building owner's conditions via negotiations with a housing fund for the cooperative housing and with a housing association for the rental housing. The adaptation to the municipal planning is being negotiated with Køge Municipality's building administration. Finally, attempts are being made to allow the possibility of special experimental conditions in counsel with various departments in the Ministry of Housing.

The conditions that are special for the experiment and therefore special objects for negotiations are:

1 the high degree of community, especially the problem of financing in relation to the collective responsibility;
2 mixed building with both owners and renters, especially the problem of the financing and administration of the major common facilities;
3 the organizational structure, especially concerning the establishment of a direct democratic decision-making process and strong, increased rights to the competent tenant bodies in relation to the existing authorities' competence areas;
4 the form of the housing scheme, in terms of the town planning conditions, traffic and subdivision principles, especially larger lots belonging to different tenant associations;
5 the building form, the employment of flexible dwellings with the possibility of expansion and, in connection with this, also the financing of additions in a later phase – progressive financing.

The programming was carried out according to two points of view: the town planning conditions, including the adaptation to the town of Herfølge, and the individual dwelling and its relations to the other dwellings and the supplementary common facilities. The project group, in collaboration with the municipal engineers and building department, participated in defining the principles for the master plan for Herfølge Township. The principles, which the project group suggested, have generally been followed in the framework that at present has been presented to the municipality.

The tenants' organization in Køge and in general

In autumn 1972, when the project group visited Køge, it was not to gather the future tenants around a completed project, but instead, together with a group of tenants, to try to figure out what their project was. In our efforts to emphasize this, we omitted bringing their attention to the fact that there were many restrictions and not many choices, regardless of who was responsible for planning. Our approach suggested that one could plan and realize almost anything. Thus from the beginning, we appealed more to the groups who, to varying degrees, were used to managing and planning things, such as their work, rather than the groups, who in their work and living situations were completely subject to the control of others, the less-fortunate social groups, who were actually the project's target groups.

We – the tenants and project group – were aware of this situation from the beginning, and we agreed to try to satisfy the target groups' more concrete and tangible relations to the housing and environment by carrying out the preparations, in other words creating the housing association and building programme and on the basis of this running a new recruitment campaign specially aimed at the housing quarters in the Køge area, which house the most low-income, elderly and single mothers. We had assumed that in the beginning of the programming process we would use a great deal of time discussing the project's conceptual content: community, solidarity and the better life, where we imagined people could live together, if their immediate surroundings functioned better and they functioned better themselves in them. In this case we had miscalculated: the groups that were actually formed had the exact same notions as we did about this side of the problem and expected us to present concrete and clarified study-group material that would enable them to plan their homes and their housing environment in keeping with the common expectations.

Autonomous groups and direct democracy

After about six months work with organizational problems, together with the groups we were able to establish the Housing Association of September 27, 1973. Its purpose was to create and administer a local society in Herfølge in which the design and operation of the dwellings, common facilities and institutions occurred according to direct democratic principles.

The association's regulations were adapted to the stipulations for a social public housing association. This means that it can be admitted as a unit of an existing housing association or establish a new, independent housing association.

The regulations are constructed so that they clearly define how the rights of decisions are tied to the areas that are affected by the decisions: the individual families or tenants have complete control of their own homes, which can be altered in keeping with changing needs.

The family groups choose their own degree of communal living and content, and make independent decisions in cases that do not imply financial obligations for the housing group. The housing group manages its own common facilities, and makes decisions in situations that do not involve financial commitments for the housing area. The main common facilities and the institutions outside of the housing group are administered by the joint meeting, which also makes all decisions concerning the initiation of substantial new building projects or alterations of the existing buildings.

The joint meeting is the association's highest authority. It elects from its members an administrative group to deal with the daily work, but does not have any decision-making authority aside from that which is delegated by the joint meeting.

If a sufficient number of project participants want to own their own homes, then a non-profit homeowner association is established, which is co-ordinated with the housing association and is tied together with it in a mutual association. The mutual association then establishes a private institution that is responsible for the establishment and operation of all the main common facilities. Municipal subsidized institutions can also be run by the private institution. The by-laws will register the contribution obligations of the private institution.

Rent strike or decentralization

The organizational form and decision-making structure in the Køge project grew out of the way of working with study groups and common meetings, which were employed in the programming work. This can be seen as an example of how the organization can be formed in a building project, which also in its physical form reflects the principle of autonomous groups and a direct democratic decision-making process. We see the tenants' collective organization as a necessary prerequisite for an improved standard of housing. The building industry's traditional decision-makers either have no interest or are incapable of carrying out decisive improvements by themselves.

This notion is not only based on the Køge project but also on our experience and observations in the user groups, which during the last few years have established themselves in the existing housing mass and attempted to solve acute problems and create connected interrelated environmental improvements. Examples of this can be seen in the Sjællandsgade and Ole Rømersgade quarters in Århus and Røde Rose, Islands Brygge and Nansensgade in Copenhagen. These tenant groups have only, under special conditions, been able to base their activities on a competence that is available in the existing legislation and practice. Otherwise, they would have been forced to rely on themselves and the voluntary assistance of random politicians and technicians. In relation to the work that has been carried out, the results must also be considered minor and completely dependent on the local administration's will.

For us, the problem can be seen in this manner:

- should the organized tenant groups carry out rent strikes and seize the "power" in their housing areas;

- or can planning be done and carried out as a decentralization of competence from the traditional decision-makers to tenant groups on the building, neighbourhood and local society level?

In this light, the Køge project can be seen as an example of action research – a practical investigation of the latter possibility. For the time being, it is only we – the architect group – who have relinquished competence to the tenants. The municipality, housing associations and finance companies have declared an interest and offered principal support. The fate of the project in the year to come will reveal if there is a real will behind their words.

The local society in a state of decline and ongoing development

Approach

Not until there has been a geographical determination of the functional and administrative framework will it be possible to carry out a goal-oriented and controlled planning and development of the local society.

Aside from being a problem of methodology, it also represents a political problem. This can be seen by the planning authorities' relationship to the efforts that different tenant groups have made to carry out and maintain improvements in their housing neighbourhoods. Despite the existing planning terminology, which is especially employed in connection with new housing areas, the tenants' efforts were confronted with a constant resistance from the authorities when trying to carry out reforms that would ensure the tenants' overview and competence. Changes such as these would of course also limit the authorities' present freedom to work according to specially defined norms in keeping with the undefined groups' interests. In order to test the immediate possibilities and consequences, and to gather a number of controlled findings, we have in a provisional collaboration with the National Building Research Institute and with the municipality and housing associations in Ålborg, prepared an experiment in three existing housing neighbourhoods.

The experiment involves the tenant governed planning of a new housing area in Svenstrup according to the same guidelines as the Køge experiment. For the tenants, who either prefer or are obliged to remain in their homes, the possibility will be offered to define and carry out a renovation and renewal of the neighbourhoods in question in collaboration with the involved local authorities.

Administration

The basic governing principle in a local society is direct democracy, and the decision-making structure is two-part. The basic unit is "the immediate cohousing" – a street council, stair council, family group – whom together form the local society's governing assembly – the joint meeting or basic assembly. The act of establishing a local society that is autonomous in terms of its own concerns in the existing social structure, also requires that primarily the municipal authorities, but also the county and national authorities relinquish a degree of competence to the local society's competent assemblies. This concerns an influence on the local planning and the assumption of responsibility for a number of tasks primarily in the areas of social services and education as well as the disposition rights of part of the municipal tax income.

As the real responsibility at the moment cannot be moved from the elected legislative assemblies, one must during the transitional phase, presume an extremely precise right to insight and record obligations.

Production

In the local societies, the communal housing must be expanded to also include the production conditions. Primarily through a balancing of the number of housing units and work places. After that through the joint ownership of the production means, including property, buildings and machines. And finally through basing the production on local raw materials and with sale to the local market.

In addition to agriculture and horticultural production, which are obvious choices outside the urban areas, certain branches of craftsmanship and industry can exist in the local society without problems. Examples of this are primarily industries that deal with foodstuffs, clothing and woodworking, graphics, building materials, furniture, small factories and workshops, all with a certain degree of self-sufficiency. These activities usually work with a very modest number of employees – more than one-third of all Danish industrial firms have less than six employees. As the amount of manpower employed in these companies is high in relation to the invested capital, they are well suited to function in a local society, especially because they can be feasibly established.

We suggest that the organizational form and the acquiring of capital are tied together with the local society's other activities in the establishment of cooperatives and other joint undertakings. Production chains will further strengthen the possibilities of production in the local society and the cooperation between different local societies. Examples of this are forestry – sawmill – woodworking factory or cattle farming – slaughtering – meat-packing factory.

Culture

The local society as a social and cultural unit cannot be realized until the local autonomy includes the necessary institutions for education and social services. This means that the local society must solve its own social problems.

Today, many of these problems are caused by the housing and work conditions, which society has developed, and will not exist in a society that is based on community and a respect for the individual. At the same time, the local society with its family group structure will be able to absorb a number of physically and mentally disabled members, who now must be sent to institutions.

In terms of education, in the local society there would be a basis for a single-track school, and a common junior high-school with eight to ten grades could be established to serve several local societies. The preschoolers and other children after school will be able to interact and participate in a number of different activities in the family groups instead of the present hierarchy of children's institutions. In the same way, the elderly with reduced work capacity, will be able to participate in production activities.

In order to give villages and local areas in larger cities the opportunity to survive as local societies, we could imagine that in the beginning the local citizens, with county support, were given the opportunity of establishing local centres, in other words activity areas, which for example could include common facilities, grocery store, library branch/book bus, medical clinic with pharmacy, post office, café, bus stop and a local municipal office. This would also offer the possibility of an untraditional work sharing.

The family group

The family group is an intimate co-housing form, a collective of nuclear families and individuals, perhaps the basic social unit, which in a new social structure can replace the faltering nuclear family. The family group is also a practical and economic arrangement: by sharing work and joint purchasing, a larger group of people can help each other and together procure goods and services, which they would not be able to on their own or in smaller groups.

In any case, the communal principle is the basic idea in the Køge project. This is true of both the family groups and on the scale of the housing area, but is most clearly evident in the family group, where problems are most similar to the traditional housing situation, and where the balance between private and common is the most sensitive.

The process of creating the family groups has naturally been the most time consuming, and the sketching of the family groups' physical surroundings has been critical. It is during this phase that the guidelines for the balance between common and private, the content of the common areas and the size of the private dwellings must be determined and the basis for the group's future norms must be established.

The family groups consist of six to eight private dwellings, grouped around a common courtyard, which is surrounded by a balcony structure. This serves as a covered walkway between the dwellings and also as an outdoor space for the first floor. The family groups' common areas vary from group to group, but in general they represent an expansion of the relatively small private dwelling's functions in terms of a common kitchen, living and dining areas, smaller workrooms (darkroom, hobby room) as well as playrooms for the children. The common areas are distributed as ideal shares for the dwellings in the group with an average of 12 square metres per dwelling.

Several family groups
The joint programme for the first housing group included workshop facilities, which were considered too extensive to place within the family groups. In addition to this there was a small laundry and a sauna/joint bath. The latter was adjacent to the common areas for the eight to ten rental rooms, which as part of the public housing section are planned to be built in connection with the common areas. Depending of the negotiations with the municipality concerning the institution quotas in the area, part of an age-integrated family institution will be located in direct connection with the common facilities.

As an area function, in other words a common function for approximately 100 dwellings, a common house will be located in the first housing group. In a similar fashion, in the other housing groups, there will be other functions that will serve the entire housing area (special rooms for day-care centres, garages, automobile workshops, and so on). In this way, the housing groups will be mutually functionally connected and be able to utilize the possibility of a greater common variety of activities.

Thus the housing group is not self-functioning, even though outwardly, the dwellings have a direct relation to the group's common facilities.

Density

Building legislation and the social housing associations' activities, up until today, have represented a reaction to slum building. The apartment block schemes around greens, and the park housing schemes from the 1940s and 1950s, were created as a reaction to the old urban fringe areas' lack of light, air and grass. These efforts during this period were cemented by the building industry's concrete apartment blocks and the standard-house manufacturer's monotonous monuments. The reaction against slum housing was an expression of the notion that sound and sensible legislation and planning in itself could solve the physical and social problems that were implicit in mass housing.

The environmental crisis reveals that this notion must be revised. Even if it requires a greater in-depth analysis of cause and effect, we will for the time being maintain that the inhabitants have been moved – often compulsorily – from one type of slum to another – from the Medieval quarter to the fringe quarters – from the fringe quarters to the suburban apartment houses.

Of course it is better to sit in a suburban bathroom than in the Medieval quarter's courtyard latrines. Many facilities have been improved and the size of the apartments has increased – that is fine, and of course the daylight and fresh air conditions are better than the darkness and stenches – but in a good social environment there is also a need for people to meet and the opportunity for contacts and activities of many different kinds, for fun and for serious activity, for long and short periods, to solve common problems and to enjoy each other's company both indoors and out.

And then we must state: we believe that there are qualities in the fringe areas with up to 300 dwellings per hectare. Here one can find inspiration despite social squalor. We feel that density can be a quality, but this requires that it is organized in an interplay with sufficient open areas, and that opportunities are provided for more activity per hectare than in the slums and single-family house neighbourhoods. In several of our projects, we have worked with a *partial density* that is greater than in the darkest Nørrebro and Vesterbro quarters, but these densities were integrated in the housing plans with a total maximum usage of about 35 dwellings per hectare, which is the equivalent of an old village like Dragør or the larger public housing schemes of the 1960s.

This greater partial density is not the result of a need to achieve the density advantages characteristic of speculative building projects, but the housing principles include a vast number of possibilities for expanding the traditional housing area's common facilities and the opportunity for future expansions of both service facilities and work places. In addition, greater density also implies an ease in creating road and supply systems, which also offers economical advantages. The economic savings that result from a higher partial density are not evident until a change in the area distribution on the family group and housing level is implemented. There will be obvious economical advantages in an alternative use of the housing area for cooperative purposes. The administration of the property line, distance and daylight regulations becomes more difficult proportionally with the increased partial usage, and there is no doubt that this has prevented the municipal authorities and housing associations from allowing the above-mentioned efforts to be realized.

Our basic notion is that the building regulations make reasonable and respectable demands, but that the interpretation and administration of the laws and the regulations on the family group level should be taken over by the residents themselves. We could say – to use the language of the law – that the family group built on its own property.

Growth

In a society such as the Danish, where we still accept that capital can freely seek the areas that give the greatest, surest and quickest profits, the fact that anything happens in the housing area is usually an expression of investment returns and marketability more than a question of any ideals involved in improving the housing situation.

During the large growth period in the 1960s, this situation has led to technocrat controlled, isolated and oversized but half-empty new apartment house areas for speculative conditioned rents, for monotonous standard house subdivisions and unsuccessful total renovations and a lack of urban renewal.

If under these conditions, and under the increasing competition for the acquisition of capital, we have any hopes of maintaining a reasonable part of the total expenses in the improvement of housing conditions, we must either nationalize the entire sector or create satisfactory investment opportunities that, as opposed to what has happened up until now, will require a constant and increasing subvention in the form of mortgage tax reductions and interest subsidies as well as rent and redevelopment subsidies.

In order to manage the investments in the housing sector, it will be necessary to define a comprehensive goal for redevelopment, urban renewal and new housing areas, and that the realization of these is carried out in a collaboration with the actual tenants who are going to pay. The investments should thus be directed in accordance with this: limited, continuous and flexible.

First, frameworks should be determined for the individual local societies, and then within these, precise goals should be created for the improvements that should be carried out in terms of urban renewal and new building situations. In this way the urban growth concept is changed and assumes the character of an increased improvement of our entire physical surroundings, and the buildings will be a continued rounding off and completion of the already existing local society's framework.

A new building tradition

The architectural competitions during the last decade — like the public housing debate in general — have constantly circled around the concepts of flexibility, changeability and variation, with this to no great extent having had any major influence on the ordinary building practice. The reason for this must in part be blamed on the condition that these concepts have arisen as a kind of negation of the building production that has developed during the building sector's so-called industrialization.

Some characteristic features of the rationalized building methods are the inflexible housing plans, the static buildings and the uniform expression. This is due to the fact that industrialization is based on production-oriented criteria without a real analysis of the product or the product needs and without, at any time, involving the user in the process. To a certain degree, one has transformed a tradition-determined product to a new technology — the mass-production of brick buildings.

The basis for a new goal for housing production must thus be a number of user-oriented building requirements:

- Dwellings should be able to be used differently and be altered depending on the needs of changing users.
- Dwellings should be able to be enlarged in keeping with the users' needs.
- There should be the opportunity for self-realization (self-building) within the house and its immediate surroundings.
- There should be the opportunity for the individual design of the dwelling — including standard demands.

These requirements are clearly at odds with the existing tendencies in housing production. Industrialized building continues to develop in the direction of larger units and a larger degree of finish. This necessarily results in a greater degree of uniformity and a total lack of possibilities for self-expression. The tendencies in the single-family housing sector are, by and large, the same, although here there exists a certain degree of individual design and the possibility of do-it-yourself activity. On the other hand, the single-family house in a town-planning context is extremely problematic due to its large area requirements and the complete lack of common areas.

A reorganization of housing production is a necessity, also in a greater perspective. The background for the reorganization of housing production to indus-trial, capital-intensive production forms was a political wish for an increase in capacity as well as an increased productivity. The stagnating population growth and the reduced tempo of economical growth will mean that society's investments in new building will decrease in the future, i.e. the pressure for increased capacity will be reduced. Compared to the fact that industrialized building has not experienced an increase in productivity – expressed in lower building and rental costs – implies that there is no reasonable argument to base the future building production on industrialized systems with concrete elements.

The possibilities of a restructuring of production in the building sector seem to revolve around two models. Either the mass production of lightweight product elements in an expanded market context, or a return to the traditional, more labour-intensive production methods. It is natural to imagine that these tendencies could result in a new kind of building tradition based on an interplay between the craftsman-dominated construction of a number of less complicated building elements and the mass production of the more complex components.

To return to the starting point, "a qualitative goal for housing production", a concept like variation will to a high degree be satisfied by the construction of the building's basic structure by craftsmen. A differentiation between the basic structure and the finishing work would allow a division of contracts, which could provide the basis for self-building work as well as minor craftsmen contracts in the finishing phase. What remains to be seen is how to satisfy the needs for flexibility and expansion. There is no doubt that additions are most easily carried out on ground level, which indicates a restructuring of housing production to low-rise buildings. In practice, the realization of expansion and flexibility implies a number of technical problems such as bearing systems, installations, use of materials and so on. It is given that the traditional production methods imply a number of advantages compared to concrete element systems, and it is not hard to imagine a combination of traditional and industrial methods, which allows a high degree of flexibility – especially in connection with low buildings with a great freedom for installation conduits (crawl spaces and so on). However, these problems can only be partially solved theoretically – only actual tests in connection with experimental practice will provide precise guidelines for the development of flexible building systems.

Basis dwellings

The enormous increase in capacity in the building sector during the last fifteen years has not resulted in a solution to the housing problem. This is due to the fact that the housing problem is not so much an expression of a lack of housing as it is a lack of affordable housing. Even though the building industry during the most active building periods has only exploited about 60 per cent of the total production capacity, today there is an overproduction in the housing sector compared to the populations' buying power.

Thus the problem is not one of capacity, but more one of economy, in any case in terms of that segment of the population that does not have the possibility to utilize the tax deduction rules in connection with private housing. The social housing associations have not been able to build in keeping with their goal: to build reasonable homes for the lowest income groups. In that the housing associations are forced to finance their projects via the general capital market, their production is subject to the ordinary market fluctuations. The result is that apartment sizes and equipment have varied at a rate concurrent with market trends. To a certain degree, this has meant an increase in cost due to interventions in the production process, but also the necessity to produce dwellings, which in terms of size and equipment, must be considered unacceptable in the long run. This situation is especially evident today, where the rental crisis (which can be further increased by the latest developments in financing conditions) has caused the housing associations to be even more cautious than required by the so-called "stove legislation".

The entire situation demands a radical re-evaluation of housing production both politically and product-wise.

Dwellings that are built with a modest size – for financial or other reasons – should have the possibility of being enlarged at a later time. This seems to be a quite natural requirement, but in fact today we are producing apartments, which as a consequence of production methods and financing conditions are completely fixed in size. Thus it is necessary to develop building and financing systems, which will allow the building of apartments of modest size that can be enlarged at a later time in keeping with the users' economic abilities and needs.

There exist plenty of good ideas: in countless theoretical projects a number of different basis dwelling principles have been suggested. In general there are two main tendencies. The first being the apartment house principle, where the floors are established as platforms with the possibility of installation hook-ups. The apartments are then built on the deck according to the user's need and later expansion is implemented by incorporating a larger area of the platform. The other main tendency could be described as basis dwellings with expansion opportunities in the form of annexes or added bays on the ground level. Which of these two tendencies is preferable could probably be ascertained via an experimental practice. Offhand, the apartment house principle seems to imply a number of economical problems. The platform principle would involve a relatively expensive basic structure, and it would require the establishment of a somewhat large basic structure in the first phase. On the other hand, the low-rise housing has inherent problems in terms of land economy and probably could only be realized as dense/low-rise housing with a ground usage ratio of the same size as the high-rise.

The most obvious solution is probably dense/low-rise housing, as expansion quite naturally is easiest on ground level both in terms of construction and installations. In any case, the basis dwelling concept offers the possibility of relaxing one of industrial housing's most problematic aspects: uniformity.

The basis dwelling principle is the basis for a dynamic perception of the home. And the expansion from a basic unit will have the character of a constant interplay between the economical and technical development as well as the changing users' different needs and wishes. The dwelling could thus be designed individually and to a greater degree express human needs rather than the necessities of economy and production methods.

The Saudi Arabian Ministry of Foreign Affairs by Henning Larsen

1987

Henning Larsen

Danish Architecture

How is it possible that since the middle of the 1700s, Danish architects have made their mark not only in Denmark but also abroad? How is it possible that a tiny country and a tiny population can be recognized not only in terms of quantity but also quality, while suffering from inferiority complexes and being afraid of foreign influences and immigrants – despite century old experiences that have proved that exchange implies inspiration, development and life instead of stagnation and death? Also today we witness the fear that Danish architecture will be infected by foreign trends so it no longer is "Dansk Arkitektur," Danish quality. But history has proven the opposite, that Danish architecture has profited from foreign inspiration through the years, and vice versa.

The first architects in Denmark were Dutch, imported by Christian IV. Later, Danish architecture was influenced by Danish architects who had studied abroad, and when the Royal Academy of Arts was founded in 1754, foreigners led it. There have constantly been foreigners who have brought new ideas to Danish architecture, and vice versa. Despite – or due to – the foreign influences in the 1700s outstanding buildings were designed by Danish architects, such as Nicolai Eigtved, Laurids de Thurah, Philip de Lange and C.F. Harsdorff.

In the 1800s architects like C.F. Hansen, brothers Hans Christian and Theophilus Hansen as well as M.G. Bindesbøll created architecture that today is still part of the world's architectural history. C.F. Hansen was very productive and built villas in Altona, the Christiansborg Palace and the Palace Church, Vor Frue Church in Copenhagen, not to mention the old Town Hall and the Court House and Jail in Copenhagen. The two Hansen brothers, Hans Christian and Theophilus, worked in Athens, where Hans Christian Hansen designed the University, the Science Society's Headquarters and the National Library – buildings that today are still considered some of the best works of architecture from that period. His brother Theophilus Hansen lived in Vienna, where he also designed a number of public buildings that are in use today and are also among the best of that period. Bindesbøll's greatest work is Thorvaldsen's Museum, which is probably the most distinguished building from that time.

Among the great international works of architecture one can include Grundtvig's Church by P.V. Jensen-Klint. It represents a clear offspring of the Danish brick tradition, but has a number of special qualities including the exceptional treatment of materials as well as the incredible scope of detailing with an extremely strict discipline – a building where all whole, half and quarter bricks form an expressive synthesis.

This is also true of the buildings from the neo-classicist period up until 1930, including the Copenhagen police station by Hans Jørgen Kampmann and Aage Rafn, Øregaard High School by Edvard Thomsen and Fåborg Museum by Carl Petersen. The police station, especially, has a great architectural strength and a wealth of nuances and a level of detailing that is unique in international architectural history. The museum in Fåborg, despite its small size and modesty has a world class architectural format.

It has not been a noticeable trait of Danish architects to theorize or nurture epoch-making ideas about architecture. Neither are there many examples of great Danish architecture historians. However, Steen Eiler Rasmussen offered an unusual pedagogical effort with his fine books, especially *Experiencing Architecture*, which is read by first-year architecture students in many countries. His book on London is still considered the best description of the city and its history. Also an architect like Poul Henningsen has a special place in Danish architecture both in terms of debate, criticism and production.

After the advent of modernism, Danish architecture split in two directions. One involved the continuation of the classical tradition, the other the modernist tradition. Looking back we can see today that despite their differences, the one being international in expression, the other more regional, and despite their two different directions in terms of both their basic theoretical background, materials, etc. they were both concretized in extremely fine buildings by Kay Fisker and Arne Jacobsen respectively. But today, we see them both as typical of their time, just different voices in the same choir. In reality they had much in common, perhaps more similarities than differences. They supplement each other in a way we find difficult to define, but many foreigners can clearly recognize in these buildings typically Danish characteristics.

After the Second World War, new faces arrived on the scene. Jørn Utzon won the international competition for Australia's most important building, the Opera House in Sydney. Despite political, technical and economical problems, the Opera House became an architectural innovation. Utzon's Opera House became not only Australia's best building and a symbol for the country, but also one of the world's most significant architectural works from that period – a brilliant synthesis of idea, form, proportions and detailing, with an effort in which all melt together in a complete product of incomparable class.

And still new Danish architects make their mark, also abroad. At one point, a third of all international architecture competitions were won by Danish architects. This reveals something about the Danish architects' competence, drive and impact. Arne Jacobsen built in Germany, and both he and Utzon built in Kuwait. In recent years there have been a multitude of Danish projects abroad. To name a few, Ulrik Plesner in Sri Lanka, Hans Munk Hansen in Africa, Vilhelm Wohlert in Tunis and Algiers, Kjær & Richter on the docks of London, Claus Bonderup in Finland and Johan Otto von Spreckelsen in Paris. And then there are all the Danish architects who have "only" built in Denmark, but epoch-making buildings in an architectural sense, and who have contributed in creating and further developing the framework around that which is known as the Danish quality of life, which is both greatly admired and seems to be greatly inspiring abroad. In addition to this there is a completely different side of the architectural profession here in Denmark, namely furniture design, where architects such as Kaare Klint, Hans Wegner, Børge Mogensen and Poul Kjærholm have added their names to the international list of Danish architects.

And why is that? How is it possible that different Danish architects at different periods of time in different countries have been able to work with different clients often without problems despite the language barriers, cultural and religious differences, different legal demands to the building's technical realization, different building codes, different levels of building methods, different climatic conditions, etc? How is it possible that Danish architects evidently have been so flexible and adroit and still so strong-willed and determined in their own *métier* that they could create things that have become part of world architectural history?

Today, it is difficult to give a single explanation for what determined this previously. But one of the reasons for the present success could be that Denmark was industrialized comparatively late, which has meant that the individual architect has had a quite intimate relation to craftsmanship during his or her growth. Many have had childhood experiences of having seen how things are created. This implies an understanding of interrelations. However, the childhood environment, with the experience of craftsmen and their work with hand and eye, has disappeared. This basic childhood background is gone and thus the life as a grown-up is also definitively altered forever.

In the future it will be more and more difficult for the aesthetic aspects of life to be recognized, which is already the case in heavily industrialized countries like the USA, where commercialization pervades everyday life. It is more difficult to escape passive television watching, a confusing, pluralistic everyday with advertisements, a commercialized leisure life, etc. – all together things that drain one of energy. Perhaps the artists, designers, architects, etc. are the only remaining "craftsmen" in our culture, where the coordination between hand and eye, sense and intellect, spirit and body, still exist in professional disciplines. And it is perhaps one of the reasons that at the moment, architecture educations throughout the world are so popular as a field, since the education and practice are almost the only place where one can deal with "the whole person." In other words, the profession in itself implies an attractive life quality.

Denmark is the mother country of the public school system and public information, and this has meant a high level of information and an effective system of information (cf. the number of newspapers, book publications, library loans, etc.), perhaps also due to the country's modest size and extremely homogeneous population. Thanks to the public schools, folk high schools, libraries, etc. public information has been able to spread throughout the country and out to the individual citizen, with ease and flow from the outside world and back again.

One of the reasons that we have been able to report back to the outside world in certain disciplines could be that in the area of design and architecture there are no language barriers. These professions are directly accessible throughout the world, as opposed to literature, theatre, drama, etc.

The architectural milieu in Denmark has strongly changed through time. Sometimes it has not even existed. Sometimes there have been very active groups who have discussed, created and developed new professional directions. But often the best have been reclusive and not participated in the common debate, but only contributed to the discussion and development through their products or completed buildings. Today, the architectural milieu in Denmark does not really encourage a honing of the professional disciplines, that is to say architectural theorization and reasoning, the artistic sensibility. On the other hand one can no doubt say that in the daily professional practice, such as at the drawing offices, there is still a fruitful environment, where many still hold the flag high and, despite increasing demands on the architect, still work hard without a resulting increase in fees. On the contrary! But in general we work more thoroughly with our projects than one does abroad. And on this level we can be compared with the best in terms of care and understanding of details and materials.

We find ourselves in the middle of profound changes in our existence, in our experience and understanding of everyday life. The world is becoming more fractionalized and intellectualized. This is also true of architecture. Great changes are taking place in architecture at this time, both in terms of education and the profession. There are more registered architects today than ever before, and this large group is inhomogeneous and disconnected. There are more architect students than earlier, aside from the boom after the period of free access to the education. The architecture schools are disjointed and lack a profile. And the great outside world is more confusing and chaotic than ever before, also in terms of architectural currents and rapidly changing fashion trends.

There exists the probability that all of this will worsen the possibilities of maintaining and renewing the tradition of architecture and architects of top class. Thus an extraordinary effort is required in the years to come.

During this period of change it is necessary to clearly consider our professional environment, which has more or less been left on its own and has simply followed along in the wake of everything else. It will be increasingly necessary to think in more constructive ways. How can we develop our professional milieu together so that the individual architect will be better equipped to address the new outside influences and the new demands in our daily lives? This is also true of the architecture education. Here a more critical approach is necessary and a more conscious attitude to the education and its individual parts, to the profession's theory and practice. In the years to come it will be vital that there is an increased awareness of the environment, debate and visions, so that the profession does not become muddled up or stagnated.

Despite the fact that our entire hinterland changes concurrently with the significant international influences, there is no doubt that one of the reasons that Danish architects have been so successful abroad is that many of them, aside from their professional competences, have met the world as open, flexible, adaptive and persuasive individuals in the positive sense of these words.

Denmark has not been a great power for centuries. Danish architects have made their mark without support from a strong government as opposed to many foreign architects and engineers in their export drives. Danish architects have come alone, without diplomacy, without a supporting government, without the opportunity of bribery, without any security such as export subsidies, guarantees or the like.

Yet still they have managed to convince clients and builders, both directly and through competitions, that they have honest intentions and are not just interested in earning easy money, they are not looking for superficial solutions, etc.

Many projects have naturally been lost due to this. On the other hand it has been an advantage to come alone, open, unarmed and, in a way, incredibly vulnerable, but with the belief that if the professional content was intact, then things would no doubt work out. At home or abroad, large or small projects – this is not of greatest importance. The most important thing is that we continue to update and renew the education of future architects, as well as the professional environment. Only in this way can Danish architects continue to be an important part in the international architecture exchange and development.

Tietgen Dormitory by Boje Lundgaard and Lene Tranberg

1992

Boje Lundgaard

The Crisis in Building Technics

We are living in a time of strange paradoxes. Never before have there been so many technological possibilities for building houses. And never before has construction been so characterized by technical shortcomings, accidents, flaws and maelstroms.

Throughout the course of history and on all levels of scale, the architect has been entrusted with the task of optimizing and linking together functional, technological and aesthetic aspects into a weighed overall solution. Of course, different eras have assigned priority to these aspects with shifting emphasis, but a salient characteristic of what we call architecture of lasting value is that considerations of form/function/technics merge into a higher balanced unity.

At a time when the profession is so marked by a need to find new standpoints with respect to form, it is explicable that this can have a deleterious effect on other considerations. However, when it comes to be the general case that buildings are being designed without any fundamental function and technical ethics, there is cause for alarm.

What I mean to indicate by technical ethics is a conscious attitude about how the choice of technology often springs from and forms parts of the entire architectonic approach and can also, in the best instances, play a role in imparting special qualities to the physical result in the aggregate formal expression, in the structure, in the materiality and in the detailing.

However, elementary respect for and insight into scientific premises, and premises related to physical construction and production, which are necessary to the profession are also part and parcel of technical ethics. And let us not overlook the knowledge about human beings' basic biological and psychological needs, which must always serve as the crucial foundation not only for the choice of technology but also for the choice of architectonic expression.

It is quite possible that parts of the modernist and function-oriented architecture movement have been preoccupied all too one-sidedly with the profession's more quantifiable elements like function-studies and technological development. On the other hand, any sense of engagement in these matters has been conspicuously absent in this last decade of the century.

But when we say that architects are losing interest in building technics, this is not tantamount to saying that the development has come to a standstill. It has merely come under the influence of other professionals like structural engineers, researchers and producers. And this is where we are right now.

So-called industrialization

Over the past fifty years, our building culture, on the basis of a technological assessment, has totally altered in content, having moved from craftsmanship-based, building-phase-allotted praxis, with a well-arranged quantity of material and construction variants to the present day's half-industrial, often entrepreneur-dominated world of construction with an opaque chaos of newly emerging building commodities and principles of execution.

Whereas Poul Kjærgaard was able to document the typical craftsmanship-based building praxis that prevailed until the outbreak of the Second World War with his *Byggebogen* in a most exemplary way, a corresponding documentation of present day building construction would, first of all, fill as much room as the architectural offices' collections of catalogues and, second, be obsolete even before it got printed.

In the building sector, industrialization has taken a different turn from what most of the pioneers were dreaming about in the 1950s. Overall, what was envisioned was that building construction would, like other sectors, benefit from an increase in standardization, prefabrication and mechanization so that the products would come to be less expensive and better and that it would be faster to produce them.

Of course, within certain areas, reductions in costs and an increase in efficiency have appeared. When we think about kitchens and lightweight interior walls, this is true. However, it is harder to spot any genuine gains in quality. Therefore, we have to ask whether there really are significant price reductions.

When it comes to other building components, it has not proven possible to develop any radical rationalization benefits, despite a colossal effort to do so.

Turning to the construction aspect, we can still – after thirty years of prefabrication of concrete elements – find examples of competitive totally brick-built buildings. I know that this fact is connected with the decline in the number of assignments and in the breadth of those assignments. But why, then, can we not adapt to the new conditions?

To put it succinctly, building construction has never become industrialized to a degree that involves genuine rationalization benefits or qualitative improvements. Rather, traditional craftsmanship and the sense of high-quality work have almost vanished in synch with the concomitant appearance of lots and lots of new dubious products and methods.

Damage to the buildings

The desire to improve how we steer and control the building's quality with the vehicle of the industrial building process stands in glaring contrast to the extensive spread of building defects and damages which has been evident all too frequently in recent decades' construction activity. Some of these flaws turn up in a relatively short time after the buildings have been put into use and occupied. In many instances, these shortcomings necessitate repairs and renewals of a magnitude that fiscally exceeds the building's original price, and by a long shot.

Seeing that the situation has gone so awry, I would venture an opinion that this is primarily due to two factors. In the first place, there is the fact that such a radical realignment process, which was brought forth with Danish industrialization, is intrinsically riddled with initial difficulties. New materials, new manufacturing and construction processes, new kinds of teamwork – all emerging at once and in a brief interval – it simply has to go wrong! And then again, these problems are amplified by the second factor: too little knowledge and not enough experience among the involved consulting architects and structural engineers and among all the performing parties. And we have not even mentioned the building research sector, which has not been sufficiently alert, critical or motivated.

Of course, all this is being regarded in the wisdom of hindsight which, as we all know, is the easiest thing to do. On the other hand, it is necessary to cast our glance back if we want to avoid making the same mistakes.

When now, for a certain period of time, buildings have been constructed badly – technically speaking – and consequently have to be renovated, some measure of delight might be taken in remembering that there are also serious problems in other areas, coming to the conclusion that many factors are in need of renewal.

What we are speaking about here touches upon factors like the overall environmental quality, the architecture, how the open-air areas are treated, the façade expression and the poverty of the experience. For this reason, it is necessary to kill two birds with one stone: improve the technical quality of the construction and simultaneously improve the so-called environmental conditions. But obviously, this is not such an easy thing to accomplish.

In fact, it is not merely a question of replacing the flat roofs with pitched roofs or of choosing new colours and panelling. And for that matter, how long will the renovation last? It is frequently the case that the buildings become more unsightly after undergoing such a process, which is generally carried out by a different architect than the one who was originally responsible for the construction. This in itself also gives rise to problems.

In any event, it provides food for thought that one of the few successful examples of renovation in recent pre-cast construction is Albertslund, which was carried out by the original architect of account. Viggo Møller-Jensen himself joked that he was the only architect who has ever been allowed to build the same city twice, in the very same place!

There is one area, however, where industrial building possesses a distinctive and not unessential quality, namely when it comes to the design of the residence. The apartments are generally large, filled with light and well equipped, with place for storage, spacious kitchens, two toilets, and so on. These are qualities that almost disappeared in the two- and three-room mania of the 1980s.

On the other hand, the prevailing construction principle – the bearing interior walls – entails an awkward deadlock in the interior design. The rooms cannot be joined together. Not even a door can be moved. The rooms are fixed and it is only seldom that the apartments can be divided up in new ways. At the same time, the construction principle has another drawback that is often overlooked. This is the problem related to sound. There is no systematic study available, but I am convinced that a large number of the residents in the pre-cast building are really suffering from having to put up with nerve-racking sounds generated by their neigh-bours. This is a state of affairs which, in practice, can be far more enervating than the question of whether the windows are waterproofed.

Indoor climate

With the sound problem before us, we are moving into the new buildings' other formidable complex of problems: the poor indoor climate. As a matter of fact, it is not only the sound conditions that have gone amiss. Evidently, it is also the air and the light.

The prerequisites for having a suitable indoor climate, however, amount to a composite web of problems. The matter revolves primarily around the air's quality and consequently, around ensuring the necessary renewal of the air (which, in practice, has become a huge problem). It revolves around the quality of the mater-ials and surfaces used inside the building and around their radiant and degassing effect. But moreover, it revolves around all the physiological/comfort-related factors that affect our physical wellbeing when it comes to daylight, heat and humidity. And factors like housecleaning, maintenance and durability also come into play.

Seeing that the indoor climate has become a growing problem in recent years, this is due – above and beyond the lack of knowledge among those conducting the design – in part to the many building materials turning up on the market that have not sufficiently been tested in the long-range and in part to sharpened legislative demands concerning the building envelope's functions.

The central problem here has to do particularly with the sharpened require-ments concerning insulation, not in the sense that insulation in itself is a problem but rather in the sense that touches upon the effects that narrow-minded insulation efforts can bring about. This can be said primarily about the increased sealing, of course, but also about the number of difficulties related to building technics to which thicker pieces of insulation material have given rise.

Decline in the detailing

Of course it is alarming that our days' buildings are collapsing almost before they are built and that people are getting sick when they stay indoors! However, along-side of these miseries, there are many newer buildings that register a blithe indif-ference to the architectonic detail. In synch with the transition from traditional craftsmanship to more industrialized construction, the understanding of the importance of the building's detailing has gradually vanished.

One only needs to think about former times' dignified (even in less expensive projects) treatment of the façade's profiling, the windows' openings, the walls' panels, the doors' profiles and casings, the ceiling's cornices and the stairways' baluster and to compare these with today's standards: facing brick wall with steel brick lintel, window casing of chipboard, wallpaper with fake texture, door of cardboard and its plastic casing, metal baseboard, aluminium handrail and so on and so forth. It seems as though architects have either given up or that they are only being remunerated for working out a sketch project or perhaps a schematic design for the authorities' approval, only to leave all the questions concerning detailing to those who are strictly setting their sights on the market's cheapest standard elements.

But then again, it is also shocking to see how much crap of the cheapest standard the market offers. We can only speculate about whether the nation's most highly esteemed designers have even considered the building sector to be an area for product development. In any event, it appears that the people producing building materials have not discovered the designers!

In Sweden, a country that has spawned such architectural talents as Asplund and Lewerentz, both of whom certainly understood the importance of detailing, it is not at all unusual to witness that architects do not take any part whatsoever in the process of solving the details. This task is entrusted instead to the structural engineer and is generally carried out in cooperation with the general contractor. Much is "taken care of on site", as the saying goes. And this can be seen!

The precondition for the architect "re-conquering" the domain of being entrusted with making a qualified detail treatment, however, is that the interest in doing this is present. In this connection, the architect's standpoint is often that it is the grasp of the whole, the large stroke, "the concept", as it is referred to these days, that engages. For all the rest – well, fortunately, we have capable building technicians for managing those tasks or else the decisions are delegated out to other firms that can perform the task!

A better way of building?

The troubled ruminations put forth above articulate a critical attitude towards the development of construction following the Second World War, as seen by an architect and as assessed on the basis of a certain generalizing point of view. Of course, I am well aware that during this same period a number of admirable buildings have been constructed, maybe even some of the best we have. But they are simply drowning in the mire of the rest of the multitude.

If one has to come up with something positive to say about the crisis that construction is presently facing, it would have to be that it invites reflection. And it is precisely these issues, giving ourselves enough time to discuss the results of a development, adopting a critical stance, and even one involving self-criticism, with respect to the patently evident problems of building construction, which are more pressing matters than they have been for a very long time.

The heart of the matter, then, is that the building sector, alongside the problems cited here, is facing enormous new challenges. These challenges have to do with the new markets and with the adoption of new technology. But most of all, they have to do with the readjustment to a new ecological reality.

Ecological objectives

As has been described by some, ecology's influence on societal relations in the industrialized world is going to have an impact of the same dimensions as did the advent of the industrial revolution.

Following this, it is also logical and consistent that radical considerations about resources on all levels will lead to very significant changes in our ordinary attitudes about growth, production and technology. Our standards of value and our political, social and behavioural attitudes are also bound to be included. In this connection, the building sector forms an important constituent part, but it is only to a modest degree that it has been involved in the discussion.

This cannot be said, however, about energy conservation. Here in Denmark, we have introduced in the course of just a few years the world's most stringent requirements about insulation and window sizes, demands that have already exerted a great deal of influence on the design of the building. In spite of this and in spite of the surrounding world's growing concern with the whole spectrum of resource administration, the profession has not really committed itself – in any event, not beyond the somewhat holier-than-thou, self-satisfied and folksy "green" architecture.

Once again, we see the civil and structural engineers leading the pack with newly established ecology departments and so-called expertise, almost before the need has been acknowledged.

Everything else aside, it should not be all that difficult to catch sight of the special gauntlet that ecology is laying down before architecture. Ecological fore-thought primarily entails thinking in wholes and in connections and if there is anything that we as a profession normally claim to have a proclivity for, it is, in fact, these very capabilities. We are accustomed to choosing materials and constructions on the basis of a long line of often conflicting requirements but with the objective of ensuring wholeness and continuity. Ecological considera-tions could accordingly play a part in both rediscovering and reinterpreting a number of the architectural practitioner's most distinctive and dignified essential features.

Ecology does not change the profession's characteristic work process but it does introduce new essential parameters that have to be involved, not merely as special extra requirements but as radical new sources of inspiration. And in this connection what occurs to me is that an ecologically conscious architect's attitude has consequences that are congruent with a long line of architectural values.

In the first place, architectonic quality in itself is of ecological value, if only because beautiful and well functioning houses preserve their value in the long run. Ugly houses with many flaws in the construction (read: typical pre-cast buildings) are, ecologically speaking, the least clever contrivances one can ever come up with, even when the building envelope is very well insulated!

In the second place, considerations about long-term sustainability imply that one can sort away a large part of the market's more dubious products, solely on this account – products that can only exist as a consequence of short-sighted con-siderations related to the economy of construction.

Third, considerations involving the production process, pollution and recycling entail that a long line of products of aesthetically poor quality can be passed over, solely for ecological reasons. This can be said about plastic windows, plastic drain-pipes, grooved plywood, chipboards, vinyl floors, and so on.

But conversely, what is important to the architect's work will be that it will once again become both well regarded and necessary to work with quality on all levels – also on the level of building technics. Time-honoured virtues like ponder-ing through the questions in a thorough manner, using common sense and ensur-ing durability and long-term value all the way down to the smallest details will be restored.

Many examples can be cited showing how the aforementioned considerations can lead to new products and new kinds of architectural expressions. In conclud-ing, I would like to call attention to the following three areas for development.

The building envelope

In the course of thirty years, the design of the building envelope has completely changed in character. From being characterized by its static function as a part of the building's bearing and stabilising structure, it is completely dominated in the present day by increasing demands related to insulation.

The history of heat insulation is not an extensive one. It was not until after the Second World War that insulation materials started to gain a foothold. At the outset, the material was only five to seven centimetres thick in those spots where it could, in fact, be placed. But, as we know, in the wake of the Oil Crisis, the thick-ness has increased especially due to sharpened requirements in the Building Code.

In reality, getting the construction industry to re-adjust itself to what is a quite radically different building practice proved, surprisingly enough, to be relatively painless. One of the explanations for this is the very close connection between the Ministry of Housing and SBI, the National Building Research Institute. Another is the all too complaisant corps of consultants. This line of development has, in fact, given rise to many problems.

Within the domain of brick buildings, there has been a deliberate attempt to differentiate the exterior and interior part of a cavity wall, with the result that the firm perpends disappeared. The interior wall could be executed in virtually any material, while only the exterior brick veneer remained (in order to satisfy the wish to obtain that "brick look"). However, on the basis of considerations about statics, the exterior wall should be divided up into small entities or should be constructed in cement mortar. People tended to choose the latter and what happened then was that the smallest movements gave rise to the formation of cracks. In terms of build-ing technics, then, the construction is therefore a dubious one. But also, aestheti-cally speaking, an apparently solid brick wall is remote from the technological reality. The ordinary Danish brick, which has been developed for entirely different purposes, is now regarded only as a decorative element.

Within the realm of light wood-frame construction, it has naturally proven easier to place the increased insulation. But, in fact, it is still not that easy. It has been necessary to develop new crossed wood-frame systems, fastened on to new kinds of insulation beams or glued plywood on mineral wool. But regardless of how the insulation itself is installed, it is necessary, as we well know, to place a vapour barrier in order to avoid condensation and this creates a new problem.

As easy as it is for an expert at the National Building Research Institute to draw a vapour barrier on a standard section drawing in a set of instructions, it is just as complicated in the real world of the building site to get the foil laid down in the correct way, to have it sealed with the requisite meticulousness and to guide it through all the tricky nodes. I do not know of even one carpenter who does not curse these solutions into oblivion.

But even when these foils are actually placed according to the prescribed drawing, we still must ask: what kind of house have we built, after all? Well, on the exterior it is a "solid" brick house and inside, it might be neatly "wallpapered". But in reality, the house is constituted by a plastic tent. Only a few centimetres behind the outer wall's paint, there is an airtight membrane! Is this really an acceptable way to build houses?

Shouldn't people sit down and figure out how a contemporary outer wall can be created? Not as a repetition of earlier epochs or other countries' traditions but one that satisfies all the demands that our own time and place poses when it comes to optimal heat insulation, natural circulation of air and the accumulation of moisture and heat and also takes into account considerations about resources, material quality, durability, recycling and, last but certainly not least, aesthetic and use-related value.

A formidable task for building researchers and designers. Who knows? We might even be able to export some of this knowledge! But really, we cannot sell our mistakes – in any event, not for long.

The window

The design of the window poses even greater architectural challenges, especially because what we are presented with here is a line of development that has become guided for quite some time now by demands dominated totally by considerations related to quantity.

Once again, sharpened legislative demands have served as the point of departure. When limits were prescribed on the size of the windows by the "15 per cent Rule", this constituted a break with an otherwise long-standing tradition of being free to place and size the windows on the basis of wishes concerning daylight, view and façade proportions.

Also here, the architects have submitted to the new requirements to an astounding extent, partly because it suddenly became interesting to deal with the cottage and picket fence idyll and partly because one could generally "get by" by placing a triple-layer of glass in the windows or by putting a little more insulation in the roof.

It gives cause to wonder that so few architects make any attempt to work with the window as an energy-regulating factor dependent on the points of the compass. In fact, when it is designed correctly, the window with a southern exposure offers the possibility of inducing more energy into the building than what-ever might be vanishing in the other direction. Passive solar heat can reduce the building's requirement by as much as 50 per cent.

In façades (and roofs) that are oriented towards the south it would therefore be feasible to operate with relatively large glass sections, even if they happen to be in excess of what the 15 per cent rule prescribes. On the other hand, when it comes to the northern orientation, it is clear that indeed, this ought to involve a conscious stance of moderation.

This trivial fact alone ought to lead to further changes in the organization of the building's plan arrangement, where the rooms that are being occupied for most of the time, or the rooms that are dependent on light and sunshine, will be situated alongside the large glass sections while the secondary, short-term occupancy func-tions can establish buffer zones away from the light.

This might sound a little bit stiff and diagrammatic and it can also easily lead to planning developments that are too oriented towards one side. The challenge, then, is seated first of all in laying out the building in plans and sections in such a way that sunlight is drawn into the building structure through special façade pro-jections, light wells, roof constructions and so on.

Also here, there will accordingly be a merging of ecological/resource-conserving considerations and important architectonic objectives, namely the essential strategy of inducing daylight and incident sunlight into the rooms. And these are not two sides of the same coin.

Many newer residential building complexes contain few variations in the plan and do not take the question of orientation into consideration. There are a great many residences that have the primary living room situated so that it faces the east or the north, as if one ought to be content that any *light* at all is coming in through the window.

The passive use of sunlight can play a role here in reviving considerations about basic qualities related to the comfort. But there are other perspectives.

Running alongside the sharpened legislation, what has occurred, of course, is an intensified development of the known window-pane constructions, aimed at improving insulation capabilities.

Regardless of whether we are speaking about thermal windows with gas, selective and diverse coatings, vacuum window-panes or three, four or five layers of glass, there can be no doubt that it will not be long before window-pane con-structions are going to be developed that will be competitive when it comes to heat loss, with insulating wall sections. Window-pane constructions might, additionally, with the inclusion of passive solar heat gain, eventually come to constitute the building's most important energy supply.

With this kind of glass it will become feasible once again to operate with large glass surfaces, not only in the form of the transparent type but also in combination with light-permeable matte window-pane types. The main problem associated with this new glass building possibility will be to avoid overheating in the summer; this can be circumvented with the intelligent use of screening and ventilation.

But there are many other problems that have to be solved first. For the time being, most high-insulated window-panes are suffering the consequences of being discoloured by the light. Similarly, their net weight often results in clumsy and stout mullions. Whether the future's demands on building materials' long-term durability can be accommodated by these rather complicated – technically speaking – window-pane types is also a pressing question.

Concurrently, architects ought to let themselves be inspired by these possibilities and look for new ways of utilizing the sunlight and new ways of designing the windows, taking into consideration everything from the overall orientation of the buildings' layout and each building's disposition with respect to natural light to a solicitous concern with the windows' placement and the proportioning of the details.

The construction

As has already been mentioned, the part of the building that has undergone the greatest degree of change in the past three decades might well be the load-bearing construction, which has been transformed from the homogeneous brick structure to wall/slab systems in concrete or lightweight concrete for the walls and the floors. At the outset, with the small spans for the slabs, the consequence was that the building's walls, by and large, were bearing concrete walls with all the flexibility problems that have been described above.

With the development of wide-span slabs it has become more and more feasible to span larger areas, such as one continuous sequence of residential units, all at once. However, this is a possibility that is only seldom being exploited.

On the basis of an ecological way of thinking, what seems logical is that long-term sustainability of as many building components as possible is going to be required – and particularly of the "fixed" structural components. And this is precisely why it is of the utmost consequence that the structures are executed in a manner that is as flexible and multifunctional as possible.

Ninety per cent of the recent decades' residential construction has been executed by inflexible wall/slab systems without any future guarantees. Keeping in mind the latest years' tendency toward building only two- and three-room apartments, this state of affairs seems all the more grotesque.

Since demands are being posed on the windows' sizes, it would also be appropriate to demand that residences in housing complexes can be changed without tearing everything asunder. For this reason, it is going to be necessary to bring forth new construction forms that will both fulfil the pressing need for flexibility and adapt themselves to the future's resource-minimal design principle.

Perhaps one could also envision that the building's structural elements could again play a role in imparting identity and character to it or maybe even serve to infuse valuable decorative qualities, with respect to both structure and detail.

Postscript

Quite recently, assuming the role of an external censor entrusted with the task of evaluating a student's final examination, I had the occasion to ask a prospective graduate who had otherwise come up with a perfectly fine and clear project what the house was to be made of. "Plaster", was the response, "on the outside and the inside." I rephrased my question: "Yes, I can understand this, but what about everything else that's *behind* the plaster?" "I'm not interested in that", was the response. I agreed that the student had passed the examination. But on my way home, I felt apprehensive about the situation.

Finnish Introduction

Anni Vartola

The Mythology of Essentiality

The austere national character of the Finns and the severe Finnish cultural climate have produced splendid modern architecture and cultivated a number of admirably skilled architects. Finland has not, however, provided a particularly favourable substrate for cultivating intellectual discussion among architects. One of the many legends cherished by the Finns is a statement attributed to Bertolt Brecht, which describes the Finns as "the only people in the world who can be silent in two languages".

No wonder then that Alvar Aalto's principle of not using paper for anything but designing has become an unwritten rule.[1] Any architects worth their salt who follow the path indicated by Aalto prefer to write their "poems in sand"[2] and say what they have to say in their buildings. Finnish architectural debate has focused mainly on practical matters in its rather limited discourse: publication of new designs and new buildings, analysis of topical architectural phenomena from the viewpoint of national aims, and the status of architects and architecture in the march of overall progress through joint action and solidarity.

Reima Pietilä, one of Finland's most idiosyncratic architects and productive writers, wrote about this in an article entitled "Why Architects Prefer Not to Write"[3] and gave eight reasons for Finnish architects' apparently poor literary ability and lack of interest in writing. The article was published in one of the principal forums for architectural debate in Finland, *Arkkitehti* (*The Finnish Architectural Review*), founded in 1903 and one of the oldest architectural journals in the world still published. Pietilä's polemical article was a response to an idea proposed by the editor, Pekka Laurila, to provide a special "Apropos" column for the discussion of topical architectural issues in direct, everyday language, but Pietilä did not hold out a great deal of hope for the success of this new discussion forum.

According to him, the reason for literary inaction on the part of the profession was not just the lack of column inches, or architects' temporary, perhaps even general, distaste for writing; as Laurila had assumed in his proposal, there were far more serious reasons. According to Pietilä, things like the gulf of non-communication that had separated one generation of architects from another due to the Second World War, the fact that the basic training was entirely non-written, the cult of self-satisfied speechlessness, the difficulty of understanding the concept of architecture, the fear of one's peers, and a distinct neurosis about theory were all obstacles to unrestricted polemic repartee among architects.

Pietilä pointed out that architects' university education was focused on technical performance and did not encourage debate. This, according to Pietilä, had led to arrogance and even malignance towards more human discussion. "The architect firmly believes that the drawing speaks for itself and the drawing says it all", he wrote. In Pietilä's opinion, the ruling dictum in 1960s architecture that "good architecture must contain no aesthetics or theory of any kind" was also an obstacle to architects writing. Pietilä saw the prevailing conflict in values between the realist and the theorist that existed in Finland in those days – and perhaps still does – as extremely significant. "The realist is a good man, the theorist a bad one", wrote Pietilä and went on to say that the reason for fear was concealed in the doggerel that "those who can't design buildings prefer to write journals. Thus the fact that a man finds writing unpleasant means that he must be a good architect". Pietilä was at his most cutting when talking about the arrogance of architects:

> Architecture is so elevated, so exalted, as to be almost unattainable. Architecture is an extremely difficult and therefore an incomprehensible issue, an issue that the layman is never capable of approaching in the right way . . . It is dangerous to explain the nature of architecture to "the people" and this undoubtedly leads to a false simplicity. The calling of architecture demands acquiescence, humility and worship from those who practise it.[4]

Pietilä's analysis provides an interesting context for the Finnish texts selected for this book. They are fine pieces of writing from a country that produces fine architecture, and yet there is a delightfully perplexing common denominator which makes them so easily recognisable as Finnish. Each one of them has been written by an architect who has shown great practical design ability and attained great respect in Finland and even abroad. Each of the texts ponders the nature of architecture and describes architecture as one complete indivisible and perhaps slightly mystical profession of artistic talent. All the texts are, in a way, frozen still-lifes in words: they are favourable portraits of architecture written as if under an obligation. They are not a matter of debate for its own sake, but tokens of faith.

Historically, the first of the texts is Eliel Saarinen's "Address", a speech given in his capacity as president of the Cranbrook Academy of Arts at the annual general meeting of the American Institute of Architects.[5] Saarinen had moved from Finland to the United States in 1923 after winning second prize in the international architectural competition for a skyscraper for the *Chicago Tribune* newspaper. Earlier, in collaboration with his student colleagues and partners Hermann Gesellius and Armas Lindgren, he had attained an important role as someone who had genuinely shown the way in a national sense. This era had come to an end, however:[6] what was needed when he wrote the speech was a new vision, new integrity and consistency, rationalism and modern architecture.

Perplexingly enough, both the setting and the agenda echo the heated debate that had been sparked off early in the twentieth century after Saarinen had won the two major competitions for the National Museum (1902) and Helsinki Railway Station (1904). Then, the opposition to Saarinen consisted of the pioneers of Finnish Modernism, Gustaf Strengell (1878–1938) and Sigurd Frosterus (1876–1956) to whom architecture was not an independent artistic issue but quite the opposite: "Architecture is – or at least should be – linked firmly with life, and interact with it."[7] In his speech, Saarinen is rewriting their modernist manifesto and calling for the same things: truthfulness from the new style and for the style to rise organically from the circumstances and the society in which we live. For Saarinen, the time for linking national characteristics with architecture is over. Yet, Saarinen, on the threshold of a new international architectural career, does not look as if he is ready to give up his idealism about his own country and his own architecture. Earlier, he had helped to build the quality of "Finnishness"; in 1931 he is helping to build the quality of universal "Westernness".

In Alvar Aalto's writing, the relationship between Finland and international affairs is also topical in a rather exciting way, but the interpretative reference framework is very different. Throughout his life, Aalto had been interested in social questions and in the renewal of architecture, and he considered technology, the advancement of society, economic growth and wellbeing to be inextricably intertwined with architecture. The number and quality of Aalto's international contacts were already surprisingly high at a very young age: warm personal relationships with many influential people in the Nordic countries and important visionaries in Europe took Aalto straight to the heart of Modernism. His circle of friends included names such as Sven Markelius, Erik Gunnar Asplund, Poul Henningsen, Walter Gropius, Sigfried Giedion, Fernand Léger and Laszlo Moholy-Nagy. Aalto made a solid contribution to the activities of many important groups intent on renewing architecture. He helped Poul Henningsen to run the magazine *Kritisk Revy*, took part enthusiastically in the activities of CIAM (Congrès International d'Architecture Moderne) from its 1929 congress onwards,[8] and in summer 1939 he founded a new cultural magazine *Den mänsliga sidan* (*The Human Side*) with Gregor Paulsson, intended to "bring to the awareness of the wider public in a practical and comprehensible manner, new phenomena observed in social life, business and politics that can be explained socio-biologically and that have begun to appear all round the world and which, taken together, are an indication of the fact that, in all probability, a decisive structural change is taking place in these areas".[9]

The Aalto text chosen for this book was written at a politically significant moment. Finland's war with the Soviet Union, known as the Winter War, had ended on 13 March 1940, and in April 1940, Aalto had been invited to the Massachusetts Institute of Technology as a visiting lecturer in the Department of Architecture. Although the Second World War was not finally over until 1945, Finland was already faced with the biggest re-housing project in European history, involving the resettlement of more than 400,000 Finnish refugees from the areas ceded to the Soviet Union. This called for immediate action, so Aalto's attention in the early 1940s focused on the housing issue, the rural building issue and town planning generally.[10] All the time and in all possible forums both in Finland and the USA, Aalto was calling for systematic, efficient, standardised housing research and housing production, but starting out from architecture. The basic question concerns the relationship between the individual and standardised architecture: "In architecture, the job of standardisation is not to aim for types, but quite the reverse, to create viable variation and richness, which in an ideal situation, can be compared with nature's unlimited ability to produce nuances."[11] Aalto was looking for an elastic standard: a flexible, adaptable, production-efficient and economic, industrial solution that would speak a universal language of architecture.

The idea of a universal architecture and how to define it remains a bone of contention in the architectural debate in Finland from that day forward. For Nils Erik Wickberg it is a question of style; for Aulis Blomstedt it becomes an aesthetic problem of a systematically dimensioned language of form. In Osmo Lappo's writing, the question goes back to a humanity-serving system theory by way of a Vitruvian whole, and for Pietilä in 1973, the universal language of architecture harks back to original sources in the spirit of Aldo Rossi: to a city, an experience and an expression of Man's existence. Kirmo Mikkola takes the question towards the trinity of art, technology and society, Markku Komonen towards the themes of rationalist structuralism in the second half of the nineteenth century, until Pallasmaa brings the topic right back to the themes of Saarinen, Blomstedt and Pietilä: a form of art which arouses peoples' memories and through them an archetypal understanding of the basis of existence. As Pietilä writes in 1967, the Finns talk about twentieth-century architecture "as if it were the one and only thing, as if there were just one correct and indivisible architecture".[12] In this way, according to English architectural critic Roger Connah, twentieth-century Finnish architecture forms an "essence mythology": to talk of meta-architecture and teasing out the meaning of architecture flees further and further from the illusion of a common Finnish reality.[13]

For this very reason, the contemporary reader lost in multiculturalism and the pluralism of cultural values may see Nils Erik Wickberg's concept of architecture as extremely confusing, as he ties architecture, the spirit of the age and the idea of Volksgeist so tightly together. For him, the art of each culture expresses the set of values of that particular culture, and the development of the architecture of each country is based on local climate, natural conditions and social mores.[14] From Wickberg's standpoint, architecture is in some way separate from the other arts; it is cleaner, freer and nobler, and it develops continually according to the law of its own autonomous evolution towards an ever more touching and refined perfection. In Wickberg's mental landscape, Finnish culture is an inalienable part of the western Hellenic cultural tradition, so architecture too is tied above all to western tendencies. By the same token, architecture can never be to the taste of the wider public or in accordance with the demands of business. Wickberg was Finland's leading expert in restoration and the history of architecture and it may be that it is precisely his thorough knowledge of the history of architecture that convinced him to believe in the inevitability of Modernism. For him, architecture was the expression of time and culture, so having entered the modern era and adopted the modern way of life, a change in architectural style must necessarily follow. Correspondingly with earlier styles, Modernism is, thus, an inevitable phase in Western cultural evolution.

Another cornerstone of Wickberg's thinking is the idea of architectural "style as the manifestation of an ideal based on a principle".[15] According to Wickberg, the architecture of the 1940s had to rely on the sensitivity of great artists, on their ability to interpret the reality around them, on the uncompromising logic of architecture, and on the opportunities architects are given to lead the whole of society towards better and more peaceful times through their unfathomable art. Like Aalto, Wickberg remained an untiring supporter of Modernism and human functionalism; in 1940s

Finland it was not permissible to turn one's gaze to the past, one had to step forward boldly on the chosen path. In Wickberg's analysis, style therefore becomes more than just a way of arranging architectural elements based on everyone's aesthetic taste; it becomes a symbol born of inner necessity to every nationally important civilisation of the new age with pretensions to great art. It is for precisely this reason that in architecture, Wickberg urges the reader to be obedient to the fundamental programme indicated by the creators of the Modern Style; they were visionaries who created the ethos of modern Finland and made it progress.[16]

As we come to the 1950s, Finland is rewarded for her logical and unbroken line on the path of Modernism. Finland becomes a world-famous land for design, and Finnish skills in joinery, glassware, furniture design, textile design and architecture are suddenly in demand as paradigmatic pioneers. In 1952, Finland concludes her war-reparation payments to the Soviet Union and the Helsinki Olympic Games are held complete with their Coca-Cola advertisements, exotic sportsmen and women and their international atmosphere. It is clear that at last, Finland is having a banquet year in the midst of its own culture.

Joy and pride can be seen at last in the architectural debate, too. The Museum of Finnish Architecture begins operations in 1956 and *Arkkitehti* is given an overhaul. It starts aiming to be a comprehensive cultural journal which, in accordance with the view enthusiastically pursued by Aalto back in the 1940s, will increase the links between architecture and accelerating design; in 1953, a separate series named *ARK* begins to be published four times a year to deal with these themes. Both Wickberg and Aulis Blomstedt rise to the top of the architectural debate because of their knowledge of culture and their sparkling dialogue; so ecstatic is the euphoria that both of them refer fascinated to the same Le Corbusier quotation from 1936: "architecture is a state of mind, not a profession".[17]

In this light, Blomstedt's 1958 inaugural lecture "The Problem of Architectural Form" represents an exciting policy definition. It defines architecture as being like other areas of art and industrial design, but nevertheless as an autonomous art form that is a law unto itself. The key question for Blomstedt is one of relationships: in the same way as the organisation of the planets is based on the mass of the heavenly bodies and the forces of interaction between them in accordance with precise physical laws, so architecture too is based on harmonic relationships. Architecture is not just a matter of artistic design, but the art of proportion, where as well as aesthetically refined spatial forms, it must have its own logic defined by mathematical precision. The architect's place in society is, as Blomstedt puts it in a lecture given in Oslo in 1956, "the place of the intellect": the architect's intellectual work takes place precisely in the area of harmony.[18] The harmony, the comprehensive synthesis, that Blomstedt is reaching for is nevertheless only possible through systematic measurement and mathematical relationships, as the Canon 60 system that he developed himself around 1960 demonstrates.

Topicality and growing criticism towards Alvar Aalto's absolute authority and position of power, plus a growing dissatisfaction with the overall quality of the built environment derived from mass production, suddenly makes Aulis Blomstedt an extremely interesting theoretician in the climate of the 1960s. He represents a new kind of internationalism, after all he had been involved in 1958 with the Helsinki

CIAM group in founding the new international journal Le Carré Bleu, which had its head office in Helsinki.[19] Blomstedt also offers new potential and a fresh, modern and rational explanation to the idea long held to be too romantic, of beauty that pleases the eye, by combining architectural dimensions with human dimensions, architectural harmony with the harmony of musical intervals, and thus architecture with the age-old natural philosophy of Pythagoras and the universal logic of nature. The long-awaited Modernism has now been realised but the promise of modern architecture has been greater than the results that can be seen in the surroundings. Finnish Modernist architecture receives a shot in the arm from Blomstedt, insofar as architecture now becomes a matter of carrying out a huge synthesis, and architects become "the last profession of synthesists in a specialised world".[20] Juhani Pallasmaa, one of the leading figures in the emerging constructivist view of architecture, writes enthusiastically in 1966 in a biting criticism of the architecture of Reima Pietilä, which favours rather more free-form themes from nature: "Art and architecture are not a matter of subjective arbitrariness, but of arranging forms in a complex and high-quality manner."[21] Blomstedt becomes a leading rationalist and constructivist figure, and the right angle becomes the norm for the new architecture, directly related to the laws of nature.

The reflections of Osmo Lappo, Reima Pietilä and Kirmo Mikkola bring their own perceptive views to this arrangement of ideas. In 1968, the era of student revolt begins and in Finland too, the students in the Department of Architecture at the Helsinki University of Technology take to the barricades with red flags flying on behalf of a democratic study environment and a curriculum that takes on social problems.[22] Robert Venturi's Complexity and Contradiction in Architecture is reviewed in Arkkitehti and the time of heroic modernist monuments is briefly over: attention focuses on international politics, social inequality, the decay of western society, scientifically based design and criticism of the élitist concept of architecture personified by Alvar Aalto.

The architect Osmo Lappo, known as a pragmatic and sensible designer, takes over the job of professor of public building design at the Helsinki University of Technology in 1967, never doubting he will have to face up to criticism from the younger generation of architects. He turns the still topical question of flexible dimensioning and human scale away from form-giving towards the practical design and building process. More fundamental than the argument about the best possible system of architectural expression is the question of multiple use and adaptability in buildings. There are obvious points of contact with the thinking of Christopher Alexander, after all Lappo approaches architecture as a matter of logic in resolving the problem between the information given at the start and the final result, not as a psychological problem besetting the creative artist. However, whereas Alexander exhorts architects to think about the image of the starting point and concentrate on careful and precise research into the requirements set for the design, Lappo trusts the professionally skilled architect and the splendid culture of Finnish architecture. For him, architecture is above all a matter of serving the public: "of creating people's entire living environment, of giving form to all those spaces where human activities take place".[23] Thus, Lappo in his interpretation turns Blomstedt's rationalist architecture into a rationalist design approach, which suddenly no longer excludes the artistic quality caught up in the rumbling scientific-techno-political revolution.

This, surprisingly enough, provides an excellent foundation for Reima Pietilä, for whom "architecture is a general form and solution developed by a designer".[24] He has already outlined a general chart of his own design doctrine in *Arkkitehti* and come to the irrefutable conclusion after a tricky, and for Pietilä typical, play on words: "a building cannot be a typical representative of architecture, but is always an individual case".[25] Defined thus, the debate about the existence of architecture now turns towards individuality rather than the universal applicability proposed by Blomstedt and the constructivists inspired by him. According to Pietilä, individuality means above all, architecture that is geographically, ethnographically and culturally local.[26] Regionalism thus defined becomes Pietilä's mission in the Department of Architecture at the University of Oulu, and with Pietilä's professorship an alternative emerges to the architectural debate that has revolved around the Helsinki University of Technology and dominated Finnish architecture: this eventually becomes known as the Oulu School. From Pietilä's standpoint, research is necessary, analysis is necessary and a systematic approach is necessary, but authenticity is necessary, too.

Kirmo Mikkola who, during the years of political upheaval in the latter half of the 1960s, becomes the undisputed figurehead of the young, radical generation of architects, defines authenticity in a crucially different way from Pietilä, however. For him, authenticity means understanding the characteristic nature of architecture as a synthesis of design, technology and economics in the spirit of Aulis Blomstedt, but in such a way that it is always linked with the prevailing political reality. Architecture is part of the society that surrounds us: architecture shapes society just as much as society influences architecture. Thus, high-quality architectural reflection is not a matter of insignificance, it is a matter of the wellbeing of large groups of people and, at best, the promotion of citizen-orientated democratic discussion about society. The gulf between Pietilä and Mikkola is so deep that the concept of ideology is given a completely different interpretation by each of them. For Mikkola, ideology means primarily, communicating the role of the architect and taking a class-conscious, socio-political view of architecture. In Pietilä's opinion however, ideology is an extremely dangerous concept, since with it, "architecture can be made into an identification mark of something that cannot be authenticated".[27]

The question of architectural form or the attempts at right or wrong that lie behind architectural aesthetics remain unresolved and so the architectural debate since the 1970s remains in a state of tension. The style of "pure architecture" derived from constructivism and its variations becomes the predominant style in Finnish architecture; other approaches such as the 1980s colourful Oulu School along with its critical writing about boxy architecture, or the austere but atmospheric architecture of Timo and Tuomo Suomalainen, are marginalised as passing phenomena or ephemeral experimental phases in the work of individual architects or architectural practices.[28] The image of a united modern Finland threatening Postmodernism could also be said to be almost deliberately reinforced, one example of this being the international symposium on "The Future of Modernism" held on the Gulf of Finland on 22–24 August 1980.[29] Additional backup comes directly from abroad, when Kenneth Frampton's *Modern Architecture: A Critical History* is published in 1980.[30] With it, Finland rises to become one of the most important countries in the world for modern architecture along with France, Spain and Japan.

Markku Komonen, editor of *Arkkitehti* from 1977 to 1980, had set up a practice with Mikko Heikkinen in 1974 and their breakthrough work is the prize-winning entry, *Heureka*, in the 1985 architectural competition for the Vantaa Science Centre. Komonen's definition of architecture is ingenious: he does not deny the apparent demise of Modernism but neither does he give in to the populist notion (in Finland) of going over to being a supporter of Postmodernism, or as Komonen himself puts it, "Neo-Nationalist-Romanticism".[31] He wants to build a new Modernism and to do it in a thoroughly Finnish style: using few words but by means of greater practical achievements – High-Tech Constructivism.

This high-tech constructivist frame of reference can also be attributed to Juhani Pallasmaa who, during the 1990s, rises to become the leading figure in Finnish architectural debate and undoubtedly the Finnish architectural theoretician most highly thought of abroad. Pallasmaa was head of exhibitions at the Museum of Finnish Architecture from 1968 to 1972 and Director of the Museum from 1978 to 1983; Pallasmaa was in practice with Kirmo Mikkola from 1976 to 1980 and was professor of principle and theory at the Helsinki University of Technology from 1992 to 1997.

In Pallasmaa's essay, Modernism is constructed anew; the old triangle of man, culture and the environment is turned on end and architecture becomes an existentialist projection of man in the spirit of the phenomenological view of architecture called for by Christian Norberg-Schulz since the 1960s. The new question set for architecture concerns purification and the return of architectural autonomy. This, says Pallasmaa, is possible in the following way:

> One way of achieving architectural autonomy and 'purification' is paradoxically to question the utility and practicality of architecture. The second is a kind of archiving, a survey of the experiential basis for architecture. The third is to return the language used for expressing architecture to the pure language of architecture, to images that are characteristic of architecture. The fourth is to detach oneself from the superficial value of the new, from fashion and the myth of individuality and focus on the poetry of the everyday, the 'other reality' behind the everyday.[32]

As we enter the twenty-first century, the circle is closed. The crisis of Modernism, critical regionalism, the pluralism of the culture and ideology of the Postmodern era, the unshakeable belief in the giving of architectural form as an art and the question of a universal language of architecture are bringing the Finnish architectural debate back to its roots, to a new interpretation of the question of "the fundamental form of the time, the fundamental form of a nation."[33]

NOTES

1   Alvar Aalto, "Artikkelin asemasta" in *Näin puhui Alvar Aalto* [*Alvar Aalto in his Own Words*], ed. Göran Schildt, Otava, 1997. In http://artikkelinasemesta.blogspot.com/ (15.7.2007), Esa Laaksonen, architect and director of the Alvar Aalto Academy, suggests that the title has deliberately been written *Artikkelin asemasta* [On the status of an article] rather than *Artikkelin asemesta* [Instead of an article], as it has often erroneously been written. Understood this way, Aalto is talking about the challenges of writing rather than the triviality of writing.

2   In the article referred to above, Aalto continues: "Of course, I have written poems – not many, but good ones naturally. But they are written in sand. And poems written in sand are not suitable for publishers and periodicals. Their publisher is the wind, a splendid publisher . . . So I don't publish poems. I'd rather publish specifications about my work . . ." Aalto in Schildt, *Näin puhui Alvar Aalto* [*Alvar Aalto in his Own Words*], p. 264.

3   Reima Pietilä, "Miksi arkkitehdit eivät mielellään kirjoita" ["Why architects prefer not to write"], *Arkkitehti* 4–5, 1961, pp. 5–6.

4   Pietilä, "Miksi arkkitehdit eivät mielellään kirjoita", p. 6.

5   For more information on Saarinen's Cranbrook period see e.g. David G. de Long, "Eliel Saarinen and the Cranbrook tradition in architecture and urban design" in *Design in America: The Cranbrook Vision 1925–1950*, New York: Harry B. Abrams Inc. Publishers, 1983.

6   On the intricate transition period between National Romanticism and Modernism in Finnish architecture, see e.g. Roger Connah, *Finland: Modern Architecture in History*, London: Reaktion Books Ltd, 2005, pp. 27–51; Kenneth Frampton, *Modern Architecture: A Critical History*, 3rd edn, London: Thames & Hudson, 1992, pp. 192–202.

7   Gustaf Strengell, "Some observations on present conditions in our architecture in view of the railway station building problem" (1904) in Asko Salokorpi and Maija Kärkkäinen (eds), *Abacus 3*, Helsinki: Museum of Finnish Architecture, 1983.

8   Göran Schildt, *Nykyaika: Alvar Aallon tutustuminen funktionalismiin*, Helsinki: Otava, 1985, pp. 54–68.

9   Schildt, *Nykyaika: Alvar Aallon tutustuminen funktionalismiin*, p. 182.

10   Alvar Aalto, "Maaseudun rakennuskysymys" ["The question of building in rural areas"], *Arkkitehti* 9–10, 1941.

11   Alvar Aalto, "Euroopan jälleenrakentaminen tuo pinnalle aikamme rakennustaiteen keskeisimmän probleemin" ["European rebuilding brings up the key architectural problem of our time"], *Arkkitehti* 5, 1941; available in Salokorpi and Kärkkäinen (eds), *Abacus 3*, pp. 121–42.

12   Reima Pietilä, "Vastaavuuspeli" *Arkkitehti* 5, 1967.

13   Roger Connah, *The End of Finnish Architecture*, Helsinki: Rakennustieto, 1994, p. 69.

14   Historical pioneers who thought this way included Voltaire (1694–1778) and Johann Joakim Winckelmann (1717–68).

15   Eugène-Emmanuel Viollet-le-Duc, *The Foundations of Architecture – Selections from the Dictionnaire raisonné* (1854), New York: George Brazillier, 1990, p. 229.

16   Connah, *Finland: Modern Architecture in History*, pp. 101–22.

17   Blomstedt in Sirkkaliisa Jetsonen, *Arkkitehti* 2, 2003, p. 75; Nils Erik Wiekberg, *Försök över Arkitektur*, Helsinki: Söderströme Co. 1963, p. 20.

18   Helena Sarjakoski, *Rationalismi ja runollisuus: Aulis Blomstedt ja suhteiden taide* [*Rationalism and the Poetic: Aulis Blomstedt and the Art of Proportion*, English summary pp. 222–30], Helsinki: Rakennustieto, 2003, p. 130.

19   Founder members of *Le Carré Bleu* included Aulis Blomstedt, Eero Eerikäinen, Keijo Petäjä, Kyösti Ålander, Simo Sivenius, Reima Pietilä and the Frenchman André Schimmerling. The journal is still published: www.lecarrebleu.eu.

20   Aulis Blomstedt, "Arkkitehtuurin vastaus teollistumiselle", *Arkkitehti* 4, 1963.

21   Juhani Pallasmaa, "Vastapoli", *Rakennustekniikka* 9, 1966.

22   Roger Connah has analysed the radical 1960s and their impact on modern architecture in Finland in a recently published book; see Roger Connah, *The Piglet Years: The Lost Militancy in Finnish Architecture*, Datutop 28, Tampere: Tampere University of Technology, 2007.

23   Lappo in an introduction to the SAFA conference on 20 October1967, published in *Helsingin Sanomat* 21.10 and in the book Osmo Lappo, "Arkkitehdin ja yleisön vuorovaikutus" in *Arkkitehtikoulutuksen asialla. Koulutuspoliittisia artikkeleita ja puheenvuoroja vuosilta 1961–73*, Helsinki: Helsinki University of Technology, 1973.

24   Pietilä, "Vastaavuuspeli".

25   Reima Pietilä, "Harrastekoirat", *Arkkitehti* 6, 1967.

26   Reima Pietilä, "Paikallinen – ei-paikallinen", *Arkkitehti* 7–8, 1967.

27   Reima Pietilä, "Arkkitehtuuri – estetiikka – yhteiskunta – ideologia", *Arkkitehti* 1, 1973.

28   On this topic, see e.g. Roger Connah, *Grace and Architecture*, Helsinki: Rakennustieto, 1998; Anna-Maija Ylimaula *et al.* (eds), *Arkkitehtuurin Oulun koulu* [*The Oulu School of Architecture*] , Helsinki: Rakennustieto, 1993.

29   Markku Komonen; Michael Graves, Charles Moore, Kristian Gullichsen, Daniel Libeskind, Michael Sorkin, Pekka Helin, Heinrich Klotz, Juhani Pallasmaa, Dennis Sharp, Kjell Lund, Timo Penttilä, "Samassa veneessä", *Arkkitehti* 5–6, 1980; see also Connah, *Finland: Modern Architecture in History*, pp. 184–209.

30   Frampton, *Modern Architecture: A Critical History*, London: Thames & Hudson, 1980.

31   Komonen, "Samassa veneessä", p. 24.

32   Juhani Pallasmaa, "Rakennustaiteen rajat – kohti hiljaisuuden arkkitehtuuria", *Arkkitehti* 6, 1990.

33   Eliel Saarinen, "Address" in this book.

Competition for the Chicago Tribune Tower by Eliel Saarinen

1931

Eliel Saarinen

Address

Louis Sullivan explained once to me his philosophy of architecture. When he finished, he said: "That is the only right thing to do."

I looked sceptical and said: "Do you think so?"

"Yes", he answered, "that is the only right thing to do – for me. You have to consider what is right for you."

I have to say the same thing to you, when I am going to explain my opinions: "That is the only right thing to do – for me. You have to consider what is the right thing for you."

There is still another point I will mention, so there will not be any mistake. When I speak about contemporary architecture, I do not mean the French modernist, as you call it in this country. I will not mention anything in this way or that way, or my personal opinions of contemporary architects and their work. I will speak only about principles and I only take into consideration architecture, which has principles and logic behind the forms.

I will not criticize. And if I do criticize, I will limit my criticism to a little story: There was a man walking crookbacked along the street. His friend met him and said: "What is the trouble with you – lumbago?"

"No," he answered, "That is not lumbago. That is modern furniture."

My topic will be: *the historical and ethical necessity of the contemporary movement in the development of our culture.*

We all know that when something new comes in our art life, minds are divided into two main parts. One part is for the new: the progressive minded; another part is against the new: the conservative minded. Both are necessary. The progressive part is the motor which gives the speed; the conservative part is the brake which prevents accidents.

There is a third group in the middle, doubtful, hesitating and asking: "Is this only a fashion for today, or will it last?"

The conservatives who are against the new are against it partly because they have grown up with the old forms and they are slow in changing their minds. They are watching to see how the new will develop. Others are against it because they are satisfied with the old forms, they are afraid of something new which disturbs them, and they do not see anything good in it.

And I have heard remarks like this: "Why all this searching of new forms? We have architecture already settled. We have the antique and the Gothic. They have been regarded for hundreds of years as basic things in all architecture. Aren't they good enough?" It is surprising that they ask this, because nobody asks: "Why all this thinking today? We have Plato, Aristotle and Kant. Aren't they good enough?", or, "Why all this composing today? We have Bach, Mozart, Beethoven."

I think, however, most of the people understand the movement. They see the logic of it, they know that a new time has to create new forms. But they may think it often goes too far. Why revolution? Why not evolution?

There is not much difference between revolution and evolution in art matters. Revolution is only evolution at more speed. All the different appearances in human culture have to develop parallel with each other. If one is slower than the others, it has to hurry. But the result will be evolution.

Suppose that our cultural life from the Renaissance to our day had developed with smooth evolution. Suppose our architecture had developed parallel with it, always moulding its forms according to the changing life, day after day, year after year. Suppose further we still would wear the Renaissance dresses, with gilded brocades and colourful ornaments. Don't you think that one day there would be quite a radical change? Don't you think that we would take off the ornaments and fit our dresses to the spirit of the time?

But now we wear golf knickers and straight cut suits and enter Greek temples and Roman palaces, and are surprised that there is a revolt in architecture – a revolution.

But, is there a revolution?

He, who still sticks to the old forms, thinks so. He who has for years been longing for new forms does not think so.

I became an architect in 1897. I had a classical training in school, but already in the school years I freed myself from the old forms and went my own way. I do not see the revolution. I see only evolution. And as I look back over those thirty-five years, I think often that the evolution is too slow.

A few weeks ago we had a dinner at the Architectural League in New York. Ralph Walker made a speech. He spoke about the individuals who do research work in contemporary architecture. He explained how they go different ways, how they solve their problems differently, and how they look upon things from different angles. He said: "We need those individuals. They are our leaders. They try to find the way for us."

That is true. And it is right that those individuals go their different ways.

But could you imagine the old styles like antique and Gothic being born if the individuals, the leaders had *not* gone different ways in those days? Quite naturally, they had to do their research work too; they had to try different ways; they had to seek just as we have to do it today.

But there was something which, as time went on, drew them together. There is a repulsion and attraction in art development just as in nature. There is something fundamental in the power of the human mind, in the power of a nation, or in the power of a cultural epoch, which directs the whole life.

I call it: *the fundamental form*. The fundamental form of the time, the fundamental form of a nation.

This fundamental form is the attractive power which leads the art development towards a coming style. We have many kinds of individuals, but only those individuals, who feel the fundamental form of our time and who can express it in an adequate architectural language are our leaders. And the strongest of them will remain as milestones in the history of architecture.

That is so in every art.

But more in architecture than in other arts the outline of the individual disappears when the time passes by and the spirit of the time comes in the foreground.

When we study sculpture, we like to know the name behind the sculpture. When we study painting, we like to know who is the master and we name the painting after the master: a Rembrandt, a Van Dyck, an El Greco. When we read literature, and go so far in the past as to the antique literature, we still like to know the name of the author.

But when we go to a town in France, Germany or Italy, we are not so much concerned with the name of the architect. We say: "This is twelfth century; this is thirteenth century." The *spirit of the time* speaks to us. And we feel the spirit of the time not only in the forms of the architecture, but we feel the spirit of the time in the entirety of life *through the forms* of the architecture. This because the whole life was conducted by the fundamental form of the time.

The fundamental form of the time was the real leader.

What it is, we do not know. Its influence comes through intuition, and it has to be felt with intuition.

In studying the architecture of old Greece, their sculpture, their painting, their crafts, in studying their philosophy, literature, drama, their whole life with customs, dresses and even their movements, as far as we can study them from their paintings and their sculptures, we feel how everything is especially Greek, and *only Greek*. There is something which draws everything together and forms it to an entire world for itself.

If we take something from Greek culture and compare it with the culture of Old Egypt, we will find that it is strange there. It does not fit. It does not fit, because the fundamental form of Egypt vibrates differently than the fundamental form of Greece.

Compare Romanesque, Gothic, Assyrian and Chinese forms with each other. And we see how each one has built his own world of forms. Each one has his own fundamental tune. No one can imitate the other, it would sound false. *Each of those great cultural epochs has had creative power to build its culture in an expressive style of its own through a fine sense for its fundamental form.*

Now, if we compare our attempts to develop a contemporary architecture of today with those great epochs of the past, we have to ask: "Does the fundamental form of our day conduct our movement, or do we still wander in darkness? Where do we find our leaders?"

The same question is asked in other arts.

Who is the leader of music today? Is it Debussy? Is it Stravinsky? Is it Sibelius?

In painting we have had in a few decades Impressionists, Symbolists, Pointillists, Cubists and so on. Each one thought it had found the key of the time.

We have Cézanne and Picasso. Many say that Picasso is the greatest painter of today. Maybe. Maybe he will found the painting of the future. Or maybe his influence will be gone in a few years, or a few decades.

Maybe there will appear some day a strong mind that will go deep into things, and the doors will open for the painting of the future. Maybe the same will happen in the art of building! Only the future can tell.

But, says someone, why all this talking about deep thinking? Our time is practical! We have to build in a practical way. Practicality has to decide the form of our architecture. If a building is practical, it is beautiful. This is what they say.

But I wonder! I wonder if it is so, because we so often see very, very practical buildings, practical from every angle, practical in every point, and they appear so terribly ugly. They have no proportions, no rhythm, no balance of masses. The colour is terrible, the treatment of materials is terrible.

So, I do not think we can say that if a building is practical it is beautiful. But, I think we could say – or rather – I *do think we should* say that *a building has to be practical to be able to be beautiful.* And further, a *practical building is able to be beautiful only if the architect has a subconscious sense for beauty*, that is, if he is a creative artist.

Is the practical really so especial a mark of our age as we think? We are inclined to think so when we see what they had in the earlier days. But it seems to me that they were more practical than we are, because they could get along with lesser needs. And on the other hand, we do not know what the future holds for our practicality. Maybe then it will be said: they were not practical at all. They used gasoline in their cars, just as in the old kerosene lamps! Why couldn't they take the power directly from the air as we do?

Every age has its own point of view regarding practicality. Practicality is one of the cornerstones of all architecture, has always been and always will be so. Nature is our teacher in the principles of architecture, and nature itself is the perfect functionalism.

When we speak about practicality, we mostly think about our daily comfort. We push a button here and a button there, we get cold here and hot there, and that is all very practical. But we do not live for our daily comfort. We have higher ideals. And the very man who preaches the coldest and hardest practicality is not always practical himself. He plants roses in his garden. Why roses? Roses are not practical. Cabbage is more practical.

Then there arises the question of our traditions.

Couldn't we take the forms from our forefathers and mould them so that they fit our time and then develop our architecture through tradition?

That is evolution!

It sounds good.

But where do we find our traditions?

If we go to the forms of yesterday, I am afraid we will arrive in trouble, because we will find so many different styles. Which of them should we adopt? Or should we take all of them and melt them together to a gay pot-pourri?

Or should we go deeper in the past and find our forms there?

We all know how well the Gothic architecture expresses the Gothic life. But life keeps changing from day to day. Instead of dry Scholasticism there comes something new in the mediaeval life. People begin to read antique literature, they begin to study antique art, and during two hundred years or more the antique ideal of man meets the Gothic ideal of God through humanism. We have a new cultural epoch. We have a new architectural form. A new style.

There are three things which together form a style:

1   the conditions of the life itself;
2   the tradition;
3   the outside-coming influences.

When we speak about the outside-coming influences, we do not mean to take foreign forms and include them in our style as they are. No, art is always creative, and if we are influenced by foreign forms, and will adopt them in our art, they have to be melted into our style *through a mental process.*

For instance, if we buy a Chinese sculpture and place it in our garden, it is still a Chinese sculpture, and will always remain so. If we take a replica of it, it is still Chinese in form. But when we are inspired by its beauty, do something of our own, maybe in the same spirit, then it is our work. It has passed our individuality, our personality, and through a mental process it is part of our culture.

Just in the same way the antique forms were melted together with Gothic forms to be a beautiful style which we call the early Renaissance.

But there soon came a change.

In the later Renaissance, men began to take forms direct from the antique world. Instead of using their intuition, they began to use dividers and rulers. They began to write theories and formulas. They began to make science for practical use of an art form which did not belong to them.

They founded schools – where they *thought* their theories, formulas and measurements. There was no need any more to have artistic intuition to do good work; a little taste and much theory was enough.

The great masters of the later Renaissance still used their intuition. They were educated in the spirit of intuition, and they erected masterpieces. But the poison of copying spread through the schools and architecture began gradually to lose its mother place among the arts. Architecture became more imitative than creative, and the strongest minds and the strongest talents of the time became sculptors and painters, and sculpture and painting became the ruling arts. Sculptors and painters disregarded the architectural principles and used architecture as the playground for their artistic imagination.

Bernini and his followers made architecture sculptural, and sculptural forms overflow cornices and columns. Tiepolo painted his theatrical effects of clouds and skies and forgot the proportions of the room limited by walls and vaults.

This developed further in Rococo. Rococo was gallant as the life was gallant, and playing ornaments made architecture purely decorative.

After the French Revolution life became much simpler. The social life was new. There was a new literature, new science. Even the dresses were new and simpler and expressed the spirit of the time. There seemed to be a strong creative power in the air.

But the gods of architecture were dead: only imitative art from old Rome, neo-classicism.

And from now on during the Romantic time and the whole nineteenth century, we see a fairy play with architectural forms. All the styles, antique, Romanesque, Gothic, Renaissance from here and Renaissance from there, towers, pinnacles, crenulations, all dancing together in this fairy play. Imitation is fashion of the time. Imitation in style, imitation in material, imitation in construction. *The logic and the meaning of style was entirely lost.*

And I ask: "Is this our tradition? Are we going to build our contemporary architecture on forms that do not mean anything?"

No!!!

If we have to find our tradition from our ancestors, we have to go to a time when *art was still creative art*, in the Greek architecture and the Gothic time.

But what is our tradition and what is our wisdom from the Greek architecture?

The Greek architects tell us: our tradition comes from Egypt. They had a dualistic construction, the support and the weight, the column and the architrave. We used this principle because it was practical for our purpose. But they had their own fundamental form. It would have been easy for us to use their form, but it would have been a lie. *Art has to speak truth as well as man has!* So we had to use our own fundamental form and develop through it a style of our own. Our architecture has been admired for thousands of years because it is truthful in form and truthful in expression. This is our advice to you and this is your tradition from our art: *Be truthful in form and expression*, and the future will admire your work.

The Gothic architects tell us: our tradition comes through the Romanesque and through the Christian architecture from old Rome. We accepted the Roman plan-form because it was practical for our purpose. We found the pointed arch in the Orient and we adopted it because it was practical for our high windows. But we had our own fundamental form, and it governed our architecture. Look at our lofty vaults and buttresses; look at our high towers. The whole is a logical organism; it rises from the bottom to the top, stone built upon stone. You can feel the power go through the material and you can follow the power line the whole way to the top. It is truthful in material and truthful in construction and therefore our architecture has been admired for centuries. This is our advice to you and this is your tradition from our art: *Be truthful in material and construction* and the future will admire your work. *Be truthful in form and in expression. Be truthful in material and in construction. This is our tradition and this is our ethics.*

Our time is quite different from the earlier times:

- We have become more or less international.
- Our time is a machine age.
- Science helps us to feel the construction of the whole universe.
- The form of our life is new.

And the form of our architecture has to be new if there will be truth in expression.

But our building problems are so manifold in comparison with the earlier times. Every day brings new materials and new construction methods. And we ask: are our architects able to concentrate themselves, to listen to the voice of our fundamental form? Do we have enough creative power to build up our own style? Style, *cannot* be artificially made. It comes or it does not come. But if it does come, it comes only through intuition. Style grows as folk songs grow. People sing their songs, and those songs which express deepest the best feeling of the nation remain as folk songs. It is the fundamental form of the nation which sings through the soul of the nation.

Therefore, those architects who have the strongest imagination are *not* the strongest leaders. They are those architects who feel deepest the silent song of the fundamental form and who can express it in forms of truth. They are our leaders. And they will build the foundation for the architecture of the future, and the architects of the future will continue their work.

When we speak about our future architects, we come directly to educational problems because the schools of architecture have to take care of the architects of the future. I am not the right man to discuss educational problems, because my experience in this line is limited to the hard task of educating myself. The function of the school is to develop, besides technical and historical instruction, in the students:

- their artistic intuition;
- their sense for the spirit of the time;
- their instinct to translate the spirit of the time in an expressive architectural form;
- their sense for truth, ethics and logic in architecture;
- their creative imagination.

Creative because art is always creative in every moment and at every point. And the devil of copying has to be kept far from the schools.

To develop those things in the students is the problem of the schools. How to do it, I do not know, and it is mostly very individual. But, I have a distinct opinion as to how *not* to do it.

Do not kill the intuition with theories. Art based on theories is a dead art.

Do not teach theories of proportions. They only disturb the sense for proportion. Theories of proportions are only for arrived men to play with when they have leisure time and do not like to play bridge. The gifted man does not need them. A man without gifts cannot use them correctly.

Do not teach theories of colour. They only mislead the sense for colour and, besides, they are all wrong, at least for art purposes.

Do not teach the students the Greek form language before they understand their own form language. You do not teach your children Latin before they speak their mother tongue.

Do not teach style in connection with design. The only style you could possibly use in connection with design is the contemporary. But there isn't any! "But", someone says: "How can we teach architecture when we have nothing to go by? We have no theories, no styles. It is difficult." It is difficult, or it is easy, it all depends. I would say: It is *impossible*, or it is *very easy*.

It is impossible if the teacher has no sense for the deeper meaning of architecture and the student has no talent. You cannot grow roses from cabbage. But if the teacher is a living artist, and if the student has natural gifts to become a living artist, it is very easy. You hardly need to teach him. He will find his path himself.

There is still one point in connection with the educational problem.

We speak so often about the lack of interest for architecture on the part of the public. We have to get the public much more interested in our doings. It would be helpful for our profession.

That is true. But how can a person be interested in a thing he does not understand?

Well, we have to educate him.

Someone asks us: "What style is this building?"

We say: "It is Italian Renaissance."

Now he knows it is Italian Renaissance because we tell him so. But it does not help him very much. When he goes to the next building, we have to tell him again about its style.

So we have to educate him. We have to go with him through the whole history of architecture; we have to explain the differences between the various styles, their characteristics and their ornamental treatments. It is a hard task, because there are so many styles and varieties of styles, a long list of French kings and English kings and queens, and so on.

When we are through, he says: "Well, now I can see myself this building is Italian Renaissance. But there is one thing I cannot see. Why *should* it be Italian Renaissance? The owner is an Irishman, the architect is a German, the contractor is Danish, the workmen and the building materials are American, and the building was built in the United States a few years ago."

"Why *Italian* and why *Renaissance*?"

"Well", we say, "it is Italian Renaissance because the architect thinks it is a beautiful style."

"What, a beautiful style! What does it mean? Beautiful forms without any meaning! I would not like to read a book filled with beautiful words without any thoughts. No, sir! I do not care for your architecture."

So there we are. He was not interested in architecture because he did not understand it. Now we have educated him to understand it, and he is not interested at all. He likes to have thoughts behind the forms. He likes to have logic. And there is no logic! Or here is the logic: I read in the paper some time ago that a person in Detroit had the intention to build a building, and he said: "I will build it in the Spanish Renaissance style because this style is so little known in the Mid West."

I could say as well: "I have to go to San Antonio and make a speech, and I will speak in Finnish because this language is so little known in Texas."

There is the logic! No, we cannot get logic in architecture as long as we use styles which are only decorative, only empty ornaments which do not mean anything and which do not have any connection with our contemporary life. We have to get rid of the styles. They are poison for living architecture, for living art.

They do not use styles in other arts, do they?

Or could you imagine someone speaking about Galsworthy's books and saying: "Is it early Italian, or is it Greek, or is it Spanish?" No. Or, could you imagine someone speaking about Tchaikovsky's Fifth Symphony and saying: "Is it early Orpheus, or late Liszt, or Middle Mozart?"

No, you could not.

You could not, because you know what it is. And everyone knows that Tchaikovsky's Fifth Symphony is Tchaikovsky, and it comes directly from his inner-most soul and goes directly into the deepest heart of the public. And the public understands it.

The public understands our language, too, if we speak directly, and if there is logic in our thoughts and if there is truth in our words.

We do not need to educate the public.

Our art has to do it.

Harjuviita Housing by Alvar Aalto

1941

Alvar Aalto

Research for Reconstruction: Rehousing Research in Finland

Here emphasis is laid on the building activity in connection with the reconstruction problems being currently produced by the European War, mainly because of the opportunities they offer for large-scale housing. But this scheme is offered strictly in the spirit of a suggestion, not as a carefully formulated plan. If it succeeds in stimulating an eventually productive discussion of the possibilities of such a project, in doing so it will have served a valuable purpose.

A new problem created by the present war

Years ago one of the first organised efforts to mitigate the sufferings that grew out of modern warfare led to the foundation of the International Red Cross. Today there is no question of the high humanitarian contribution of this undertaking. Out of the last World War a new problem developed outside the strict province of Red Cross activity. This was the problem of resettling refugees and transplanting various political and ethnic groups in the realignment of international boundaries. From a humanitarian viewpoint, the work in this field accomplished by leaders such as Fridtjof Nansen stands only second to that of the Red Cross. Each war brings its own problems to be solved. And new forms of human activity grow up to meet new needs.

The present war – "total war" – has already shown the sort of problem it is carrying along in its wake. It is an old problem which has taken a new aspect due to its increased scale, that is to say, the number of human beings involved. The scale of the problem indicates the scale of the activity required to meet it.

The nature of today's problem
Today one sees that the root disaster of this war is the unprecedented destruction of human dwellings that is being effected, from great cities to the humblest shelters, and the consequent disruption of the social group. This war is destroying the first and oldest human protection – the home and the community – and is being effected on such a scale that life in certain areas has become practically impossible. For example, in a city in eastern Finland 149 houses were destroyed in an hour, while many small Norwegian mountain villages were completely wiped out with equal rapidity.

The fact is that the technique of the present war destroys more buildings in non-military areas than it does human beings. The population feels the full weight of the present war first of all in this indirect way – through the destruction of its homes.

There are few climates in the world where society can exist without the protection afforded by buildings. The result of a lack of such protection will be epidemics and other war and post-war sufferings in catastrophic proportions.

Reconstruction and building activity on a large scale is, therefore, an absolute necessity. This, if it is done with both speed and efficiency, will be the most helpful activity in the present situation.

The lesson of former attempts

At the close of the last war a similar need of reconstruction existed. Compared with today's need the problem of twenty years ago was minor. But, for all that, the slow, unmethodical mode of reconstruction employed in Belgium and in certain parts of France doubtless was in great part responsible for the epidemics that had such tragic consequences during that period. And the physical sufferings imposed on the inhabitants of many of the war-torn regions by the makeshift character of these first barrack-shelters probably played a serious psychological role in fostering social unrest among these people.

Now there are again signs that a similar sort of clumsy, unsystematic approach to reconstruction may be undertaken. But there is a grave difference in the present crisis which must be kept in mind. Today mistakes such as were made after the last war will be a hundred times more costly due to the difference in the scale of destruction.

Organisation a necessity

Today Red Cross activity and that of many other relief groups offering direct aid to suffering humanity is highly organised. But, there are still no organisations or group-efforts aimed directly at discouraging haphazard, unscientific reconstruction activities.

Today, compared with other forms of destruction, the indirect threat to human life through the destruction of even man's most elemental shelters is proportionately many times greater than it was after the last war. This is why the organisation of scientific and humanitarian methods of combating this indirect disaster is vitally and urgently necessary. An organised, scientifically conducted work of reconstruction must be undertaken in connection with a laboratory centre where the most desirable methods of meeting actual building problems may be studied.

Architectural research and the post-war reconstruction problems

From a structural viewpoint the problem of post-war reconstruction is closely related to ordinary peacetime housing problems. In times when the cultural development maintains an even tenor the organisation of social groups and buildings also grows evenly and harmoniously. In times when the basic character of the cultural structure changes abruptly, due to the more speedy development of certain elements of society than others, the organisation of human dwellings, of cities and even patterns of living, become confused, uneven and full of conflicting currents. In such times there is especially need for some controlling body or group.

The human factor

There has always been a great deal of attention given to technical research in building. This, however, has most frequently taken the character of a stress on separate details without any scientific attempt to study them in their direct relation to human life. There has never been a large and scientifically conducted research centred immediately around human needs in building problems.

Now if building activities are frequently haphazard and confused in peace times, it is clear that in building periods like that of post-war reconstruction the activity will be even more confused and wasteful.

Post-war reconstruction problems of earlier wars in comparison with those of the present one were elementary. Consequently, today the mistakes committed through haphazard building will have much more disastrous effects on the growth of society in the future. Therefore we should build on the experience of similar situations of the past, an activity which will give assistance in the present crisis and change the former unplanned approach to reconstruction to a more methodical one.

The problem in the past

The period of social construction which in most ways resembles our present period are certain stages of frontier colonisation. In colonisation building periods – that of the American Gold Rush, for example, in spite of its exaggerated character – we see certain similarities with the conditions that face us today.

In such periods of rough colonisation we have a crude development of the social unit. In the first phase of such colonisations buildings take the character of hastily constructed primitive shelters – temporary barracks. These barracks, however, will not meet the demands of a more highly organised mode of living. As a result they have to be torn down and replaced by buildings of a more permanent character. This second town in its turn usually lacks the qualifications for supporting a higher standard of living. As a result a third town often has to be built. Sometimes even this has to be demolished to make room for the step towards a more highly developed form of society. The wasteful character of such a process of demolition and reconstruction in wave after wave is obvious.

The time element

Now, in both the case of colonisation building and of post-war reconstruction, speed is clearly a vital consideration. The buildings were needed for immediate use. Construction under temporal pressure may be a feature also in ordinary peace-time housing projects, we have an example of it in a government project such as the Russian Five Year Plan. Yet in such cases, even if we admit that the quantity of building aimed at has been very great and the time for the work frequently limited, the result rarely matches the original aims. In many cases the original plan gives way to confusion and makeshift solutions. The lack of regard for the natural organic growth of the social community is fundamentally to blame. But makeshift solutions for the sake of speed are also economically unsound. They do not accord with the fundamental principles of good organisation. In the present situation, with a building problem of the magnitude of that which now faces us, such an approach would be disastrous.

Still the magnitude of today's catastrophe makes speed once again a vital consideration. Therefore, it is up to us to create a system where the restrictions of time will receive an equal consideration with such other factors as the satisfaction of biological needs and the need for permanency. But the desire for speed in construction must not receive such an emphasis as to eclipse the other two factors and bring back the barrack-shelter situation.

A programme to permit expansion

To satisfy the need for human shelter in an organic way we must first of all devise a shelter which will provide the essentials of protection for the individual family and for the community. At the same time it should be possible for this shelter to develop, step by step, with the social group.

In the present situation there is immediate need for an elementary human shelter that can be produced in large quantities. But at the same time, the permanent character of human life requires that such shelters should be of a nature that they may be developed into shelters on a higher level – that is to say, be turned into "homes".

Therefore, our problem today must envisage three factors, each of which must receive equal consideration. Our problem demands:

- speed of construction;
- satisfaction of biological needs;
- construction which will envisage a degree of permanency.

By this last feature, permanency, we should understand a possibility of expansion in step with the needs of a developing society – a system of construction that would not require demolition and reconstruction with each step in the progress of the communal unit.

The "growing house"

The prime objective then should be a building system which would provide a community, first, the most elementary protection and then gradually more and more fully developed forms of human dwellings. Our ideal should be a "growing house" so constructed that higher levels of the living standard can be reached and developed without the destruction of any part of the first elementary constructions or the elementary communal skeleton first worked out.

This means we should give the people, first of all, walls, a roof, and a primitive system of ordinary services. In the next step the construction will be developed to a higher degree. This procedure should be maintained until the house, in the final building period, will have reached the quality of a complete human "home".

Different forms of utilities should follow the same line of development; for example, first, a primitive type of temporary heating system, then later a more fully developed one. Other supply services which in the primitive stage will be collective for the sake of economy or facility of construction, will later be worked out on a private or individual basis. Sanitary equipment, especially, will follow this line: the first phase of hygienic convenience will be established on a collective basis and later on the basis of a smaller social unit such as the family.

Each of these stages of development can and should constitute a development of earlier forms rather than a replacement of them. The desirable plan of construction should permit a biological growth of the social unit without requiring the usual wave after wave of demolition and rebuilding.

The social group
Such a system will not confine itself merely to construction or to the problem of the individual house. It is a question that covers the whole field of human society from the planning of the community with its problems of traffic, sewage, and the like, down to new forms of houses – even to patterns of living. It covers the question of harmonious transition from the first primitive solutions of utility and shelter problems on a collective basis, to a higher development of them for smaller units within the social group. In this way the problem also embraces questions of the protection of the individual's privacy and that of small social units against the pressure of larger groups in collective living.

Scheme of an experimental town, combined with a commercial subdivision. This map shows in a schematic way all the necessary elements of a complete town. When built, the various units will have to follow natural local conditions and actual topography. The map shows the following units: a is the experimental part of the town consisting of one-family houses, row houses and apartment houses. Units d (one-family houses), e (small apartment houses) and f (row houses) show additional buildings which will be erected after the models developed in the experimental section as a usual real estate operation or with governmental subsidy, b is the community centre, and c school and athletic field.

The need of a testing ground

An experimental housing group must be built to embrace a number of houses of different types as well as all essential constructions needed for serving a community as a collective-living basis. This "experimental group" must be large enough to include all the buildings necessary for a careful study of the essential problems of a normal community.

At the end of the first building period we should have a communal unit embracing both primitive shelters and a higher development of the same. After the first "building period" this laboratory group will be turned over as dwellings for families and individuals to serve as a living centre for refugees. In this way the laboratory field then begins to fulfil its task directly to humanity.

During the second phase or "dwelling period" the field will be kept under scientific observation while further developments will be watched. And the results of observation of this period, like those of the "building period", will be published and distributed for academic and scientific use.

The organisation

If really good results are to be obtained this research work must be the product of a world-wide organisation working in many different countries, under many different conditions, but with its centre in an industrialised and scientifically progressive country, for example, the United States.

Such an organisation must be politically independent and must have no connection with local commercial building enterprises. It must be free to cooperate with any local building activities of a suitable character in a given location. The main purpose of such an organisation is to be able to give real aid in an emergency completely independent of local conditions, just as the Red Cross aims at doing. But at the same time this organisation must have a creative end. Its aim is not merely to alleviate temporary sufferings, but beyond that to work out of the opportunity provided it by the present crisis, new forms for normal peacetime housing – forms that will have a more profoundly humane and scientific justification.

To achieve the proper results the organisation and its subsequent research work must be directed, or at any rate supervised, by an American university or technical institute where technical and scientific faculties are available and can collaborate. This is important because the planning, supervision and observation of the experimental and research work in the field and the combination and analysis cannot be satisfactorily effected without the aid of various scientific and technical groups or experts.

A centre for the collection of the data obtained must be located in this same university or technical institute in the form of an "Institute for Architectural Research". The parent institute will have to deal only with technical and humanitarian issues – not with financial problems.

The institute will be primarily a scientific centre where all results obtained through the fieldwork are collected, analysed and published. The actual research work of the institute will be done in the field, in different countries under conditions differing as widely as possible in order that a variety of results may be obtained for comparison. The complete research building groups will still be kept under observation by the institute for a certain time after the termination of the building period.

These research groups will be parts of housing areas, or building projects aimed first at satisfying humanitarian needs and only secondarily at commercial objectives, should they exist.

To make the plan financially feasible the institute will be authorised to enter into agreements with foundations and with local authorities.

The institute will also serve as a teaching tool in arranging practical research work in the field for graduate scholars and in the undergraduate preparation of students for this activity.

Introduction to the programme

To illustrate the manner in which this plan might be put in to practice, we will take Finland today as a typical research field. We take Finland merely for the sake of a concrete example and also because it happens to be the terrain with which the writer is personally most familiar. From a practical point of view, Finland offers special opportunities for research work of this character: rich topographical variations; a building industry developed in keeping with other productive activities of the country; extremely low costs for all kinds of building in relation to existent conditions in other countries and a comparatively high standard of living. However, it must be understood that such an approach is not intended to limit the field of such work to any particular country.

On this basis we may assume that the initial research field is to be established in Finland in a district designated by that country's government. It should be located north of the capital, Helsinki. It should be conveniently accessible to the capital itself, to the industrial areas close to the capital, as well as to certain smaller industrial towns. At the same time it must have ready communication with one of the larger agricultural areas. The location is very important because the houses to be constructed in this research field are afterwards to be used for ordinary dwellings. Therefore good connections with several industrial centres and agricultural areas are vitally necessary.

The research field, during the work and all activity in connection with it, is to be under the joint supervision of an American university or technical institute and a local committee, including representatives of the supervising research Institute and the State of Finland. All technical advisers in the local committee are to be approved by the supervising American university or technical institute.

The area for the research field is to be provided by the Finnish State for this purpose without any expense to the collaborating American university or technical institute. Highways and principal streets and electrical power will be arranged by the local authorities. The area for research construction will cover at least 200 acres, excluding highways.

The local staff, including a chairman responsible to the collaborating American university or technical institute, is to have headquarters at Helsinki as well as on the building field itself. A part of the staff is to be comprised of American graduate architects and graduate engineers maintained by American travelling scholarships. The chairman of this committee is to be responsible for the academic assignment of work to the student members of his staff.

The research field will be divided into five sections which when completed will constitute a communal unit. The research work will be carried on independently in each section, but with a view always to the coordination of the sections.

Section one: the embryo human shelter

The work in this section will deal mainly with experiments in minimum dwellings as temporary shelters for families of various sizes and for single individuals. The location, planning and construction are to be of such character that buildings suitable for a permanent mode of living may be developed without demolition of the basic structures or serious changes in the general plan.

Part of the work will be related to the problem of grouping primitive shelters so that several of them may form a complete family unit. Another part of the work will be related to the problem of transportable elementary shelters. Special attention will be given to technical problems such as the study for suitable foundations to make buildings independent of seasonal conditions, climatic conditions, and the like.

This section will contain the following buildings:

- 12 units (1). The problem of absolute minimum shelter to be examined through one room unit-cells.
- 8 units (2). Combination of different cells into a primitive 2, 3 and 4 room shelter.
- 4 units (3). Development of (1) and (2) by additional building into more complete shelters. Each finished unit will be at a different stage of development.
- 6 units (4). Group buildings of embryo shelters with a semi-collective living room which later can be used as a private living room of one family. Each finished unit will be at a different stage of development.
- 4 units (5). Transportable buildings of type (1) and (2).

Two-thirds of the above buildings will be prefabricated, one-sixth will be assembled by unskilled workers from factory made standard units and another sixth will be built by local craftsmen.

Section two: the one-family house; a product of prefabrication and industry

In this section the main problem of building, period by period, will be examined. All buildings will have fixed sizes and they will meet different levels of living standards.

There will be the following points of research:

a   Examination of the minimum standard: the most primitive form a house can have and be suitable for healthy living for a short period.

b   Examination of several houses showing different stages of development from a primitive to a complete house.

c   Examination of the relationship between individual and collective living. Examination of what services can be collective during the first period and for what size groups of buildings and families. Transformation of this system of collective services step by step into a system of services for smaller groups and individuals.

d   Examination of the same problems in (c) in connection with town planning. In the first period there will be a simple system of roads and streets; to be developed later into a system more suitable for individual living.

e   Questions dealing with the shortage of materials in post-war periods; for example, the examination of possibilities of installing temporary heating systems in such a way that they need not be destroyed later.

All these problems will be examined with standardisation and industrial production as the chief consideration.

Standardisation here does not mean a formal one with all houses built alike. Standardisation will be used mainly as a method of producing a flexible system by which the single house can be made adjustable for families of different sizes, various topographical locations, different exposures, views and so on.

This means that practically every house will be different from the next in spite of the fact that there will be a strict standardisation of elements and building cells.

Special attention will be given in this section to a system of standardisation that permits flexibility. Sixteen units are to be built in this section in each of six types, (a) to (f). One unit of each type is to be used for special laboratory purposes (six units). The types (a), (b), (c), (d), (e) and (f) are all of various sizes with variations from 45 square metres of net area to 80 square metres. The size of each of these types will depend on the size and character of the different families.

Different stages of development demonstrating the flexibility of standardisation will be carried out. A temporary field laboratory for the test of technical details will be established in connection with this section (one unit). Nine units will be built for collective services.

Section three: the one-family house; a combination of industrially made units assembled by unskilled workers

The third section will cover the same purposes as section two, but the difference is to be in the method of assembling. Altogether 32 units will be built, with the same variations in size and location as in section two. Three units are to be built for collective services.

Section four: the one-family house built with the aid of local craftsmen

In this section, factory made standards will be used only in the smallest possible quantity. Special research will be carried out in this section to explore the combination of permanent and temporary buildings in accordance with the following schedule. A total of 32 units will be built:

- 16 units with the same variations as in section two.
- 8 units showing a combination of temporary and permanent houses.
- 8 special units for examination of transportable houses of larger size than in section one.
- 1 unit for collective services.

Section five: row houses on level and sloping grounds

In this section five different apartment houses will be built to examine the important problem of building step by step (five units). The research field in this section begins with two types of houses: the terraced row houses on sloping ground (three units with six dwellings in each unit); and row houses on level ground combining concrete, brick and wood (three units with 20 dwellings in each unit). It is estimated that these five units are enough for examining the problem of the growing house; however, it is more important here to examine the problems particular in row houses.

A special part of the research in this section will be the examination of the use of prefabricated systems and prefabricated units as part of row houses and apartment houses. This will cover the difficult question of combining prefabricated elements with local materials.

All of the above-mentioned houses are to be built with the ultimate purpose of investigating the possibilities of providing the maximum privacy in single family units. Half of this group of apartments will be built for the investigation of the most primitive stages and half will show various developed forms of higher living standards.

Estimate of cost

It is suggested that the Experimental Town will be built from funds of combined foundation's grants and an international or domestic loan approximating 60 per cent of the total cost. The houses when completed will represent at least an actual value of 75 per cent of the total cost.

It is expected that the grounds will be granted by the local authorities. The local authorities will put into immediate use the technical results of the Experimental Town by building neighbouring units.

The builders of the Experimental Town will make an agreement with the local authorities concerning the use and the financial management of the total unit. Aggregate rental income in excess of 60 per cent of the cost should be used for future field experiments.

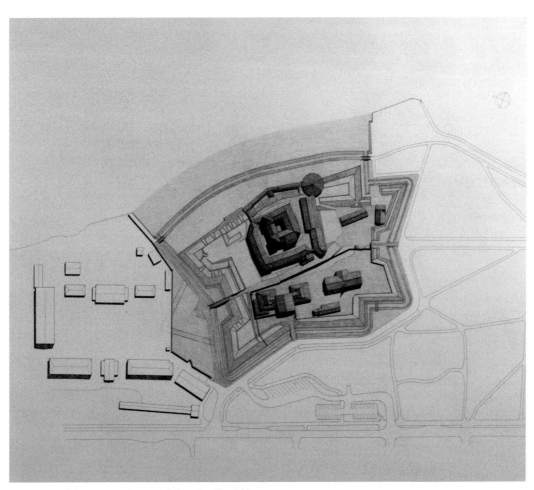

Restoration of the Hämeen Linna Castle by Nils Erik Wickberg

1943

Nils Erik Wickberg

Thoughts on Architecture

What makes a work of art – a poem, for instance – interesting, and gives it perman-ent validity, though the subject and meter may have been endlessly repeated, is its personal ring. In some tribe or nation on the other hand, we are fascinated by its particular national characteristics. When we travel in a foreign country it is not the outside influences and impressions found there that interest us primarily; the most brilliant imported works leave us indifferent. What we like to experience is national themes in what may be vastly more modest and less striking works. It is sympto-matic that in its first edition a major work on European art history was arranged in the established fashion, horizontally layered according to period throughout: first Romanesque, then Gothic, Renaissance and the other periods. The new edition, however, has gone over to a vertical division, according to nationality: Italian art, German art and so on.

Thus our contemporaries seem to appreciate national art in its deeper meaning, art which has permeated an entire nation and become its property, so that it is encountered both in the big cities and in the most remote rural areas. One of the most recent European examples of such a phenomenon is south German Rococo. It is a joy to see how genius even emerges from the rank and file, always keeping in close touch with its native soil. They are no demonic supermen, no rebellious eccentrics rising in arms against a hated and apathetic present; they are merely the noblest, the most exquisite flowers of their tribal heritage, the highest embodiment of its specific, inherent potential. A couple of the great masters – Johan Michael Fischer and Dominikus Zimmermann – never went beyond the borders of Germany, the latter not even beyond the immediate vicinity of his native district. They never attended any academy and they built mainly in rural areas, per-taining to the strict limitations of the guild system. And yet they created interiors with a wealth of ideas and perfection in execution that, if anything, exceeded what was being done at the same time in Paris and Rome, and even constituted a late perfection of the monumental spatial art that started with the Pantheon and the Byzantine Hagia Sophia and which is a great contribution to Western architecture, unparalleled anywhere else in the world. It merely adds to the fascination of these resplendent, light-flooded halls that we know so little of their creators; they retain something of the provocative and venerable anonymity of the unknown master builders and sculptors of the Middle Ages.

In Bavarian-Swabian Rococo, architecture, sculpture and painting merge into an absolute unity such as has never been achieved before or since. It is easy to say that this architecture is "unarchitectural", "musical", the sculpture "non-sculptural", "picturesque", and so forth. But one does not have to use these hackneyed expressions; it can be called "total art", "unisono" art, which is what it is, in fact. Everything depends on the whole, and the whole depends on all the individual details. It cannot be denied that the various art forms individually lose weight in the process; if a decorative detail is taken out of context it seems more or less meaningless. At the same time the whole suffers, for the architecture itself is not enough on its own, either. In other words, the "totalitarian" principle has been carried to the extreme. And all this inexhaustible wealth is finally merely an instrument on which light can play. With unceasing inventiveness, everything is formulated so as to catch and diffuse the light, and make it a composition. The most important agent in this art is light, and the next is colour. Thus it is not without justification maintained that we have here a phenomenon which occupies a place in architecture comparable to that of Impressionism in painting 150 years later.

Strangely enough, the backbone of this late and exquisite art was formed by rural masters. Does not Zimmermann's shrine "Die Wies" stand like a blossoming apple tree in the home meadow, with the dark forest and the gleaming ridge of the Alps in the background? Zimmermann is one of the most lovable, pure in heart and harmonious artists that ever lived – a Fra Angelico of Rococo architecture, or its Haydn, to use a less remote comparison.

To a northern European, those old cathedrals which seem to have grown organically, changing their shape over the centuries, hold a rare charm. On to a dim, severe, long-shaped Romanesque building, during late Gothic times an airy choir, flooded with light has been built, during the Renaissance and Baroque times funeral crypts added, and at different eras pews, chandeliers and altars; the choir perhaps has been decorated in playful Rococo, the organ loft and façade shaped in the Neo-Classical style, and on to the sombre, massive colossus of a Medieval tower Baroque masters have casually and unselfconsciously added their graceful rounded caps. And yet everything fits together, though this harmony is not the fruit of a uniform plan drawn up in advance but rather of some intrinsic vegetative principle which allows widely varying components to grow together like the multifarious trees and plants in a forest. Such a northern cathedral is the direct antithesis of the Greek temple, which from the very beginning stands in consummate perfection – absolute, like a Platonic ideal.

Intellectuality carried to the extreme, is certainly a disease, though a highly admirable one. It has a tendency to end up with the thought that "the cosmos is a blemish on the purity of non-existence". Le Corbusier's words on the imperfection of the orange compared with the geometrically perfect beauty of steel spheres and cylinders, his assertion that the machine, devised by man, is the "goddess of beauty", infinitely superior to all natural growth, not only sound blasphemous but already strangely out-dated and irrelevant. These days there is certainly no reason to idolize the machine. The great problem of our times, so difficult to solve, is, on the contrary, how to *master the machine without annihilating it.*

"We must envisage our living space as compartments or cabins. We must consider the house as a machine for living in or as a utensil."

It is written in a language that has no word for the concept "home". Behind lurks the ideal of a society like a rational beehive, a society which must seem like – and is, to the extent it has been implemented – a degradation to mankind. To innumerable modern people the home is the only place where they do not function like rats in a treadmill, where they can, at least to a certain extent, *exercise their creativity freely*. The home is the last defence against the mechanization of life. If Functionalism is to have a future, Le Corbusier's rationalist Romanticism must be overcome. Aalto realized this when he advocated more flexible and more abundantly varied standardization and points to the pattern set by nature's own standardization – which is unattainable, of course – its inherent capacity to produce an infinite variety of combinations from similar cells. If Le Corbusier is the Voltaire of modern architecture, Aalto is its Rousseau (such comparisons do not stand up to close scrutiny!), who points out the decisive importance to human life and coexistence of irrational and immeasurable forces. After all life is not what Monsieur Teste and other "anchorites in the desert of the intellect" – to use Novalis' words on the philosophers of the Enlightenment – seem to say that it should be: a mathematical problem.

Concrete, the material used by Le Corbusier and Functionalism, also has somehow to be overcome or neutralized, in residential architecture at least. Concrete is perfectly adequate as a building material for those with a mechanical and materialistic ideology. It has never been fire, never been stratified in beautiful marked layers or acquired vivid hues, as natural stone or brick has. It has never been a living organism like wood; it lacks every quality of beauty. It is abstract, unnatural, as if merely a necessary means of giving visible shape to mathematical formulae. Here again, Aalto has been guided by a true instinct in once more bringing wood to the fore. It is the only building material that has itself once been a vessel of life. Another alternative is the plain or patterned facings so masterfully used by Frank Lloyd Wright.

That Aalto the individualist has plunged into the problems of standardization with such fervour is not, of course, because he loves uniformity. On the contrary, he has realized that we have reached the point where a thoroughgoing standardization in the field of building is unavoidable, and that it must, therefore, from the start, be steered on the right course, allowing as much leeway as possible for freedom of creation. *That* is why Aalto has tackled standardization. If the task has to be accomplished it is safer that the master takes the initiative than for it to get into the hands of amateurs. But the principle that standardization should apply only to building elements, that – to use Aalto's simile – the architect's relationship to his norms should be that of the poet to the dictionary, is far from considering the "machine à habiter", or the endless repetition of serial houses the ideal on the horizon. He has in mind more a standardization of the type represented by the Japanese dwelling.

Japanese house architecture is one of the strangest phenomena in the history of art. In Europe, the most grandiose and unique contribution in the field of building is perhaps the monumental interior, a place for festivity and worship: the

Pantheon, the giant halls of the Roman baths and the basilicas, Hagia Sophia, the Gothic cathedrals, Baroque churches, banqueting halls, stairwells. In East Asia, above all in Japan, monumental spatial architecture, those bold techniques of vaulting, is notable for its total absence. How limited, how strangely similar over a period of one thousand five hundred years East Asian architecture seems to us beside the European, with its changing styles, sudden reverses and constant ability to renew itself. There are, of course, shifts in style there, too, and that they seem less different from one another than their European counterparts depends no doubt to a certain extent on the unifying distance. It is probably indisputable, however, that the changes really have been greater in the West than in the Far East, and that the fruitful mobility and unrest of the European spirit, its world-embracing taste for adventure, is reflected in a wider amplitude in the swing of the pendulum of formal and artistic expression.

Already the fact that Japanese architecture is architecture in wood (the earliest stone houses were erected by Portuguese Jesuits in the sixteenth century) implies considerable limitation. There is nothing even to approach the gigantic concrete structures of the Romans, or the dressed-stone Gothic cathedrals, reaching up to heaven, with their stained-glass windows in flaming colours. But within this limited world, which does seem to a detached observer to have been marking time for a long while, an architectural miracle is growing. This miracle is not expressed in terms of magnificence, but in absolute perfection, polish, an utter refinement surpassing well-nigh everything built by the hand of man: the Japanese house.

In terms of absolute perfection it equals the Doric temple. But it has qualities that make it more widely prolific in our times than the temple. It has been said that Greek temple architecture is standardized, but it is a standardization which rides dangerously near to the concept of a uniform house type that Aalto is fighting. Not only the elements but their composition, the spatial whole, is strictly according to norms (throughout time cult buildings have been more or less "standardized"). It is here that the Japanese house asserts its superiority as a source of inspiration for contemporary architecture. Since it is not the whole but only the elements that are standardized, it allows the possibility of varied combinations according to taste and space needs. If you compare the Parthenon to a polished crystal, in which every line, every surface is calculated exactly, and nothing can be taken away or added without spoiling the whole, then the Japanese dwelling house can be compared to a bush, or a tree, putting out new twigs and shoots in different directions without the free equilibrium being upset.

In the course of time, despite the vast distance, Europe has absorbed no small measure of artistic influences and stimuli from East Asia. Well-known examples of this are Medieval silk fabrics from Lucca, glazed earthenware, porcelain, furniture and interior art of the Baroque and Rococo, the English landscape garden, the graphics and handicrafts of Art Nouveau, modern European ceramics and garden art. But none of these can be compared to the basic importance that the Japanese house has had, and will have for a long time to come, for contemporary Western architecture. Bearing in mind the freely expansible plan, the large windows, the innumerable sliding doors enabling the whole apartment to be converted into one large volume in which the individual rooms flow into one another, the abundance of built-in cupboards, the opportunity to open the rooms on to the garden, the intimate connection with the natural setting throughout, to say nothing of the actual artistic design of the detail, with large, empty surfaces or discreetly patterned ones, a lot of unstained wood, plaited straw – an aim to let materials speak for themselves without the burden of ornamentation – in a word, without the stimuli from Japan, contemporary Western architecture would not be what it is today.

In some quarters one notices a tendency to again regard what has gradually grown up more highly than the outcome of rational thinking, the organic, as it were, as superior to the geometric. According to this the symmetry introduced by the Renaissance in place of the freer style of composition of Gothic times would seem to be a lapse, the lifeless and unrelieved chessboard pattern of the Renaissance town plan a clumsy abomination beside the meaningful hierarchy of large and small, wide and narrow, of the Medieval town, its organic adherence to the terrain, its supple adaptation to wind and sun. The relationship of the Medieval town to the ideal town of the Renaissance is like that of a juicy sun-ripe orange to a polished, geometrically perfect steel sphere – to use the image quoted earlier. But it should not be imagined for that reason that those Medieval towns were created haphazardly, *purely* by instinct. They are more than one at first thinks the fruits of practical calculation and a conscious sense of beauty. The difference is mainly that the town builders of the time were greater artists than the architects of the Renaissance, who – as the Swedish romantic poet Atterbom put it – got too wrapped up in a sheer idea. During the nineteenth century the last remnants of this wonderful ability were lost, the ability that enabled earlier people to build their houses and towns so that they seem as natural where they stand as rocks and rivers, forests and meadows, so that they seem to belong to the surrounding countryside as though they had been there since the beginning of time.

"Functionalism", "the new architecture", or what you will call it, is the offspring of the age of bourgeois Liberalism. It has found its most cherished tasks in industrial buildings, housing and business buildings; it has scoffingly put "monumentality" inside quotation marks and is therefore somewhat taken aback when confronted with the new demand for monumentality. Like the idols of earlier epochs – the church during the Middle Ages, the Baroque princes, progress under Liberalism (temple – palace – "the temple of Mammon", "the bank palace") – the god of our times, the State, demands homage in the form of monumental buildings, our new "sacred buildings".

It is, incidentally, a strange coincidence that two of the great pioneer works constructed in glass and iron – the Crystal Palace in London and the Glaspalast in Munich – were both erected during the first part of the 1850s and both burned down around 1930. Rarely is an important era in architectural history brought so clearly to a close.

A dream has been nourished of a "telluric" culture, a culture common to the entire world which would assimilate all the best achievements of different peoples. Far-reaching evolution in this direction would, however, involve the danger of losing all distinctions, resulting in a sort of spiritual "thermical death". Something of that sort is already discernible in the common Hellenistic culture of the Mediterranean countries during late Classicism, and there the area was both limited and, geographically speaking, fairly uniform. Take architecture as an example. An "international" architecture is already something unnatural for the simple reason that the world is not the same all over. The cupola roofs on the bazaar buildings of the Eastern Mediterranean countries are as naked as Greek athletes. The "play of muscles" in the construction can be observed in abounding sunlight, whereas in our Medieval churches the upper side of the stellar vaulting is concealed under a saddleback roof, in the same way that people cover their bodies with warm clothes in a country where two-thirds of the year are more or less wintry. With present-day methods of insulation, vaulted constructions can very likely be made without an outer roof, even on the Arctic Circle, and probably there is nothing to prevent churches on the Mediterranean from being built with high saddleback roofs. But all that is possible is not necessarily natural. When the hecklers of Functionalism called the famous "Weissenhofsiedlung" in Stuttgart, where there are buildings by Le Corbusier and other renowned architects, "Stuttgart's Casablanca", the criticism was without doubt to a certain extent legitimate. It also may be justifiable to resume the use of building materials and the methods of construction characteristic of various parts of the country which were swept away by the effect of equalization in big city architecture. But such a reaction should not stop at a protest, because then it would easily result in the stale atmosphere found at Skansen in Stockholm: one should aim at a synthesis with the scorned Functionalism. It cannot be argued that modern concrete architecture never existed.

As a writer, Le Corbusier's role in doing away with the surviving prejudices and putting things straight has been of inestimable importance. But the philosophy of life propounded in the theses he formulates in brilliant rhetoric and with lyrical verve seems to us arrogant and hostile to life. He is an object lesson in "Der Geist als Widersacher der Seele", and seems to idolize the leaning toward the mechanization of human existence which D.H. Lawrence opposed so passionately. Nothing is as off-putting to a northerner as a lack of "heart", or "temperament", which by no means is the same thing as sentimentality (the most coolheaded intellectual may very well be sentimental). To understand what is meant here, just think of old Frank Lloyd Wright. He has what Le Corbusier lacks – a touch of the wide-open spaces, smells, wind, sun, rain; Walt Whitman and *A Midsummer Night's Dream*.

Le Corbusier is an unusually downright and fanatically one-sided proponent of the Latin spirit. Others before him had created architecture in iron, glass and concrete. All the architectural theorists of the Renaissance and Baroque were Italians or Frenchmen, and now again, it called for the Latin intellect to classify the new architecture, to write its law tablets, to *form a school*. However much Le Corbusier warned against "L'école Corbu", that is just what we have seen grow up. It is astonishing how again and again one encounters among young architects all over the world proposals and solutions first put forward by him. Le Corbusier has become the Palladio of Functionalism. His plan for a city of three million inhabitants is, in its magnificent and complete symmetry (every idea is presented of necessity more or less "symmetrically"), a worthy latter-day descendant of the ideal towns of the sixteenth and seventeenth centuries: the arrangement of the lamellar housing is a direct reminder of Jacques Perret's ideal project.

However, though Le Corbusier's greatest significance may have been as a preacher, one should not forget that he was at the same time a superb architect, worthy of inclusion in the ranks of great masters of the past. In the world of architecture one seldom gets such an impression of intensive purity, clearness and lightness as is encountered in his works. And if there are things one does not approve of, which invite opposition, his buildings and projects are in any case stimulating; they make you want to actually plan and build yourself.

The elements of modern architecture were to a large extent in existence before Le Corbusier. The open plan is found, for instance, in English domestic architecture, in Frank Lloyd Wright's work and in the villas of the 1880s, with their projections and glass verandas, to say nothing of examples as famous as the Japanese house, the East Karelian farm house or the castle layout of the Middle Ages. Nevertheless, if anybody is to be honoured with the title "father of modern architecture" it should be Le Corbusier. His everlasting service is that he has collected the odd elements and welded them into a new organic whole, in roughly the same way as the Gothic master builders combined and interpreted motifs already in existence – the ogival arch, the rib vault, the portal that recedes inwards, the twin-towered west façade – and created from them a new style, the most individual style brought forth in the Western hemisphere before the emergence of contemporary concrete architecture.

Le Corbusier's aversion to Gothicism is one of the most surprising results of his one-sided classical aestheticism, which only approves of the simplest stereometric forms, among which the Gothic pointed arch cannot be included. And yet Gothic is nothing less than the only historical example of a skeleton construction consistently carried through in fireproof material. In buildings from earlier times – for example the concrete constructions of the Romans – the wall mass was always over-dimensioned. It was the Gothic builders who first scaled it down to the indispensable minimum and as a result of this broke up the walls with huge windows. When Le Corbusier moves the supporting columns on the outer walls inwards and turns the walls into uninterrupted glass surfaces, it is merely a logical sequence to the Gothic idea.

But Le Corbusier prefers the temple to the cathedral . . . And yet one would think that the cathedral, related as it is to modern constructions, would for that very reason be more prolific in our times than the Parthenon. In the field of architecture, the cathedral represents the declaration of the coming of age of the Western spirit, and in comparison Renaissance architecture is an atavism, an interlude, a return to older and more primitive means of construction and a conventional spatial concept. As far as spatial concept is concerned, the Baroque did overcome this outside element and represents a return to original sources.

Le Corbusier, the obstinate Classicist with Romance background, does not seem to see that it was Gothic and Baroque, the styles he dislikes – not the Greek temple, which is mainly intended to be seen from the outside (the interior is really only a superfluous empty space lighted only through the entrance) – that represents the preliminary stages on the route to the flowing, dynamic sense of space which is expressed so consummately in his mezzanined villa interiors. In the Gothic cathedral the eye is not drawn exclusively to the absorbing vertical movement of the nave; one also seeks out, between a forest of columns, the side aisles, the transept, the rich garland of chapels surrounding the choir, and everywhere a bewildering wealth of perspectives is perceived, a stimulating play of light and shadow. And how typical of Baroque that the splendid, imposing stairwell became the favourite subject of its secular architecture; the stairwell, where movement is the soul and the beauty of its constantly changing perspective can only be fully appreciated during a "promenade architecturale". That is the genealogy of modern spatial expression; the Parthenon plays no part in it, nor the Pantheon.

(An historic predecessor of Le Corbusier's great mezzanined living room is found, incidentally, in the Hanseatic burghers' "Diele", the spacious two-storey hall with its views of the adjoining rooms, its balconies, spiral staircase and large windows; sometimes one could, in fact, speak of a glass wall.)

Why this deep concern with Le Corbusier, why argue with him? Because he is one of the spiritual leaders of our times who, in his field, has meant as much as Freud, for example, did in his. One cannot make light of his achievements, as they have tried to in Germany, any more than psychoanalysis can be spirited away. You can conquer a continent but you can't force it to read German type, and the Germans have had to learn this.

It would not be surprising if one fine day the Germans sounded the retreat on this point, as they have on the question of German type; they might even proclaim that the new architecture is actually their discovery! And they would do so with a certain justification: Jahrhunderthalle at Breslau showed decades ago that monumental effects can be achieved with modern constructions, and no other country put so-called Functionalism into effect so early or on such a large scale in residential buildings. This last may well have contributed to the reaction in Germany: the public was not ripe to accept so much that was new and the architects were not ready to use the new forms rightly. How different it was in France, for instance! At that time – during the 1920s – there were only a few art enthusiasts there who had villas built for them according to the modern construction forms. France lacked a counterpart to the innumerable settlements which sprang up like mushrooms on the outskirts of all large and medium-sized German towns.

Leppäkertuntie Housing by Aulis Blomstedt

1958

Aulis Blomstedt

The Problem of Architectural Form

The topic I have chosen – the problem of architectural form – is such an extensive one that I shall be able only to throw a limited amount of light upon it within the framework of a short lecture. However, it is of major importance because it is one of the key issues of architectural design. It appears as a central problem, a problem that demands an answer, in all the practical tasks of the architect.

Architectural form is akin to an iceberg: the part that can be seen is only a fraction of the whole. Insofar as the invisible part is, in fact, the iceberg itself, and the visible part is effectively only a sign of a more profound reality. This is something that every architect knows. To us, the drawing board has two visible, load-bearing supports of exactly the same significance as the invisible part between them. The essential elements of architectural design are mainly abstractions. As Lao-tzu said: "The value of what is depends for use on what is not." A chimney that you can see certainly has its worth, but it is the flue you cannot see that is really useful.

The home of architectural form is an unseen world of different relationships and proportions. Imagine what would happen to visible, architectural form if the towers of Notre Dame were to shrink to half their height, or the building mass of the Parthenon were to grow three times higher. Or, if the balconies at La Scala in Milan, which allow you to watch the performance from different angles and different levels, were to be removed.

Unfortunately, our northern languages do not include a precise vocabulary that we could use to operate in the various branches of the world of relationships and proportions with sufficient clarity. In the major civilised languages, things are different. For example, the French words "rélation", "conception", "position", "rapport", "distance", "dimension", "proportion" with their precise meanings are available for explaining the intricacies of architectural form. Compared with this, our own vocabulary is poor – and seldom sufficiently unambiguous. Any attempt to explain architectural form is liable to become confused right at the start, because of the terminology.

Because of this, I have chosen to supplement my talk with another method of presentation, a visual one, with which we are more familiar. But this method of presentation, that is to say an architectural entity broken down into projected illustrations forms a reality that is, of course, contrary to our ideas. (Showing still transparencies of the shapes of countries, or of novels, or of functions, would of course be even less helpful.)

I had hoped to be able to find you an enlightening example of a public building that has actually been built. Perhaps the famous pilgrim chapel at Ronchamp, where contemporary architectural form is illustrated taking on various monumental tasks. However, this excellent piece of work is too plastic in its vocabulary of expression to be a typical example of pure architectural form.

What then is architectural form?

I will mention a few imprecise shapes that can hardly be called architectural forms: the three-aisle church, the two-storey family house, panorama restaurants, catacombs, water towers, sun-terraces. These do not yet tell us much more than that they are vague groupings (or constellations) of space, or references to such groupings.

Architectural form is certainly something that has more shape, and is more solid and fixed. Everyone knows that the architectural design is not in itself the building, but it is perhaps fairly rare that the design is not meant to be built. Nevertheless, the design can be presented as a completely finished architectural form – in the same way as a score for a piece of music.

Paul Nelson's study *La Maison Suspendue* (Suspended House), published as a slim volume about twenty years ago, is perhaps the clearest possible example of architectural form that has emerged in full bloom, complete and about as solid and fixed as it could be. It is no longer an ovule or an embryo as are the examples I just gave you. (It is more like a fully developed walnut in its shell. Let us try to crack the shell and peep inside.)

What we see is a rather special approach to a house, where the geometric basic shape fits inside the silhouette of two parallelepipeds. The higher of these is suspended monolithically from a metal frame. The structure is a surprising organization of interior spaces, as we shall see; most of the rooms are suspended from the roof structure forming free groupings or constellations (of rooms) in an otherwise empty spatial universe.

This can be seen from the section. We can see the groups of rooms suspended from the roof, in the upper part of the section. The diagonal division of the façade is apparent from the suspension; it does not carry the roof in the normal way. The windows are of translucent, opal glass. Visibility outwards and inwards is limited to essential points.

The author himself has set the parameters. The basic premise is Nelson's idea that unnecessary areas of space (spaces that are anonymous as far as actual use goes) are also an essential part of a person's dwelling.

The lower part of the living room is on the right, low down in the middle is an oval dining room and above it two staircases, the one on the left is a service stair that goes right up to the top floor. To the left of this is a circular kitchen. Upstairs on the left are the servants' quarters and downstairs is a garage. The main entrance, with its auxiliary spaces, is upstairs in the centre. The four columns that carry the high part can be seen as dots from outside the house.

The left-hand side of the visible square of the living room is a balcony, with both the stairs leading to it. The stair on the right ends at this level and changes into a gentle ramp, curving upwards. Three rooms branch off the ramp at the lower end, the circular library and two studies, and the ramp leads on up to the bedroom wing. Above, on the left, is the parents' bedroom with an en suite bathroom and a balcony.

The uniform block of rooms that fills the lower part of the building makes up the children's (and perhaps the guests') sleeping wing which is connected to various auxiliary spaces, a children's playroom and a large balcony. The plan shows the hierarchy of the different levels projected onto a common horizontal plane.

The concept of conventional architectural form as a set of storeys one on top of the other has effectively disappeared. Here, in free space, we are only higher or lower, without any major steps in the vertical direction.

We will leave La Maison Suspendue, through the white main entrance door. As we leave, we get an overall idea of this curious house design.

Laszlo Moholy-Nagy, one of the most important teachers at the original Bauhaus, said that the *core* of architecture lies in the problem of space and building is simply a matter of construction. Nelson's house design is a spatial problem handled as a key issue, but it calls for a certain form of construction and a certain lifestyle. New *architectural form* is a synthesis of these.

The architectural form of La Maison Suspendue is thus so distinctly articulated that one might even talk about completely classical architectural form in connection with it. But with the proviso that we also give Classicism a wider and more universally applicable meaning than is usually the custom in architecture.

The Roman Vitruvius Pollio set these three requirements for proper architecture: firmness, commodity and delight, that is to say proper architecture has to fulfil three criteria, it has to be structurally sound, it has to be functional and it has to please the eye.

Nelson's house plan fulfils these three criteria. Its beauty lies in the rhythm of the interior spaces, not in any plastic aspect. The visual language of form in La Maison Suspendue is a little clumsy as is often the case when a really new, ingenious idea takes its first steps in the world of formal conventionality. I used the word ingenious, with complete justification, since Nelson's score shows us for the first time, no more no less, the *spatial model for twentieth-century architecture*. Along with it emerged a new style of architecture – but not in the conventional external sense.

Somebody may have noticed that there are plenty of curved lines and surfaces to be seen in the examples. But architectural form is not made up of lines, neither straight lines nor curved ones. As a meaningful concept, relying on the completeness of the proportion, it is really invisible.

In the same way as the iceberg I mentioned at the start, its essential part is invisible, completely at a deeper *level of thought* than just within the realm of the sense of sight. It is just that we are used to thinking in a way that seduces us into identifying architectural form with plastic form, which to my mind is a mistake.

Firmness, commodity and delight are the autonomous pillars of a healthy architecture, but in the very best architecture, the highest principle of form is represented by a synthesis of all three of them: *architectural form*.

Over the last few decades, we have become used to labelling products of architecture that imitate forms which are exaggerated, illogical or superficial, as

Formalism. But in science, this word has almost the opposite meaning. As I see it, bad architecture emerges precisely where a deeper and stricter understanding of architectural form has become dimmed, or undisciplined, or has completely disappeared.

It is said that mathematics is at its most practical when it is at its most abstract. It is precisely this abstraction that makes architectural form such a sharp *instrument.*

It would be fair to say that if you compare people who have never had any long-term design education, very few of them would be able to resolve even the most modest tasks of building composition in a satisfactory manner. They do not have viable experience of pure architectural form – mainly the problem of space *per se*, not to mention any familiarity with ways of controlling it.

The concept of architectural form varies in different cultures and at different cultural levels. At the same time, it is subject to shared development – as is everything else that comes within the sphere of culture. Thus, the architectural form of the house design I have shown you seems to have some connection with the contemporary astronomical worldview. Its spatial composition is reminiscent of a planetary system with an invisible centre of gravity that is in fact the architectural form that controls the whole.

Nelson's house has not been built at full size and probably never will be, but since its score has been in existence, it has already managed to bring about a kind of Copernican revolution in architecture.

That being the case, it is not appropriate to be surprised by what Wassily Kandinsky, one of the greatest pioneers of our time when it comes to artistic concepts, has said about the Nelson house: "His work is a synthesis of everything we attempted to do."

Of course, the development of architectural form does not stop here. We can already see signs of more than three-dimensional design, for example in that we try to think of the milieu that has to be designed as a field in which changes of form also take place in the dimension of time. As always happens in reality. But closer examination of this development does not lie within the scope of this lecture.

Leppävaara Swimming Bath by Osmo Lappo

1967

Osmo Lappo

The Need for Flexibility: A Problem of Modern Architecture

Close on nine months after the Danish architect Jørn Utzon gave up the planning of Sydney Opera House, after much disagreement, the architects who had started to continue his work there announced that it was impossible for them to meet the demand that the great hall should simultaneously be an opera, concert and meeting hall. Without giving any further thought to the question of whether the original designer could have honourably met the demands made of him, we can draw a couple of conclusions bearing on the subject of this lecture from the announcement I just mentioned. First, we can say that the client would like a flexible space suitable for more than one purpose, that is, more use of his expensive investment. Second, we note that the designers cannot fulfil this requirement. The question is probably of a demand for flexibility which is – with present means, anyway – almost impossible to attain without compromising over the quality of the finished product.

There are, of course, many planning jobs where we have long been used to the demand for flexibility. One example is the office block: one of its fundamental characteristics is a window axle distribution based on the size of the work points, making it possible to divide up the floors into rooms of different sizes with light, movable partition walls. Here, the need for flexibility is well-founded, clearly defined and relatively easy to produce.

It is, however, by no means always possible to inform the architect in advance what kind of flexibility is expected. In the case of many building jobs, flexibility is even thought unnecessary. Function is conceived of as something static, the present situation permanent. In many cases, only a few years after the completion, the architect may see to his amazement that the space is not being used at all in the way he had planned. What goes on in the building is not following the line mapped out beforehand. A good example of this is Paul Rudolph's plan for the new building of the Department of Architecture at Yale University, which is certainly not being used in the way the architect originally planned. The students have divided up the central hall, which was designed to have a monumental effect, into separate little working cubicles with paper walls and bits of curtaining. Or to come closer to home, when have you ever seen the 4th year drawing room in our own Department of Architecture full of hardworking architecture students?

The need for flexibility – the chance to make changes – always exists, even where no one expected it beforehand. There are also sectors of planning for which we know in advance that we can absolutely certainly expect changes. An example is modern university planning, where it is almost impossible to predict the development of research in various fields and in which rises in student figures bring unexpected surprises. When giving directions to the architects, Professor Boris Ford of Sussex University said: "Never believe the Vice-Chancellor, because when the building is at topping-off stage he will come to you and say, 'Excuse me, but we will have to make the building for twice that number of students'."

Advance programming is, of course, an unbeatable aid to the planner, who can use it to examine his planning commission in a sufficiently long chronological perspective. Good programming also helps us to define the factors which will probably be subject to change, in other words to specify where flexibility will be required and what kind of flexibility it should be. A situation like this, however, where the architect has at his disposal a complete set of programming, with functional and developmental schedules, is rare, and most of us have never experienced it. We must also be prepared to find inexactness and mistakes even in good programming. The number, of course, decreases if detailed research on which the programmers can rely can be used for the programming. Research is, indeed, the watchword of the hour. Usually, however, there are no research results available when we are faced with the sheer necessity of building something.

In this kind of situation it is quite natural that planners are dogged by the problem of how to plan systems – buildings, towns – which allow for internal changes and external growth, yet which are entities. How can we create a framework in which various functions are possible and which provides a favourable setting for unpredictable development? We must literally plan for the unknown future.

To examine flexibility in the various forms in which it appears, we can, to simplify handling, divide it into internal and external flexibility. By the former I mean ways of making changes, shifts of walls and functions, inside the building; by the latter, the way in which a building can be extended in a way organic to itself and its surroundings.

Internal flexibility calls for a structural solution with as few fixed structural parts as possible, since these are obstacles to re-organization. A mere pillar framework, however, is not enough to make a building flexible. A modern building is a complicated piece of technical apparatus whose whole mechanism must be worked out with an eye to flexibility. In other words, we need a technical service system which will operate in many variations. One condition of good flexibility is, indeed, that the technical system to be installed be worked out systematically and usually on a wider scale than originally needed.

Many years of experience have shown that our neoclassical buildings still justify their existence relatively efficiently, though now used for quite different purposes than for which they were originally planned. Their solid building masses and regular window division provide fine conditions for the flexible use of space. Although they were built with bearing walls, their brick structure makes it much easier to make new apertures than in our modern concrete-walled housing. In spite of the fact that the technical fittings of these buildings are modest, the great room and intermediate floor height make it possible to add new horizontal installations. Whatever our opinion of such alterations from the point of view of architectural history, we have to agree that these buildings have two important qualities from the point of view of flexibility: systematic arrangement and internal reserves.

The universal inheritance of classicism transferred to steel and glass makes its first consistent appearance in the 1940s, in Ludwig Mies van der Rohe's Illinois Institute of Technology in Chicago. Having said that he could not in any way predict the developments to be expected as regards the technical laboratories, Mies van der Rohe concluded that the only real function of a building is that it can be used flexibly.

The demand for internal flexibility brings with it many technical and architectural problems. The external flexibility of a building, on the one hand, faces us with a totally different kind of problem. Here, the character of the whole building's constructive being, its "structure", is involved. Is it definitive right from the beginning or does it permit additions, and in what way? To throw light on this question, it is a good idea to examine certain properties of various kinds of structural forms in general.

A composition is a closed, complete entity. If we add something, its internal equilibrium suffers and the tension between the various parts is lost. In architecture the use of pure composition presupposes an exactly specified building commission with regard to both environment and content. A composition does not have the potential essential for expansion.

Nowadays composition is the most generally used and an often fully justified planning principle. Le Corbusier's Chandigarh and Oscar Niemeyer's Brasilia are closed, complete compositions. Both are also permanent national administrative centres.

In a system where one powerfully expressive element dominates the whole, we can make small-scale changes within the sphere of influence of this overwhelming dominant, without harming the total effect. A varying, changing pattern of buildings, small in form, sit very comfortably in the shadow of a huge cathedral or factory. The curving walls of Alvar Aalto's Finnish Section at the 1939 New York World Fair form a powerful theme which only too gladly permits the arrangement of exhibits in varying ways on the lower level. Aalto has in other works, too, proved himself a brilliant exponent of the dominant, and is able to use quite freely forms which may even seem startling in the "shadow" of the main theme developed.

A structural scheme used a lot in recent years is "similar form". The elements, which must be similar in form, can change position within the framework of a particular law, for example a rectangular grid system. The system is very flexible, for the most vital thing is not the location of the elements but the internal cohesion of the system which decides how they shall be located.

If we intend to start using a similar form, that is, group form, as the point of departure for a flexible system, it is important that the units in the system can be ready-planned in size and shape. It is, of course, possible to make internal changes to the basic units if they have internal reserves. We can, nevertheless, consider it a general rule that similar form is suitable as the basis for a flexible system only in cases where we can be sure of the permanence of the form of the basic unit. Changing needs, the development of technology and new constructions may easily mean that the guiding thread of similar form will become the straitjacket of planning.

The principle of similar form has been used a lot in the group planning of private houses and in the planning of housing in general, where the house or flat

Alvar Aalto's Finnish Section at the New York World Fair, 1939

itself forms a suitable and sufficiently compact multiple unit. The most important suburb built on this principle in Scandinavia is probably Albertslund in Copenhagen, where the large size of the area would in fact stand more variety in height.

The forms of building I have described have, of course, been very much simplified, and may appear in combination in various kinds of architectonic entities. The need for flexibility is a functional need growing out of changes in activities. We tend to imagine that activities develop smoothly or in components of a particular size. Perhaps we also make our plans for this kind of stage-wise growth. We easily forget that all growth – including changes in function – is organic in character and rarely groups itself according to arithmetical series. Even a child's weight and height do not go up regularly – not to mention his mental development.

Often planning, too, must allow for irregularity of growth, its varying extent. This can be done by allowing for a quality called "continuity" in the basic solution. There is, for example, no reason to divide up a whole surface area permanently more than is essential merely because of an unconsidered positioning of, for example, stairways or other fixed parts of a building.

The well-known American architect Louis Kahn designed an architecturally important laboratory building in Philadelphia around the end of the 1950s – the

Richards Medical Research Building. The solution is based on a skilful grouping of building masses of the same shape and made to a square plan. The system has good external flexibility – it withstands very well the addition of similar units – but the internal, functional flexibility is hampered by the fact that internal changes can only take place within the square sections. In other words, the plan has no internal flexibility in the horizontal.

Striving towards continuity leads naturally to a system which finds expression in the form of a network or grid. Growth can occur in various directions along the arms of the network or grid via the points where they meet without hampering continuity. In a labyrinth, only one road leads through, but in the grid or network each road does so.

The flexibility of the grid is, however, questionable if the internal properties of its arms do not permit the building on them of various kinds of premises or if there are no internal reserves in a network system. Internal reserves in this case mean that there must be unconstructed areas within the network. A grid, which is built up right away and which lacks internal flexibility in its arms, is an inflexible structure, and the grid form is then just a bluff as far as flexibility is concerned. The hidden potential of a network system arises from the fact that the system is unfinished, but already clearly formed as an entity.

The use of totally formed, though at the same time incomplete, systems without any doubt offers a promising, though difficult, answer to the planner aiming at flexibility. It is then important to work out the flexibility field of each system. The old grid plan for urban construction offers a suitable example. This is a clear rectangular network with an overall form, and contains built-up blocks and blocks left unconstructed, that is empty spaces and squares. If a single building is missing in a built-up block the grid plan requires the space to be filled in, since it will not stand the void. But when a new building is put up in place of an old one and the old façade changes, the system usually stands up to this quite well. In other words, we can consider the flexibility field of the grid plan the façades of the blocks. There is no need – indeed no reason – to build the same kind of façade as the block next door, and this is also an important factor. The urban entity is complete and even an unsuccessful façade cannot spoil the townscape too much. The grid plan has another flexibility field, the yards of blind blocks, where architecture can flower in peace, close to life as it is lived.

The grid plan system has worked almost perfectly for centuries now. Each new generation has made its own fruitful contribution to this townscape. There would be no reason to abandon it if only it were able to cope with the needs of today's dominant motor traffic. This it usually cannot do without basic structural alterations. The most important job of urban planners at the moment is to try to find new comprehensive systems with flexibility fields which can be defined exactly in advance. The recently decided Espoo centre international competition showed clearly how difficult this is.

In countries with a fast population growth in particular, for example Japan, planners have developed various megastructures, even entire town areas, where housing is sited inside a gigantic construction. Although the reason for these plans is usually the lack of suitable land for construction, they can also be considered interesting efforts to find new comprehensive systems. The technical structure is

International Competition for Espoo Centre Plan, 1st Prize, Finland, 1967

the dominant and prescriptive feature, and changes can take place subordinate to it. A constructive basic structure has, it is true, been used in the same way earlier. Venice's four-hundred-year-old Ponte Rialto takes a whole set of tiny shops. The idea is old, but the scale is new – and frightening.

The architect is, of course, interested in the problem of where the border lies between limitation, or conclusiveness, and variation. What can we consider conclusive and what should be left open? It is probably impossible to give a generally true answer to this, since planning jobs and human judgements are so different. However, one function is common and essential to all people – movement. I pointed out above that the old grid plan is being destroyed by man's new way of moving around. Its structure is unwilling to withstand changes in ways of movement, for these affect its conclusive parts. The system of movement is, indeed, usually the basis for functional comprehensive structures. This is true both of buildings and towns. Briefly, we must plan a movement system in which guided freedom is created around the fixed route which this takes. The dilemma of conclusiveness and variation is of course not to be solved in this way. It is a complex problem and one which touches on everything, right down to detail. Like the grid plan, each system has its own laws which decide the quality and extent of the freedom obtaining in it.

The need for flexibility in a building also affects the style of the building, of course. The architect consciously stresses the building's conclusive parts, its primary elements, floors, construction, and so on. In planning, the various types of factor must be separated hierarchically and the aim must be to make the expressive force of the various conclusive parts such that the whole withstands adaptation in the parts. "Beauty is the fulfilment of invariance", as Eino Kaila has put it.

Nine years ago, giving his inaugural lecture on the theme "The Problem of Architectural Form", Professor Aulis Blomstedt ended his speech as follows:

> The development of architectural form does not stop here. We can already see signs of more than three-dimensional design, for example in that we try to think of the milieu that has to be designed as a field in which changes of form also take place in the dimension of time.

Today we can say that the random signs then visible have become an easily recognizable signpost pointing out the direction that will be taken by architectural planning in the future. We can now say that the problem of flexibility is also the problem of architectonic form.

Taking the time dimension into consideration in planning is, of course, hampered by certain features connected with human existence and behaviour. It is natural that man, with his brief time span, should hope to get returns from his investments in building pretty well immediately and not many years later. As we well know, this human characteristic is usually one of the biggest obstacles to long-term economic planning. Architectural planning aiming at flexibility meets the same kind of difficulties. The need for flexibility may, indeed, in the form of, for example, technical solutions or preserving internal reserves, involve expenses which we want to avoid. In English university planning it has been noted that in general the cheapest of the premises to be built – the student halls – call for least flexibility, whereas the expensive premises, the technical laboratories, need a high degree of flexibility. Economic benefit is felt later, after several changes have perhaps been made. In general, the need for flexibility is felt most in buildings which are the expensive type and where there are great changes in function, such as research centres, colleges, production plants and hospitals. Ultra-expensive military aircraft are outdated in a year or two.

A planner who consciously tries to compensate for deficiencies in programming by drawing up a plan which in his opinion offers flexibility, easily finds himself in the thankless position of a prophet, crystal-gazing for the future. The architect who in this respect defends the importance of flexibility is considered a dreamer, the proponent of impossible utopias. The private client who himself draws up and carries out his own working schedules every day may well understand the importance of a plan aiming at flexibility. But when the client is a corporation, a direct exchange of views about function is often not possible, and the holy regions of "room planning" prescribe the solutions, where flexibility is not known. The need for flexibility is, however, in fact great in civic buildings planned for anonymous consumers, in the planning of which the architect all too rarely knows who will actually be using the building's premises and what they will need.

Luckily man is a flexible and adaptable creature. He can live and work in the most primitive conditions and make his surroundings pleasant. He can also, to the horror of the aesthetic eye, redecorate our neatly planned, balanced accommodations quite differently – and again be perfectly happy there.

The need for flexibility involves taking into consideration the multiple forms of life, its everyday character, in all planning. It leads to an architecture of many possibilities, to a life-giving environment. A sterile environment produces the situation shown in an Enrico drawing where the lady next door is shouting to her friend, on catching sight of the planner: "Quick! Take the plant out of the window. The architect's coming!"

Dipoli Students' Union Building by Reima and Raili Pietilä

1973

Reima Pietilä

Architecture and the World of Techno-culture

And [I] proclaim:
1. That Futurist architecture is the architecture of calculation, of audacious temerity
and of simplicity; the architecture of reinforced concrete, of steel, glass, cardboard,
textile fibre, and of all those substitutes for wood, stone and brick that enable us to
obtain maximum elasticity and lightness;
2. That Futurist architecture is not because of this an arid combination of practicality
and usefulness, but remains art, i.e. synthesis and expression;

. . .

5. That, just as the ancients drew the inspiration for their art from the elements of
nature, we – who are materially and spiritually artificial – must find this inspiration in
the elements of the utterly new mechanical world we have created, and of which archi-
tecture must be the most beautiful expression, the most complete synthesis, the most
efficacious integration;

. . .

8. From an architecture conceived in this way no formal or linear habit can grow, since
the fundamental characteristics of Futurist architecture will be its impermanence and
transcience. Things will endure less than us. Every generation must build its own city.

(Umbro Apollonio, *Futurist Manifestos*, London: Thames and Hudson, 1973, pp. 171–2)

I have just read some passages from a manifesto on Futurist architecture written by
the Italian architect Antonio Sant'Elia. This document, published on 11 July 1914, is
like a cross section through our own contemporary architecture – like a survey of its
very essence.

From the traditional point of view of contemporary architecture, in order to
understand the passage of its development, it has to be noted that sixty years ago
it was already possible to see the background forces which created present-day
urban reality. Young Sant'Elia, who was only 26, succeeded in mapping the potential of his own time almost in its entirety.

Thus the ambitious goal of modern architecture remained the same for
decades: the task of architecture is to embody the real nature of the age.

The goal of Sant'Elia and of Futurist architecture as a whole was even bolder:
when new principles and new prerequisites come into being, there has to be a
reform of architecture, too – from the very foundations. In that way alone architecture will be what it should be: a uniform and logical synthesis. And the architecture
of synthesis is incomparably more than just building.

Firm faith and trust in people's ability to build reality on the basis of an inner view was characteristic in the first decade of the twentieth century. Correspondingly, the Bauhaus in the 1920s saw training in building design and industrial design as a synthesis of art and technology. Thus the architecture of functionalism was born.

After the Second World War, Finnish architecture of the 1950s was based – at least I assume so – on the spatial concept of the Futurism of the 1910s and the object concept of the functionalism of the 1920s. The aim was still an artistic and technical whole.

What is an artistic and cultural concept of architecture?

Behind architecture is a weighty view of the status and task of art as a cultural force. A building is more than a tangible object intended for use. It has its own internalised picture of totality. It arrives at an expression that surpasses practical need. Architecture itself wanted to describe society from all sides and shoulder a heavy responsibility – one that society saw as superfluous, even dangerous.

What, for example, is the view of architecture as a genuine picture of the times? Achieving it called, in individual cases, for a lofty expression of space and form, which the task in question scarcely demanded.

This superfluous message, the idea of additional existence, is precisely characteristic of artistic culture. In artistic and cultural architecture, form has to be allowed to grow on its own, as a kind of language: the building speaks. The building is personified. As a system, it exceeds the language of simple function. The building gives the impression of personification divorced from people. There is a rhythmic movement in its form, which plays on the feelings. It is filled with mystic emanations of existence.

When talking about the essential nature of architecture in the 1950s, architects used their own reference language. A few examples of the vocabulary of this sort of jargon or working language will illustrate what we are talking about.

- Wholeness and oneness: a synthesised building complex of any size grows into an indivisible whole consisting of form, structure and function.
- Originality: architecture has a characteristic space and form of its own.
- Reality: architecture is at one with the modern way of life and architecture is a true and positive reflection of the times.
- Authenticity: the use and treatment of building materials correspond with the experience of authenticity we find in nature.
- Functionality: functionality is the common denominator of all other factors – it also describes the social responsibilities of architecture.
- Human: an architectural work is characterised by scale to suit the needs of living, and by recognisable and comprehensible form.
- Synthesis of form: a building is a cultural and artistic work at the same time as it is an article for daily use and a consumer commodity.

These and other similar requirements forced Finnish architecture in the 1950s to aim high, perhaps too high. Presumably, observing these rules was accompanied by an internal surplus growth in reserves of meaning and pluralism – unresolved pluralism instead of striving for oneness. Perhaps architecture served the tasks which, in the final analysis, the architects themselves did not require.

In Finland in the 1950s, we were approaching an architecture that was a synthesis of art and culture – a degree of premium form. Society viewed this sort of building culture as foreign. Architecture proclaimed the solemn message of integrity, but it was recognised as utopian. It did not correspond with the *realpolitik* of the time and its pragmatic economics.

As we progressed into the 1960s, architecture had to face up to an ever stronger headwind. Several bursts of development took place, but together they worked against architecture.

Synthesis in the grip of techno-culture

The 1960s became the decade of simplification and reduction
What does this mean?

- Industrial mass production brings with it an irreconcilable conflict between quantity and quality.
- The idea of social equality is realised with the help of standardisation. The sameness of basic housing needs calls for more or less the same kind of construction.
- The international markets of distribution and consumption upset requirements for local quality and local differences.
- Organisation and scientific research create new rational models for thought and action.
- Respect for individual artistic intuition collapses.

The basic architectural content of buildings also experiences a series of rapid and radical changes. The following list illustrates the transformation that appears in ways of thinking in the 1960s – the building is now an object and an item of production, where the aim is:

- to minimise choices – to eliminate the ideal of abundant choice;
- to produce buildings that can be repeated *ad infinitum* – to eliminate the basic idea that limits are essential;
- to find a universal application, that is a building suitable for everywhere and every use – to eliminate the ideal of individuality in a specific case;
- to find a scientifically developed solution – to eliminate the possibility of something being invented by chance;
- to find a system of division that runs through the whole and a logical connection of each part to form a system – to eliminate the idea of an indivisible undifferentiated whole;

- to divide the building into a planned field of structural dimensions – to eliminate the picture of a spatial architecture that changes through growth;
- to assemble a building from finished components – to eliminate the opportunity to create a building where the overall entity is made up of (ever smaller) unique details;
- to assemble buildings of arbitrary size by repeating the same components horizontally and vertically – i.e. the whole is nothing more than the sum of the parts – to eliminate the rule that says the whole is more than the sum of the parts;
- to construct the same buildings in more diverse places and more diverse surroundings – to eliminate the requirement that the building should adapt to the site and to nature – to eliminate the complex relationship between the building and the surroundings;
- that the crucial dimensioning in the surroundings is derived from traffic planning and municipal engineering – this eliminates the possibility of buildings fitting together and the task of buildings to balance out urban space so that it is recognisable.

This list is far from being complete. It is just a representative sample of a chain of events resulting in the piecemeal crumbling of existing experience – the viewpoint of synthesis.

The successor to the architecture of synthesis, the new environmental state of techno-culture, radiates many kinds of threats and the pressures of monotony. Its architectural desert is dominated in turns by suffocating superfluity and by a complete dearth of ideas to the point of tedium.

The excision of content that has taken place over the last twenty years or so has been too great. The natural expectations that we, as individuals, as groups and as society, attach to the built environment are fulfilled only in part. We know that there is not that equivalence in our cities that we demand emotionally and by right.

Sant'Elia's ill-fated futuristic vision comes to mind once again: *"the fundamental characteristics of Futurist architecture will be impermanence and transience. Things will endure less than us. Every generation must build its own city."* Our generation has not been particularly successful in its efforts.

The more the cities grow, the poorer their quality will become – to the point where the minimum need, which might be seen as proximity to one's surroundings and experiencing them as an expression of safety, will generally speaking no longer be fulfilled. The voluble expression of gesture and symbol in established cities is today that something that we long for, that something that the new can never be.

Our own city is nothing more than a collection of unnamed places, insignificant spaces, surroundings that nobody could ever identify with. Our cities are no longer syntheses, no longer great silhouettes we can identify with.

Sant'Elia's dream was the idea of identification, just the same as the genuine dream of the Futurists of the 1910s – feelings and inward experience had to be in parallel with the articles and events of the outside world.

Today's mechanistic techno-culture environment is out of proportion with humankind. It is an alienated species of reality and it has nothing to say in terms of creating human closeness. The viewpoint that shapes the city culturally has been thoroughly ruined and that is a problem! So too is the reason why modern architecture looks as if it has been barbered down to the hairline! Why does the city create an impression of nothing but abundance and quantity without leaving us any clear impression of quality?

Perhaps the cultural goals of a great synthesis are not just surplus ballast after all. At least throwing them away has tended to make the development problems of urban culture worse.

The deep structure of traditional culture in the environment – in other words the comprehensive task of architecture – has not been invented in vain, but is natural, that is to say a response to basic human needs.

Supplementation strategies

For some time now we have been aware that building design and environmental design have been suffering from a deficiency disease. We have been eagerly searching for, and indeed finding, ways of combating the sterility of techno-culture or at least covering it up and alleviating its alien features.

So far, several programmes have been found to repair and adjust this development. The thing shared by all of these is that they divert attention from the building to the environment, to a wider objective reality, its programming. At present, town planning is governed by the idea of the environment as some kind of galactic pluralism. Urban space is made up of numerous fields nesting inside each other and mutually interacting at the same time. The character of these fields can be illustrated by the following list.

1 The flight into history
Fleeing to the realms of pre-industrial urban culture. Arousing the idea of the new small town. Trying out old, alleyway towns with labyrinthine buildings. The emphasis shifts from genuinely searching for something new and of high quality, to putting everything into restoration. The idea behind this is that by preserving at least a little bit of the old, it is easier to accept even a lot of the rather unpleasant new.

2 Environmental art
Works of art as big as buildings used as landmarks, as local identification marks, or as stimulating arrangements of signals.

3 Major technical components of the environment
Tunnels, bridges, flyovers, parking decks, pedestrian decks, seen and experienced primarily as substitutes for buildings in urban space.

4 Imaginary and entertainment environments
"Disneylands", zoos and funfairs act as places of refuge from the dreariness of the urban surroundings.

5 Event and participation environments
Pedestrian precincts, children's villages, centres for performances and musical events, multipurpose halls and gymnasia all help with the problem of what to do with one's spare time.

6 Shaping space and green landscaping
Takes care of visual hygiene, redistributes masses and articulates the space between buildings, hides and patches up unsightly views of buildings.

7 The cult of displaying objects and products
An ever-growing environment of objects of interest has emerged. City centres are unbroken product display areas. The eye is no longer able to switch from the objects and display windows to see the buildings, the streets and the people themselves. They are seen as passive.

8 The city as a script
The city consists of a whole series of urban situations nested one inside the other, which write the script – command environments, guided-movement environments, purchase-stimulation environments, environments that distribute enlightening and educational slogans.

9 The strategy of open form
The city that has an open form consists of a freely adaptable network of areas, buildings and objects. Structures are not limited but grow as the situation permits. The environment is governed by the continuous, the relatively incomplete, that is, the direct opposite of the finality of the architecture of synthesis. The city is fragmented, formless, unrecognisable – incomprehensible?

The absolute hierarchical stiffness of technical systems and the open anarchy of non-technical types of environment form at the same time an unsatisfactory team of workhorses. Too many components are standing in for each other. The feeling of uncertainty and insecurity can be warded off for the moment, but soon they return again in a new form, in a different context.

In the final analysis, the strategy of supplementation is only a substitute. It cannot be used to condense reality so that people's basic need – the need for a place to live – gets a response. The city of unrestricted growth cannot achieve this almost cosmic relationship with nature, which is characteristic of cities in history.

Urban man feels this lack of bonds as a general feeling of transience. He experiences the unreality stemming from the current quality of the city.

Architecture's breakthrough in terms of knowledge

Architecture is not sufficiently well equipped with knowledge instruments for it to accomplish the tasks that pile up on it. Straightforward methods that hark back to a combination of techno-cultural strategies and supplementation strategies do not genuinely favour the opportunities architecture can offer. Returning to the design synthesis used formerly does not succeed except in limited individual cases. Architecture suffers from knowledge and procedural crises.

The error has been particularly in the fact that there has been no pause to begin thinking about and developing a knowledge tradition for architecture as a whole. People have given in too easily to development optimism. In other words, there has been too great a rush to identify current information on technical practice with information about architecture. Too much trust has been placed in information being superseded and previous experience being written off.

An impenetrable wall has risen between the concepts of rationalist and humanist architecture. Each side becomes obsessed with its own special viewpoints and differences in phrases to such an extent that in Finland different schools speak almost in different tongues. It is only in the very last few years that we have begun once again to strive to reach a more universally applicable way of understanding. It becomes clear that architecture cannot survive – retain its importance – simply on the basis of collected information. We have to take research into knowledge principles into account as well. Thus we will presumably have to confess that a whole series of questions of knowledge theory that are characteristic of this field are part and parcel of architecture.

Knowledge analysis is a matter of returning bit by bit to the problems that belonged to the sphere of art and architecture in historical times.

The description of content – what we are talking about is precisely the field of contemporary architecture – must be carried out in a revealing manner, using the most efficient concepts available. The demystification of the 1960s was a complete condemnation of "the old". The critical approach of the 1970s is already constructive:

- to illuminate questions about the character and nature of architecture;
- to clarify important ideas about the whole, the parts and proportion;
- to examine impartially the importance of art and culture to the community;
- to develop a general theory of environmental space in which the space occupied by the building is linked with other spatial factors.

It is thus possible to show that contemporary architecture is not yet ready in any way. It is only halfway through its development.

This generation has to try and obtain a better overall picture of the reserves of ways and means that exist in architecture. This information is vital in trying to steer techno-culture building, which has now grown to worldwide proportions, in a direction that is more favourable to people.

House Thorsbo by Kirmo Mikkola

1974

Kirmo Mikkola

Architecture: Its Ideals and Reality

The architect today is clearly losing status. There is a lack of confidence between him and society, and the architect's own self-confidence is shaky. The result is a deterioration in motivation and professional security. From half a century of development, the rationale of efficiency is all that is left of modern architecture. With this, technicians, business men and politicians are building an environment which is at the same time destroying its own psychological and biological conditions. The business world uses architects more to underline its own status than to create a good working environment. Architects are also used as a kind of scenery builders. The monuments they design are used as fallacious proofs of respect for culture or social-mindedness. We have drifted far from functionalism's dream of a democratic architecture.

The background

Externally, the background to Finland's post-war reconstruction was roughly analogous to the premises from which continental functionalism developed in the 1920s. There was an immense need for housing, which was further increased by the halt in building caused by the war. Legislation promoting subsidized housing production was passed, and large developments gradually got under way. The problems of reconstruction had already been studied during the war on the initiative of architects, and the Association of Finnish Architects had taken an important step by setting up its standardization institute. The idea of elastic standardization proposed by Alvar Aalto pointed the way for Finland's post-war architecture rather as Le Corbusier's Domino did for the functionalists of the 1920s. Aulis Blomstedt's modular studies created the basis for industrialized building. In the early 1950s a big housing reform competition was arranged, with a special construction technology series, and Revell, Ervi and Siren, for instance, studied the problems of prefab building in practice. But at the same time there was an anti-mechanical and anti-collective reaction to features conducive to socialized building production. This meant that architecture hid its head in the sands of romanticism, and in urban planning this led to the illusion of individual and mid-nature housing. The conflicting goals of Anglo-American anti-urbanism and continental functionalism were, however, reconciled in a quite harmonious synthesis in the most important experiments of the early 1950s, the first stage of Tapiola and the Otaniemi campus.

The few civic buildings of the period were marked by an idealistic unpreten-tiousness which did not, however, exclude artistic expression related to the func-tion of the building. All in all, it looked as though orthodox functionalism had been developed in a more psychologically and geographically successful direction. This picture was soon to be shattered, however. Why? Some reasons may already be clear, though from the historian's point of view we are still very close to events.

Ideological labyrinths

The leading architects of the 1950s had at the time adopted the socially oriented ideology of functionalism, but because of the war they had to wait for commissions in vain. The ideological situation after the war was confused. The concepts of col-lectivity and individualism became blurred in the machinations of international politics. The world's first socialist state had banned functionalism, yet it began to win a foothold in the cradle of capitalism, the USA. Biological mysticism replaced the machine culture, vitalism the mechanistic view of nature.

Aalto was the most important interpreter of the new ideas, and his fine build-ings gave power to his words. Aalto's thinking, which stressed the individual right from the start, and his close relationship with America, Frank Lloyd Wright's individ-ualistic concept of democracy, and Jeffersonian anti-urban thinking may well still prove one key to the architectural ideology of the period.

In the 1940s societal arguments began to give way to philosophizing about the inner nature of architecture in the debate between architects. Unnoticed, a picture began to form of an architect who was apolitical, or above politics. The idea of the servant of society was, of course, still valid. The ideological change merely gave the concept a new meaning.

The emergence of criticism

By the end of the 1950s, Finnish architecture had taken on features against which we angry young men of the 1960s rebelled. The main emphasis of architecture shifted to civic and commercial building. Revell won the Toronto City Hall competi-tion; Aalto went to work for the "German miracle" in Wolfsburg and, with his Vuok-senniska church, started a period of expressive church architecture, with its many large-scale competitions. A typical planning feature of the time was a complex of cultural and administration buildings called a "monumental centre", the kind that was at the end of the 60s branded the very bastion of technocracy and the élite culture – in brief, bourgeois hegemony. At the same time as this boom in civic building, the developers worked out their concrete panel systems – the straight-jacket of today's environment. The role of architects in this work of development was almost non-existent.

The new role of architecture was, of course, a result of economic develop-ments. Patriarchal capitalism – which could well produce a Käpylä Garden Suburb, Sunila or Tapiola – started to pave the way for iron-fisted monopolies. The angry

Viljo Revell's Toronto City Hall, 1965

Kaija and Heikki Siren's Chapel in the College of Technology Village, Otaniemi, 1957

young men did not, though, criticize the programmes of the plans so much as the style, which they considered anti-social. Aalto was accused of exclusiveness, Pietilä of subjectivity and Revell of formalism. These accusations combined both aesthetic and social moralizing in a verbalized pathos which was as powerful as the plastic expression to which it was objecting. The alternative was considered to be an anonymous, aesthetically controlled, logical, mathematical, and consumer-oriented architecture utilizing the knowledge provided by interdisciplinary search and the full potential of technology. Emphatically technological system architecture was preceded by a return to the sources of functionalism. At the beginning of the 1960s Aulis Blomstedt and Aarno Ruusuvuori had a major influence on their students at the School of Architecture.

Debate about the architect's responsibility gradually spread to the global scale and to the brave new world of futurology. At the level of architecture, Mies van der Rohe assumed the role of prophet, and on a wider scale the ideas of Archigram or Buckminster Fuller were eagerly taken up. The result was rather paradoxical: on the one hand, architectural absolutism (the revolutionary youth of 1968 called this "design fascism") and on the other, anti-architecture!

Alvar Aalto's Wolfsburg Cultural Centre, 1963

The younger generation criticized Reima Pietilä especially sharply. Pietilä was one of the central figures of the 1960s, building his prize-winning competition entries. Aalto, who had become a national institution, was eventually left in peace. The angry young men, as assistants at the University of Technology, prevented the emergency of a Pietilä School (which was actually on its way), and the trial of strength between Pietilä and Juhani Pallasmaa in the *Finnish Architectural Review* after the completion of Dipoli is already one of the classics of Finnish architectural debate.

Gradually some adjustments of attitudes proved necessary. On closer study, a too straightforward interpretation of Pietilä's architecture as "built ideology" does not seem to hold good. His starting point is more likely a view of the inner nature and logic of architecture than of its relation to society – and the same can be said of his opponents in many respects. Gradually, as one began to see how multinational business had adopted the Miesian style as its architectural image, attitudes to Pietilä's architecture also began to change, however irrational it was. In the hurly-burly of the EEC debate some people even saw similarities between the political role of Pietilä, and that of the National Romanticists of the turn of the century.

Reima and Raili Pietilä's Kaleva Church, Tampere, 1966

All in all, the new social and technological-minded generation nevertheless considered the Finnish architecture of the day anti-social. The answer to this accusation could be that architects do not themselves choose what they are commissioned to do. Obviously. But architects can both privately and collectively take a stand on the interest which their limited resources should serve. They can also express ideological values in the style of their architecture. And the style of architecture does not always merely reflect the economic basis of building. It may also mould it. First we make things that *look* cheap and social. Then we really make things that *are* cheap and social. That's how the functionalists began in the 1920s. At the next stage they believed that the new style would spread and affect the whole of everyday building. And everything did work to start with, but then world politics overturned the chariot of progress. When, after the war, society was ready to adopt the forms of functionalism, many of those who had created them were no longer sufficiently interested. They were already creating new forms for new things, individual expression to serve the interests of a small minority. The social field of building was neglected. But what alternative were the younger generation of the 1960s offering?

The heirs of functionalism

"Acceptera den föreliggande verkligheten!" "Accept the reality that exists!" could have been the battle cry of the young, as it was of the Swedish functionalists. The older generation's talk of humanism and play with forms was to be replaced with aesthetics derived from the newest science and technology, and social good would follow automatically. In fact this was very up-to-date, and concentration and efficiency grew. But the social analysis was lacking – after all, the science of architecture that emerged in the 1960s and was so eagerly adopted here came from the cradle of planning liberalism, the USA. Soon they stood wondering just what goals they were supporting. Town centres did not turn out to be airy meeting places for pedestrians, but rather selling machines intended for car-owners outside the town. Housing areas did not turn out as cosy urban fabric, but an ironic, inhuman interpretation of the theme: "Die Wohnung für das Existenzminimum". And uncritical reliance on interdisciplinary cooperation and technocratic planning methods paved the way for the consulting monopolies which today replace the old fruitful interaction between public planning and studio work. Architects' tendency towards utopian thinking had again borne fruit. The weapons they had chosen to increase equality had fallen into the hands of enemies of democracy.

The amazing thing in the younger generation's optimism is that they did not notice that Sweden had gone through the same stages somewhat earlier, that the exemplary housing of the "people's home" had become a harsh oligarchy of producers. Perhaps the very power of our own expressive architecture (Sweden had nothing like it) confused them. They thought that it was the main guilty factor explaining the social weakness of our architecture.

In fact, this kind of utopianism has dogged the steps of modern architecture even since its early stages, since Ruskin and Morris. It was particularly fine and

Aulis Blomstedt's Annex to the Workers' Institute, Helsinki, 1959

strong in the optimistic belief in progress of the 1920s, until the iron fist of fascism shattered all the dreams. Utopian thinking did not die, though.

In the 1960s a new view of society spread among planners, behind which lurks the Three Sector Model of Jean Fourastié. The scientific and technical revolution is expected to eliminate the old class structure as a *tour de force*, and any new problems will be common to the whole industrialized world.

The main emphasis is on the constantly expanding third sector of the economy and its effect on planning and building. This theory (also adopted by many planners in socialist countries) is clearly also behind the statistical thinking, computer worship and futurological dreams of the young men of the 1960s. This is the path to a new utopia and a new aesthetics, a unified brave new world in the sunshine of technology! Who could bear to bother with day-to-day policies!

The Marxist young

The young people in Finland today no longer talk about techniques or beauty or the relation between them. They project themselves into the conflict between work and

Reima and Raili Pietilä's Dipoli Students' Union Building, Otaniemi, 1966

capital, and demand a clear stand on the class struggle. The contrast to the ideo-logically inarticulate 1950s is sharp, but there is not much in common between the heirs of functionalism and the class-fighters of today. The young have advanced into political purpose out of the enchantment of the neo-leftist student revolution which in Finland, too, threatened the window-panes of the School of Architecture.

The more pragmatic line is a parallel phenomenon to Sweden's Alternativ Stad or Norway's Kanal. This Scandinavian form of "advocacy planning" defends the existent environment and the rights of residents faced by the constant threat of growing economic monopolies and international trading integration. The residents' movement started by architects have in fact gained considerable influence on plan-ning, and they have prevented many a fatal mistake. Side by side with the resid-ents' movements has gone the philosophy of conservationist renovation based on reasons of cultural history and economy. The clash of the latter with the renewal ideas of the functionalists has been a historical inevitability.

Rigid class thinking, on the other hand, opposes compromise reforms, wishing to strip bare the class nature of our society and awaken people's political aware-ness as an element of revolution. The School of Architecture in Helsinki has been a fortress of the class consciousness, and it will be interesting to see what influence

Aarno Ruusuvuori's Printing House Weilin+Göös, Tapiola, 1966

the Marxist-Leninist young people of today will have on the building of tomorrow. So far there is no specifically socialist theory of architecture, and in style, too, the architecture of socialist countries has been related to general Western developments, once it rid itself of the monumentalism of the Stalinist period. Thus the future prospects of the class fighters have basically been of a general political nature.

The stalemate of architecture

The present situation is not exactly simple from the point of view of the development of architecture. The quality of new building, which was the central issue of functionalism, is easily ignored in the debate, if the builder becomes a lawyer or a politician. However, the large developments today affect the largest proportion of our society, relatively speaking, as well as those who have no opportunity to choose their environment themselves. What is the architect's responsibility in such

Bengt Lundsten and Esko Kahri's Kortepohja Housing Area, Jyväskylä, 1969

a situation? Is it like that of a surgeon in the operating room or that of a politician in a parliamentary national health debate? In the end, the alternatives are not mutually exclusive, as long as one can distinguish between short and long range action. And because of our human limitations, different people do get selected for different tasks.

Max Planck Institute of Molecular Cell Biology and Genetics by Mikko Heikkinen and Markku Komonen

1995

Markku Komonen

Construction, Technology and Art

Why did I choose a subject and a viewpoint like this at a time when the operational requirements for architects have deteriorated to the point of collapse, and the whole field of design and construction seems to be metamorphosing into a form where the synergy of forces that architecture demands can no longer materialise? Perhaps it is at just such a turning point that we should examine the fundamental issues facing the profession.

The essence of our profession is written in its Greek name *Arkhitekton*. Woven together in it is a double imperative of quality and construction, art and technology. At a lecture he gave at the centenary celebrations of Helsinki University of Technology in 1949, the famous Frenchman August Perret described the architect as a poet who thinks and speaks in terms of construction. According to his strict canon, the architect who hides a load-bearing column makes a mistake, but the architect who constructs a false column commits a crime. He also emphasised that requirements that are affected by nature are permanent, but requirements that are affected by humans are temporary.

A method of building, a flash of technical inspiration, has often meant a direct point of departure for architects. We all know the architectural chain of events set off by the invention of vaulting, for example. Massive logs and the skilfully made joints that held them together formed the structural basis for a rich architectural tradition much closer to home.

Quite apart from structural solutions, other technical innovations have often formed a direct point of departure for architects, too. The Eskimo igloo is a small dwelling heated and lit by small whale-oil lamps, which together with its complex entrance arrangements forms an efficient device for combating the cold. The traditional buildings of the hot desert areas of the Sahara and the Middle East consist of ventilation systems designed to catch the breeze, in which the entire spatial arrangement combined with special structural solutions promote the flow of a cooling stream of air. In ancient Indian architecture, there are efficient cooling systems based on the evaporation of water connected with the function of pools of water used in religious rituals. Not all traditional building has been exemplary from the technical point of view, but the history of architecture offers us plenty of evidence of the skill of combining materials, construction and spatial arrangements into a whole package which responds inventively to the demands of climate, landscape and way of life.

Recently we have been able to learn from the excellent *Animal Architecture* exhibition that the structures of the animal world, developed during the long evolution of nature, are supreme achievements compared with the efforts at building produced by the human race in its short history. Even the finest steel constructions cannot compare in tensile strength with the spider's web. Nor can any ventilation adjustment system that we control compare with the complicated but clearly functioning system in a termites' nest. Against this background, it is of course paradoxical that in the last blink of an eye in human history, also referred to as the "Age of Technology", the construction sector has finished up in a situation that is in many ways untenable.

Modernist architecture included the essentially sound idea of applying advanced technology to building, but it was also associated with a blinkered approach to experiments with new materials and new technologies. In architecture and in other areas of culture, the romance of the machine age, which made a fetish of technology, was more or less an expression of puberty. The buildings that were manifestations of the wonders of technology did not always show control of the technology – far from it. It is worth bearing in mind that at a time when the silicon chip and the micro-cosmos of the circuitry contained within it would already have accurately described the state of technological development, fashionable high-tech architecture still expressed the steam-age aesthetic. In this context, it should be pointed out that the environmental reality that horrifies us all today has not arisen from some untenable architectural ideal, but from much greater and more corrupt social vectors. The sanctification of technology and the machine in architecture was, however, a clear reflection of a worldview, a vision of a simple mechanical order, of mechanical domination of the world.

In recent years, the counterpart to this techno-architecture has been the architecture of chaos. It looks as though popular discussion of chaos theory has found reinforcement for this kind of explanation of the world, that is, that the world is now mixed up and without any fixed points anywhere. From recent trends in architecture we can easily recognise interpretations of a new superficial worldview. Rudolf Arnheim, 90-year-old Harvard emeritus professor of the theory and psychology of the history of art, recently commented wisely on the fashion for chaos. He said that the atmosphere today is very similar to the atmosphere that existed when Einstein's theory of relativity was published. The popular interpretation then was that the theory showed that nothing was objective, nothing was certain. Arnheim points out that the interpretation was completely at odds with the actual content of the theory of relativity. In fact, in the early years, Einstein had tried to call his theory the "invariant theory". Invariance, fixed points and some kind of fragments of order were what chaos theoreticians were probably looking for when new, more multi-dimensional fields of view were opening up in front of them. Architects, too, should scrape together the fragments of order into their own profession rather than building unsustainable scenery from a trivial interpretation of science and technology. The challenges that are facing us of developing building and putting it on a more sustainable foundation, call for a new kind of integration of the work of architects and engineers. There is a great deal of research and development ahead within the sphere of building materials, construction technology and equipment technology, but above all, what lies ahead is the need to integrate the separate sectors with each other.

Ecological building is an area of technology where integration comes under the spotlight. It calls for traditional methods and control of sophisticated technology and the ability to combine the two together in a flexible manner. The buildings of our time have often been examples of incompatible partial solutions. Spatial arrangement, structure and circulation have not been in synergy. In outlining the outlook for the development of technology, it is still worth bearing in mind the Ancient Greek wisdom contained in the story of Icarus. What we know about this generally is only that it involved an audacious flight and a tragic ending. However, there are several dimensions to the myth.

Icarus was the son of Daedalus, the architect who built the famous labyrinth for King Minos of the island of Crete. At the end of this mammoth task, however, the king threw the architect and his son into jail. The only chance of escape lay in developing the technique of flying. They found a technical solution to the problem and at the moment of departure, Daedalus gave his son some guidance on the importance of choice of flight path, warning him not to go too close to Helios the Sun-God. They both arched their wings and took off towards freedom. Daedalus navigated wisely, but Icarus's mind was overrun by an intoxicating feeling of omnipotence – hubris. In Greek mythology it is an attitude and a state of mind that the gods punish immediately with death.

Thus, with Daedalus, the responsible tradition of wise consideration was transferred to architects as well as technical skill. Daedalus was *Arkhitekton*, a building artist whose task had been to erect the palaces and monuments of Minos, which would guarantee the king immortality. The architect's inescapable task is to create built monuments, to immortalise the intangible value of materials linked with our culture, our collective memory. Ludwig Wittgenstein, who was also a dilettante architect or an architect *manqué*, said that it is a requirement of architecture that there is something to extol. If there is nothing to extol, there can be no architecture. But isn't talk like this about monuments in sharp contrast to what I have said about wisdom and sustainable development? Not at all, if we give up the vulgar interpretation of the word monumental. Let us take a look at this question of semantics. After all, "monument" in the context of architecture, is one of the most erroneously used concepts, but nevertheless, it is one of the key words of the art of building and indeed of all culture. The meaning of monument or monumental has become distorted in a pejorative manner to mean, in normal conversation, something large in size and pompous in spirit, not to say ostentatious. Nevertheless, even the most modest architectural task should include the dimension of monumentality. It is in precisely this dimension that the humanism of architecture is crystallised. Monumentality has nothing to do with large size or small. The Pyramids are monuments, but so too are the togunas or meeting canopies of the Dogon people of Mali, which are dimensioned from a free sitting height. One might say that the veranda of every Finnish lakeside sauna is a built monument in miniature.

More than twenty years ago, Aulis Blomstedt and Reima Pietilä had a brief but pithy exchange about the concept of "monument", in which Blomstedt quoted a Shakespeare sonnet which crystallises the idea thus: "Your monument shall be my gentle verse which eyes not yet created shall o'er read." Here, the monument is a gentle verse which carries a memory, an idea, value and meaning beyond time. It is thus a question of something that is in some way a complete opposite to boastfulness and arrogance. The strictest definition of architectural values is linked above all to monumentality and artistic quality.

The same thing is expressed in Chinese calligraphy by the term "Qi", the vitality that a line is charged with. It is deemed to be one of the most important features of calligraphy.

In the 1920s, the young geologist and poet Aaro Hellaakoski examined artistic aims with these thoughts:

> There is still a good deal of clumsy and wooden material. Of course, I am entertained more by sketchy rough-hewn work than polished work. I cannot stand eclectic manipulation. My verse does not aim for any special suppleness or flexibility. I am happy if the words feel natural and true. I feel that poetry should be genuine metal which gives a metallic ring when you strike it.

I am going to bother you with yet another literary quotation in an attempt to show that architectural study material is scattered far and wide, outside the palisade of our profession. At the turn of the century, Anton Chekhov advised his young colleague, the writer Maxim Gorky, about his work thus:

> They are splendid things, masterpieces; they show the artist who has passed through a very good school. I don't think that I am mistaken. The only defect is the lack of restraint, the lack of grace. When a man spends the least possible number of movements over some definite action, that is grace ... The descriptions of nature are the work of an artist; you are a real landscape painter. Only the frequent personification (anthropomorphism) when the sea breathes, the sky gazes, the steppe barks, Nature whispers, speaks, mourns, and so on – such metaphors make your descriptions somewhat monotonous, sometimes sweetish, sometimes not clear; beauty and expressiveness in nature are attained only by simplicity, by such simple phrases as "The sun set," "It was dark," "It began to rain," and so on.

The energy at the core of art is a conscious aesthetic intention somewhere below the surface. Creating art is a matter of digging out this core. Development can appear in science and technology, but not in art. We have progressed no further in art today than the painters at Lascaux and Altimira, but it is the same thing that keeps us going.

To conclude, I will tell you briefly about a building that fulfils the criteria of monumentality. I saw it quite by chance about twenty years ago in northern Portugal. It was a small paper mill that used rags and waste paper as raw material. The building was set beautifully in a rolling landscape with a little stream running through it. The lower floor was built of massive blocks of stone. The hot paper pulp steamed inside this dimly lit production space. The figures of the mill-workers moved about between the shafts of light filtering in from the little windows. The upper floor was built of wooden louvers with light flooding in between the slats accompanied by a fresh breeze. A web of metal wires was strung across the space where the finished sheets of paper hung up to dry. The scent of drying paper filled the silent space that was bathed in light. The subdued sounds of work echoed from below.

House of Silence by Juhani Pallasmaa

2007

Juhani Pallasmaa

Space, Place, Memory and Imagination: The Temporal
Dimension of Existential Space

The time perspective in architecture

Architecture is usually seen in futuristic terms; novel buildings are understood to
probe and project an unforeseen reality, and architectural quality is directly associated with its degree of novelty and uniqueness. Modernity at large has been dominated by this futuristic bias. Yet, the appreciation of newness has probably never
been as obsessive as in today's cult of spectacular architectural imagery. In our
globalized world, newness is not only an aesthetic and artistic value, it is a strategic necessity of the culture of consumption, and consequently, an inseparable
ingredient of our surreal materialist culture.

However, human constructions have also the task to preserve the past, and
enable us to experience and grasp the continuum of culture and tradition. We do
not only exist in a spatial and material reality, we also inhabit cultural, mental and
temporal realities. Our existential and lived reality is a thick, layered and constantly
oscillating condition. Architecture is essentially an art form of reconciliation and
mediation, and in addition to settling us in space and place, landscapes and buildings articulate our experiences of duration and time between the polarities of past
and future. In fact, along with the entire corpus of literature and the arts, landscapes and buildings constitute the most important externalization of human
memory. We understand and remember who we are through our constructions,
both material and mental. We also judge alien and past cultures through the evidence provided by the architectural structures they have produced. Buildings project
epic narratives.

In addition to practical purposes, architectural structures have a significant
existential and mental task; they domesticate space for human occupation by
turning anonymous, uniform and limitless space into distinct places of human
significance, and equally importantly, they make endless time tolerable by giving
duration its human measure. As Karsten Harries, the philosopher, argues:

> Architecture helps to replace meaningless reality with a theatrically, or rather architecturally,
> transformed reality, which draws us in and, as we surrender to it, grants us an illusion of
> meaning . . . we cannot live with chaos. Chaos must be transformed into cosmos.[1]

"Architecture is not only about domesticating space. It is also a deep defence
against the terror of time", he states in another context.[2]

Altogether, environments and buildings do not only serve practical and utilitarian purposes; they also structure our understanding of the world. "[The house] is an instrument with which to confront the cosmos", as Gaston Bachelard states.[3] The abstract and indefinable notion of cosmos is always present and represented in our immediate landscape. Every landscape and every building is a condensed world, a microcosmic representation.

Architecture and memory

We all remember the way architectural images were utilized as mnemonic devices by the orators of antiquity. Actual architectural structures, as well as mere remembered architectural images and metaphors serve as significant memory devices in three different ways: first, they materialize and preserve the course of time and make it visible; second, they concretize remembrance by containing and projecting memories; and, third, they stimulate and inspire us to reminisce and imagine. Memory and fantasy, recollection and imagination are related and they have always a situational and specific content. One who cannot remember can hardly imagine, because memory is the soil of imagination. Memory is also the ground of self-identity; we are what we remember.

Buildings are storage houses and museums of time and silence. Architectural structures have the capacity of transforming, speeding up, slowing down and halting time. They can also create and protect silence following Kierkegaard's request: "Create silence!"[4] In the view of Max Picard, the philosopher of silence: "Nothing has changed the nature of man so much as the loss of silence."[5] "Silence no longer exists as a *world*, but only in fragments, as the remains of a world."[6] Architecture has to preserve the memory of the world of silence and to protect the existing fragments of this fundamental ontological state. As we enter a Romanesque monastery we can still experience the benevolent silence of the universe.

There are, of course, particular building types, such as memorials, tombs and museums that are deliberately conceived and built for the purpose of preserving and evoking memories and specific emotions; buildings can maintain feelings of grief and ecstasy, melancholy and joy, as well as fear and hope. All buildings maintain our perception of temporal duration and depth, and they record and suggest cultural and human narratives. We cannot conceive or remember time as a mere physical dimension; we can only grasp time through its actualizations; the traces, places and events of temporal occurrence. Joseph Brodsky points out another deficiency of human memory as he writes about the composite images of cities in human memory and finds these cities always empty: "[The city of memory] is empty because for an imagination it is easier to conjure architecture than human beings."[7] Is this the inherent reason why we architects tend to think of architecture more in terms of its material existence than the life and human situations that take place in the spaces we have designed?

Architectural structures facilitate memory; our understanding of the depth of time would be decisively weaker, for instance, without the image of the pyramids in our minds. The mere image of a pyramid marks and concretizes time. We also remember our own childhood largely through the houses and places that we have lived in. We have projected and hidden parts of our lives in lived landscapes and houses, exactly as the orators placed themes of their speeches in the context of imagined buildings. The recollection of places and rooms generates the recall of events and people.

> I was a child of that house, filled with the memory of its smells, filled with the coolness of its hallways, filled with the voices that had given it life. There was even the song of the frogs in the pools; they came to be with me here,

reminisces Antoine de Saint-Exupéry, the legendary pilot and writer, after having crash-landed with his plane in a sand desert in North Africa.[8]

The mental power of fragments

In his novel *The Notebooks of Malte Laurids Brigge*, Rainer Maria Rilke gives a similarly moving record of a distant memory of home and self, arising from fragments of the grandfather's house in the protagonist's memory:

> As I recover it in recalling my child-wrought memories, it is no complete building: it is all broken up inside me; here a room, there a room, and here a piece of hallway that does not connect these two rooms but is preserved, as a fragment, by itself. In this way it is all dispersed within me . . . all that is still in me and will never cease to be in me. It is as though the picture of this house had fallen into me from an infinite height and had shattered against my very ground.[9]

The remembered image arises gradually, piece by piece, from fragments of memory as a painted Cubist picture emerges from detached visual motifs.

I have written about my own memories of my grandfather's humble farm house, and pointed out that the memory house of my early childhood is a collage of fragments, smells, conditions of light, specific feelings of enclosure and intimacy, but rarely precise and complete visual recollections. My eyes have forgotten what they once saw, but my body still remembers.

Buildings and their remains suggest stories of human fate, both real and imaginary. Ruins stimulate us to think of lives that have already disappeared, and to imagine the fate of their deceased occupants. Ruins and eroded settings have a special evocative and emotional power; they force us to reminisce and imagine. Incompleteness and fragmentation possess a special evocative power. In medieval illustrations and Renaissance paintings architectural settings are often depicted as a mere edge of a wall or a window opening, but the isolated fragment suffices to conjure up the experience of a complete constructed setting. This is the secret of the art of collage but also some architects, such as John Soane and Alvar Aalto have taken advantage of this emotional power of the architectural fragment. Rilke's description of the images of life lived in a demolished house triggered by the remains and stains left on the end wall of the neighbouring house, is a stunning record of the ways of human memory:

But most forgettable of all were the walls themselves. The stubborn life of these rooms had not let itself be trampled out. It was still there; it clung to the nails that had been left there, it stood on the remaining hand-breadth of flooring, it crouched under the corner joints where there was still a little bit of interior. One could see that it was in the paint which, year by year, had slowly altered: blue into moldy green, green into grey, and yellow into an old, stale rotting white.[10]

Spatiality and situationality of memory

Our recollections are situational and spatialized memories, they are memories attached to places and events. It is hard to recall, for instance, a familiar or iconic photograph as a two-dimensional image on photographic paper; we tend to remember the depicted object, person or event in its full spatial reality. It is obvious, that our existential space is never a two-dimensional pictorial space, it is a lived and multi-sensory space saturated and structured by memories and intentions. We keep projecting meanings and signification to everything we encounter, I have rarely disagreed with the views of Joseph Brodsky, one of my house gods, but when he argues that after having seen touristic buildings, such as Westminster Abbey, the Eiffel Tower, St Basil's, the Taj Mahal or the Acropolis, "we retain not their three-dimensional image but their printed version", and concludes that "Strictly speaking, we remember not a place but our postcard of it",[11] I have to disagree with the poet. We do not remember the postcard but the real place pictured in it. A recalled image is always more than the once seen image itself. In my view, Brodsky presents a rushed argument here, perhaps misguided by Susan Sontag's ideas of the power of the photographed image in her seminal book *On Photography*.[12]

Pictures, objects, fragments, insignificant things, all serve as condensation centres for our memories. Jarkko Laine, the Finnish poet, writes about the role of objects in his memory:

> I like looking at these things. I don't seek aesthetic pleasure in them . . . nor do I recall their origins: that is not important. But even so they all arouse memories, real and imagined. A poem is a thing that arouses memories of real and imagined things . . . The things in the window act like a poem. They are images that do not reflect anything . . . I sing of the things in the window.[13]

The significance of objects in our processes of remembering is the main reason why we like to collect familiar or peculiar objects around us; they expand and reinforce the realm of memories, and eventually, of our very sense of self. Few of the objects we possess are really needed strictly for utilitarian purposes; their function is social and mental. "I am what is around me", argues Wallace Stevens,[14] whereas Nöel Arnaud, another poet, claims: "I am the space, where I am."[15] These condensed formulations by two poets emphasize the intertwining of the world and the self as well as the externalized ground of remembrance and identity.

A room can also be individualized and taken into one's possession by turning it into a place of dreaming; the acts of memorizing and dreaming are interrelated. As Bachelard puts it: "The house shelters daydreaming, the house protects the dreamer, the house allows one to dream in peace."[16] A fundamental quality of a landscape, house and room is its capacity to evoke and contain a feeling of safety, familiarity and at-homeness and to stimulate fantasies. We are not capable of deep imagination outdoors in wild nature; profound imagination calls for the focusing intimacy of a room. For me, the real measure of the quality of a town is whether I can imagine myself falling in love there.

The lived world

We do not live in an objective world of matter and facts, as commonplace naïve realism tends to assume. The characteristically human mode of existence takes place in the worlds of possibilities, moulded by the human capacity of remembrance, fantasy and imagination. We live in mental worlds, in which the material and the spiritual, as well as the experienced, remembered and imagined, constantly fuse into each other. As a consequence, the lived reality does not follow the rules of space and time as defined and measured by the science of physics. I wish to argue that the lived world is fundamentally "unscientific", when measured by the criteria of western empirical science. In fact, the lived world is closer to the reality of dream than any scientific description. In order to distinguish the lived space from physical and geometrical space, we can call it existential space. Lived existential space is structured on the basis of meanings, intentions and values reflected upon it by an individual, either consciously or unconsciously; existential space is a unique quality interpreted through the memory and experience of the individual. Every lived experience takes place at the interface of recollection and intention, perception and fantasy, memory and desire. T.S. Eliot brings forth the important pairing of opposites in the end of his fourth quartet, "Little Gidding":

> What we call the beginning is often the end. And to make an end is to make a beginning . . . We shall not cease from exploration. And the end of all our exploring will be to arrive where we started. And know the place for the first time.[17]

On the other hand, collective groups or even nations, share certain experiences of existential space that constitute their collective identities and sense of togetherness. We are, perhaps, held together by our shared memories more than by an innate sense of solidarity. I wish to recall here the famous sociological study by Maurice Halbwachs that revealed that the ease of mutual communication between old Parisians living within a distinct quarter was grounded in their rich and shared collective memories.

The lived space is also the object and context of both the making and experiencing of art as well as architecture. Art projects a lived reality, not mere symbolic representations of life. The task of architecture, also, is "to make visible how the world touches us", as Merleau-Ponty wrote of the paintings of Paul Cézanne.[18] We live in the "flesh of the world", to use a notion of the philosopher, and landscapes and architecture structure and articulate this existential flesh giving it specific horizons and meanings.

Experience as exchange

The experience of a place or space is always a curious exchange; as I settle in a space, the space settles in me. I live in a city and the city dwells in me. We are in a constant exchange with our settings; simultaneously we internalize the setting and project our own bodies, or aspects of our body schemes, on the setting. Memory and actuality, perception and dream merge. This secret physical and mental inter-twining and identification also takes place in all artistic experience. In Joseph Brodsky's view every poem tells the reader "Be like me".[19] Here lies the ethical power of all authentic works of art; we internalize them and integrate them with our very sense of self. A fine piece of music, poetry or architecture becomes a part of my physical and moral self. The Czech writer Bohumil Hrabal gives a vivid descrip-tion of this bodily association in the act of reading:

> When I read, I don't really read; I pop a beautiful sentence in my mouth and suck it like a fruit drop or I sip it like a liqueur until the thought dissolves in me like alcohol, infusing my brain and heart and coursing on through the veins to the root of each blood vessel.[20]

Remembering is not only a mental event; it is also an act of embodiment and projection. Memories are not only hidden in the secret electrochemical processes of the brain; they are also stored in our skeletons, muscles and skin. All our senses and organs think and remember.

The embodied memory

I can recall the hundreds of hotel rooms around the world, which I have temporarily inhabited during my five decades of travelling, with their furniture, colour schemes and lighting, because I have invested and left parts of my body and my mind in these anonymous and insignificant rooms. The protagonist of Marcel Proust's *In Search of Lost Time* reconstructs similarly his very identity and location through his embodied memory:

> My body, still too heavy with sleep to move, would endeavour to construe from the pattern of its tiredness the position of its various limbs, in order to deduce therefrom the direction of the wall, the location of the furniture, to piece together and give a name to the house in which it lay. Its memory, the composite memory of its ribs, its knees, its shoulder-blades, offered it a whole series of rooms in which it had at one time or another slept, while the unseen walls, shifting and adapting themselves to the shape of each successive room that it remembered, whirled it in the dark . . . my body, would recall from each room in succession the style of the bed, the position of the doors, the angle at which the sunlight came in at the windows, whether there was a passage outside, what I had had in mind when I went to sleep and found there when I awoke.[21]

We are again encountering an experience that brings to mind a fragmented Cubist composition. We are taught to think of memory as a cerebral capacity, but the act of memory engages our entire body.

"Body memory is . . . the natural center of any sensitive account of remembering", philosopher Edward S. Casey argues in his seminal book *Memorizing: A Phenomenological Study*, and concludes: "There is no memory without body memory."[22] In my view, we could say even more; body is not only the locus of remembrance, it is also the site and medium of all creative work, including the work of the architect.

Memory and emotion

In addition to being memory devices, landscapes and buildings are also amplifiers of emotions; they reinforce sensations of belonging or alienation, invitation or rejection, tranquillity or despair. A landscape or work of architecture cannot, however, create feelings. Through their authority and aura, they evoke and strengthen our own emotions and project them back to us as if these feelings of ours had an external source. In the Laurentian Library in Florence I confront my own sense of metaphysical melancholy awakened and projected back by Michelangelo's architecture. The optimism that I experience when approaching the Paimio Sanatorium is my own sense of hope evoked and strengthened by Alvar Aalto's optimistic architecture. The hill of the meditation grove at the Woodland Cemetery in Stockholm, for instance, evokes a state of longing and hope through an image that is an invitation and a promise. This architectural image of landscape evokes simultaneously remembrance and imagination as the composite painted image of Arnold Böcklin's "Island of Death". All poetic images are condensations and microcosms.

The modernist architecture of the Paimio Sanatorium projects images of hope and healing. Alvar Aalto, Paimio Tuberculosis Sanatorium, Paimio, 1929–33

The Meditation Grove on the hill is an image of hope and resurrection. Gunnar Asplund and Sigurd Lewerentz, The Woodland Cemetery, Stockholm, 1915/1932

"House, even more than the landscape, is a psychic state", Bachelard suggests.[23] Indeed, writers, film directors, poets, and painters do not just depict landscapes or houses as unavoidable geographic and physical settings of the events of their stories; they seek to express, evoke and amplify human emotions, mental states and memories through purposeful depictions of settings, both natural and man-made. "Let us assume a wall: what takes place behind it?", asks the poet Jean Tardieu,[24] but we architects rarely bother to imagine what happens behind the walls we have erected. The walls conceived by architects are usually mere aestheticized constructions, and we see our craft in terms of designing aesthetic structures rather than evoking perceptions, feelings and fantasies.

Artists seem to grasp the intertwining of place and human mind, memory and desire, much better than we architects do, and that is why these other art forms can provide such stimulating inspiration for our work as well as for architectural education. There are no better lessons of the extraordinary capacity of artistic condensations in evoking microcosmic images of the world than, say, the short stories of Anton Chekhov and Jorge Luis Borges, or Giorgio Morandi's minute still lifes consisting of a few bottles and cups on a table top.

Slowness and remembering – speed and forgetting

"There is a secret bond between slowness and memory, between speed and forgetting . . . the degree of slowness is directly proportional to the intensity of memory:
the degree of speed is directly proportional to the intensity of forgetting", suggests
Milan Kundera.[25] With the dizzying acceleration of the velocity of time today and
the constant speeding up of our experiential reality, we are seriously threatened by
a general cultural amnesia. In today's accelerated life, we can finally only perceive,
not remember. In the society of the spectacle we can only marvel, not remember.
Speed and transparency weaken remembrance, but they have been fundamental
fascinations of modernity since the proclamation of F.T. Marinetti in the Futurist
manifesto almost a full century ago: "The world's magnificence has been enriched
by a new beauty; the beauty of speed",[26] and Karl Marx's prophesy: "Everything
that is solid . . . melts into the air."[27] Today, even architecture seeks the sensation
of speed, instant seduction and gratification, and turns autistic, as a consequence.
The architectural confession of Coop Himmelblau illustrates this aspiration for dra-
matized architectural action and speed:

> The aesthetics of the architecture of death in white sheets. Death in tiled hospital rooms. The
> architecture of sudden death on the pavement. Death from a rib-cage pierced by a steering shaft.
> The path of the bullet through a dealer's head on 42nd Street. The aesthetics of the peep-show
> sex in washable plastic boxes. Of the broken tongues and the dried-up eyes.[28]

In my view, however, architecture is inherently a slow and quiet, emotionally a
low-energy art form in comparison with the dramatic arts of sudden affective
impact. Its role is not to create strong foreground figures or feelings, but to establish frames of perception and horizons of understanding. The task of architecture is
not to make us weep or laugh, but to sensitize us to be able to enter all emotional
states. Architecture is needed to provide the ground and projection screen of
remembrance and emotion.

I believe in an architecture that slows down and focuses human experience
instead of speeding up or diffusing it. In my view, architecture has to safeguard
memories and protect the authenticity and independence of human experience.
Architecture is fundamentally the art form of emancipation, and it makes us understand and remember who we are.

Architectural amnesia

There are different kinds of architecture in relation to memory: one that cannot
recall or touch upon the past and another that evokes a sense of depth and continuity. There is also an architecture that seeks to remember literally, like the architectural works of Postmodernism, and another that creates a sense of deep time,
and epic continuity without any direct formal reference, as the works of Alvar Aalto,
Dimitris Pikionis and Carlo Scarpa. These are products of a "poetic chemistry", to
use an evocative notion of Bachelard.[29] Every significant and true work sets itself in

a respectful dialogue with the past, both distant and immediate. At the same time that the work defends itself as a unique and complete microcosm, it revives and revitalizes the past. Every true work of art occupies a thick and layered time instead of mere contemporaneity.

There is yet another dimension in architectural memory. Architectural images, or experiences, have a historicity and ontology of their own. Architecture begins with the establishment of a horizontal plane; consequently, the floor is the "oldest" and most potent element of architecture. The wall is more archaic than the door or the window, and projects a deeper meaning as a consequence. Modernity has suffered from another kind of amnesia as architectural elements and images have become abstracted and detached from their origins and ontological essences. The floor, for instance, has forgotten its origin as levelled earth, and turned into mere constructed horizontal planes. In fact, as Bachelard suggests, human constructions of the technological age have forgotten verticality altogether, and turned into mere horizontality. Today's skyscrapers consist of stacked horizontality and have lost the sense of verticality, the fundamental ontological difference between below and above, Hell and Heaven. Also, the floor and the ceiling have become identical horizontal planes. The window and the door are often mere holes in the wall. I do not have the space here to elaborate on this theme of the historicity of architectural images and the current architectural amnesia resulting from the loss of the historicity of experiences; I merely point at the mental significance of this dimension.

The tenses of art

I venture to suggest that in its very essence artistic work is oriented towards the past rather than the future. Brodsky seems to support this view as he argues: "There is something clearly atavistic in the process of recollection, if only because such a process never is linear. Also the more one remembers, the closer perhaps one is to dieing."[30]

In any significant experience, temporal layers interact; what is perceived interacts with what is remembered, the novel short-circuits with the archaic. An artistic experience always awakes the forgotten child hidden inside one's adult persona.

There are fabricated images in today's architecture and art that are flat and without an emotional echo, but there are also novel images that resonate with remembrance. The latter are mysterious and familiar, obscure and clear, at the same time. They move us through the remembrances and associations, emotions and empathy that they awaken in us. Artistic novelty can move us only provided it touches something that we already possess in our very being. Every profound artistic work surely grows from memory, not from rootless intellectual invention. Artistic works aspire to bring us back to an undivided and undifferentiated oceanic world. This is the *Omega* that Teilhard de Chardin writes about, "the point from which the world appears complete and correct".[31]

We are usually conditioned to think that artists and architects ought to be addressing the future readers, viewers, and users of their products. Joseph Brodsky is very determined, indeed, about the poet's temporal perspective: "When one

Looking through a window is a profound architectural encounter rather than a visual design of the window itself.
Caspar David Friedrich, "Frau am Fenster", 1822

writes, one's most immediate audience is not one's own contemporaries, let alone posterity, but one's predecessors."[32] "No real writer ever wanted to be contemporary", Jorge Luis Borges argues in the same vain.[33] This view opens another essential perspective on the significance and role of remembrance; all creative work is collaboration with the past and with the wisdom of tradition. "Every true novelist listens for that suprapersonal wisdom [the wisdom of the novel], which explains why great novels are always a little more intelligent than their authors. Novelists who are more intelligent than their books should go into another line of work", Milan Kundera argues.[34] The same observation is equally true of architecture; great buildings are fruits of the wisdom of architecture, they are products of a collaboration, often unconscious, with our great predecessors as much as they are works of their individual creators. Only works that are in vital and respectful dialogue with their past possess the mental capacity to survive time and stimulate viewers, listeners, readers, and occupants in the future.

NOTES

1 Karsten Harries, "Thoughts on a Non-Arbitrary Architecture" in David Seamon (ed.), *Dwelling, Seeing and Designing: Toward a Phenomenological Ecology*, Albany, NY: State University of New York Press, 1993, p. 47.
2 Karsten Harries, "Building and the Terror of Time", *Perspecta: The Yale Architectural Journal* 19, 1982. As quoted in David Harvey, *The Condition of Postmodernity*, Cambridge: Blackwell, 1992, p. 206.
3 Gaston Bachelard, *The Poetics of Space*, Boston, MA: Beacon Press, 1969, p. 46.
4 As quoted in Max Picard, *The World of Silence*, Washington, DC: Begnery Gateway, 1988, p. 231. Kierkegaard writes: "The present state of the world and the whole of life is diseased. If I were a doctor and were asked for my advice, I should say: Create Silence! Bring men to silence."
5 In Max Picard, *The World of Silence*, p. 221.
6 In Max Picard, *The World of Silence*, p. 212.
7 Joseph Brodsky, "A Place as Good as Any" in *On Grief and Reason*, New York: Farrar, Straus and Giroux, 1997, p. 43.
8 Antoine de Saint-Exupéry, *Wind, Sand and Stars*, London: Penguin Books, 1991, p. 39.
9 Rainer Maria Rilke, *The Notebooks of Malte Laurids Brigge*, M.O. Herter Norton, trans.; New York and London: W.W. Norton & Co., 1992, pp. 30–31.
10 Rilke, *The Notebooks of Malte Laurids Brigge*, pp. 47–48.
11 Joseph Brodsky, "A Place as Good as Any" in *On Grief and Reason*, p. 37.
12 Susan Sontag, *On Photography*, Harmondworth: Penguin Books, 1986.
13 Jarkko Laine, "Tikusta asiaa" in *Parnasso* 6, 1982, pp. 323–24.
14 Wallace Stevens, "Theory" in *The Collected Poems*, New York: Vintage Books, 1990, p. 86.
15 Noël Arnaud, as quoted in Bachelard, *The Poetics of Space*, p. 137.
16 Bachelard, *The Poetics of Space*, p. 6.
17 T.S. Eliot, *Four Quartets*, San Diego: Harcourt Brace Jovanovich Publishers, 1971, pp. 58–59.
18 Maurice Merleau-Ponty, "Cézanne's Doubt" in *Sense and Non-Sense*, Evanston, IL: Northwestern University Press, 1964, p. 19.
19 Joseph Brodsky, *On Grief and Reason*, p. 206.
20 Bohumil Hrabal, *Too Loud a Solitude*, San Diego, CA: Harcourt Inc., 1990, p. 1.
21 Marcel Proust, *In Search of Lost Time: Swann's Way*, C.K. Scott Moncrieff & Terence Kilmartin, trans.; London: The Random House, 1992, pp. 4–5.

22   Edward S. Casey, *Memorizing: A Phenomenological Study*, Bloomington, IN: Indiana University Press, 2000, p. 148, 172.

23   Bachelard, *The Poetics of Space*, p. 72.

24   As quoted in Georges Perec, *Tiloja ja avaruuksia*, Espéces d'espaces, original title; Helsinki: Loki-Kirjat, 1992, p. 72.

25   Milan Kundera, *Slowness*, New York: HarperCollins Publishers, 1966, p. 39.

26   As quoted in Thom Mayne, "Statement" in *Peter Pran*, Ligang Qui: DUT Press, 2006, p. 4.

27   "All fixed, fast-frozen relations, with their train of ancient and venerable prejudices and opinions, are swept away, all newformed ones become antiquated before they can ossify. All that is solid melts into air, all that is holy is profaned, and men at last are forced to face . . . the real conditions of their lives and their relations with their fellow men."

28   Coop Himmelblau, "Die Fascination der Stadt" in Anthony Vidler, *The Architectural Uncanny*, Cambridge, MA: The MIT Press, 1999, p. 76.

29   Gaston Bachelard, *Water and Dreams: An Essay on the Imagination of Matter*, Dallas, TX: The Pegasus Foundation, 1983, p. 46.

30   Joseph Brodsky, *Less Than One*, New York: Farrar Straus Giroux, 1986, p. 30.

31   As quoted in Timo Valjakka (ed.), *Juhana Blomstedt: muodon arvo*, Helsinki: Painatuskeskus, 1995.

32   Joseph Brodsky, "Letter to Horace" in *On Grief and Reason*, p. 439.

33   As quoted in Norman Thomas di Giovanni *et al.* (eds), *Borges on Writing*, Hopewell: The Ecco Press, 1994, p. 53.

34   Milan Kundera, *The Art of the Novel*, New York: HarperCollins Publishers Inc., 2000, p. 158.

Norwegian Introduction

Elisabeth Tostrup

Effective Words on Behalf of the Architect(ure)

The 1900s was the century Norway became an independent state and a monarchy after the union with Sweden was dissolved in 1905, after 400 years as a colony under the rule of Denmark up to the resolution of the Napoleonic Wars in 1814. It was the century that the country was under German occupation for five long years during the Second World War, followed by a strict national reconstruction programme which marked the work of architects for many years. It was the century when Norway, the poorest among our neighbouring countries, became unbelievably rich due to oil and gas deposits in the North Sea. Aside from these specific Norwegian factors, the country has, like other western countries, gone through comprehensive industrialization with moving to the cities, a doubling of the population, globalization in all areas, and in the last ten years a strong increase in ethnic and cultural diversity.

While the population has increased from 2.3 to 4.7 million over a hundred years, the number of architects who are members of the National Association of Norwegian Architects (NAL) has been multiplied from around 100 to 3,300.[1] It was not until 1910 that the country had its own programme for training architects at the Norwegian University of Technology (NTH) in Trondheim. Before that Norwegian architects studied out of the country, in Stockholm or Copenhagen, but also at German technical universities. After the union was dissolved, the NAL was founded in 1911 and their own publication *Byggekunst* (*The Art of Building*) in 1919. This very brief description gives the background for the Norwegian architect's situation, their ideas, attitudes and opinions, and the fantastic changes which have taken place in the general framework in the course of the last century.

Before *Byggekunst* came into being, there were two publications in Norway where architects published their work: *Arkitektur og dekorativ kunst* (*Architecture and Decorative Art*), which came out as an offprint from *Teknisk ugeblad* (*Technical Weekly*) from 1909, and *Kunst og Kultur* (*Art and Culture*) from 1910. *Bonytt*, a magazine for interior decoration and applied art, was established in 1941 and was an important forum for architects far into the 1970s. It included design of furniture and other objects, especially "Scandinavian design" in the early postwar period, and in addition more theoretical articles about the production of artistic objects and the building of houses and recreational homes. In 1945 *Arkitektnytt* was established as a debating and information forum for members of NAL.[2] Such material had been published earlier under the name *Tillegget* (*Supplement*) in earmarked pages of *Byggekunst*, where material from architectural competitions was also printed. The magazine *Konkurransen* (*Competition*), later renamed *Norske arkitektkonkurranser* (*Norwegian Architectural Competitions*), did not come out until 1953.

Architects as authors of books are rarer. There are architects that have specialized in textbooks, like Odd Brochmann and Christian Norberg-Schulz, and others
who by virtue of their positions as editors or museum directors have published
books, generally monographs, about individual architects. But, as literary scholar
Mari Lending points out, there is a large vacuum to fill in passing on Norwegian
architects' activities and works in book form.[3] One area has been the object of special
issues under the direction of architects: Norwegian house building and timberwork.
During the war a group of architects collected material for a comprehensive book
called *Norske hus* (*Norwegian Houses*), which came out in 1950.[4] Even though all the
authors were functionalists, over two-thirds of the buildings were from before the
twentieth century. Starting in 1963, Gunnar Bugge and Norberg-Schulz presented
old, Norwegian wooden houses in each issue of *Byggekunst* – popular articles which
came out in book form under the title *Stav og laft*.[5] The last books which the Association of Norwegian Architects has published on this subject are the Timber Awards
starting in 1961.[6] Architects have also written historical articles in connection with
anniversaries, whether it be for *Byggekunst*, the local architectural associations or NAL,
where the task was to write about a certain period in the past of Norwegian architecture. Along completely different lines, some architects have been frequent contributors to daily newspapers, especially Odd Brochmann, P.A.M. Mellbye and more
recently Thomas Thiis-Evensen, Didrik Hvoslef-Eide and Jan Carlsen. Qualified
articles on architecture in the Norwegian press have nevertheless been on a much
smaller scale than in our neighbouring countries.

The most common type of architectural writings are articles written as part of a
presentation of buildings and projects. Sometimes such texts can sound like a manifesto or a stated professional ideology such as Knut Knutsen's article in this book,
but more often professional ideology is implicit in the text. Illustrated travelogues
are also a genre which, through choice of destination and what is to be described,
express one aspect of what architects are concerned with. Sverre Fehn's "The Primitive Architecture of Morocco" from 1952 is an example of this.[7] The chosen texts
written by architects impart opinions which have the character of a manifesto, which
express the architect's professional programme, their ideas and thoughts: typical
points of view which were shared by different groups of Norwegian architects in the
course of the last hundred years.

With the emphasis on logic, science and international models

Johan Ellefsen's lecture for Oslo Architect Association (OAF) in October of 1927 with
the title "What is Contemporary Architecture?" was immediately printed in *Byggekunst*.[8]
When this article was called the manifesto of functionalism in Norway, it must have
been because the milieu was ready to accept it and that the article had a lasting quality:
it was a rhetorical success. Prominent architects and intellectuals had for a long time
spoken up for a radical confrontation with the past in the field of architecture, art and
design. The fight for "the new objectivity" was the struggle against "the 19th century's
hopeless search through every imaginable historical style's chaos", against national
romanticism and neoclassicism which dominated around 1920–25.[9]

The article imparts Le Corbusier's message from *Vers une architecture* and argues for the use of reinforced concrete, right angles, flat roofs and mass production. At the same time, by connecting the ties from the present to the great Egyptian and Greek epochs in western architecture, Ellefsen encourages his listeners to identify themselves with this long and proud historical fellowship.

The article is a work of art in embracing and inspiring a broad audience within the profession. It balances general cultural knowledge with specific architectural references and clear reasoning. It is not too heavy theoretically, and its elements of pathos seem universal and appropriate through well-chosen metaphors; it is not objectionably controversial.

Reference to Aristoteles' guideline *mean*, the ideal of keeping to the centre so that there is nothing to add or subtract, runs like a connecting thread throughout the article and gives the impression that the message is objective and important, like Le Corbusier's term "axis". In Ellefsen's elegant conclusion the architectural profession, and mankind, are seen as

> rowers on two sides of the same boat. If one side should stop rowing, the others would then row in a circle. If the rowers on one side of the boat are displeased with the course, they may begin to row forwards, so that the *mean* in Norwegian architecture can be attained.

In this way he can propagandize for an absolute extreme in architecture, and legitimize it by emphasizing the ideal of *mean* and a steady course.

PLAN's "Our Agenda", published six years later, springs out of the same movement – in this case younger champions of modern architecture and functionalism – but has an explicit political centre of gravity with emphasis on housing, lack of housing and living in cramped quarters.[10] PLAN consisted of members of the Association of Socialist Architects and called for "fundamental change in the profession's social circumstances – in the material and economic basis for its activity". The problems of architecture could be perceived as a social problem. The group accuses and criticizes the politically neutral functionalists, including Le Corbusier, for seeing this architectural problem too narrowly, for not taking a stand in this ongoing class conflict.

According to PLAN, architects have to go further than the Danish *Kritisk Revy* and the Swedish *Byggmästaren*, they must be an active part of the political opposition and put their professional knowledge at the disposal of the struggling working classes and "contribute towards dissuading the working class from following an unsound housing policy during the years remaining before our nation, too, will achieve the reality of a socialist planned economy".

The article encourages logic and a scientific approach and it gives a more matter-of-fact impression than Ellefsen's article, even if it is sharp in its criticism. "Our Agenda" accuses the majority of architects of suffering under "the illusion that the housing issue can be solved within the capitalist society". The group itself, however, suffers under the illusionary notions: first, that capitalism will be conquered, and second, that the working class will share the architect's taste and views on what is proper architecture.

Nevertheless, PLAN's work had an impact. Some of the members were instrumental in the public planning. The principles of extensive public planning, of social housing with subsidized purchasing of the site and state financing through the Norwegian State Housing Bank was a part of the Norwegian Labour Party's regime for several decades after the Second World War, up until the 1980s when market forces took over. From the 1960s on, PLAN's activities were a reference point for politically active, radical architects who criticized the stagnant technocratic planning, and who involved themselves in different ways to the advantage of residents and users.[11]

About twenty years after PLAN, and with the Second World War as a dividing mark, a new architectural revolution occurred which also called on international resources, but which was apolitical in regard to the architect's work in relation to the social and political arena: PAGON (Progressive Arkitekters Gruppe Oslo, Norge) represented a counterweight to explicit politicizing of architecture. PAGON's leading article "CIAM" is a sharp criticism directed at society's everyday, domestic architecture which they maintain is characterized by "cosiness" and "history's most pronounced era of petit-bourgeoisie . . . when we sit, every man in his castle, guarding a tin of deep-frozen living standards".[12] They are referring to the so-called new empiricism or neorealism which has dominated in the Nordic countries since the last half of the 1930s. PAGON evokes the vitality and innovating radicalism that far exceeds the political significance of which the years between the world wars were full. A central aim was to free oneself from national restrictions and rise up into a universal cooperative effort; the national can only mean a regional distinctive feature, a variant, within this larger context.

It is striking that this article also emphasizes scientific methods in combating sentimentality and the "subjective exhibitionism in architecture". But PAGON's article is more demagogic than scientific; it appeals to the feelings and ignites the architects' fighting spirit. The manifesto does not appeal to ordinary people, but to architects who have the demanding pedagogical task to "awaken the needs of fellow citizens, teach them to see and coax them out of their sentimental routines".

The section "Meccano of the Home" elaborates on these thoughts, and the title became a term Arne Korsmo (1900–68) used in his lectures, first at the National College of Applied Arts and Crafts (SHKS) in Oslo, later at NTH in Trondheim. Teaching at SHKS was about interiors and space, which is reflected in this section. "Meccano of the Home" is a clever rhetorical move: even though the word "Meccano" has scientific, technical and engineering associations, it refers to a play-building system, "Meccano", which was quite popular in the 1950s. It consisted of a number of rods with holes in them which could be screwed together to make thousands of different things, which could then be taken apart and reused to make new devices. Thus, the most urgent and impelling paragraphs in this section are about freeing people, stimulating them to play, to take command of space and form one's own surroundings to rich variation with simple means and under knowledgeable guidance by the architect.[13]

This section was far ahead of developments in Norway in relation to "open form", structuralism and user influence. It is not pragmatic, and its alluring and positive tone takes the sting out of the crass criticism. Look at the conclusion: "In the wholeness of interaction lies the chance for the greatest encounters of energies and thereby the highest unfolding of life." PAGON heralds modernism recapturing the hegemony in Norwegian architecture after the Second World War, a hegemony which would last and still does at the beginning of the twenty-first century, when one includes the nuances and variations which are modern at all times.[14]

The environment and human architecture

Knut Knutsen takes another approach, accentuates other qualities. Knutsen does not advocate a radical break with tradition and local building practices.

> To create an architecture that focuses on people, one can draw on architecture from other periods and use the numerous shapes in nature as inspiration . . . Respect and reverence for the landscape must be prevailing values. Respect is not just a matter of making buildings subordinate to the landscape, but also to emphasize it, develop it, maybe even create a new nature.[15]

"People in Focus" is written in a light tone and is easy to follow. Knutsen's message is to promote "continual architecture", an architecture carried out consistently from century to century, where the whole must be evaluated before the individual building. He takes up arms against styles and trends, which he says are detrimental to the whole. At the same time he finds himself in the spirit of modern architecture where he stresses the importance of creating something original and not an imitation.

The title "People in Focus" is taken from the exhibit "We Can" in 1938, which according to Knutsen had the title as its motto. "We Can" was a big exhibit on the 100th anniversary of Oslo's Crafts and Industry Association, where Knutsen had won the architectural competition in 1935 along with Arne Korsmo and Andreas Nygaard. The exhibition was seen as a follow-up of the Stockholm Exhibition in 1930, and was often used by Korsmo as a reference in his campaign for a more radical modernism than Knutsen's. After the war Korsmo and Knutsen became prominent figures in two conflicting directions in Norwegian architecture, the one internationally directed with the emphasis on industrialization, the other more connected to local materials and artisan traditions.[16] With the title and introductory illustration from the "We Can" exhibit, Knutsen puts himself in the centre of Norwegian modernism, and points out that the PAGON wing does not have a monopoly on putting "people in focus" with accompanying rhetoric.

As an author of books and articles on architecture Norberg-Schulz is unique in Norway, due to his extensive international activities, his intellectual capacity and his comprehensive writings. After studying under Sigfried Giedion in Zurich in the late 1940s, he took the initiative for PAGON and was an active member in the group's projects in the 1950s. Norberg-Schulz was an avid advocate for bringing back modernism in Norway, and he was especially enthusiastic about Mies van der Rohe. His work as a practising architect gradually gave way to theoretical absorption and several long periods abroad. In the USA in 1952–53 he took courses in psychology, sociology and semiotics at Harvard University.[17] Later he received a research grant and lived in Rome 1956–58 and 1960–63 where he finished his doctoral thesis 'Intentions in Architecture', which he presented in 1964.

The article "Order and Variation in the Environment" is bursting with knowledge and pedagogically formulated reasoning, with thoroughness and clarity. It was written at a time when Norberg-Schulz was editor of *Byggekunst* and newly appointed professor in architectural theory and history at the Oslo School of Architecture (AHO).[18]

Even with a wide perspective, the concrete physical conditions are central in his presentation: it is form and figure, the tangibility of the senses, and the comprehensive physical nearness of things. His presentation was an attempt to benefit the endeavours of Norwegian architecture, which at that time were influenced by Team X and the ideas of "open form". "Dense-low" and structuralism were about to break through. Shortly afterwards the architectural milieu, and even Norberg-Schulz's job at AHO, was shaken with uproar and political activism. "Order and Variation in the Environment" points to Norberg-Schulz' later works, his continual search for a meaning in architecture and his theoretical works where a poetic, phenomenological approach takes over for early modernism's scientific rationale. As always in his observations, his article bears the message of totality, order and coherence, regardless of whether his architectural preferences reach from Mies van der Rohe to the Finnish Reima Pietilä, from orthogonal clarity and simplicity to figurative and pluralistic architecture.

"Adaptation" is a theme that is often taken up in debates about architecture since the 1970s. "Tradition and Distinctiveness" by Wenche Selmer was published in an issue of the magazine put out by the Society for the Preservation of Norwegian Ancient Monuments which was devoted to this problem; it concerns the adaptation of new architecture to existing surroundings. Selmer says that adaptation should not be associated with something resigned and passive, but a "conscious act which is the result of sensitivity to people and surroundings". The goal is to give quality to the new in the best possible interaction with the existing surroundings. Pastiche – a potpourri of different style fragments – must be avoided, at the same time as understanding the importance of "not introducing wrong proportions in an especially fine and balanced environment".[19] She campaigns against laws and regulations which reduce the architect's chances for creating human architecture. The article clearly refers back to Knutsen's ideas – he was her teacher. But Selmer's text is narrower, more matter-of-fact: she keeps to her own experience and reflects over general architectural problems by examining architectural means in detail, the working process including measuring old houses and observing the site's qualities at close range.[20]

The text is unassuming and low-key in form and argumentation, but the message is clear and demanding enough in practice: there are not many architects today who go into such a detailed collecting of knowledge about the site and its characteristics, nor do they create and build new buildings with the same humility over what is given. Here there are no elaborate theories or a soaring choice of words. The presentation builds on her own experience as a practising architect, and it imparts the architect's competence in the decisions she considers to be central to an audience both within and without the professional sphere. Perhaps a lot of architects, both men and women, who do good, respectable work throughout the country, will find support and inspiration in articles like Selmer's.

The realization of freedom?

"Structuralistic Architecture" is written by Kjell Lund, probably one of Norway's architects who has most consistently carried out big building projects in structuralist architecture for many years.[21] Like Selmer's article, his presentation comes right to the point, describes the principles and the reasons for them without philosophizing too much or referring to authorities of theory. One goal is that the buildings shall provide maximum freedom in meeting changing needs for use: "The structuralist organization of constructions and technique is originally functionally motivated and adapted to industrial production." In addition to giving flexible interiors, structuralism also makes possible a systematic and ordered additional expansion in small and large building complexes.

It almost looks as if this is the answer to PAGON's "Meccano of the Home" from the 1950s. "Structuralism may be classified as differentiation and specialization of functionalism via constructivism", writes Lund, and he discusses the development from the fixed constructions from their first projects to the open, three-dimensional skeletal structures. The square is the recurring basic geometric shape in all their projects. At the same time, the juxtaposition of the units to buildings has the figure characteristics that Norberg-Schulz evoked in "Order and Variation in the Environment".

The article has an almost scientific level of precision. It is as compact and readable as filigree work; one has to think carefully and imagine visually in the mind, link for link. At the same time, it is not postulating. The word "may" is often used: the explanation is one of several possible and is to convince with its logical credibility, not as an authoritative statement. At a time when the echo from American postmodernism was a disturbing element in Norway – a style which the Norwegian architectural hegemony generally rejected – the author sets structuralism up as the opposite of cliché-like symbols and coulisse architecture. One may question whether the rhetorical reservations, the inviting openness, are adequate to lead this sensible message through prosperity's growing pressure for more individualized, figurative and spectacular works of architecture.

Architecture's autonomous space – openings in the hedge?

In 2004 a collection of younger Norwegian architects were presented in *A+U* (*Architecture and Urbanism*) as successors of Norway's most important architect Sverre Fehn (1924–), who is a contemporary of Lund. Some of them, such as Jarmund and Vigsnæs as well as Jensen and Skodvin, had been Fehn's students at AHO.[22] These younger architects are trying, each in their own way, to articulate their architectonic ideas and points of view.

"Is a House Interesting Seen Through a Hedge?" by Håkon Vigsnæs takes as a point of departure a journey where he visits world-known architect-designed houses in Los Angeles and reflects over the single-family house as task for architectural experiments and a challenge in the architectural practice. It is a well-informed and thoughtful text which deals with many different aspects of the problem. The author sees architecture as a social tool and argues in favour of the houses' – the small individual architectural commission – significance in the professional process. The text is also interesting as it takes up the span between the detailed, purely professional problems and their social implications on a larger scale, from the building industry to the social and ethical challenges out in the world. "The hedge" becomes a well-chosen metaphor which covers both the concrete architectonic reference – the single-family house – and the containment or isolation of architecture's autonomous space.

Jan Olav Jensen's "Affinity" brings to mind Norberg-Schulz, Knutsen and Selmer, in that it cultivates the site and the unique work, closeness to the materials and the production process itself. Jensen takes as his point of departure reflections on the deeply personal in every creative person's work. What characteristics and opportunities are given a person from where – God, karma, genes and other factors – at birth, and what is provided and shaped throughout life? This is a big question which cannot be answered here. But there is good reason to give the personal dimension in architectural works great credibility.

In contrast to the architect's usual project materials which are pre-figurations of built work (drawings, models, and so on), and which here are referred to as "instructions", Jensen presents a method whereby the work comes into existence in close interaction with the site, its topography, vegetation and other characteristics which are given by the larger surroundings. The "instructions" are the described detailed principles for the single parts where the whole constellation is first formed when the single elements and the principles are adapted to the given site. Shaping things in their context, according to Jensen, is a method and an instrument in bringing out certain architectural qualities that overshadow each work as total composition. While the conventional realization of a building is compared to a musical performance based on the composer's notes, Jensen and Skodvin's methods should be looked upon as improvisation – an improvisation which requires both finely tuned sensuousness and a deep practical knowledge of the instrument's capacity. The "darling" is the moulding situation which occurs in the confrontation between the working architect and the site's complex materiality, and which becomes unique through the move from the abstract level of the office drawing table to the final work's physical birthplace. Such a reflection and communicating of essential processes in architecture's autonomous space is truly praiseworthy. Pseudopoetic and pseudophilosophic interpretations are avoided, but on the other hand the article denies a wider perspective in society and the world.

The different architect's articles can be regarded as a plait running through time: first the one, then the other, so the third in changing positions from side to side. Different architects may represent different professional and political positions, but at the same time share a common cultural characteristic which is expressed in the message or style of writing. It may look as if the Norwegian architects in the early period had a wider perspective concerning the architect and the role of architecture in society; they speak with more general cultural knowledge and commitment. But they exercised, too, overconfidence on behalf of science, rationality and progress. The Norwegian architectural milieu is, at least after the Second World War, characterized by anti-academic, anti-intellectual attitudes, as Karl Otto Ellefsen points out.[23] In spite of his warning around 1986 about "cracks in Norwegian consensus", these are attitudes which are common for different Norwegian groups of architects. "I draw houses, I don't write", is the usual comment from practising colleagues. This provides a breeding ground where mystification and prophetic speech is well on the way to being successful if it is presented by people one respects professionally. Nonetheless, it is not an accepted truth that man's search for "his inner source" has to include an unconditional cultivation of master and élite, and that the way forward has to go by way of mesmerizing "creative lies", as Jensen says when he refers to Fehn as a teacher.

It is claimed that the professional architect's position and status in Norwegian society has declined at an accelerating rate in the last decades. Their influence is curtailed as other professional groups have taken over the architect's leading and coordinating role in building and planning. At the same time we witness an increasing cultivation of design, star designers and star architects on the part of the media, thus giving a freer certain liberty and a touch of glamour to some very few professionals. Perhaps the architects' intense efforts within the autonomy and immanence of the subject have something to do with these new circumstances. And perhaps there is an appropriate realism in a positioning which is directed towards the professional community, but which at times seems too subjective to try out on society. Norwegian consensus in regard to expanding the limits of architecture to include a pluralism without radical confrontations basically conceals a struggle for the power to define. It is the professional milieu that decides what is to count as certified knowledge in the field, and it is here the architects contribute to the collective understanding of things through linguistic acts which separately are persuasive for their case.[24] To what degree society accepts the profession's certified knowledge is another matter. The articles, along with reference architecture, give a historiography of Norwegian architectural ideology, a historiography where the distinctive rhetoric gives a further insight into the individual's and the group's range of understanding.

NOTES

1 Earlier architects were members of the National Association of Norwegian Civil Engineers and Architects which was founded in 1874. Local leagues were established in the larger cities before NAL: Nordenfjeldske Arkitektforening in 1902 (Trondheim), Christiania Architect's Association (Oslo) in 1906 and Bergen Architect's Association in 1908. A lot of people with other backgrounds worked as architects at that time, primarily a group of builders who were in transition between being architects and builders.

2 *Arkitektnytt* came out in a stencilled version from 1945. From 1952, no. 9, it came out in print.

3 Mari Lending, "Arkitektur i skrift", *Prosa* 13 1, 2007, p. 55.

4 Eyvind Alnæs, *Norske Hus en Billedbok*, Oslo: Aschehoug, 1950. The group's main contributor was Georg Eliassen, a leading functionalist in the 1930s.

5 Gunnar Bugge and Christian Norberg-Schulz, *Stav og Laft i Norge*, Oslo: Byggekunst, 1969.

6 Dag Rognlien, *Treprisen* 1961, 1962, 1964, 1966, 1971, 1973, 1975, 1978, 1981, 1983, 1986 = Thirteen Norwegian prize-winning architects, 3rd edn, Oslo: Arkitektnytt, 1988; Odd Ellingsrud and Beate Hølmebakk, *Timberwork*, Oslo: Arkitekturforlaget, 2000.

7 For an English translation, see Sverre Fehn, "The Primitive Architecture of Morocco" in *A+U* 340, 1999, pp. 41–42.

8   Ellefsen, who was educated at the Norwegian University of Technology (NTH), shared his office
     with Finn Bryn (1890–1975) from 1922. Their projects were initially characterized by neoclassi-
     cism, later functionalism. They won the architectural competition for the University complex at
     Blindern in Oslo in 1926.

9   Harald Aars, "Byggekunstens utvikling gjennem de siste 25 år", Byggekunst 5, 1931, p. 8. The occa-
     sion was Oslo Architect Association's 25th anniversary, where Aars, Oslo's town architect, wrote:
     "Even if the struggle for ... 'the new objectivity' had been going on in many countries and in
     many ways in the years before the war, it was that which made things fall into place ... And now
     we have come so far that Norway too is a part of this huge orchestra that is trying to give the 20th
     century its wonderful rhythm and melody through form and colour in stone, glass, concrete
     and steel."

10   The periodical PLAN came out with four issues from 1933. The editors consisted of a group of relat-
     ively newly educated architects who were members of the Association of Socialist Architects. They
     all had their background in "Arkitektstudentenes Broderskap" (Architect Student's Brotherhood)
     and the student strike at NTH in the 1920s.

11   An example of this is Anne Sæterdal and Thorbjørn Hansen, Ammerud i planlegging av en ny bydel,
     Rapport/Norges byggforskningsinstitutt 58, Oslo: Norges byggforskningsinstitutt, 1969. The archi-
     tect's social commitment at this time was also visible in a number of architectural competitions on
     housing, in the Tett-lav (Low-dense) movement, Bo-serviceforeningen and other grass root move-
     ments and protest campaigns where architects were central figures.

12   The group was a subdivision of CIAM and consisted of young architects with the older, pre-war
     functionalist Arne Korsmo as leader. Both Richard Neutra and Sigfried Giedion had been guest lec-
     turers in Oslo in 1949, and Giedion returned when the group was founded in 1950. According to
     Korsmo, the group had been connected to CIAM since 1948, see Arne Korsmo, "Til unge arkitekt-
     sinn", A5: Meningsblad for unge arkitekter 1–2, 1956. Several of the members had participated in the
     CIAM congress at Bergamo 1949 and at Hoddesdon in 1951.

13   Kosmo had been in the USA for a year in 1949–50 as a Fulbright Fellow and had come to know many
     prominent architects, artists and researchers within the fields of social psychology and education.

14   See in addition Elisabeth Tostrup, Architecture and Rhetoric: Text and design in architectural competitions, Oslo
     1939–97, London: Andreas Papadakis, 1999, about modernisms hegemony which is especially pre-
     vailing in architectural competitions.

15   Knut Knutsen was a prominent functionalist in the 1930s. His prize-winning project in Aftenposten's
     small house competition in 1930 was pure, striking functionalist in contrast to the winner Ove
     Bang's more moderate hybrid project. Ove Bang was later known as one of Norway's great cham-
     pions for international functionalism, while Knutsen is associated with regionalism.

16   This is pointed out by Peter Davey, among others, who was the editor of The Architectural Review in his
     article "Norwegian reflections", Byggekunst 4–5, 1986. At times the front between the two flanks was
     so irreconcilable that "blows were dealt", see Wenche Selmer, "Knutsen skolen – norsk arkitektur
     på sidespor?", Arkitektnytt, 1986. In 1972, after both were dead, the National Association of Norwe-
     gian Architects arranged an exhibition on the two architects Arne Korsmo and Knut Knutsen at
     Høvikodden Art Centre outside Oslo. The exhibit brought out their differences clearly and the
     Danish architect Nils-Ole Lund, who had worked with them both, reflected on this and also talked
     about the likenesses between the two. Nils-Ole Lund, "To norske arkitekter: Arne Korsmo and Knut
     Knutsen", Arkitekten 22, 1974. Korsmo's and Knutsen's architecture is also discussed in Nicola Flora,
     Paolo Giardiello and Gennaro Postiglione, Arne Korsmo – Knut Knutsen due maestri del nord, Architettura
     Progetto 20, Roma: Officina Edizioni, 1999, in both English and Italian.

17   There he met Anna Maria de Dominicis, a student of literature from Rome, whom he married
     in 1955.

18   Norberg-Schulz had a grant from, and presented his thesis at, the Norwegian University of Techno-
     logy, where Arne Korsmo was professor in the Department of Architecture from 1956. Norberg-
     Schulz was editor of Byggekunst in the years 1963–78 and professor in architectural theory and
     history at the Oslo School of Architecture from 1966.

19   Selmer had her architectural practice alone, and was appointed assistant professor at AHO in 1976.
      See also Elisabeth Tostrup, *Norwegian Wood – The thoughtful architecture of Wenche Selmer*, New York: Prince-
      ton Architectural Press, 2006.

20   Selmer took meticulous measurements of the plot with a measuring tape, sighting sticks and level-
      ling telescope. In the area where she designed holiday cottages there were only land consolidation
      maps before around 1970 on a scale of 1:5000 and an equidistance of 5m. Younger architects like
      Carl-Viggo Hølmebakk and Jensen & Skodvin have learned their thorough registration work in the
      field from Selmer.

21   Kjell Lund had his architect practice together with Nils Slaatto, see also Ulf Grønvold, *Lund & Slaatto*,
      Norske arkitekter 4, Oslo: Universitetsforlaget, 1988, in both Norwegian and English.

22   "Norway. Fehn and his Contemporary Legacies", *A+U, Architecture and Urbanism* 411, 2004, pp.1–125.
      See also Jensen & Skodvin et al., *Jensen & Skodvin architects – processed geometries 1995–2007*, Oslo: Unipax,
      2007; Håkon Vigsnæs et al., *Lost in Nature, Jarmund/Vigsnæs Architects: La Galerie d'Architecture, Paris, April–May
      2007*, Oslo: Jarmund/Vigsnæs AS arkitekter, 2007.

23   Karl Otto Ellefsen, "Tendenser i norsk arkitektur 1986: sprekker i den norske enigheten", *Byggekunst*
      7, 1986, p.N4.

24   Scientific rhetoric is a field which is the object of increasing attention, see Jonas Bakken, "Kunsten å
      overtale sine forskerkolleger – en introduksjon til vitenskapsretorikken", *Arr* 1, Vitenskapens prosa,
      2007. Here situations are discussed in depth which also relate to architectural rhetoric. See also
      Tostrup, *Architecture and Rhetoric*, 1999.

University Complex by Finn Bryn and Johan Ellefsen

1927

Johan Ellefsen

What is Contemporary Architecture?

There are two types of imagination that create art. The first and original one is the imagination of primitive people. It is not guided by strict logic, but its wealth of images is as a rule influenced by a specific environment within which these people are sequestered. We still find today in remote valleys the results of primitive peoples' rich but introverted, subjective and non-innovative imagination.

Another kind of imagination is at the base of all modern science and technology: namely, imagination grounded in logic.

It is to the credit of the Egyptians, and to an even greater extent the Greeks, who were the first to apply strict, objective logic as a control and measurement for their creative imagination in art.

"Every art does its work well", Aristotle says, "by looking to the intermediate and judging its works by this standard – so that we often say of good works of art that it is not possible either to take away or to add anything, implying that excess and defect destroy the goodness of works of art, while the mean preserves it." Furthermore:

> It is possible to fail in many ways (for evil belongs to the class of the unlimited, as the Pythagoreans conjectured, and good to that of the limited), while to succeed is possible only in one way (for which reason also one is easy and the other difficult – to miss the mark easy, to hit it difficult); for these reasons also, then, excess and defect are characteristic of vice, and the mean of virtue.

This clear and conscious guideline for art is the antithesis of the primitives' notion.

Since the days of the Greeks, all great epochs of art have been founded from the outset on internationally recognized premises of logic. And the strong, advancing current in the field of art has always had a distinct direction: ideas emerged only when new, contemporaneous demands were manifested, and this was in the larger cultural centres of southern and central Europe. From here they spread throughout other countries. In this manner all of the various styles came to us earlier. The stronger our social structure and its spiritual life were, the more rapidly the currents came. Thus we raised Trondheim's Cathedral about the same time as similar constructions were built in Central Europe. The current then coursed out of the cities and across the country into the various remote valleys, where it was met by a more and more subjective popular imagination and formed together local whirlpools and shallows. These whirlpools and shallows have managed to remain in place and with approximately the same content for centuries because of the poor communications with the outside world.

The fact, in contrast to all historical art traditions, that we now should seek renewal in these whirlpools and shallows rather than daring to venture out into the main stream, as we did previously, seems unreasonable. We will inevitably be pulled along with the mainstream at any rate, because it is bound by natural laws as much as the Gulf Stream, and we might just as well accept it sooner rather than later, but at the same time trying to direct its course as well as possible and trying to ready ourselves for the consequences – to the extent that this is feasible.

The ideas that have created the new movements in architecture in Europe have manifested themselves during the course of the past fifteen to twenty years, but they did not have fair winds until the post-war period. They have developed somewhat concurrently in the central European countries and in America. The compulsion for a renewal in architecture, like all of the other fields of art, appears to have remained latent for nearly a half century. As precursors for a modern conception of art, one might include the various -isms that have emerged during this time, as well as the Jugend style that fizzled out, when it lost touch with its constructive logic. The various emotionally charged and individualistic currents of art have not demonstrated that they have led to anything more than dissolution and chaos either, nor to any expression of contemporary life and thought.

During all of this groping from one extreme to the other, technical advancement has celebrated its triumph across the world. It has increasingly attracted the attention of the entire world at the expense of the other fields of art. I say deliberately other fields of art, because in retrospect we have come to the realization that the leading art of our age is precisely technology. We became aware of this first and foremost in the central European countries and in America, because the advent of technology became important first in these places. It is no longer, as earlier, the poets, architects, painters and sculptors who have most clearly shaped and expressed their age, but rather the scientists and the engineers.

What is the cause, then, of modern technology's great aesthetic accomplishments that we find in machines, automobiles, aeroplanes, and so on? Through seeking the causes of these results, one aimed to find a clue that could be applied to the other fields of art. Modern technology's results come on the one hand from science's knowledge about nature that has been accumulated from generation to generation. On the one hand, technology's quest for the correct and purposive forms – for the mean, to use Aristotle's word – from standard to standard. This quest is liberated from national boundaries and sentimental constraints. Technology with the aid of the natural sciences has defined the aesthetics of the era. We all feel, when we see a modern automobile, aeroplane or a locomotive on the Bergen line, if you will, that these represent forms that are entirely new and peculiar to our age. They are not characteristic of it merely in their dynamic and powerful traits, but also the conciseness and usefulness of these objects' form appeal immediately to contemporary man.

The line of thought in modern technology is closely related to classical Greek thinking. The historical development of the car and the aeroplane in this sense is also parallel with that of the Doric temples. The latter's form was likewise gradually refined in that each new temple was built based on its forbears with minor changes leading to increasingly greater clarity and expressiveness in proportions. A relative of the Doric spirit is revived in machine technology, a spirit that expresses our era's dynamics just as clearly as the spirit in the Parthenon is expressed through eternal balance and order.

The architect Le Corbusier writes in his book *Vers une architecture*:

> There are millions of countenances constructed on these essential [facial] lines; nevertheless all are different. We say that a face is handsome when the precision of the modelling and the disposition of the features reveal proportions which we feel to be harmonious because they arouse, deep within us and beyond our senses, a resonance, a sort of sounding-board which begins to vibrate. An indefinable trace of the Absolute which lies in the depths of our being.

He goes on to say:

> This is indeed the axis on which man is organized in perfect accord with nature and probably with the universe, this axis of organization which must indeed be that on which all phenomena and all objects of nature are based; this axis leads us to assume a unity of conduct in the universe and to admit a single will behind it. The laws of physics are thus a corollary to this axis, and if we recognize (and love) science and its works, it is because both one and the other force us to admit that they are prescribed by this primal will. If the results of mathematical calculation appear satisfying and harmonious to us, it is because they proceed from the axis.

Out of this a definition of terms is possible: the factor for concord with the innate axis in the human being and thus also with the universal "Return to universal law".

Le Corbusier's axis dares to respond somewhat to Aristotle's mean. In nature we find an infinite number of forms that correspond to Aristotle's mean and Le Corbusier's axis. The following are a few examples from this world full of beauty and richness: the lion's mane and strength, the eagle's wings, the sheep's wool, the peacock's feathers, the flower's blossom, the ear of corn, the leaves of trees, the spider's web, the mussels' shells, and so on. All are forms that Darwin has shown to have a historical development parallel with what we have seen in the Parthenon and the aeroplane – namely a foundation in the law of natural selection and of survival of the fittest.

In this respect, nature, art and mathematics form a triangle.

All of them follow the same inviolable laws.

We find it necessary to admit that in our modern art of building, the axis has yet to be found. Le Corbusier and others have sought to point the way towards progress. By using the construction methods in the building art of our era and showing the utmost consideration for contemporary life and its demands – consistently and with mathematical logic – one will be able, he thinks, to achieve the objective in the long run.

Le Corbusier shows that great results have already been achieved by American engineers using their new industrial facilities, as well as partially in skyscrapers, bridges, and so on – in brief, in constructions that have come into existence based on the same conceptual basis as the machine. He also shows beauty in the pure geometric forms: the cube, the cylinder, the cone, the sphere, and so on, and shows how fine architecture from the age of the ancient Egyptians and Greeks employs these forms. The Gothic alone broke from this tradition, but the Gothic in its highest form was not built on free logic, either. It seeks to express the improbable and superhuman and exists essentially in a context with the mysticism and dogmatic beliefs and strongly religious attitude of the entire era: it is a religious drama; it is, I think, an expression of the era's will to find latitude for its thinking, to seek upwards – in the absence of the opportunity to seek outwards.

Le Corbusier underscores the capital importance of a conscious mathematical proportioning such as Antiquity employed, and he emphasizes how the architecture of our time should strive to attain the same pure, logical clarity as Antiquity and to learn from its devotion to the right angle. In this respect he means the right angle as properties of the trabeation and bearing elements. In making buildings the right angle is the only natural alternative with the construction methods of our age, iron and concrete. To apply lancet and semi-circular arches over common window openings and the like is to create for oneself complications that have been overcome several hundreds of years ago. Likewise, there is little point in applying excessive wall thicknesses, especially where plots are expensive and the price per cubic metre of construction is high. In addition, out of concern for light, such wall thicknesses with their deep mediaeval window niches are objectionable in modern buildings.

Architecture based on predominant and distinct window surfaces and a light and airy appearance should be able to provide a truer and thus more beautiful expression of our age's working and living environment rather than palatial façades with heavy and imposing wall surfaces.

Another factor of paramount importance is that the application of concrete permits the use of completely flat roofs. Gable roofs were originally necessary since they were constructed of wood. They constricted the shaping of our cities to a great extent. With the use of flat roofs made of concrete one achieves, besides fireproofing and a valuable roof terrace, a far greater freedom of design, both for the individual buildings and the streets. In detached houses, one avoids the symmetrical axes that pointed roofs normally constitute, and one is thereby freer in outlining the individual rooms on the exterior. In the streets one is no longer restricted to placing the buildings in a line, but can instead stagger them and thereby take advantage of sun and light from all directions. Modern architects in the central European countries put inordinately great emphasis on the social aspect of modern architectural issues. They point to the fact that architecture's tasks today have become different and more comprehensive than in earlier times.

The primary and greatest requirement for architecture is the demand for a plan for both the city and the individual buildings – and this plan must solve traffic, sanitary and economic prerequisites, all of which are new to our age.

All of these requirements entail demand for saving labour – both in the construction of the buildings and in their use. Labour saving, in the opinion of these same architects, should in most cases be attainable through the use of modern materials and a consistent typification and standardization of both the building's specific parts and the buildings themselves in the same manner as automobiles. These architects therefore foresee the future of housing as one of mass production, whereby every type will be tested and subject to improvements aimed at optimal utility. They imagine construction sites of the future as huge factories with modern work methods.

Architects of various nationalities have worked with these issues, and the newer architectural concepts have already created nationally and locally distinctive forms.

We will scarcely be able to adopt and develop these new ideas here at home before we have addressed our great enthusiasm for our nation's heritage and submitted it for some revision.

This enthusiasm has had, and still has, a great mission. Without it, there would have been no 1905. However, in recent times it appears, in our architecture at least, that it points backwards rather than forwards in time. An organization has been created, and with public sympathy for the effort, to preserve our heritage; this deserves all due respect, and the organization should well serve as a model for work in the future. If one examines it sober-mindedly, however, one must admit that our traditions, at least with regards to monumental architecture, are extremely meagre. For more than five centuries, from the cathedral in Trondheim to the royal castle and the university, we can hardly point to a single monumental building of European dimensions.

Therefore, we probably face a long-term process of development in this area.

There are two types of infatuation with our past that are of interest to us.

The first is the enthusiasm for our old rural culture. It was originally a wholesome national pride and interest that has now in part become a caricature. The imitations of our good rural buildings, which one frequently finds in urban residential areas, are distorted misrepresentations of our rural culture. Rural art was created by a spirit that through daily toil was in contact with nature, and this can never be interpreted or reproduced by urban romantics with drafting pencils and rubbers between their fingertips without losing its character and aesthetic value. This is a manifestation of the upper class's flirtation with the primitive, just as with jazz music and the like. The continually recurrent comparison between the rural dwelling and the monumental building appears to rely on a high degree of confusion of terms.

Our other infatuation with the past is an interest in surviving styles. This was also originally a very healthy interest. Its importance is in achieving an understanding of what old styles entail in regard to ideas. They appear to be expressions of certain eras' ways of thinking and living in certain places and have all developed on the basis of the construction methods of different ages. As ways of thinking and living have changed and the various ages' arsenal in the battle between materials and perishability has developed, so also have styles changed. Because changes in living and thinking and principles of construction have come from the outside, as previously indicated, so have the changes in our styles come from the outside. A style dies when a new way of thinking, way of life, emerges, just as an animal species dies out when a new, stronger one emerges, or as the method for producing saltpetre is abandoned when a new, better one comes along, or as an older, previous model is discarded when a newer, better one is found. This does not preclude that one can continue to preserve old Ford models and old styles and old species of animals in museums, and that in special cases they can still fill certain needs. When, for example, a building for the Oseberg ship is to be made, it may be appropriate to accentuate the silent wave of national reminiscences that are an expression of the fact that the building houses a faded, yellowed page of our history. But imitations of old styles cannot be living art because the living environment is lacking.

The consequences of this reasoning are wide-ranging. It is unfortunately not possible to "revive the Gothic spirit in our time", as was proposed in connection with the restoration of the Trondheim Cathedral. In such as case, one of two procedures must be chosen.

On the one hand, one can place historical interest ahead of the architectonic and try to create a Gothic that is as close to the original style as possible, accepting that it will none the less never be a living work of art. And eventually the result of this approach will also be a historical self-deception since one will never know exactly how the church originally appeared.

On the other hand, one might proceed in the manner of all previous, conscious art eras and continue to work based on the spirit of our own time and seek to express ideas that are in harmony with contemporary circumstances. It may then perhaps become a living work of art. In the days of Archbishop Eystein, no one entertained the thought of continuing the project as it had begun: in the Romanesque style. Instead, renewal was sought in the contemporary ideas of Europe at the time. During recent years we have worked our way through a maze of styles. We have witnessed the construction of residences, one after the other, with interiors in every style imaginable, like small museums of architecture in the most tasteful designs.

The generation that tumbled into all of this ten years ago reacted instinctively against this equilibrism. One had to ask oneself: is it really possible that all of European humanity's ways of thinking in all their diversity and spanning a couple of millennia can be kneaded together and baked into a tasty bread, even though the sourdough is Norwegian? The result was a quest for contemporaneity, simplification, clarity and unity in purpose. Later, everything that was unnecessary and deemed useless was thrown overboard, with the exception of that which was most closely related to this approach, namely: classicism. Here at home, and certainly also in other countries, we have undergone quite a struggle for liberation.

We have now come so far in our development here that we have planted our feet firmly on Norwegian ground and want to try new approaches.

I take the liberty straight away of making a certain reservation concerning Le Corbusier and some of his contemporaries. Their watchword is that the house is a machine for living. This is perhaps nothing more than a motto, an artistic overstatement, but in its consequences it entails a new romanticism: machine romanticism. It is just as wrong as calling the machine a house of forces. On that basis, the machine would never have attained its axis. A house is a house, and that should suffice.

There is an essential difference between what we commonly understand by the terms machine and house; we become aware of the difference already in the comparison of, for example, a canon or a turbine with machines that people come into contact with in their daily lives, for example, an automobile. By nature people have a certain urge for superfluity. A room can be built on the principle of the machine and executed with all of the noblest art, but something is lacking. The moment we get some pictures on the wall or perhaps a well-dressed table, it becomes a house. But not just anybody can achieve this, and particularly not in a form that harmonizes with the character of the rest of the house. In this respect it is the architecture itself that must provide something.

Everywhere in nature we find superfluity as a paramount factor in beauty. The tail plumage of the peacock is completely superfluous – but not for the peacock himself. This urge for superfluity is important to take into consideration. It is what creates the perpetually recurrent development in art from Classicism to the Baroque. We might term this minor or major superfluity which people always covet as the "smile" in our existence. It must be admitted that technology already has gone far in the direction of providing us with this "smile". All we have to do is sit in a common Ford to feel that Fortune is smiling upon us, and if you and I, gentlemen, were to take a ride in a Rolls Royce or take a jaunt over the Atlantic in an aeroplane, we would certainly feel that we were on the way to celebrating victory over all surmounted difficulties, which one might call technology's baroque. Superfluity, however, must always lie within the framework of unity in purpose.

With this reservation, we will return to the basic notion in the new, yet otherwise very old ideas: it was that the architect should first and foremost dedicate himself to creating unity from all of the factors that each individual task entails. That is to say, not only factors such as materials and finances, and so on, but also factors of climate and terrain and people's temperament – in brief *all of the common and local factors* must be taken into account. To proceed in any other way precludes attaining the axis. The whole is like a finished painting from which no single colour can be removed or borrowed from another painting, or like an unending chain from which no single link can be removed without severing the whole. Olaf Bull says:

> But everything in distant orbits scattered
> That darkly whisper at each other yonder
> Must somehow die – and as mere spirits wander
> And gather 'neath my forehead's heaven tattered

If we turn to the treatment of these things in the scattered orbits, examine their character, we can then suitably classify them in the following manner:

1 consideration of climate and terrain;
2 consideration of construction and materials;
3 consideration of planning requirements;
4 economic considerations;
5 the architect's personal contribution.

The first point: *consideration of climate and terrain* is the constant factor we have to deal with, a constant to each individual site.

If this consideration were the only one we had to take into account, it is clear that architecture would eventually find a final type, like the bees' cell, which would be the only right one for each place, a local classicism that we would be obliged to accept. But things are not this simple. The consideration of local factors will obviously have a great impact on the design of the buildings. If the terrain is steep, one must seek other solutions than for flat terrain, just as a harsh weather climate requires other forms than a mild climate does. These local conditions compel us in the long run to find local building traditions. And the local building traditions comprise a very valuable corpus of practical experience and, in addition, of popular temperaments. The conditions mentioned here naturally impede development. They have not been so imposing, however, that they have prevented us here or in our neighbouring countries from keeping pace with all international currents of style. Even our local building traditions have gone through continual changes.

If we look at *the consideration of materials and construction principles*, we encounter the factors that have always created development in our traditional architecture. These factors essentially compel modern Norwegian architectural methods to be different from those of earlier eras. Since concrete and iron constructions primarily build upon mathematical calculations, one must also primarily build on international experiences with these materials' properties, as long as the law of gravity persists in being an international standard.

One must expect that concrete and iron will be used increasingly in our cities. But shouldn't one also expect that they will be used more and more in the residential suburbs? Solely from the point of view of the fire risk when using wood, this alternative must be considered of national, financial benefit. The consistent use of concrete also implies that one should construct roofs of this material and that they should be cast flat. There is no impelling reason to continue to keep the slanted roofs typical of wooden constructions. On the contrary: considerations of light and the danger of snow slides from rooftops, which entails an increasingly greater risk the higher one builds and the more traffic there is, are compelling arguments for using flat rooftops here at home as well. Besides this, our building traditions show that in intensely cold areas during winter, there is a tendency to construct roofs such that they retain snow as long as possible over the building.

A change such as this – a transition to the use of flat, concrete roofs – will constitute a radical change in the appearance of our cities. The slanted roof is the factor in residential areas that forces us to make urban dwellings in a straight line. With the disappearance of slanted roofs, one can at the same time adopt the newer principles involving the staggering of houses in relation to one another in order to take maximum advantage of sunlight and fresh air. This concept is very suitable to our conditions.

Another freedom that concrete offers, and which must be regarded as equally revolutionary in our building traditions, is freedom in the span of openings.

Thanks to the possibilities of concrete and iron, the appearance of our commercial buildings and particularly of shop windows should be able to undergo a fundamental change. What purpose is served with shop windows only a few metres wide and tediously covered with rounded arches when one can build them five metres wide and more with these materials? Our shop windows, at least in larger commercial buildings, should be able to become small theatre stages with lighting effects and more. Thus, the appearance of our streets can be given a larger and more daring scale, as well as a festive aura. The horizontal design of windows must be considered as having practical application to our residential areas. The sun is low in our country and casts its rays relatively far into the rooms. But it is weak, and it is advantageous to preserve sunlight for as much time during the day as possible. By the same token, this is a desirable effect since we use low storey heights in order to conserve heat. In our traditional log constructions in the valleys, wide and low windows have frequently been used.

If we follow the natural dissemination of ideas out to the rural districts, we see that the new materials have also begun to compete with other materials in certain areas. Especially in foundations as well as in barns and stalls they will undoubtedly become more and more common and will characterize our rural buildings. The Norwegian farmer has always been receptive to any practical and technical progress. Concrete is easy to apply and the materials as a rule are readily available.

The third concern is *the consideration of planning requirements.* Requirements that arise are often closely related to the ability to meet them. Because modern technology has solved problems in the areas of construction, traffic and finances better than ever before, requirements have emerged in terms of the best possible exploitation of the accomplishments of that technology. Here we encounter Darwin's law of the survival of the fittest. The age of overly thick walls, of picturesque but impractical plan effects, is over. And how are they faring, our beloved old wooden roof trusses and raftered ceilings and cross-vaults that looked so attractive in our plan layouts about ten years ago?

All of them, unfortunately, have had to yield to modern requirements for fire safety, finances and cleanliness. About 400 years ago Michelangelo won immortal honour as the greatest genius of his age when he constructed the St Peter's dome, namely in 1558–1560. Today any brick mason can build a dome in iron and concrete just as large and in as many months as Michelangelo used years. In terms of constructing coverage of space, these materials seem to offer us absolutely fantastic opportunities. And why not take advantage of them?

If we then look at *the social and economic consideration* in modern architecture, many, including me, will undoubtedly feel they confront a much uncultivated field. Our age has created entirely new ways of perceiving. As mentioned, French and German architects stress the importance of a consistent standardization and typification, with the goal in mind to save labour.

Sporadic attempts have been made here at home with certain technical components: windows, doors, and the like, but so far they appear to have come out of our "national" chaos of style and individual tastes. In the old days of the "alen" measuring unit, there was at least one form of standardization here in this country that could be profitably returned to, and that was the standardization of the length of wooden materials. After the individualistic ideas of the Romantic era victoriously swept the country, along with the metric measuring system, it seems to have become a point of honour for a person to build the living room 20 centimetres wider than the neighbour's. If one could return to the old measuring system, there would undoubtedly be many a joist end saved. And although our market is small and personal desires many, one might wish that the ideas of the modern age could lead to a further increase in standardization and that our construction budgets could be improved accordingly.

The commonly shared urge to have one's own house independent of all others and located in the centre of one's own little kingdom, has resulted in urban residential areas emerging around our cities during recent decades. Satisfaction of this urge will presumably be revealed to be very expensive in the long run, if it will occur in the forms seen thus far. It requires vast areas of valuable land. A major part of this land, in a country that is poor in arable land, could be more profitably used for vegetable nurseries, and so on, which could then serve as the natural kitchen gardens for our cities. Because they now are located far away from the city, all agricultural products supplied to the city have become more expensive. At the same time, the owners of suburban residences are further and further removed from their place of work, and society is subjected to great costs for the construction and maintenance of a considerable network of roads, septic and water systems, and so on. The design of residential gardens is impractical, and the buildings are costly. In addition, since experience shows that these residences are completely demolished when fires occur, common sense should dictate that it is time for a revision of these building principles. During the years 1920–24 a total of some 125 million Norwegian kroner has been paid for fire losses. If one calculates uninsured losses, it can be calculated that damages have amounted to between 140 and 150 millions. This level of loss can be attributed primarily to the fire hazard nature of our building methods. The question is whether we can afford in our impoverished nation to subject ourselves and our descendants to fire-loss costs in this manner?

A residential area constructed of modern concrete buildings and placed wall-to-wall, or staggered in relation to the street line providing light and fresh air and with deep, narrow gardens – must be considered a more contemporary and economical solution to this problem. In other countries there has been a transition towards splitting up newly regulated developments of this kind and delegating to the individual architects the task of planning the entire street in order to achieve the necessary unity. In this connection, we might mention the German architects' ideas concerning application of colour in the urban environment in order to bring in overall atmosphere and beauty. These are ideas that can be suitably applied to our nation as well.

But in order to implement ideas such as these, it will require organization and promotion. Is it not a task of architects to make people aware of the fact that the way the country is to be built is a greater and more important question in society with regard to economy, sanitation, morals and culture than the majority of issues that politicians adopt as election platforms? Impractical building arrangements cannot, unfortunately, be removed by popular referendum. They will remain as our descendants' heritage for hundreds of years.

We then come to the final point in this development: *the architect's personal contribution.* Those who must assume the task of adapting the ideas are architects. We thus broach the subject of Norwegian distinctiveness and personality in architecture. In order to be an indispensible link in the structure of society, it should be the architect's task in our age to evaluate all requirements objectively in relation to one another, including to seek out what Aristotle called the mean. The greatest identity and the greatest degree of Norwegian distinctiveness is then found in that which gathers the largest possible amount of objective considerations such as they are found in Norwegian circumstances today, with a unity as objective. It is therefore self-evident that development must be based on what the history of art has taught us: that the strongest national and personally informed architecture as a rule emerges at the end of an epoch. The national, local and personally informed architecture is the final goal of the development. When this goal is reached, architecture fades like autumn leaves in a richness of nuances and eventually collapses in introspection. Even though the requirements for architecture in our time are greater and more numerous than at any other time previously, there should none the less be a need for Norwegian distinctiveness and for the invisible personal power to attain something other than meaningless ornamentation. It is not convincing when one purports to possess a distinctively Norwegian point of view.

The Norwegian temperament has always manifested itself as receptive to the impulses of all eras of style, with a pronounced aptitude for proportions, a simple and powerful artistic idiom and healthy common sense. The Norwegian temperament is the product of a daily struggle and co-existence with a natural environment that comprises all nuances, from the pleasant idyll to the lush fertility and voluptuousness of mountainous nature. As a result, there are many types of Norwegians: from the miller boy who sits watching the cascading whirlpool beneath the millstone wheel and plays the fiddle, while the waterfall gushes next to him and overwhelms him with its rush against the mountain wall, blurring his vision as it gushes over the trunk of a birch tree, to the man who harnesses the waterfall in pipes, builds a factory and provides light for the valley.

It is true that there have always been and always will be two forces that are prevalent in a national development, the one extroverted, seeking and fumbling after an expression of the life and thoughts of the contemporary, the other introverted, collecting from the prism of time the popular temperament that will colour these thoughts. Neither can do without the other, for there are few people who harbour an equal degree of both forces within them. Specifically in our age, when considerations that must be forged into a unity are so many and so varied, it is superhuman to think that this can be done through a single individual or a few. One has time and development on one's side. We might consider one another as rowers on two sides of the same boat. If one side should stop rowing, the others would then row in a circle. If the rowers on one side of the boat are displeased with the course, they may begin to row forwards, so that the mean in Norwegian architecture can be attained.

Sketch by Carsten Boysen

1933

PLAN

Our Agenda

All intellectual life, all theoretical thinking, is dependent for its development on the existing material and social context of the time.

When within a certain profession there is a crass difference of opinion, when there are sharp theoretical oppositions, it is the result of the occurrence of a fundamental change in the profession's social circumstances – in the material and economic basis for its activity.

Norway has been left behind in the social development that has caused a profound international revolution in the architect's work and way of thinking.

This applies not only to our profession's technology; to an equally high degree, it applies to the profession's social side. In other countries, the new architecture has not been merely a breakthrough in the field of building methods. It has meant not only a break with the aesthetic premises of the past, but with the entire old apparatus of style. It has also been a social current. New social demands have forced architects to assume new working methods that rely primarily on scientific analysis of the functions that must be met and of the constructive possibilities that currently exist. The architect has become the organizer of construction activities. At the same time, however, in his urban planning he has been confronted with the task of organizing people's lives. The lack of a solution to the housing problem, the insolvability of urban planning problems within the framework of existing society have resulted in many architects, through their organizational work, being driven out of their traditional professional isolation and into increasingly more conscious social activity.

The functionalists' endeavour to establish optimal planning and purpose in the building industry is not only a technical tidying-up operation. In reality it represents a reaction – at least an unconscious reaction – against the lack of planning in capitalistic society. What the functionalists have lacked is a clear acknowledgement of the fact that the roots for this lack of planning are found in social circumstances. But one does not acquire an understanding of the social developments that are unfolding by isolating oneself in one's work within a special professional field. Only when the professional considers his field as a link in a larger social context will he begin to acquire a comprehensive overview of it.

In a number of European countries, groups of architects have come into existence that share a conscious social attitude towards the problems in building and urban planning, groups that have also discerned the political consequences of this view of society. The theoretical clarity that these groups represent is a result of three factors – of open-minded debate on professional issues, of socialist studies and of active participation in the struggle of the working class. An objective discussion of the problems of our profession, just as in all other professions, leads out of logical necessity to a socialist conclusion.

In a certain sense, functionalism's purely technical propaganda is a necessary intermediary for a socialist notion of architecture. Functionalism entails a technical-scientific view of the work of architects; it is necessary to have acquired this perspective and to have spurned all forms of artistic dilettantism if one is to be able at all to recognize that the problems of architecture are a social problem.

But as socialist architects, we direct the objection against politically neutral functionalists that they see the problem of architecture in too narrow a perspective. They do not carry reasoning to its logical conclusion; they will not take a stand on the class struggle that is ongoing. They refuse to acknowledge that it is this class struggle alone and its result, the working class's conquest of power, that can establish the foundation for making their own ambitious work agenda reality.

In the larger countries, functionalist propaganda has cleared the ground for the socialist architects' further theoretical efforts. Here in Norway, the land to be cleared is overgrown. But even though our task is made difficult because we are unable in Norway to find support in any "functionalist" forbears' theoretical work, we can nevertheless reap benefits from the fact that we are delayed in the international development. We can learn from the experiences of our predecessors in other countries, and we can attempt to avoid the pitfalls.

It is natural for us to question and examine their work as we launch the publication of a socialist periodical for architecture.

Our predecessors

Le Corbusier is the name associated with the first comprehensive modern theory that treats urban planning in the context of layout and architectonic design of the individual buildings. And Le Corbusier's buildings remain textbook examples not only for sober modern architecture, but also for Funkis.

The premises for modern architecture are on the one hand the industrialized method of production, and on the other, the new, complicated needs that have emerged. Le Corbusier embarked on a discovery journey in the fairy-tale land of new technology; he refined on the basis of intellect all of the possibilities available to the engineers and architects of our age, and he gave free flight to his own fantasy and demonstrated the kind of superior results that can be accomplished with the aid of technology.

Applying an equally keen view, he synthesized in the broadest sense the sanitary requirements of both the dwelling and the city – requirements for airiness, spaciousness, all of the dwelling's remaining requirements designed to serve both the basic living functions and the more complicated needs that characterize the modern dweller.

In Le Corbusier's mind, all of these factors were crystallized for the first time in unified theory.

His practical works must be regarded essentially as experiments. In certain isolated building projects, he attempts to realize the wide-ranging planning opportunities that society is not yet mature enough to implement in the urban organism as a whole.

Le Corbusier's new "style" was not popular amongst the general public. France is a nation of petit bourgeois. And their lack of self-confidence makes him more strongly bound to tradition than the upper middle class on the one hand, and the working class on the other.

When Le Corbusier met approval, it was from a number of art connoisseurs and bourgeois cultured gentry in his circle of acquaintances. His practical activity would consist principally in building their villas. These were people in pursuit of the romantic *Zeitgeist*; people who fervently wanted to express their infatuation through their own surroundings, in their residences and their places of business.

Because Le Corbusier was unable to achieve any interrelations between his practical works and the general building industry in society at large, his theories were often characterized as pure flights of fantasy.

Le Corbusier has no grasp of the social and economic factors that cause the currently insolvable traffic and housing problems in the large cities. His plans for the future cities represent a somewhat one-sided, technically oriented architect's daydream.

These cities of the future are in their planning organized strictly in a technical sense; the traffic problems are solved by overpasses at all intersecting points, by elevated railways and underground trains. Skyscrapers are conceived to house offices for business and administration that we find today in the urban centres. Le Corbusier does not comprehend that the very existence of the urban concentration – the creation of cities with vast business complexes that have no direct tie to production and transport of goods – is precisely the result of the capitalist lack of planning.

The technical planning solution that Le Corbusier fantasizes to be a solution to urban problems has as a prerequisite a society organized as a planned economy. But with this planned economy, the very need for a city complex, as imagined by Le Corbusier for his future city, disappears.

Le Corbusier's Gratte-ciel project is the work of an imaginative poet. It demonstrates in a graphic way the possibilities of modern technology – but as a serious attempt at solving the problems of the large cities, it is a kind of gigantic future anachronism.

In terms of form, we encounter already in Le Corbusier a tendency that has been incorporated in all "functionalism", namely the tendency to apply the forms of industrial technology even to those areas of production still based on the work of craftsmen. The germination of "functionalist" tendencies – of formal superficiality, of mechanical romanticism and steamship motifs – was already present in Le Corbusier.

Germany

The German architects have contributed greatly towards solving the problem: the minimum dwelling type. First, the German municipalities' building associations made these kinds of dwellings *en masse*. During the enormous building activity in the post-war period, the Germans developed and refined all of the specific building designs that modern architecture uses today. Modern principles for urban planning were also scientifically informed during this period in conjunction with wide-ranging practical applications.

It may appear surprising that such an abundance of tasks arose during precisely the time when Germany was, economically speaking, on her knees and with all of her resources practically exhausted. It is necessary to become aware of the social premises for this construction activity in order to understand how it would eventually transform the architects' way of thinking.

The great building activity in Germany during the post-war years was a phenomenon of crisis.

On a grander scale than ever before, we see repeated here a characteristic phase in the crises of capitalist society. At a point in the development of the crisis when industrial production has totally collapsed, no new capital is placed in industrial activity. Available capital then gravitates to the building industry, which still offers a profit potential for a while longer during the crisis. Because building is relatively unprofitable during normal times, it is frequently neglected during periods of high conjuncture, with a resulting increased demand for housing during the period. This in turn contributes towards making housing production once again profitable during the time immediately following the breakout of the crisis.

This ordinary crisis development that had come to bear during the pre-war years was greatly exacerbated in its consequences because of the particular social and political conditions that existed in Germany during and after the war. Although private capital – entrepreneurs and producers of materials – reaped considerable incomes from residential construction, the undertaking was administered and planned by the public sector. German social democrats inherited administrative power after the revolution. The intense level of housing construction that aimed to a great extent at meeting the needs of the working class was a tribute to the "victorious" German working class. It was an effective means of dulling the revolutionary murmurings of some of the workers who were not entirely content with the social democratic victory. The fact that this was implemented with an extremely hard-handed disregard for property owners' rights through widespread expropriations was first and foremost a benefit for German industrial capital. A further inflation of property owners' rights through high tenancy fees in newly constructed buildings would have necessitated higher wages; and this would have weakened German industry's international competitiveness during the post-war reconstruction period.

Because the intense level of housing construction was carried out during an era of extreme impoverishment, when profitability was possible only through the application of industrial methods of production and the use of appropriate materials, it naturally followed that all sentimental and formal, aesthetic concerns had to be disregarded.

Out of this hard-handed process came the new basic forms of construction that lay the groundwork for the new architecture.

The new ways of building were welcomed as examples that could be emulated equally as well in private residences as in commercial complexes. They became effective guidelines in the hands of anyone who was clever enough to put them into play. The new materials were no longer merely exploited for their economic capacity – iron, glass and concrete were pushed to the breaking point.

The German architects became intoxicated on architectonic forms. But this dramatic architecture was at the same time a means by which to strengthen the illusion that Germany was experiencing a new period of economic vitality.

Some of the architects who were active in this period of intense building would eventually look back on both the construction activity as a whole and their own contributions from a social point of view. In their later work, these people have also carried out a considerable propaganda campaign, an aim concentrating on Bauhaus Dessau and Frankfurt am Main.

In addition, the German architectural press, which should actually provide the clearest expression of the guidelines that the profession as a whole follows, has assumed the form that is common to all architectural periodicals around the world, a form that has apparently become permanent once and for all. The primary task is seemingly to provide pictorial coverage of the latest architectural compositions – a rewarding task that is not difficult to accomplish to the satisfaction of all. The new residential buildings have indeed enjoyed wide exposure in the German periodicals. But when the buildings become the object of theoretical examination, they are frequently seen only from technical or aesthetic perspectives. The German architect profession as a whole, out of deference to its own social position and its financial dependence on the bourgeoisie, cannot acknowledge the real social basis for the new current in architecture. They will absolutely not acknowledge the true nature of their own social position. The German architectural press, then, is cut off from being able to consider building issues from a social angle. Their comments concerning the undertakings of architects are therefore doomed to lose contact with reality, to become loftier and loftier and more and more prone to philosophical jargon.

One factor that contributes to forming the character of the architectural press is simply that many of the periodicals operate as veritable publishing companies, or represent special interests of the producers of building materials. The fact, therefore, that this objective – to appeal to the affluent public's taste – will point the way for these periodicals, is obvious.

Denmark

But is it after all impossible to imagine an architectural periodical that consciously attempts to spearhead the development of architecture rather than merely following in its wake?

Why shouldn't such a periodical be able to stand in opposition to the architect's narrow professional interests as well as to the affluent public's demand for the most recent fashion in architecture?

Fate has not decided that such periodicals must be content with the quite cloudy notion that there are countless interactions between the construction industry and rest of society's processes. On the contrary. Nor is there anything preventing us from imagining an architectural periodical that generates propaganda openly and directly: propaganda for a lucidly led, socially-oriented construction industry as its primary task, and for a sober design as one of many subordinate tasks; propaganda opposing dawdling and incompetence on the part of public institutions, and opposing unconscionable speculation on the part of private interests.

One might expect to find such periodicals in those countries where the development of society is most advanced and the class oppositions are sharpest. This is because the most conscious, theoretical clarity always emerges in conjunction with the class that is on the verge of taking over power in society, and which is aware of its own growing strength.

Therefore, it is surprising at first glance that the only architectural periodical which has to a certain extent possessed the ideals we have listed, surfaced in Denmark.

Kritisk Revy – eleven editions that were published from 1926 to 1928 – did not arise due to the fact that Denmark had witnessed new societal needs that made new demands on the building industry and architects. What characterizes *Kritisk Revy* is that the periodical represents, so to speak, the only tangible result in Denmark of all of the new impulses from German architecture and German building activity. The architects who founded the periodical had no other important field of work that could serve as an outlet for their professional competence and passion for performing rational, socially edifying work.

Housing construction in Denmark was not implemented under the same economic pressure as in Germany. The Danish cooperative housing associations built traditionally for a petit-bourgeois public and were basically uninfluenced by any current whatsoever from the rest of Europe. The steadily uninterrupted prosperity with good opportunities to earn profits in all fields made it entirely unnecessary to resort to any forced housing projects in order to allow capital to generate profits.

Kritisk Revy experienced to a very great extent that its struggle for rational and grand-scale housing construction encountered crucial societal obstacles. It was of course impossible to transfer German accomplishments to Denmark. The societal needs and opportunities for meeting them were much too different for that to happen.

Kritisk Revy was read by the Danish bourgeoisie because of the periodical's wit and because it had the character of a mondaine European radicalism.

Regarding the opportunity to realize the periodical's true agenda, the editorial staff itself had abdicated. Already in the first editorial it was said that "productively and creatively, we can solve only a humble part; but critically and pedagogically, the right direction can be shown".

And the criticism that the periodical published was indeed vociferous. The entire Danish petite-bourgeoisie – in terms of housing, representational edifices, bric-à-brac artistry – was highlighted in all its absurdity. The periodical's staff proved to be mature and experienced journalists who had mastered the art of administering fatal thrusts of the sword.

The "pedagogical" part of their activity consisted in propagandizing for technical and aesthetic purity, hammering in the point that an efficient and rational solution to the working class's housing problem was the most significant task that architects of the time had to face.

In terms of further practically carrying out this task, *Kritisk Revy* had little confidence – as well they shouldn't – in the sitting social democratic government. In what way, then, could the periodical establish the solid groundwork that would be necessary for the carrying out of their task?

It was on this issue that the staff lost focus. They failed to draw the consequences of the fact that a solution to the housing problem is a matter of the power relationship between the classes of society. *Kritisk Revy*

> works within the practical area and not the political . . . we do not wish to weaken the effort by entering into political discussions, even though we are fully conscious of a shared common agenda – the socially oriented way of thinking – and the shared common goal – better conditions for the general population.

Kritisk Revy could therefore not end up in any other way than it did. "We have no readership among the workers, and we have not assumed the task of educating the working class . . . We have assumed the task of influencing a limited circle of the intellectually interested bourgeoisie."

However, *Kritisk Revy* did not succeed in convincing this limited circle of the intellectually interested Danish bourgeoisie to reform the remainder of Denmark's petit bourgeois citizens.

Indeed *Kritisk Revy* was aware – and this in itself is true enough – that one becomes ineffective if one treats architecture in isolation; the act of building is not an isolated phenomenon, it must be seen in context with the rest of society's activities.

Kritisk Revy therefore discussed all manner of current issues. They did not limit themselves to Otto Linton's excellent articles on the art of engineering and bridge building, to evaluations of new building materials and techniques, or to the critical slaughter of the prevalent mania for environmental conservation. They also discussed the danger of cultural degradation in the field of music, they discussed the temperance movement, and Otto Gelsted wrote articles on religion and on the concept of society, in which he treated these issues from the perspective of Kant's philosophy.

Kritisk Revy itself considered this development thus:

> We wanted to create a periodical for the profession that would be read, and in that we have succeeded . . . The support that *Kritisk Revy* has by virtue of being a periodical for the architectural profession is sufficient to ensure its financial solvency for the time being . . . Let us now attempt to create a Nordic periodical for art.

Considering the technical realism that characterized the periodical at its inception, the proposal of this subsequent goal for its work can only be regarded as a decisive step backwards.

One result of *Kritisk Revy*'s activity, however, was that the publication's own staff eventually became increasingly aware of their own respective views, and thus also of the principle issues that would accompany development and gradually become divisive. The only reason for the periodical's demise was hardly the one given by the editors themselves – that they forfeited the battle because of the lack of talented adversaries.

Subsequently each member of the staff found his way to other pursuits. Poul Henningsen, who most strongly fronted the periodical, has developed towards a hybrid of bourgeois radicalism and lofty philosophy of art. Edvard Heiberg, on the other hand, who wielded the periodical's sharpest and most lucid pen – despite the fact that he wrote at the time primarily about shop furnishings and window displays and even criticized the bourgeois wholesale dealers for not doing these things elegantly enough – later went on to an active political career in the Communist party.

Sweden

After *Kritisk Revy* ceased publication, the role of leading architectural periodical in Scandinavia was assumed by the Swedish publication *Byggmästaren*.

Byggmästaren is the official organ of the Swedish Association of Architects. But when compared with other official architectural periodicals it holds quite a unique position. The periodical not only propagandizes for technically sound architecture; it does so from a perspective that is to a very great extent socially conscious. *Byggmästaren* is not afraid of launching sharp attacks on public authorities in cases where bureaucratic inflexibility puts excessively large obstacles in the path of rationally planned architectural endeavours. And *Byggmästaren* is absolutely adamant in its refusal to grant unconditional support in favour of the architectural profession's demand for a monopoly in work undertakings.

The Swedish architects are clearly different from their colleagues in other countries in certain respects. What are the special circumstances underlying this difference?

In the turbulent post-war years, Sweden was one of the European industrial nations in which social conditions were most stable; and during these years Sweden was inundated with capital that was transferred out of the uncertain central European states. The practically uninterrupted industrial and financial high conjuncture in Sweden during recent years is due precisely to this extraordinary influx of capital from abroad.

This high conjuncture has been significant not least of all for the building industry; it is seen not only in the scope of building projects, but also in the exterior design of the architecture itself. Through a furious process of expansion on the one hand and the nation's growing self-awareness on the other, its architecture has emerged in purified and clear lines. Even the youngest Swedish architects, because of the abundance of building commissions, have been able to attain a solid professional position and a financially successful existence. It is greatly due to the efforts of these architects that the new general European currents have influenced the new building industry in Sweden.

The prolonged prosperity in the industry has also caused salaried functionaries and the well-paid groups of workers to make greater demands on life, and at the same time has provided them with the financial resources to satisfy these demands.

The Swedish architects, therefore, have enjoyed more than the one-sided task of designing architecture for private residences and commercial buildings. In the intense cooperative construction of housing for the class of salaried workers and the worker aristocracy that has taken place, an entirely new field has in addition hereto opened up to architects, a field in which many of the impulses of building technology and planning techniques from Germany could be implemented. Due to the fact that this cooperative housing construction has been carried out method-ologically on a grand scale and over a lengthy period of time, the opportunity has arisen for collecting experiences, for designing rational plans for housing types, and for industrializing the construction work itself.

Furthermore, the large cooperative architectural firms, through their work in direct conjunction with a wide range of the population's classes, have gradually become conscious of the profession's social character. This consciousness has not been without influence in the rest of the architectural profession.

The Swedish architects, then, have avoided being relegated to work in isola-tion with their architecture; because of the prevailing circumstances, many of them have acquired a truly responsible relationship to their profession. In this way they have adopted the premises that have made it possible for them to free themselves from aesthetic formalism's restrictive constraints. The idiom of form itself is no longer what is primary. The design of buildings emerges, conversely, as an end result of competent, professional work in the service of housing design.

Functionalism does not mean, for Swedish architects, a style that they choose to follow; it is first and foremost a work agenda. Functionalism for them means housing construction executed with the most modern and effective technical aids.

This attitude shared by a decisive proportion of the Swedish architects was first strikingly expressed in the Stockholm Exhibition. But the Stockholm Exhibition also demonstrated that the architects had acknowledged their limita-tions in terms of solving the housing issue via an architectonic approach. The cal-culations that were presented show with full clarity that a satisfactory minimum dwelling can be built only at a price that would require a much greater mortgage than the common worker can afford to pay at the present time.

Here the architects have discovered during their technical work an entirely decisive factor. But they have not drawn the consequences of their discovery. They have yet to openly acknowledge that the most important issue in housing is to increase the wage level of the working class. Only a few of the Swedish architects have drawn the conclusion that the housing issue can be addressed by the worker class itself through the development of a socialist planned economy.

At any rate, it cannot be expected that the majority of the younger Swedish architects will take any significant standpoint on the current class struggle. Their contact with the working class, after all, has been limited to the wealthy, socially conservative, social-democratic worker aristocracy.

Byggmästaren has been led by the radical wing among architects. It is none the less obvious that when this group has been able to maintain their independent position – in relation to architecture, to the prejudices of their readers, to reac-tionary forces both within the profession itself and in the bourgeoisie at large – it is because of the prosperous times that have been enjoyed not only by the architec-tural society, but by Swedish trade and industry in general.

How will that attitude develop now, with private building stagnating, with the wage levels, including the portion of the working class that constructs housing, in rapid decline, when there is a risk that the number of new building commissions will decrease to a minimum?

It is obvious that the earlier grounds for *Byggmästaren*'s radical politics are crumbling.

There are scarcely more than two possibilities for further development. Either the leading people behind the periodical will be forced back into a neutral passivity and the periodical itself will become devoid of meaning, or a new, conscious group of socialist architects will emerge and carry the radical effort further, whether it happens within *Byggmästaren* or outside it.

Our agenda

For both *Kritisk Revy* and *Byggmästaren*, it can be said that they have gone to their task – propaganda for more rational building and urban planning – with professional responsibility and a social conscience. It is just as certain that they have hesitated in their propaganda at the critical points where the architects' opposition against professional subjectivity must necessarily translate into political opposition, in order to have any effect at all. Both periodicals capitulated in face of the obstacles of a social nature that impeded a consistent implementation of their technical and social work agenda.

This capitulation is first and foremost due to the fact that the people who issued the periodicals were unable to carry out an analysis of the true content of these obstacles. They abdicated and sought to soothe their consciences with the illusion that a competent professional effort requires political neutrality. But this neutrality relied to a great extent on the fear of taking a stand out of anxiety for losing one's livelihood. In reality, this fear represented a constraint on the theoretical work that they as professionals were to carry out. It brought about a clouding of issues and often diffuse, muffled terminology.

This periodical is unwaveringly and unequivocally grounded on the workers' movement. Through a consistent, socialist position, we will be able to overcome the kind of obstacles that stopped our predecessors amongst the radical architectural periodicals. If we achieve this, it will be less important whether the technical basis here in Norway is much narrower, because in our country there has not been the same kind of comprehensive and technically rational building as has occurred, for example, in Sweden.

The architectural profession in reality stands at the core of the transformational process that is occurring in society. The fact that the future holds tasks of unfathomable dimensions for the organizing and scientifically working architect is certain. But it is just as certain that the architect profession does not possess the subjective prerequisites that will be required. These prerequisites must be acquired through a conscientious effort. They comprise not only the factors pertaining to our profession's technology. They consist in an equally high degree of knowledge of societal conditions affecting the work we are to do. Our organizational work under the planned economy of the future will necessarily require a real under-standing of society's laws of development, of the social structure of cities, of relationships between the classes, industrial conditions, of their link with and eco-nomic independence from the rural areas, and so on. It will be asked of us to be able to work anonymously, in collaboration with social economists and hygienists, and that we actively participate in the socialist transformation in the service of the working class. But we will be capable of doing this only if we already now, while the working class wages its struggle against the current societal system, are willing to participate in this struggle and to place our professional knowledge at the disposal of the working class.

As the organ for an association of socialist architects, this periodical's primary task will be to discuss all of the issues involving construction from a socialist point of view.

Our goal for architects will be to demonstrate that building activity as it is cur-rently organized will be unable to fulfil the needs that are current and impending in society. We will seek to demonstrate the specific forms that capitalistic production anarchy takes in the special areas of the architectural profession, to demonstrate why this production anarchy is a result of capitalism in general and will remain so as long as capitalism exists.

Our goal in relation to the working class will be to attempt in our periodical to adapt the professional knowledge of architects in such a way that it can profitably be used in the ongoing working-class struggle. We must seek to demonstrate to what extent the existing technical possibilities are not being utilized in the con-struction industry which thus far has been operated for the purpose of meeting the housing needs of the working class. We must seek to make readers aware that thus far, only outmoded, impractical and overly expensive housing types have been built, and that this is partially due to the static, inflexible division of labour in the construction industry as it continues to exist today, causing building activity to stagnate at the craftsmanship stage.

Most architects still harbour the illusion that the housing issue can be solved within the capitalist society. Even within the working class itself, and among archi-tects who closely associate with the working-class movement, the standpoints taken on this paramount issue are hazy and hesitant. The technical material of the profession that currently exists provides a copious resource for dispelling this illu-sion when seen in context with the working class's present economic position and the current development of society. We will present this material, we will place it in its proper social context, and we will thereby contribute towards dissuading the working class from following an unsound housing policy during the years remaining before our nation, too, will achieve the reality of a socialist planned economy.

Own House by Arne Korsmo (with Christian Norberg-Schulz)

1952

PAGON

CIAM

The years between the world wars were full of vitality and renewed radicalism in far more than a political sense. But what has become of this vitality, of functionalism and of the power and enthusiasm with which its adherents once fought?

Today functionalism is thought to be hard and cold, devoid of humanity and of respect for the emotional. The result is the new cosiness in style that manifested itself during and after the war. Functionalism, however, was not a style; it was an agenda and a working method. It would have been better to further develop the socio-psychological factors in the agenda, rather than to abandon the entire programme. The latter leads one to venture astray in sentiment and unconscious respect for unsubstantial concerns of the day.

Functionalism was no panacea. It demanded that one immerse oneself intelligently in a working method and then apply it. Functionalism intended to associate the newly found opportunities with science's need to know, to organize and to apply. Today the patient is suspicious because the medicine failed to work instantly. The working method did not put down roots in this country; we addressed formal rather than structural issues and the result was Funkis, a functionalist style, rather than functionalism.

We stabilized our national values before the First World War. We raised our buildings with sound honesty, but this does not mean that we must refrain from expanding and altering them as we become more aware and acquire a better understanding of the interactions with the world around us. Paradoxically it can be said that our buildings must have the potential to be changed tomorrow; it is only then that we truly own them. The value of tradition is not denied, but because we understand and appreciate how the forms of the past emerged out of other circumstances, we do not wish to emulate them.

In spite of all, the world is headed towards an increasingly larger unity. Architects must acknowledge that the national can mean only a regional distinctive feature, a variant, within a larger context. But rather than develop a free and stimulating co-existence between all people who are on a similar economic level, a state that we are beginning to achieve, the struggle for material wealth has led us into our history's most pronounced era of petit-bourgeois tendencies. Our sense of the greater context drowns in narrow-minded concerns. There are only two options: stagnation or teamwork and development.

We cannot stagnate. If we do so, what then would we have to show for thirty years of social toil? Nor is teamwork easy, when we sit, every man in his castle, guarding a tin of deep-frozen living standards. The goal was to provide security for people in order to give them freedom to become active, so that the material and the intellectual could be fused into a common opportunity. But in our insecurity, we grasp at scattered fragments and knowledge from unfamiliar areas, and we concentrate on details without a context. What is the good of sparing a housewife two paces if, in the meantime, she has become divorced?

Is it not time to realize that the influence of architects can be greater than following a diluted development without raising a finger? Architects shape our surroundings. They must become aware that this is an educational task. They must awaken the needs of fellow citizens, teach them to see and coax them out of their sentimental routines. They must accept, understand and use the working methods of science and oppose subjective exhibitionism in architecture.

We are fully aware that architecture today is dependent on such tangible things as the national budget, the labour market and local politics. But it might be put another way: architecture is an expression of society as a whole and its relationship to other societies. Only by liberating ourselves from a personal and national narrow-mindedness and by joining a universal collaboration can we hope to achieve something of significance for our time. And this collaboration begins with group efforts, teamwork, at home. It requires both confidence and self-criticism.

The time is ripe to look at the agenda anew, to revise it in the light of new knowledge, to consider our resources and our needs. The potential for solutions are found in more advanced technology, independence from conventions, greater imagination. The time is ripe for an architecture that does not stabilize, out of fear, an outmoded state, but rather one that can stimulate and activate all of the surroundings in our increasingly changing lifestyle.

We must find the courage to reach out towards the future.

Housing?

The word "housing" today is associated only with a single, unchanging basic concept: a roof and walls for all citizens. This is correct. It is also a natural requirement for any nation that respects its fellow citizens. But how?

We build based on a number of premises established through residential planning and urban planning research. A house is designed to provide shelter for a family. The family is of a certain size and with certain particular interests, workplaces are located here or there, and based on these factors . . . we build.

A conclusion will generally be valid only if the premises leading up to it are correct.

The conclusions upon which we build are more and more critically scrutinized, first by ourselves, then by others.

A Swedish voice on the subject of a new residential area. Here precisely nothing takes place. A few children sit and play in a sandbox. A housewife goes down to the dairy shop and exchanges a few words with the shop assistant. This is a dead dormitory town in miniature.

Why does this occur? Why do artists live in attic flats rather than in three-room flats? Why do architects go to the pub – no matter how artificial it may be – rather than to any number of modern restaurants that they have designed themselves? Are the premises wrong, perhaps?

Is the family still a valid core unit, even though an increasingly growing divorce rate disintegrates marriages and creates bachelor fathers and single mothers with informal sexual relations in their newly transformed lifestyle?

Nursery schools, day care centres and similar institutions have children from crawling age until age seven – from morning until evening so that the mother can "be utilized in productivity". Industries have an increasing tendency to expand continuously and to centralize production geographically, so that young people must move from their homes to their place of work, resulting in the break-up of families earlier than previously.

Military service is beginning to approach a two-year period and will in all probability encompass both sexes.

Didn't someone propose a number of years ago that the very best parenting involved avoiding all disagreement with children? Is the nuclear family still a valid unit, and do we or do we not want it to remain so?

We build an urban residential area for 1,000 such families. It has "neighbourhood" and "common facilities" and "playgrounds" and a host of things that have been lacking before. It is completely designed, contracted and built in great haste because construction firms have become so large and have such large administrations that things must proceed quickly in order to be profitable. 4,000 people are provided shelter.

Yes, then it exists – the residential area. 4,000 people arrive by train, sleep, leave by train again – restless, rootless. A conscious person cannot avoid the feeling that one has been shovelled in along with 3,999 presumed equals. It is perhaps edifying to read in newspapers that one belongs to the 37.5 per cent who have become accustomed to eating in the kitchen, or the group of 59.3 per cent who no longer buy tables with lion legs. So what? What is wrong? We sometimes use the term "organic" out of deep respect for nature's simple laws of development.

To build an urban residential area consisting primarily of permanent, uniform housing is in itself fundamentally and flagrantly non-organic – and thus inhuman. One can logically posit that *no single* house is *entirely correct* for the family that will inhabit it. All of them are calculated based on the statistical average – and the statistical average is the theoretical expression of *the least amount of error*, but is in every single case *wrong*.

We have become modest in our demands – "It's good enough".

Can such a new residential area be compared at all with an old-fashioned, untidy, self-developed, non-differentiated residential area? (assuming the same technical benefits in both cases)? It is easy to dismiss the thought as romantic, but we then also dismiss one of our premises. The issue remains: what is most human? And it is still people we build for and humanity we seek to serve – more than ever before!

The American electric razor that shaved all faces alike had its method. The same method will apply in this issue and is making great advances. Via all approaches *we* are attempting to reach the point where residential statistics cease to differentiate: at the point where there are no deviations from the average!

Architects have two alternatives:

1   Continue the current development. Assume that the development is correct. Build larger and larger segments with more and more finished residential units out of rational concerns, and try to include in the new buildings those things that statistical surveys show we have neglected in previous ones. Probable result: the housing need will be met and the necessary main volume is constructed. Everything has gradually become better, but in reality only less incorrect, and still wrong. It exists, however, and will continue to exist.

Those who think that empirical reasoning, generic analysis and statistics are able to satisfy the subtle needs of individualists can safely continue to pursue this path.

2   Assume that the current development is wrong. Accept the existing economic conditions and demands for rationality, but approach the task in a new way: use the mechanical aids to first create the *framework* for a house, and thereafter produce a large selection of all of the elements of which a home can be thought to consist. Leave to each family the creation of a dwelling that is most suitable and give both its interior and exterior expression. Stimulate the desire to wear one's hat as one likes.

Refrain from believing that individual fulfilment can be bought in the form of a washing machine or a television.

In brief, but poorly formulated (because it builds on conventional forms): build high-rise constructions consisting of stairs, pillars and floors, and rent them out as building lots. Allow the tenants themselves to choose or not choose façades, windows, verandas, partitioning and interior decoration. Supplement the residential craftsman with a large number of machine-produced building elements that can be easily assembled in infinite variations of individual dwellings.

In principle: supply everyone who builds or arranges accommodation with a sufficient supply of attachable, inexpensive parts that permit all to design and build up their own home environment. This will entail a certain amount of disorder, perhaps, but within a framework. And isn't a certain amount of disorder within a community framework one of society's most revered hallmarks? Who wants total order?

Impertinent French voice on the subject of Sweden: "Sweden – a giant refrigerator where people are condemned to luxury . . . A society of sanctimonious and self-righteous experimental guinea pigs waiting for – well, it is difficult to say – a certain progress . . . They live in a mechanical and nickel-plated world wherein each person accepts fate like a train ticket and each independent thought constitutes a pathological act."

If one chooses the latter opportunity – to delegate the initiative to one's fellow citizens – one does not purport to solve their problems *for* them with the help of statistically based, "average" patent solutions.

In recognition of our fellow citizens' independent will, and of their need to "enjoy", "feel at home", "settle down" and seek creativeness, we concentrate on solving the architectonic task of finding parts for the material framework around them and at the same time to develop, create, advise and stimulate choices leading to beauty of expression and poetic life form.

Proceeding from the same material basis, both paths are open to us!

"Meccano of the Home"

Economic problems have forced us to rationalize housing surface areas. The dwelling has been pressed together to such a degree that it can truly be said that

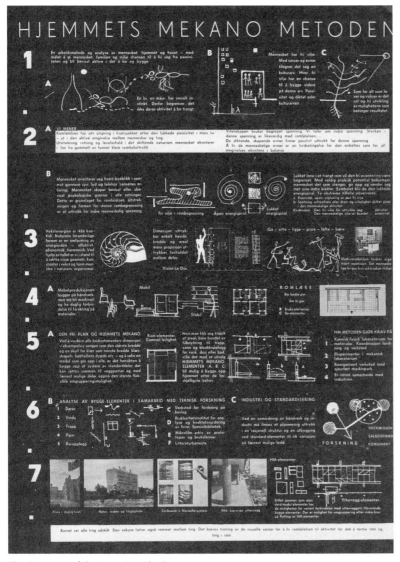

The "Meccano of the Home" Method

rooms have become like matchboxes. The conventional types of housing with several separate rooms are being continually retained. The rooms have therefore become narrower and narrower and increasingly less suitable for the conventional types of furniture that are still in use. The result is that the dwelling can no longer satisfy all varying needs. Vital family life and social interaction are inhibited by the cramped environment. One attempt at improving this is to make furniture smaller and lighter, but this means basically that one retains the same unsatisfactory solution as in the traditional dwelling, that one keeps the conventional types, just squeezed closer together and made cheaper. One might say that the misunderstanding is total and constitutes the issue. The demand for a more fundamental change must be put forward.

We know the consequences of people not having housing and of their living packed tightly together. The unequivocal need to provide housing is understandable. But we must not forget that it matters what kind of housing people get. We are aware that the 80 square metre limit is a reality and that there are also financial limitations for the dwelling's utility items. But we are also aware of the unfortunate psychological effects of tiny rooms. Although people are happy to own a flat, they are unconsciously affected by the "anxiety impulse" triggered by the small rooms.

The room and the items and the usefulness cannot be separated when the entire complex of "needs" is addressed. This should become the object of scientific study and assessment by some "institute for usefulness". Neurological therapy studies conducted on the ill or on underdeveloped people have shown that doctors are also frequently uncertain and unknowledgeable in this field, perhaps because it lies outside scientific methodology. The kitchen alone, as a very important space for the housewife, should not be the sole object of science and research. The entire living area and housing areas should be included in a coordinated plan of study and be pursued along with a structural study of the environment and population groups.

Form, colour, that is design, must be submitted to more scrutinizing assessment rather than an external rescue operation by showcase propaganda and pamphlets. This must also fall under the methodology of science and research and be coordinated into a whole.

Organizations and institutions should be able to adopt a communicative form of teamwork. Problems in the area of activity in public health, both physical and intellectual, make this demand pertinent.

In the case at hand, the world of common home furnishings is a web of complex issues. For example, a chair is an enormously important physical, psychological, social, personal and environmental factor.

In this context the discussion is not so much about the mobile objects as the heavier, more static ones, let us say from the bed to the wardrobe, which by the requirements they express entail separate rooms. A study of the objects' transformation into "mobile" utility items that are "removed" on occasion to free the room for use in meeting new needs, releases the fixed constraints of common plan dispositions.

If we look at history, we will see that this is not an entirely new concept. In the 1920s, Bauhaus Dessau conducted analyses on housing and rooms and attempted to identify standard elements that could be built together, for example a wardrobe against a wall. Marcel Breuer went one step further and said that these elements could be placed freely on the floor surface and form walls. In a sense, he introduced the entire issue. At the same time, Walter Gropius built houses with elements that were suspended from a skeleton frame. Still these houses, as well as the contemporary houses of Frank Lloyd Wright, were perceived as one solid, completed whole. In the "Meccano of the Home" we rather want to discuss the idea in Le Corbusier's system house from 1916, where one can create rooms freely with the aid of units specific to their use that can be built together.

What is the purpose of so doing?

In a lecture last summer, Dr George Scott Williamson spoke of his experiences with the Peckham Health Centre in London. Peckham Health Centre was a sort of community hall where people in the neighbourhood could meet and socialize together. The first shocking experience in this experiment was that there was about 90 per cent total passivity in the average urban population. The most human, the active, is totally suppressed. The positive result was that after some months using the centre, passivity decreased to 10 per cent. The psychologically stimulating surroundings had, to the greatest extent, a developmental effect. Alvar Aalto expressed already in 1942 during the reconstruction of Finland that the purpose above all else was to put people in an active role in terms of building, give them the experience of building on their own rather than putting them into rows of standard housing that would offer them shelter, true enough, but the wrong kind of psychological experience. Activity is an utmost necessity in order to raise our consciousness.

Science makes such great demands on active consciousness that a "vacuum" is created between science and human beings if they do not set their will to activate into motion so that they become participants in the cultural context, in the whole that science aids in creating. It is not a question here first and foremost of collecting knowledge, but rather of becoming more alert in order to react. One must counteract the dividing tendency of our time with a total sense of human existence. One must attempt to stimulate the child and the adults in family life to possess this activity together. In school it may be necessary to educate one to think and actively experience colour, surface, space. This is also Herbert Read's educational concept, among others. Human thought must be liberated in favour of personal activity and assessment so that people are able to communicate.

It is no wonder that educators are concerned with these issues. The common cultural context, despite the high level of consciousness in science and research, displays chaos. But we have recollections of order in history. One example: the Norwegian rural house from the Middle Ages until the eighteenth century, displays a sense of order and coherence based on a positive, clear regard for seasons and daily rhythm. Or look to Japan, which with its highly developed standardization nevertheless displays an extraordinary variety. The Japanese managed to produce a flexible form of housing in favour of which we now must make a dedicated effort to liberate ourselves.

Standards in the dwelling and in objects are not unknown in a European context. During the previous century a number of standard items emerged. The Vienna Chair, for example, was a technical solution that engendered an entire regrouping of handicrafts to a standard. The chair was lightweight, it was portable and it had a high degree of utility. One finds it throughout the world, just as one now finds Aalto's and Breuer's chairs. A chair does not need to be subjectively individual if it has a certain utilitarian quality.

Reminiscences from the rural environment's utility items live on in many countries. For example, we have the Budal Chair. The standard, however, is hardly developed and the manner in which it is forced in place is unsatisfactory. In order to bring the home's entire world of utility into analysis, the word "meccano" has been adopted as an expression of the interaction of objects to form a coordinated whole, a catchword for research within a professional field. It is an effort of analysis and study that provides education with a tendency and a direction.

The essence of the meccano of the home is the spatial experience, the variation in the rooms themselves and not actually the objects. The spatial experience is a requirement for being able to entertain the idea of transforming the accustomed objects to other types. The problem is simply that we have a limited surface area available and must assume that it is a lasting state. This is a state that is a necessary consequence of the social development towards a more equitable distribution of wealth. "The 80 square metre surface area" is actually a symbol of a universal state. The conclusion follows that our time makes demands on people who possess the ability to adapt to entirely new structural conditions. In order to get the biological and the psychological to counterbalance, it is therefore necessary that the "Meccano of the Home" be conducted as an analytical effort which will hopefully result in a synthesis of quality.

As suggested above, a free plan disposition is the basis for the meccano of the home. This free plan solution expresses the will to activity, to take into use the aids of the time, to create a basis for positive communication with fellow citizens, to perhaps achieve a better and more honest life together.

The meccano of the home denotes "units" or standard modules with which one builds in this free room disposition. For construction of the units, it is fundamental that people become knowledgeable about their own bodies in relation to the things that surround them. One must understand, as Le Corbusier and others did, that the body has a modular quality of its own and that it clearly and logically must be combined with the dimensions of the utility items with which people surround themselves. Housing surveys have worked with this, but they have not gone any further than to posit a sort of minimum; the effort stops there. The problem lies in freeing oneself to a maximum development via the "little we must be content with" to the maximal sense of the room we need, "rich variation by simple means".

The task consists of analysing throughout each case of need in relation to the human being, in relation to different environments. All of the dimensions one finds must be coordinated into a standard module. One must solve the issues of combinations and how the units are to be built materially. We must seek out the suitable materials and also strive for the least possible number of joints for the richest effect.

"The free art forms" have been significant for these thoughts because we are aware that the entire liberation towards the feeling of space today, the free plan, has developed in interplay with the free arts' accomplishments. From Cézanne to

Calder there is a continuous line, with the acknowledgement of human potentials for space and mobility as a result. The human being goes from perceiving himself as an integral unit to becoming a mobile unit in relation to other mobile units. The communicative emerges.

One prerequisite is that one must have what we might call the will to research and the urge to research. To a certain degree Europe is somewhat handicapped because there have been so many internal problems caused by wars. The biological-psychological factors have been so intense in trying to free themselves from the historical that we have not yet moved beyond the static space. The will to research provides means of expression for creativity. What is essential for humanity is that one manages to be so active that the instant containing positive life for a brief second will be able to unfold. People form a dynamic configuration, not a nihilistic one, but with the higher consciousness permitting the choice between qualities for the best possible development together with fellow citizens. It is a matter of building up the whole. In the wholeness of interaction lies the chance for the greatest encounters of energies and thereby the highest unfolding of life.

Own Summer House in Portør by Knut Knutsen

1961

Knut Knutsen

People in Focus

"One thing we agree on – something must be done. But what must be done, we will probably not agree on."

Robert Storm Petersen

Human architecture – liberated from style – will be able to bring architecture nearer an idiom which has a more lasting value. One must build for people, not systems. Systems change and artistic idioms change with them. If one builds for systems, architecture will lack an inner coherence and therefore be inharmonious – one sees this all over the world.

To create an architecture that focuses on people, one can draw on architecture from other periods and use the numerous shapes in nature as inspiration. Impulses can be found in our log houses, in Japanese paper houses, in the south's small villages and farmhouses, in the igloos of the Eskimos or in the huts of Africa. Good impulses can even be found in the interiors of ships and railway carriages.

However, the prototypes must be used in a completely different way than before. It is not the style that is to be the model, but the human content. We can learn a lot from the conciseness, the need for economy and the emphasis on the functional in the plan arrangement of a ship. The non-regulated expansion of small villages and farmhouses in southern Europe is a thought-provoking example. The intimacy and continuity in Japanese houses, the crudeness of our log cabins, the climatic considerations that are the basis for the igloo and African huts – these are values that are essential for the designing of architecture. Respect and reverence for the landscape must be prevailing values. Respect is not just a matter of making buildings subordinate to the landscape, but also to emphasize it, develop it – maybe even create new nature.

Continual architecture is architecture that is consistently carried out from century to century. It should be evaluated in its entirety and not each individual building. A building – it can be a really good one – will always be weakened by its surroundings if there is no connection between them. The difficulty arises in trying to adapt the new to the old buildings when the old buildings lack human content.

If one understands architecture in this way, every designer will then work in the same direction and not work against each other as they now do, to which the results around us are witness. With architecture less bound to the system, our surroundings would be more harmonious, enrich our imagination and inspire. To be able to bring about a human and continual architecture, we have to create a new way of thinking.

Architects have through the ages worked for systems and for people who wanted to show their power, their own greatness. It is only now that architects are beginning to solve the problem of building for ordinary people. And it is in our own time that the individual is respected and has attained rights and protection.

Architects today are in part responsible for how the world will look in the future. They have to take into consideration nature and economize with the resources of the world so that things of value are not unnecessarily wasted. The architect should view his or her work globally, not just locally or nationally. His task in the long run is to redesign society and hinder the prevalence of speculation and personal conceit. He is to organize reality for the benefit of the individual.

Style and trends *have to* lead to a bad result, *must* be destructive for the whole. I cannot see that anything other than continual architecture with a human content and artistically created is the only architecture that can lead to harmony in a larger context.

We have to stop using architecture as an expression of the thoughts and ideas of the times. New materials should not create new design just like that. The architecture is not there for the sake of the material and should not serve the ideas of the times. It is there for the sake of the unchanging person.

This idea of *another* way to create architecture ought to make it easier, freer and more imaginative. It is the essence of art to deepen perception, create movement and life, and organize diversity into something harmonious. The solution ought to lead to results equally rich as the profusion of the trees, the variations of the mountains or life in the sky. In our mechanized and rationalized civilization it is extremely important for people to try to understand nature and take inspiration from it.

Today one has to search to find a harmonious area where houses and nature connect and where groups of houses "fit" together. Buildings in our whole country are inharmonious and therefore destroy the landscape. Architects and builders are now doing their best to ruin pearls of nature everywhere. Building trends and speculation have resulted in badly designed and inharmonious houses. Buildings like that also fall quickly in value. A good example of this are the houses built for speculation during the 1880s. The architect's ambiguity about criteria for architecture has in its turn led the developer, the contractor and the man in the street to build badly. Almost every house today is designed based on trends. Imitation of the superficial results in the absence of art.

Our society teaches us from childhood to be imitators. We do not appreciate things until they become popular, trivial and like something we are familiar with from before. Too little is done to teach people to be original. Is not television the latest great leveller as regards creativity? The world of entertainment in itself is causing its ruin. Even travelling, to look and experience, has become passive entertainment. To create a house for people who cannot become enthusiastic about something is like stepping out into a void. The excitement found in spatial effects, in form, in movement, in proportions is completely incomprehensible for the majority of people today.

We have not had any clarified architecture since the 1920s, almost no solid building that is completely designed all the way through. No idea of the whole, no ideals that are sustained for more than a few years.

The architecture of the future must create a counterbalance against the monotony of machines. The human being must undergo an apprenticeship in nature. Only people who have studied nature will command machines in such a way that they serve society at large, harmoniously placed in the whole. Only people like that will be protected against the ruinous effects of mass production and against the "mass unemployment" that leisure time is turning out to be.

Architects have served the ruling classes for hundreds of years. Up to our time they have only been interested in grand schemes. They have not, even in addition to these tasks, been interested in architecture for people. When the light finally dawned, they had no background for finding solutions with people in focus.

The rebuilding of our country after the war reveals a lack of necessary knowledge – the solutions are without a consistent, comprehensive view.

We must be humble in relation to our tasks and remember that our work is often a result of that which has been done before. For example, today we copy, either consciously or unconsciously, Frank Lloyd Wright and Le Corbusier. With them we find an exemplary design that *they* have brought with them from the past, but which they have developed in a personal manner and added a new way of thinking.

The governing bodies of society have to help us to carry through the person-oriented, continual architecture for the common good, to preserve values that would otherwise be lost. The task is so formidable that perhaps only a few can succeed, but we must not thwart this or view it passively. Architecture is an important branch of art – it concerns everyone. Handled in the right way, it can enrich the individual's life.

Today we are obliged to build in clusters in order to preserve arable land. It is necessary to build in harmony with natural habitats and not follow pre-arranged programmes that are supposed to cover all eventualities. One should build tall and compactly, low and spread or protectively sheltered – everything based on the natural environment. The climate will also have an influence on the architecture so that houses will vary in different places in the world. The wind will be decisive in one place, heat and cold in another. Light may also be a significant factor.

People all over the world live according to the same principal pattern, now as before – they sleep, eat, make love, take care of their children, play, mourn. By freeing houses from styles and trends, the *functions* will be universal. Material values must and should be shared by everyone so that general living conditions will be the same for everyone.

The housewife has always struggled with the house. Privileged families have had help for this and had bigger houses. If people are to maintain the same standard in the future when hired help disappears, machines have to take over. The needs of the newly married are usually modest. The same goes for the elderly, so the nucleus of a house does not have to be big. But living units should be flexible – units should be able to be added and some areas should be able to be divided up. Houses being built today are not fit for use for more than 50–100 years because trends in plan layout and design dominate and flexibility does not exist. By building functionally and harmoniously, the lifetime of a house can be extended, values can be retained and society's resources can be used in a more sensible way. When it is claimed that houses have a lifespan of only 50 years and one builds based on this, society suffers while the individual is enriched. But these houses too should give people a harmonious, living environment as long as they last. If one consciously builds with the thought in mind that a house *will* have a short lifespan, then the architect is either ignorant or an enemy of society.

Great artistic ability is necessary in order to create life in houses in large developments. Materials, the colour of the materials, tectonics, the relationship between light and shadow, the significance of where the doors and windows are placed, the proportions of the structure, contrast between open and closed spaces, contact between the indoors and the outdoors, flexibility – all these are demands that must be met. With nature-based building structures and materials one shies away from the superficial and the search for sensational effects.

Tectonics, the use of materials, climate, function and economy in the building industry are things everyone can learn. But to create music, to make the materials, the proportions, the light, the construction to sing, to live, to give universal meaning – is a talent given the few. Here talent is required and talent must be cultivated. Today's tendency to evaluate architectural projects only with regard to function and economy often will result in bad houses. A *good* architectural project can adapt to both function and economy – not the other way around.

The professional sphere of the architect may encompass everything from regional planning, planning in detail, landscaping, the building of roads, bridges, houses, their details, function, construction, economy, feeling for space and furniture. Architecture touches everyone's field of interest, but specialization – which is the role of science – does not lead to results in architecture. The tiniest detail can affect the whole decisively. Therefore, the architect's working field is an indivisible whole which must be under the control of one person, no matter how difficult that may be. One and the same person cannot be an expert in all these detailed areas, but as a director he must coordinate and lead the whole in order to get a homogeneous result, and to do this artistic talent is an absolute requirement.

These are thoughts about architecture which I have repeatedly put forward and which I have tried to put together during the last twenty years. It is an architectural point of view that I have wished to explain to students and assistants in the same period and which I also have tried to make known during my time as chairman of Oslo's Architectural Association. Since everything has probably been thought of before and even said before, these thoughts are not new. But the time seems to be ripe to have them understood and carried out. The architects of the future can develop these ideas further.

Own House "Italiesin" by Christian Norberg-Schulz

1966

Christian Norberg-Schulz

Order and Variation in the Environment

In the book *Feeling and Form*, the American philosopher Susanne Langer defines architecture as "a total environment made visible". She clarifies this further by saying that architecture is a "symbol of humanity". Implicit in this is the idea that the word "environment" covers something more than the physical things which normally surround us. Above all, it stands for meanings and values, which give us a feeling of security and belonging on the one hand, and the possibility of expressing oneself on the other. We are therefore all aware that the word "home" means something *more* than the walls, roof and other building parts of which a house consists. But at the same time Langer suggests that it does not mean *something else* than that. It is in the building and how one organizes it that the home becomes *visible*, becomes real for us. In other words, it is the task of the architect to create a suitable frame around our way of life, not only a practical frame, but a frame that helps the individual and the community to obtain a psychological foothold. This is true, of course, not only for the building, but for settlements and also for the city in its entirety.

The problem for discussion has two aspects that are already included in Langer's definition. First, it is necessary to define the word "environment" by naming the human functions, needs and values it is associated with. It goes without saying that the result of this investigation is culturally conditioned and will change with time and place. Second, one must account for how the architect can make the "inherent qualities" of the environment visible. It is an artistic problem which is possibly dependent on the "artistic idiom" that an epoch more or less professes, but which also seems to be tied to certain relatively "timeless" principles of *order* and *variation*. In the following I shall try to clarify these principles with a view to our present situation, especially as regards the question of "scattered or concentrated settlements".

I mentioned above that environment should give us a feeling of security and solidarity on the one hand and freedom of expression on the other. In principle, a feeling of security arises through identification. This happens not only when we recognize things, but most of all when we really *live with* them, when we know that they have certain *qualities* we can make use of or avoid, depending on our needs at that moment. Certain qualities mean, however, that things have a certain *character*, which in turn implies that we are dependent on an *organized* world where things are "arranged" according to their similarities or differences. Knowing that we belong to such an order is a prerequisite for being able to orient and express ourselves. But in the term "express ourselves" is the underlying requirement of "freedom". We do not want to belong to an order where our role is established once and for all. We want to have the opportunity to *make choices*. In other words, the environment should be so varied that both individual differences and changing individual needs are taken into consideration.

The word "variation" implies that it does not indicate coincidental ideas but a "variation over something", that is, a new juxtaposition of known elements. It is important to emphasize this because in our time one has the tendency to understand "order" and "freedom" as irreconcilable opposites instead of realizing that they are two necessary sides of the same story. An order which has no room for variation can best be described as "purely theoretical" because it does not take into consideration the dynamic aspects of one's way of life, while a "freedom" which has no relation to the known is necessarily "meaningless". Meaning can only be defined in reference to a system of meanings we (to a certain extent) are familiar with. "Order and variation" are therefore basic categories for all human self-expression.

I have interpreted Susanne Langer's expression "visible" as "able to be seen", but could just as well have chosen "comprehensible". What is it that makes something comprehensible? I have already suggested the answer, which is that the thing has to have a certain order or *form*. The psychology of perception, the study of how our senses perceive, has long ago studied the basic characteristics of visual shapes and the theory of information has given us insight into what is implied by "meaning" and "variation". But these results are all too little known to architects and planners. To be able to make use of these results, it is above all necessary to have them transferred to our own problems at hand and illustrated with examples from architecture.

The problem of order and variation concerns us in three different ways. First, we should look at the relation between landscape and settlements, second we are interested in the inner organization of the settlements, and finally we ought to give the single elements, the buildings, a satisfactory form. It is natural to start with our relation to the landscape.

The landscape, nature, is an overall part of human activity. From earliest time the placement and character of human dwellings have been decided based on the given premises of nature. Climatic conditions, agricultural possibilities, raw materials and natural communication have been the basis for human self-realization. At the same time, these factors set limits for self-expression. And in this way, by being both encouraging and restrictive, nature contributes to giving human activities the character of a way of life. Therefore, nature concerns us all, but especially those whose role in society is to shape our environment by intervening in a way that helps people make use of nature. Originally these interventions were modest. They consisted of mainly *setting aside* areas where one could seek refuge from enemies, the unpleasant climate and all kinds of "demons". Thus, the *enclosure* was the first man-made structure to put itself in opposition to nature, as an organized and stable world in contrast to the dangerous and incomprehensible environment.

Little by little man-made structures have become more extensive. While they used to have the character of a more limited "island" in nature, the opposite is now becoming the case. Therefore, the relation between "landscape and man-made structures" has become a problem. The growth of man-made structures has mainly been random and reserved for narrow interests. It has not taken a satisfactory *form* while at the same time it has become so conspicuous and extensive that it disturbs the character of the landscape.

Let us therefore see if it is possible to give a general definition of the role of the landscape and man-made structures as a whole as a first step in trying to win back the lost order. This, I think, is possible. First, we can establish that landscape shapes are relatively diffuse, it is only in exceptional cases they have clearly defined boundaries (for example a lake, a single tree and on rare occasions a topographic formation). Vegetation and the topographic shapes rarely cover each other exactly. A certain correspondence very likely occurs, such as when a cultivated plain is situated next to a wooded ridge, but usually the boundaries are undefined and vague. The vegetation contributes to making the character of the landscape's shape diffuse. In addition, the landscape seldom contains elements having an approximate geometric form. However, we do especially take notice of such unique formations. Mount Fuji in Japan is traditionally thought of as holy, and Vesuvius excites precisely because of its even contour, which emphasizes the mountain's unobstructed location.

That being said, we do not consider the landscape to be *without form*. The formless landscape may of course exist, but it does not interest us to the same degree as a landscape where large and small elements accentuate each other, and where space and mass inspire our notion of how it would feel to take possession of it by moving through it. Landscape manifests itself in an infinite number of ways. It can be magnificent or intimate, sombre or smiling. But all these expressions have a *general* character which is characteristic of the experience of nature. Exactly because nature is not man-made, it keeps us at a distance and provides wonderful, relatively homogeneous experiences. At the same time the landscape consists of relatively "rough" topological factors. We speak of mountain ranges and valleys, and of "far out in the blue". This is accentuated by the scale of the landscape. In principle, it will always have the character of a *continual background* in our field of vision, a background that everything else is silhouetted against. It dominates in essence, therefore, over the man-made, and the first condition for visual order must be that this relationship not be distorted. If that happens, we stop talking about landscape.

The condition we have tried to describe has its parallel in one of the basic principles of perception psychology. A "comprehensible" form will always be perceived as a *figure* silhouetted against a *background.* This figure does not of course have to be a single thing; it can also be an ordered placement of a larger number of elements. If the placement has no definite boundaries, but is comprehensible thanks to its characteristic organization, we may speak of an "open form". The decisive factor in any case is that the relation between the figure and the background is clear. If this does not happen, the experience will be vague and meaningless.

From this we may conclude that the first demand for visual order must be that the settlement should appear as a *figure* in relation to the landscape, and that the task of the architect is to create such "figures". How this is to be done in each case will naturally depend on the landscape and the type of settlement, but a few general principles may be stated. The buildings should either be so spread out that they appear to be *individual units*, or so close together that they become *clusters*. Perception psychology teaches us that the simplest form of order is established through *proximity*, and every old village or farm illustrates this. It is this point that is most sinned against today. The desire to have one's own house, combined with the economically possible size of the building site, creates a scattered settlement that is neither spread out nor clustered, and which therefore loses every appearance of being a figure, while at the same time breaking up the coherence of the landscape.

This being said, it does not necessarily mean that the building should isolate itself and appear in *contrast* to the landscape. It is of course important for the building's relation to its *immediate* surroundings that it does not appear completely isolated, but is integrated with the help of "half-architectural" elements such as walls, terraces and stairs. These elements can also help us when we want to join several buildings together to form a group. But first and foremost these elements are important when we want to create visual order "at close range". "At a distance", that is in relation to the landscape as a whole, is where the more general aspects of a grouping are decisive. Sometimes it may also be necessary to *hide* the settlement when we want to preserve nature as such. The architect Knut Knutsen has given us an excellent example of this with his summer house in Portør.

I have already mentioned two such "groupings": the clearly limited area and the close cluster of houses. The word "cluster" has in recent years become a label to describe many of the experiments in new forms of settlements, and we understand that the objective is among other things to clarify the relation to the landscape. The word cluster implies a relatively irregular order, which above all is characterized by its density. It is of course possible for us to create more exacting *groups* where a fixed geometric order is decisive. But both because of the terrain and the different functions required, it will seldom seem natural to give a wide-ranging group a form that is too rigid. Therefore, the proximity factor will always be of primary importance when we speak of larger entities.

The problem of variation does not need to be focused on to the same degree as the problem of order when we are talking about the landscape. The shape of the terrain and the changing size of the groups will generally result in adequate variation in the whole. Since most present and past settlements usually consist of related or standardized houses, it is important for their adaptation to the terrain that they have variable *characteristics*. (I do not mean foundations of varying heights which we know from post-war building in Norway!) Utzon's housing project for Birkehøj is a good example of such adaptation through the use of a variable type.

The comprehensive picture I have outlined here may best be described as a *scattered concentration*, an idea which seems to be the only possibility if we want to preserve nature as it is, and not reduce it to isolated "nature museums". At the same time we see that the settlement can become a "thing" with which we can have a certain relation. Yona Friedman, the city planner theoretician, goes so far as to want to gather the main bulk of the European population into very large groups which would create a "structure of points" across the entire continent. In this way the landscape gets back its continuity and character as background for the man-made. In principle, Friedman's idea means that the structure that was characteristic of Europe up until the last century is re-established, just far more roughly meshed and consisting of much larger concentrations in keeping with today's needs and communication possibilities. We notice that Friedman shows only one concentration point in Norway, but we do not need to take this so literally that we depopulate the rest of the country. Naturally, we need secondary concentrations which make up a subordinate structure of points. What is important is that such structures are built up and that the general tendency toward scattering is counteracted.

Now let us "go into" the settlement and examine how our demands for visual order and variation can be satisfied "at close range". Even if the entities we will be dealing with are of extremely different size, entities that will be described as "housing areas", "villages", "towns" and "cities", we can begin with some general comments.

It follows from the preceding discussion that settlements should be relatively concentrated. The question that arises is whether this density is also motivated from within or whether there exists a clash of interest in the demands from the relationship between landscape and settlement. The first thing we can ascertain is that cities and villages everywhere throughout time have had concentration as their distinctive feature. It seems as though this feature satisfied an elementary human need. It is natural to think of the need to defend oneself, and this has probably played a central role, but density occurs too where the need to defend oneself is not present. Thus, the motivation must lie deeper. Now, we know that villages and cities have always been associated with the need for identification; it is apt that the Egyptian hieroglyph for "city" could also mean "mother". The city has therefore always been thought of as something near, warm and embracing. At the same time it was a *meeting place* for people. It was initially in the village and the city that people could exchange experiences and trade goods. The city was the *form* that made this possible, and naturally enough it developed the characteristics that best fit the purpose.

We understand that density is also motivated from within. Generally we can place it on an equal footing with the demand for *human scale*. This does not necessarily mean the same thing as small proportions. A big city can also have human scale. Human scale means that there are forms we can identify ourselves with, that is forms that are adapted to our needs and tasks, forms that are *comprehensible*. In scattered concentrations we have acknowledged the most elementary example of comprehensive forms in our environment. The concentrations can of course take many different forms and it is this problem we shall now look at more closely.

Perception psychology is based on three different elementary principles for order: *nearness, continuity* and *containment* (after which comes the more general principle *equality* as a fourth factor). This means that a collection of elements is ordered in either a cluster, a row, or an enclosure. These arrangements may also occur in combinations, as when a cluster is given a clear outer boundary. But we do not need to look to psychologists to recognize this. Every village from any continent is based on these principles. In central Europe one talks of three village forms: a cluster village, a row village (along a road or a river) and a circular village ("rundling"). And we have the same thing in Norway. In a significant article on the geography of architectural tradition in Norway, Halvor Vreim has shown that we know three characteristic yard shapes, which occur in three distinct geographical areas: the cluster yard in the western part of Norway, the yards in rows in Setesdal and Telemark, and the square yards in the eastern part of Norway – three variations on the theme of containment, undoubtedly the result of different regional conditions. And each variation may of course again be varied endlessly.

Today the elementary orders seem to be forgotten, here in Norway anyway. Certain architects have only recently started to use these "timeless" principles again, clearly inspired by the anonymous architecture. We are here witness to a new attitude towards the past: one does not copy its motives, but uses its general experience.

These three fundamental principles will also be decisive for larger concentrations, such as the establishment of cities. In this way the *district* is understood as a more or less clearly limited cluster or grouping, the *city street* (and especially the main streets) is fundamentally a row-formation, and the *square* or market place is an enclosed area. Even when it concerns American cities of today, Kevin Lynch has found out that the terms *district, path* and *node* are the best way to describe their structure. He defines "district" as a characteristic cluster, which is recognized by a special "texture" in the repetition of certain types of buildings and so on, while the term "path" is defined as a continuity which can exist in a characteristic spatial context, in a façade that repeats itself, or even in a certain activity that takes place in the street. A "node" is, finally, "a distinct and unforgettable *place*" which creates a kind of centre of gravity in the city's structure.

The main point in Lynch's significant book is that our idea of the city we live in should be fairly clear and coherent for the city to be satisfying as an environment. Thus, he says: "A good environmental image gives its possessor an important sense of emotional security." And he continues by emphasizing that "different environments resist or facilitate the image-making". In his fascinating analysis of the formless Los Angeles, he quotes a characteristic statement from one of the interview objects: "It's as if you were going somewhere for a long time, and when you got there you discovered there was nothing there, after all." The challenge for the planner and the architect lies in this understanding that the organization of our environment is decisive for us to develop a sense of identification. They must be able to create a city structure that satisfies the basic need for order and variation.

The recognition that the basic elements in the organization of a city are the district, the street and the square is in direct contrast to the characteristic tendencies in today's city planning. The district today dissolves into scattered apartment blocks which make a visual understanding of the area difficult (except from the air), which in turn results in weakening the feeling of *belonging* to the place. The streets have become pure arteries of communication without any architectural definition. Even if pedestrians are separated from cars, which do not need the same architectural environment, it has up to now been commonly accepted that pedestrians should preferably move freely around out in the open air. And the square, Lynch's "distinct and unforgettable place", has given itself up to drive-in cinemas and malls. Sidewalk cafés in the old squares are becoming more and more disagreeable, thanks to the traffic that is pushing nearer and nearer.

Let us look more closely at the visual problems and the problems of form that are tied up with the district, the street and the square.

The *district* is the least definite of these three. In older towns there is seldom a clear division between the districts. To be sure, many cities are divided in two by a river, and other topographic conditions may also contribute to characterizing certain areas. The Seven Hills of Rome are a well-known example from history. In any case, it seems to be important that *some* division and boundaries are established. (But they should not be so marked that the city is divided into fragments.) If we take away the rivers of Paris, London or Rome, a picture of the cities would be much more difficult to imagine. Yes, even in such a city as big as New York a certain structure is given through the natural division into districts. Manhattan is to a great extent characterized by the fact that it is an island. Therefore we always have a limited contour to which to refer. Manhattan is also an example that a district can be quite large, without stopping being comprehensible, as long as it has a clear shape. In addition, Manhattan is divided into many more or less well-defined subsidiary districts. Greenwich Village is a well-known example. Here are the crooked streets and changes in the proportions which characterize the area, and it is typical that especially artists and intellectuals seek to settle here. New York has thus a kind of hierarchical structure with primary and secondary parts, and this is probably a natural form for a city. (To avoid misunderstandings I would also like to emphasize that New York without a doubt also *lacks* a number of things!)

That the district has its own *definite character* is even more important than its being divided up with limiting boundaries. It is this that makes it different from the others and which gives a feeling of belonging and gives it substance. As previously mentioned, character is defined above all by the "texture" that is created by the course of the street system and by the concentration, height and proportion of the buildings. Moreover, the repetition of certain types of buildings plays a decisive role. Since the network of streets and density are usually connected to the choice of building type, these factors become dependent variations. The idea of *buildings typical of a district* should be stressed at a time when one seeks for practical reasons to repeat the same kind of building everywhere, even over the whole country. The district's changing character gives the city the most elementary form for variation and assures the individual's *choice.* While we have up to now spoken of "neighbourhood" as mere functional units, the idea of characteristic districts first and foremost is a result of the need for visual order and variation, in other words for a meaningful environment.

The street is a form which is more easily comprehensible right away. In the old towns the streets were what Professor Hans Peter L'Orange appropriately has called "a little universe", where the character of the district and the city becomes apparent while one walks through it. The street represents so to speak a section of life in the flesh and history is outlined on its walls, from graffiti to the Coca-Cola sign. Even in a city like New York the street still has this function. When we see Miss

Chinatown pass by on the district's festival day, it is the street that gives the parade a setting and brings it to life.

In today's new cities, the street form has largely been lost. This, of course, is the result of the common scattering of settlements, and traffic would at any rate make most other functions impossible. But the problem has several aspects. It is also the result of the *large building units* that more and more often influence the street scene. In the first place, we can only with difficulty identify with the new scale, and second, the lack of variation and spontaneous details is depressing. It is with this in mind we should understand Le Corbusier's reaction to the "corridor street". Kevin Lynch's studies have shown, however, that it is important to win back the street as a basic link in the structure of the city, something that is only possible within a new "pedestrian urbanism".

Four factors are decisive in the creation of any outdoor space. First, the space's own shape, "the space form", that is if the space is round, square, elongated and so on. Second, the treatment of the walls or "interfaces" which surround the space. Third, the formation of the floor (for indoor rooms the ceiling must also be considered). And fourth, the proportions or "scale".

The shape of the street can most simply be described as "elongated", but it is not necessarily straight. In old towns crooked angles and curved lines create a "closed perspective" which give the experience a completely different element of surprise. (In Peter Smithson's Berlin Capital Master Plan this experience is made use of. His pedestrian streets vary in breadth and direction and branch out in variations of space.) It is important for the spatial effect that the houses appear as *surfaces* and not as masses. If the mass effect is dominant, each house will appear as a figure and together with the spaces between the houses, the street will be reduced to a subordinate "background". For the street to be a true *form*, it must *itself* have the character of a figure. This is achieved above all by a surface continuity, which does not only require a certain concentration, but also that the houses are similar, that they belong to the same "family". L'Orange has in addition pointed out how important it was for the old street space that it lacked a sidewalk. Sidewalks accentuate singularly the corridor effect of the street and force the pedestrian to sneak along the walls of the houses. The street without sidewalks rather *unites* the row of houses and creates a whole space.

The desire to have the houses all belong to the same "family" naturally may bring with it the danger of monotony. In the old days this was counteracted by variation in the treatment of surfaces, or by the houses being variations over the same theme. It is not easy to describe in detail what constitutes such a "wall theme". It can simply mean that a relatively fixed house size is repeated, or that the houses have one or more prominent features in common, like the shape of a gable or an arcade on the ground floor. The theme should allow for *complete freedom* in the choice of details. When the street façade is understood as a repeated variation on a theme, this implies a division into relatively small units. The larger units therefore not only spoil the proportions, but also prohibit the street from attaining the varied continuity which is its essence.

These principles were in common use far into the last century. It was only recently that it became common to introduce parallel building lines and joint cornice heights as the most important ways to create order. Historically this has its roots in *procession streets.* In the 1800s the main streets were no longer thought of as an intimate pedestrian environment, and thereby easily lost its human scale. The boulevards in Paris are saved only thanks to their being divided up into several parallel zones: first a wide sidewalk where there is plenty of room for cafés, then an access road, then a row of trees, and finally, far removed from people, the fast-moving traffic.

In addition to the type of street we have outlined above, there are other, simpler streets that first and foremost serve as access to the houses. These will usually be more neutral and have a more homogeneous character than the main streets, but here too a certain continuity is necessary for experiencing the whole. We are dealing with a differentiated system of streets, which satisfies the demand for variation and order if they are made in an adequate way.

Within this system the *street crossing* is especially important. The crossing is not really a *goal*, it rather represents the possibility of choice by being a contact point for several directions. Therefore pulsating life reaches maximum intensity in the street crossing. We even have the expression "to meet down on the corner". At the end of the 1400s, on extending the city of Ferrara, the architect Biagio Rossetti grasped the importance of the street crossing. By marking the corners that surround the crossing, he defined the "street crossing space" rather than the buildings.

The *square* or marketplace is finally the most clearly defined element in the city's structure. As a finished "thing" it is the most easily comprehended; it means a fixed point, a goal for movement. Paul Zucker has fittingly designated the square as "a psychological parking place within the civic landscape". In the old city atlases there were generally two things that were portrayed: a bird's-eye view of the city, that is the city as a whole organism, and the marketplace, that is the "heart" of the city. It was not until one came to the square that one had reached one's *destination.* That is why one is naturally led toward the marketplace in most of the old towns; the streets are pointed in this direction. Returning to New York once again, we can see that even in a city of 16 million people, a couple of squares function as centres of gravity for the social environment: Times Square for entertainment and Washington Square for "everyday life". Even under typically "modern" conditions the square seems to fill an elementary human need.

The square is determined by the same factors as the street space, only with the difference that here it is the continuity of the buildings *around* the space that is decisive. That this actually is generally known is shown by the fact that "plassveggen" ("square wall") is not a professional expression but a commonly used word in the Norwegian language. Here, too, the building *masses* have to step back and be bound into a relatively continuous surface. A square will usually, depending on its shape, consist of different "zones". This is important so that several activities can be carried out, and so that the spatial experience in itself will have a certain variation. It is usual that this division occurs by means of monuments or fountains, with the expression of the floor, or more seldom, that a building is placed in the space. This is often an especially important building, like a city hall or a church. It is also important that the zones are somewhat different in character, either thanks to the spatial form or the shape of the limiting walls. A monumental square which is arranged symmetrically around a memorial is probably divided into zones, but here the zones are equal and the square will look monotonous.

Because of its relative size in relation to the streets, the square gives us an opportunity to have some distance to the city's most important monumental buildings; it creates so to speak a background for them. In this way the character of the monumental building takes the form of a "landmark" that we use to orient ourselves, physically as well as psychologically, and we understand that it goes against the essence of the city to remove important common functions from its "heart". In this way the square will generally be characterized by a contrast in proportions, which provides a highlight in the visual experience of the city. But there should also be *contact* between the small and large scale so that our identification with the whole picture is made possible. In many of Europe's old squares this is attained by having monumental buildings serve as especially spectacular variations over themes, which are found in more modest buildings.

In the preceding analysis I have constantly drawn the single *building* into the discussion. While the building forms and creation of outdoor spaces we have looked at up to now have had a relatively abstract character, the building is highly tangible and concrete which, to all appearances, is easily understood. The public's *conscious* interest focuses first and foremost on single buildings. It is therefore natural that we, parallel with the "liberation of the individual", have experienced a "liberation of houses". A standard house today is thought of as a necessary evil rather than a means to attaining visual order. A strong urban form can tolerate, however, considerable individual stunts. Manhattan is again a good example; it is only in the scattered apartment blocks from recent years that its form has been broken up. A theoretically interesting, but utopian solution is suggested by Friedman, who imagines whole cities arranged into continuous building structures, "infrastructures", that have such a strong influence as regards order that the single houses which are placed within the structure can be formed completely freely. It is more likely that in coming years we will again resort to the more *variation-friendly* types of houses.

I have pointed out that order and variation are two sides of the same story, and that both are based on the idea that things which are to be ordered and varied have a *definite character*. In the above I have tried to indicate how settlements as a whole can attain a certain character. It now remains to be seen if a building can satisfy the same demands. When we say that houses without character are the most dominating feature in today's visual chaos, it implies that we have criteria for defining "character".

The word "character" is equal to "inner consequence". Inherent in this is that a form should not contradict itself, if it is to be fitting. Architects have known about this for a long time, and it has been expressed in theory and practice down through the ages. Alberti says it thus: "It is the function and duty of lineaments, then, to prescribe an appropriate place, exact numbers, a proper scale, and a graceful order for whole buildings and for each of there constituent parts." Le Corbusier's Modulor is also a typical expression for this desire for consistency and unity, but the Modulor is at the same time an example of the relatively abstract point of view which up until now has been made part of the architectural form. In my opinion it is necessary to go forward in a much more concrete way.

An example of *lack of consistency* can show what we mean. The design of a house from Trondheim, which originally had quite a definite character, is disrupted by the introduction of a completely foreign element, such as a window, which clearly arises from another kind of architecture. A bigger window is equally as meaningless as a Gothic arch would be in a Greek temple. But why is it really so meaningless? The original character of the house is clear: it consists in its look of a well-defined volume. All the details are built up around this: the simple main form, the unifying hipped roof, the small latticed windows which unite the surface. When a hole of a completely different size breaks through, it is as if a living organism has been injured, not to mention it looking like a pirate with a black patch over its eye.

This example shows that one cannot do just anything with any old house. But it also illustrates a new need which has been attempted to be satisfied within a framework where it really does not fit. In other words, it expresses a demand for a *new artistic idiom* which is adapted to our way of life. We cannot go into this here, but I would only like to emphasize that it is time to examine this problem more closely. Actually, it is a whole other subject for a conference.

I hope that it has become clear that landscape, settlements and buildings are *dependent variables*, a relationship that was also discussed in Erik Langdalen's speech. Luckily, we can say, the "inner" and "outer" demands put upon settlements support each other. These were completely obvious things as long as man lived in pact with nature and understood the landscape and the man-made as cooperative elements of the same whole.

I have tried in the preceding discussion to list some of the most elementary principles which are the basis for visual order and variation. When I have chosen many of my examples in the past, it is because I have wanted to point out "timeless" principles rather than special motifs. However, I could just as well have illustrated my points with examples from our own time. In many recent city planning projects we find concentrated groupings, successful pedestrian environments and open, growing structures based on a limited number of variable units. With the word "timeless" I do not indicate any special *solutions*, but general *possibilities*. Each solution means that these possibilities are used in harmony with the conditions at hand. It will therefore not be "timeless" at all, but distinctly characteristic of the period and contemporary. The expression "*scattered concentration*" does not refer to a certain solution, but to a principle that as far as I can see we *must* follow if we want to attain visual order in our environment. Theoretically the expression is timeless, but it will stop being *applicable* the day people have eaten up nature.

I have noticed with interest that Director Erik Brofoss, Gullik Kollandsrud and Erik Langdalen came to the same conclusions, the former based on economic premises, the latter two based on a functional analysis. When it has been asserted that we do not know if density is advantageous for the *creation of environment*, I would like to emphasize that everything points to the fact that density and the quality of the environment are inseparable. The good environments we know from the past are all concentrated, and today's scattered settlements have again and again been characterized as completely "lacking in environment". I have tried to explain this by saying that comprehensible forms are the most elementary prerequisite for the creation of an environment, and we have seen that comprehensible forms must have a "dense" character. When big cities breed juvenile delinquency and neuroses, factors other than density *per se* are undoubtedly responsible.

The other main question is which *shape* these clustered settlements should have. Nils-Ole Lund is correct in stating that nothing is as depressing as the sparse Norwegian town. It is seldom they have a real urban quality. It is up to us architects to re-evaluate this fundamentally. The debate over one-family house *contra* apartment blocks, which usually is brought into the discussion in this connection, is as far as I can tell already out-dated. Today we know of types of dwellings that unite the advantages of the one-family house with the concentration of apartment blocks.

Finally, I would like to point out that the relevant "developmental tendencies" in architecture and city planning seem to go in the direction I have outlined. In addition, it is a fact that people *seek* densely populated areas. I see this as a reaction, conscious or unconscious, to the disintegrating tendencies Johan Galtung pushed to the extremes with his flying carpets and private TV-channels. We must not forget that *concreteness* is the basic criteria for reality. Mechanical means of contact will never replace physical presence. We must therefore preserve forms of settlements that make it possible to *meet* other people, spontaneously and accidentally. Life does not just consist of *conscious* decisions, but includes the richness of surprise. This is the real urban freedom, which I would call "*the environment of possibility*". Louis Kahn says it this way: "A city is a place where a small boy, as he walks through it, may see something that will tell him what he wants to do his whole life."

Holiday Cottage by Wenche Selmer

1978

Wenche Selmer

Tradition and Distinctiveness

Many good and applicable words have become overused. "Adaptation", which is the working title for this issue of the magazine, has unfortunately become misunderstood and misused. It is often associated with resignation and pastiche. Adaptation is not a passive concept. In architecture it is a conscious act which is the result of sensitivity to people and surroundings.

As the person staging the scene, the architect is responsible for the final result in a long decision-making process. In spite of a large portion of goodwill, the overall planning contributes to reducing the architect's opportunity for creating human architecture. It seems that the desire to attain the common good and a good environment by means of legislation, overall control and rules governing credit make it difficult to build further on tradition and distinctiveness. This has serious consequences for the individual house, both for year-round and recreational use, which still dominates building activity around the country.

Today, these houses are made more by laws, regulations and credit conditions than by an active understanding of adaptation. Demands regarding room size, areas of glass, storey height, stairs and so on strain the proportions of a small house. The same can be said for regulations concerning how the rooms are divided up, how the room is furnished and too many rules about how the building is to be used. Ideas as to the use of the basement in expanding a permitted, limited living area lead to high foundation walls with huge window holes. When a coincidental and inharmonious prefabricated house in addition hereto crowns a shattered foundation, the value of the nearest surroundings is lost. Without taking into consideration time and place, these soulless houses are set up all over Norway, from the North Cape to the southern tip of Lindesnes.

Wherever streets and the neighbouring houses in towns and villages become direct objects of adaptation for a new building, the site's topography and vegetation should be decisive in the design of the free-standing building. No matter how isolated the house is situated, it will always belong to an area with a special architectural practice. New houses must have a mutual connection with the old, even though it is behind the next rock or the next promontory. This has to do with an understanding of shapes and proportions.

Work on many projects in southern Norway, carried out in cooperation with Jens Selmer, has given me a rich opportunity to study problems of adaptation. In our work we have tried to avoid pastiche while at the same time we have been aware of not introducing wrong proportions in an especially fine and balanced environment. The houses have undergone many different designs before reaching the anonymous simplicity presented here.

Our first assignment nearly thirty years ago, a house "typical" of southern Norway with the main entrance in the middle of the longitudinal wall and two windows on each side of the door, was initially not done *con amore*. However, it led to studies of great interest. We spent a whole summer measuring, drawing and searching for explanations for planning decisions and technical solutions. In spite of the hopeless task, we became older and wiser. Our investigations gave us insight into the area's special design and proportions which had arisen out of basic needs, climate, westerly connections and last, but not least, the sailing ship. The old houses for living and for boats are situated in small coves and inlets with amazing confidence. Shoulder to shoulder, the houses stand along the beach, well protected by rocks and knolls. Everything is well worked out, concise and finely proportioned. The scale and design are characteristic of planners with a clear idea of what the basic needs have been.

Holiday cottages do not demand the same requirements for protection against the winter storms that a year-round house does. The lack of undeveloped, sheltered coves has led to the development of skerries and knolls, which no genuine Norwegian southerner would have considered a few years ago. It is therefore important to fit the house in as well as possible, connect the building to the terrain, not at the highest point, but at the foot of the knoll, not in front of but behind the crooked pine tree. Everything depends on this choice. If the point of departure is wrong, further work is futile. All the senses must be called into play when evaluating the surroundings, near and far, the topography and the vegetation.

Knowledge of how to use a measuring tape and a levelling telescope comes in handy when planning any house. In the hilly, coastal landscape, with a sea chart as the only map source, it is necessary for solving the task to measure each knoll in detail; in this way one can avoid blasting. The familiarity one gets with small and big differences in height, moss-covered stones and future doorstops is a welcome companion to bring along to further work. When the view, compass points and protective elements are registered and stereoscopic pictures are taken, there should be adequate basic data. Experience with outdoor life under primitive conditions has provided information about what is necessary and what one can get along without. When dealing with scantily allotted living space, we have tried to give individual activities comfortable and adequate elbow room, but not any more than that.

In 1964 we were visited by a speculator who wanted to try his luck in prefabricated houses. The assignment was to design a holiday cottage for prefabrication for coastal and lowland areas, a "foolproof" house without serious problems of adaptation. The result of the endeavour was a little house, encircled by a porch at floor level under a large roof. In the shadow of the roof, wall sections with or without doors and windows could be mounted wherever one desired, taking into account the sun, the view and entrance accessibility. In the shadow of the porch, the house's posts could stretch freely down until they met firm ground. Our idea was a good one, but the organization failed and the company went bankrupt. About thirty houses have been put up, fourteen of them at Hovneset near Homborsund.

The project seems to have supplied an acceptable solution to a number of problems.

There are no unequivocal guidelines for adaptation. The ability to understand proportions on several levels in natural and man-made surroundings must nevertheless be said to be a decisive factor for an architect. With ability and a fertile imagination, one can bring an element of quality into the established environment. A subdued form of expression growing out of honesty and sensitivity is not to be disdained.

The Norwegian Veritas by Kjell Lund and Nils Slaatto

1983

Kjell Lund

Structuralist Architecture: Strapped or Free?

Structuralism – as we know it from the middle of the 1960s as a style and fashion trend in architecture – may formally be characterized as a principle of composition based upon added geometrical units with intermediate zones which may vary in size and character.

Functionally, structuralism as geometric organization aims at establishing zones in the total building volume for special practical, technical and constructive purposes, so that they may be independently altered within the dimensions fixed in the primary systems.

The primary systems establish the areas of applications served with high flexibility and generality, physically delimited by frames with nodal points and specially designed detail solutions. Within the areas of application there may be established independent secondary systems for varying functions adapted to the module units of the primary systems.

The geometrical pattern consists of application zones (main zones), communications zones (secondary zones), zones for construction and technique (intermediate zones). The dimensions of all physical sections are determined in relation to main and secondary modules and coordination of the modules is a condition for the defining of the dimension of the axes and the net dimensions of the sections.

Even if the systems are able to function independent of one another, a formal adaptation between the individual components is required. This does not necessarily imply character-allied design. Different planning premises may motivate different formal solutions.

The structuralist organization of constructions and technique is originally functionally motivated and adapted to industrial production. This implies the necessity of thorough studies of details in the smallest dimensions of all physical sections with a view to prefabrication and erection of section parts. The structuralist building should in extreme consequence geometrically be referred to a three-dimensional coordinate system as composition reference.

A basic grid may easily turn into a straitjacket and lead to formalist solutions in cases when rationality conditioned by certain presuppositions in one field binds freer artistic and architectural development in other fields. It is important that the extent of the physical structure has exact references to the functional conditions and is minimized as far as possible.

New postulates in the development of architecture are the result of theoretical studies combined with practical experience. Structuralism may be regarded as a nuanced further development of constructivism, taking care of increasing and changed technical installation requirements and optimum industrial production. The thoroughly structuralized building volume functions with generality and flexibility through the standardizing of specialized components.

Structure characterizes the way in which the single sections are combined into a whole. It is understandable that in a breakthrough period the structuralist systems are exposed purely as an architectonic medium of expression. In the aesthetic organization of practical reality the history of architecture shows innumerable variations in which different structures are mutually integrated or combined into complex patterns. During the actual planning of buildings the question arises on many levels whether and to what extent the conditions given require the formation of new formal syntheses through integration of different basis structures or are added upon in direct combinations.

The structuralist order is to a varying extent a necessary presupposition for the concrete shaping of buildings in the industrial society. It is the responsibility of the architects to substantiate that structuralism as projecting method and geometrical organizational system, which offers artistic freedom to create buildings with the required emotional contents.

Some projects worked out by our office during the past fifteen years may in posterity be characterized as being structuralist projects even if this in the main is not due to a deliberate ideological attitude. The structuralist principles of organization are primarily postulates put forward on the basis of experience gained from our own projects. As can be seen from the projects, there is a gradual development from more simple constructivism to more nuanced structuralist orders. We have made the experience that the greater insight one gains in the "rules of the game", the more articulated the architecture can be formulated.

The tendencies to rigidity and emotional poverty which systems and repetition of units entail, are first and foremost due to schematic thinking and limited appreciation of the complexity latent in most geometrical and organic patterns. In recent years many buildings have been realized which on a high-quality level substantiate that structuralism is not a hindrance to poetical and emotionally stimulating architecture, but on the contrary under certain financial and production-technical circumstances are a necessary presupposition for further development and renewal of the art of building – particularly in respect of great and complicated building projects.

In an issue of *Byggekunst* from 1967 there is a reference to Dr Nic Wall's clinic in which some views as to positive and negative form, open and close system, fixed and flexible structure, special and general character were illustrated by four small figures. These can to some extent predict a development which later runs through the projects of the office from static forms via constructivism into structuralism. The experience has to a varying extent also been utilized for projects in which structuralist organization is just a secondary element, in order to comply with necessary constructive and technical requirements.

Theoretically, the principles of composition developed by structuralism should have an architectonic renewing effect without ending up in formalism.

Structuralism may be classified as differentiation and specialization of functionalism via constructivism. Optimum rationality is the justification and limitation of structuralism. Total rationality forms a contrast to spontaneity as emotional reaction. Rationality is often symbolized by a squared net and lattice, whereas spontaneity is often characterized by curves and freer forms.

The combination of both form-themes may among other things be said to symbolize the relation between reason and emotion and between static and dynamic principles. Because rational behaviour has become a necessity as a result of society's forced level of efficiency in an increasing number of fields, there is also in architecture a need for symbols representing emotional freedom and spontaneity. This finds expressions in many buildings and projects. In Pietilä's library project in Tampere, in Hollein's Art Museum in Mönchengladbach and in Utzon's church in Bagsværd there are refined constellations of structures of different characters. These projects establish closer ties to historic architectural traditions at a deeper level than to the side scene architecture of postmodernism.

Structuralism and postmodernism represent now in their extreme manifestations in architecture the ultimate bounds in the field of tension between the rational and the irrational. As ideological trends they function as symptoms of and tools for various real needs. The schizophrenic splitting of architecture between rigid rationality and cliché-like symbols of relationship and identity can only be overcome by an architecture redeemed by a deeper integration between thought and emotion.

Svalbard Science Centre by Einar Jarmund and Håkon Vigsnæs

Håkon Vigsnæs

Is a House Interesting Seen Through a Hedge?

To squeeze through the bamboo jungle and reach Rudolf Schindler's own house in Hollywood is like coming to the city in Italo Calvino's chapter titled "Zaira" from *Invisible Cities*:

> The city . . . [consists] of relationships between the measurements of its space and the events of its past . . . The city, however, does not tell its past, but contains it like the lines of a hand, written in the corners of the streets, the gratings of the windows, the banisters of the steps, the antennae of the lightning rods.

It is almost as if one can see the restless and frail tunic-clad Schindler in the vegetable garden, in front of the shaving mirror, in front of the fireplace. The architecture is so clear and sensual that time has stopped, protected only by the leaves against the passing noise around it. Old photographs show the house situated in an undulating pasture and explains the garden's idealized cultural landscape: Los Angeles in the 1920s represented the Garden of Eden for immigrants, something that clearly was mirrored in a down-to-earth, but at the same time future-oriented architecture. Schindler combines a vegetable garden with a house which is programmed for the dissolution of the nuclear family.

Are the good examples absorbed?

Have all the extroverted, optimistic, but fenced-in pearls in Los Angeles designed by Lloyd Wright, Schindler and Neutra had a lasting influence on the architecture of the area?

Paradoxically enough, it looks as if a happy combination of time and place as architectural inspiration, such as in Schindler's house, has perhaps been more important for the international history of the profession than for the local identity of the site and building customs.

Schindler's house is today a museum, owned by an Austrian foundation. Perhaps the city has changed too much to make the architectural icons in Los Angeles relevant beyond themselves. But the isolation of these explicit cultural expressions is at the same time a feature of this culture: for the dreams to work as fuel, the ideals are raised and made not easily accessible. This, in turn, affects the architecture: the good examples are not immediately ploughed back into the public soil.

Villa at Jæren by Einar Jarmund and Håkon Vigsnæs. The design of this replacement dwelling protects the interests of the public. Seen from the road, the house is located below the horizon line.

An exception in this connection is Frank Lloyd Wright's magnificent Hollyhock House. This complex originally faced the city, and the park and the house, after a long rehabilitation, is soon to open its doors to the public. But the influence is not all positive: through the years Wright's architecture has given rise to a comprehensive and careworn replica architecture in the surrounding neighbourhood. An architecture which originally arose from new ideas about the connection between indoor and outdoor, topography and style of life, has been reduced to half-hearted reproductions of ornamentation and surface treatment.

The industry-related single-family houses from the post-war period, for example "Case Study Houses Program" (Eames, Ellwood, Koenig *et al.*), are therefore more interesting with their refined treatment of generally available products and economic systematization. And not to mention in later years Frank Gehry, his fantastic treatment of underestimated materials such as fence netting, building plywood and corrugated metal in his own house from the 1970s, which still causes local irritation in a well-groomed Santa Monica.

We can in these examples see a fruitful connection between the conditions of society and a single-family house architecture: with ordinary and easily available means an architecture is established which actually says something about the many possibilities that lie in the ordinary.

Cabin in Nordmarka by Einar Jarmund and Håkon Vigsnæs. A statement about being in keeping: black-and-white colour coding and the building addressing the lake follows local tradition.

Architecture as a tool of society

The last few years has seen a reintroduction of the belief in architecture as a tool of society in a broader sense, after we have put the criticism of modernism, followed by a period of aesthetic compulsive ideas behind us. Architects are again trying to have as their point of departure ethical problems in connection with recycling, ecology, technology, global perspectives and urban challenges. This is a clear theme in several of the national pavilions at this year's Biennale in Venice. The Nordic exhibition's focus on the relation of architecture to nature in our part of the world, tentatively explained through examples of regional contemporary architecture, cannot be said to be representative for the trend of the Biennale. The theme for the 7th Biennale in 2000 was: "The city: less aesthetics, more ethics."

Has the planning of single-family houses in the traditional sense any significance for the architects' regained broader horizon; has the lesson from the small and secluded task meaning for a more officially responsible work? Or shall we calmly let the hedges grow high and wide to protect the pearls of thought from the more swine-like reality? My contention is that the design of single-family houses still has professional significance broadly speaking. Or more precisely: personal experience with practical design on a small scale is to a growing degree a requirement in giving the profession generally the necessary legitimacy.

Backyard house, Vålerenga by Einar Jarmund and Håkon Vigsnæs. Located in a worn-out backyard building, the urban dwelling can be tested in new conditions.

Villa at Nesøya by Einar Jarmund and Håkon Vigsnæs. Durability is important. The cost of the copper façades is written off in just ten years compared to painting and maintenance on timber panelling.

"Those who are very strong must also be very kind", says Pippi Longstocking. Along those same lines one may assert that those who think big and aloud for many, must also be able to think small and locally for the individual. That kind of depth perspective is necessary in order to gain critical knowledge from the twentieth century's more dogmatic architectural excesses.

Today's official planning is mixed up with private development in a way that makes the prettily drawn plan regulations of the 1960s fairly irrelevant. There is a need for varied planning tools as a tactical means to carrying out strategic visions. It could be equally relevant with a tool in the shape of a communication plan for the whole process, as the development of detailed provisions for qualities connected to the use of light and materials.

Planning should retain flexibility in regard to programme, time and economy in order to survive the economic and political ebb and flow. The ability to develop and communicate architectural qualities in examples which are closely focused will often be decisive for how an overall plan is received. Academic authority does not necessarily carry weight in the public sector, abstractions are suspect, the need for physical concretization of visions is a public right. Great leaps between different scales and genre are a necessity for communication.

Architecture is a slow profession

Architectonic ideas related to programme or technology risk being left behind by the rapid development of society when it comes to the physical implementation. Slow decision-making processes and routines for quality assurance (a solution should in principle have been used before to be acceptable; nobody wants to take the responsibility for trying something for the first time) often prevent architectural answers to social requests in the form of quick social and technological development. The design of a single-family house is often exempted from this sluggishness. Here new ideas about materials, details and spatial understanding are tested, based on architectural motivations. Not until later is this knowledge transferred to bigger projects, which are more conservatively controlled.

Even if smaller public building projects, often tied up to the infrastructure, manage to translate an idea into reality relatively quickly, the rest areas and bus shelters will no doubt lack the programmatic intensity which the house project still represents.

The design of single-family houses makes a direct collaboration with the user possible. In this collaboration the limits for a pure professional discussion are most often stretched. In most of the other design processes, the planning is taken care of by professional project administrators who have a far cooler eye and little or no desire to take a risk beyond their often limited commission. In the larger housing projects the estate agent often functions as an empirically controlling filter between the architect and the conception of reality.

This is not unnatural when you think of the increasing number of professions present in the building industry: architects are a part of a constantly more specialized reality. Nevertheless, the simple and direct relationship between the owner and the architect can perhaps be the ideal solution. Often personal communication is based on trust, without a lot of correspondence and keeping the minutes of a meeting, a place where a profound understanding of the task is possible. A strong personal engagement on the part of the architect and owner is probably a common denominator for these processes. Both the question and answer have to be clear. This does not mean that collaboration will be without friction; the owner is usually an amateur in the field, with high hopes, no time and a lean purse.

The building branch prefers the familiar

The health and durability of a house is often given priority in collaboration with an owner who plans to build only once in a lifetime. On a small scale it is possible to experiment with types of paint, principles for weather sealing, alternatives to normal treatment of building materials and so on, solutions where close collaboration around the study and its follow-up is necessary.

Trade standards have a tendency to not catch the environmentally attractive alternatives such as, for example, using alternative insulation materials or the use of porous membranes in the roof. Products and technology that are new or fill a niche are seldom dealt with in standard building details or the trade organization's general recommendations. Safe, mainstream solutions are given priority over alternatives where experience is more limited. It appears too as if technical building research is concentrated around solutions for existing problems solved with known means.

The building contractor loves to tell the builder how impractical and expensive the architect's solutions are. They laugh at us, and we laugh at them. We love to hate each other. But nevertheless I would say that they think it is fun all the same, at least as long as they are not on a piecework contract based on standard tasks. To have materials that come together without covering it up and to have the precision of millimetres instead of centimetres are clearly challenges in a business which continually becomes more efficient through standardized solutions with a liberal demand for accuracy.

In connection with single-family houses it is usual to use small and relatively flexible building firms, which unfortunately often are relatively fragile structures. These boys became workers because they wanted to build, not plan. If the project is priced too low because of sparse background material, problems having to do with economy and the will to carry out the project will usually turn up. Subcontractors and employees disappear astonishingly fast as a result of poor liquidity. In addition, the psychology in a building project – the atmosphere on site – has often greater significance for the result than one would think.

In spite of the fact that standard solutions dominate, the unique challenges of craftsmanship have a tendency to appeal to those involved, and an interaction emerges around solving the details on site.

It is the direct and frequent contact between the architect and the contractor responsible on site that primarily separates the implementation of a typical single-family house from a larger building. This can result in professional problems being solved on site and makes possible architectural adjustments in the building period as well.

Sometimes the competence of the contractors can be decisive in the choice of solutions. The building process remains mobile to a greater degree than if the entrepreneur's contractual management is limited to the reporting of discrepancies and controlling standardization in building meetings that have too many participants and too much bad coffee.

What can we learn from single-family house design?

Can we pick up some general knowledge about living forms from single-family house design? As regards the development of ideas around living forms, one could perhaps wish for more diversity and more experimentation around specific situations. It is an open question as to whether there are grounds for this in today's society: the dream of having one's own house is often formed by imagery in glossy magazines about interior design. The desire to copy styles jeopardizes the development of innovative concepts where fundamental ideas about function, place and technology are rather the basis for comprehensive architecture. This applies to architects as well as owners. Nevertheless, it seems as though Norwegian architect-designed single-family houses are often smaller, with more compact, precise, albeit flexible solutions than what applies for the typical prefabricated house.

To hire an architect today is no longer the privilege of the well-to-do. The result is that the customary ideas about size and expectations concerning the established norms for quality are challenged in the process also for economic reasons. A tight budget can lead to a fresh way of thinking.

The transfer of knowledge from single-family house design to larger housing planning is not something to be taken for granted. It is often the architectural firm that does not involve itself to a large degree in single-family house design who is involved in what is mainly a property market steered by the developer and vice versa. A broader discussion about living forms, which includes all kinds of projects and is interdisciplinary, would absolutely be desirable.

Today it is the difficult sites that are available, especially in urban areas. Much housing is built in a contextual and regulated border area or no-man's land. Often these sites are not obvious places to build, and the design is not at all considered natural by the surrounding milieu. This may apply to typical density projects, and also to housing in connection with an existing building mass, such as rehabilitation, recycling or "freeloading".

In such a situation the single-family house can work as a tool in the fine-tuning of a planning apparatus and as a mirrored result of the limits and possibilities of these conditions. Building customs and the quality of place are continually discussed by the public and redefined on the basis of one or a few examples; a negotiating situation often arises within the area between individual and collective considerations which today take up a large part of the building authorities' capacity. This is nevertheless not an unnatural situation, and it challenges the architect's ability to solve problems and communicate.

Small problems give precise answers

Architecture can be paralyzing for architects, the restraints in many big projects seem claustrophobic, and the time perspective often demands too much of one's patience. When carrying out building projects on a small scale, it may be simpler to challenge the usual questions and we can allow ourselves a certain rudeness when confronting professional conventions and common expectations.

A limited problem makes a precise answer possible; this knowledge strengthens the ability to also answer more complex challenges in a direct way. General problems can be examined on a small scale and knowledge can be ploughed back into public grounds. And not least, the inexperienced architects who are eager supporters of systems can achieve their practical satisfaction, whereas the experienced architects who are tired of systems can get their needed boost.

We have moved on. Parked on a curve by Silver Lake, far above the smog of Los Angeles, I have just found a nice little peep-hole in a hedge. Some shimmering

Neutra. Sulking children nagging for ice cream in the back seat suddenly come excitedly to life when the gate to the residence opens and Richard Gere sweeps out in an open racing-green Aston Martin. Real life. Here and now!

That was all it took.

We had all gotten our glimpse of paradise and could quietly return to the lowlands.

Mortensrud Church by Jan Olav Jensen and Børre Skodvin

2007

Jan Olav Jensen

Affinity

Without a doubt architects have different aims, ideals and interests. In addition, architects of the same generation and school have substantially different and quite personal ways of going about things. However much they may take their experience from the same kinds of projects, and however much they may share an outlook, architects consistently come up with different solutions to the same problem (for example in architectural competitions). This indicates something more deep-seated than background and contemporary discussions about architecture, and opens for an aspect that is not the outcome of choice. Something about the creative being appears to be deeply individual. Perhaps it can be called affinity, a personal preference or a propensity. I want to expand on this theme: the personal architectural insights one attains as an architect, those not chosen, but in some way handed out, and which lead you to become different from other architects, and may allow you to achieve your best as an architect. This article is about a specific group of architectonic tools frequently used in our office in order to realize architecture. It is personal, but at the same time also collective, and has certainly been developed over the years by a number of individuals. Looking back, I think it is correct to say that certain methods and ways of regarding architecture are part of a professional culture specific to our office. In the time that we have practised, these tools have developed and become more sophisticated, with the result that what we build today is closer to what we think it ought to be than in our earlier works.

This can be illustrated by an example from my very first building, the Leper's Hospital in India.[1] I can still clearly remember how dissatisfied I was when the walls began to go up. We were students of architecture, twenty-two and twenty-three years old,[2] and had designed a building which I both wanted and expected to be built just as it had been thought through and designed. But during the building process, however, mistakes were made, and in addition one mason used a different technique than the others.[3] There were deviations from plan and differences in expression which for a long while during construction were extremely frustrating. Gradually, and very slowly, I began to like these events – especially the personal contribution of the various craftsmen, the fact that one mason's work was clearly distinguishable from that of another. Thus the building came to incorporate the history of its production, a fascinating history untraceable in our drawings, and far more complex.

Leper's Hospital by Jan Olav Jensen and Per Christian Brynildsen

Works possible to represent

Given that a realized building is the goal, architects almost exclusively determine architecture by means of instructions which stand apart from the building as such, much in the way composers use notes as their primary instructions to an orchestra. A composition can therefore be performed, or a building design be built, a number of times on the basis of the same set of instructions. The performances may vary due to differences in interpretation and quality, and may comprise mistakes, but the determination or plan on which the performances are based is the same and stands apart from any performance of the work.

Such work may in other words be performed again and again, and if the originator does not want this to happen indiscriminately, it may be necessary to take legal steps to prevent unauthorized use. It is possible to think of the work as an ideal or a norm, and the performances/buildings as a striving to get as close as possible to this norm. Often, one might be able to arrive at the original instruction, and the determination of the norm, simply by studying the performance or the building. A correct performance of a Mozart symphony may, for instance, be the basis for reconstructing the original notes.

Works impossible to represent

The author Dag Solstad says that he wants to tell stories that cannot be retold.[4] This may appear to be an impossibility when referring to text. Traditionally, various disciplines within the visual and decorative arts have been the ones to provide works impossible to represent, first and foremost because there is a long tradition whereby creators build their own work, thus dispensing with the need for any precise plan. In the case of an artist working with oils, it is obvious that a work cannot be repeated exactly, only approximately. The same may be said about jazz musicians improvising a piece of music, or a potter shaping a pot. The work is created there and then, with no ideal plan to obey to the letter. Attempts at repeating such performances quite exactly are bound to fail in the sense that the work will always turn out a little differently, but this is in the nature of the process. The distance from thought to hand is as short as it is possible to make it. One may call such works unique. The work resides in no representation apart from the appropriated object. It is impossible to define it or represent it outside itself.

Transformed into a versatile architectonic tool

When we take stock and look back at our practice, it is easy to single out the project which has been most meaningful to us. The Liasanden rest area along the Sognefjell

Liasanden Rest Area by Jan Olav Jensen and Børre Skodvin

Mountain Road from 1995 preserves an insight which has influenced most of our projects since, however different they may appear to be at first glance. It is a project we have a lot of affection for and which we see as our most crucial work. What we understood with this project was that an idea can be a complete architectural idea, even if it does not have a definite shape or configuration. Exactly the same idea would result in a completely different configuration or outcome in a different place. To us it looks as if this type of geometry can be attained deliberately only by accepting unpredictable results, with configurations which are partly unforeseen and which are a result of processes that are indeterminable before they take place. For us this insight opened a whole landscape of architectural possibilities in related fields, for example the relationship between the original/copy, a unique product/a type, composition, precision, tolerances and the irreproducible. Below I shall explain the application of this architectural insight by looking at quite different samples selected from our works.

Liasanden rest area: precise approximations

The first idea for this project was conceived in the summer of 1995, just before we set up our office. At the Liasanden rest area,[5] along the Sognefjell Mountain Road, we investigated if it would be possible to retain the qualities of light and space that can be experienced in a forest, and whether the ground vegetation could be preserved. We recommended an old pine forest along the highway as the site of this project. The rest area consists of a new side "road" about three hundred metres long, varying in width from about three to twelve metres, weaving through the pine trees. A slight declivity in the forest is filled – like a riverbed – with gravel to a required datum. All blasting and digging is eliminated. All interventions are pure additions. Studies showed that if the addition of gravel was carried out very carefully above the ground line, while varying the gravel's density from the bottom up, it would be technically possible to preserve the existing large pine trees. All trees are thriving twelve years after completion. The gravel, a material with no inherent shape or module, was carefully raised to the level we wanted with backhoes and shovels. The gravel surface did not need to be horizontal, but could rise and fall according to circumstances. The scheme was based on determining the appropriate level of the gravel, so that from the first day the entire complex became a garden complete with vegetation in the form of existing plants and trees. The concept required cars to steer around the trees. Very accurate computerized maps of the trees and topography helped us to identify possible routes for cars, to make sure that driving was viable without cutting down trees. The trees in the "road" have been protected with an element capable of being adjusted to fit any tree on the plot. The "shoreline" of the gravel and the trees create spaces of various sizes. Some are suitable for car parking, some for resting. Working drawings for the project were first done on site using about 400 small wooden sticks put in place by us. The stick positions were surveyed and added to the digital map so that an accurate plan drawing could be generated as a tool for calculating quantities. The contractor, however, used the sticks as the primary "drawing", for obvious reasons. The site is an indispensable condition for establishing the geometry of this plan, if the idea is to emerge into a specific configuration or layout. Without a site, the architectural idea is nevertheless complex and advanced, but has no exact configuration.

Railings at the Videseter Waterfalls: simple instructions, complex results

A scenic spot at the edge of the precipice at the Videseter waterfalls required new railings.[6] Annual avalanches had damaged existing railings repeatedly. The rock on which the vantage point is located had been blasted long ago to improve accessibility. The new railings are constructed of steel rods, 90mm in diameter, mounted in holes drilled at the exact same level in the rock, with 10mm steel sheets between the rods. This structural principle resulted in a highly stable geometry. A repairing concrete surface was cast on top of the rock that forms the vantage point, damaged by earlier blasting. The horizontal datum admits the higher parts of the rock to form

Videseter Waterfalls railings by Jan Olav Jensen and Børre Skodvin

"islands" in the concrete. The handrails on either side of the cliff leading down to the waterfall were generated very differently. We made principal sections of three types of railings (according to building legislation requirements) and placed the railings in plan according to the curves of the site. Then we gave some simple instructions to the welder, requiring him to build the railings on site, with the poles not closer to each other than 0.6 metres, and not further apart than 1.5 metres. They were placed on stones, the height of the vertical posts being 0.9 metres and the vertical curves of the railings forming continuous curves in conformity with the terrain directly below the railings. These instructions, combined with this particular process, made detailed working drawings of these very complex three-dimensional curves redundant. The curves may actually not even be expressible as they have been realized, but a close likeness could have been produced had we chosen to use very advanced technology, and if we had had access to the resources needed for such a planning and building process. It would have required a large number of drawings, advanced programmes and highly skilled architects and engineers to plan and build it. It would have been far more costly, and the chances of getting things wrong during such a complicated and, according to conventional wisdom, a more determined and secure process would have been far greater.

Twenty-two rowhouses in Ole Reistadsvei: monotony and variation
The site borders a nearly continuous forest surrounding Oslo. The pine forest extends into the plot from the east, ending at the top of a small rocky ridge, about 10 metres high, with a view over the city to the west. We were required to design twenty-two apartments. The site was divided strictly equally by size, but existing trees provided "exceptions" to the uniformity, challenging the complexity and adaptability of the chosen type. As there were twenty-two identical programmes, on identically sized plots, the random configuration of trees on each plot provided an opportunity to study the core programmes and the dimensions of the rooms in a house related to its margins. Which rooms, or parts of rooms, had large enough geometrical margins to be used as a tool to make spaces for the trees? And what kind of construction did this generate? The public entrance area divides each plot, the garage and storage to the left, and the other rooms to the right. The trees generate variously shaped and differently placed atrium gardens in each house. Similar plans will only occur by chance; otherwise the similarity would be forced. When a tree dies the positioning of a new tree will relate to the court, as the positioning of the court relates to the old tree.[7]

Mortensrud Church: complete fragments
The church is situated on the top of a small crest with large pine trees and some exposed rock.[8] Geometrically, the church is an addition to the existing ground surface. No blasting or excavation was necessary, except for the careful removal of a thin layer of soil. A number of trees are preserved in atriums within the enclosure. Some of the rock formations emerge like islands in the concrete floor of the church, between the congregation and choir. Thus, the church takes its major divisions from elements already on the site. This is possible because there are relatively

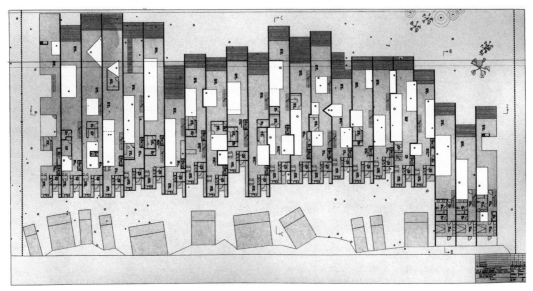

Ole Reistadsvei Housing by Jan Olav Jensen and Børre Skodvin

large tolerances in dimensioning the rooms. No module has been used to determine the exact positions of the gardens. Rather the materials and structures were chosen so that a non-incremental adjustment of dimensions, without steps or modules, was possible. The tension between the wish to create a "silent" self-referring room, and a variety of obstacles limiting this possibility, was deliberately chosen as a strategy to architecturally "disturb" a process in which a wide range of people and interests are involved, and which otherwise would have been heavily laden with conventional and historical references. The main structure is a steel framework with a stone wall carrying the roof. The stone in this wall has been laid in place without mortar, thus letting light through. There is one even side, and one uneven. The uneven side of the internal stone wall is exposed to the outside through the glass façade on three sides of the church. The pattern that emerges in the wall with these stones will never repeat itself, thus creating a geometric object, the main church room, that compositionally coheres as one thing and is unique. It is not constituted by a number of similar modules or elements, for instance suggesting that it could have had a number of different sizes. Another aspect of the same thing is surface treatment of similar pillars with transparent oil, thus leaving all the marks and scars from the manufacturing and production process, making every pillar unique, and letting its story be readable. In this case we found it appropriate to underline a quality of extreme individuality in all objects, using different techniques with unpredictable outcomes to achieve this.

The Norwegian Design and Architecture Centre: building nature
The Norwegian Design and Architecture Centre, DogA,[9] decided to move to an old transformer station in 2003. The planning and building work was done in approximately fifteen months, resulting in an extremely hectic process. The building

The Norwegian Design and Architecture Centre by Jan Olav Jensen and Børre Skodvin

consisted of a conglomerate of different additions and alterations from around 1860 until 1980. We thought it would be not only interesting to reveal this intense and dramatic history of continuous physical change by uncovering as many "voices" from the past as possible, but that it would also create rooms that would be appropriate backdrops for all the hyper-modern design objects that continuously are on display in the building. This was done with different techniques developed during the building process, such as never covering anything that had been uncovered and removing only the plaster that was in bad shape. We asked the masons to knock on the plaster with their hands so that by listening they could determine the border between good and bad plaster. The bad plaster was removed and the result was left just like that, without any further repairs. The resulting line is in a manner of speaking the identification of a ruin. One could also say that it has a nature-like quality because of the immense amount of complex information it contains; the structure in the plaster allows no margins at all, it attains the same kind of critical precision one finds in nature. Our hypothesis was that by revealing such a huge amount of extracted parallel architectural information we would come close to some sort of a very complex natural quality, a sort of white noise that would constitute a different kind of white box for all the objects on display. The new additions inside are constructed with primitive and very simple Cartesian geometries, making them stand out in a ruin-like environment, because of the simple instructions necessary to define them.

Sverre Fehn and precision

Even though I have argued that the professional concerns I have raised cannot be fully explained by our education or other external factors, I want to point out some aspects of the education at the Oslo School of Architecture, and especially at the studio run by Sverre Fehn,[10] which I think at least contributed to the formation of our architectural field of interest, if not to the particular tools I have described. As students at the school we repeatedly heard teachers enthusiastically elucidate the "precision" of different great works of architecture. Possibly it was one of the most frequently pronounced words at our crits. Precision was described as an indisputable goal, something absolute, and one of the distinguishing marks of great architecture. When this concept was explained by a good teacher, as by Sverre Fehn, architectural precision might be illustrated in the most surprising and spellbinding ways. It might for instance be a question of the acoustic properties of Le Corbusier's great hall at Chandigarh, and how the organic shapes of the muffling panels in the walls had turned out to correspond exactly to need. And best of all, that Le Corbusier had found these shapes by "sensing" and "hearing" them in the company of an expert in acoustics, finding the answer intuitively. "He was so good that he could draw sound," Fehn said in his lecture. This was of course an undisguised celebration of how far professional mastery could be taken, and a tribute to individual capabilities that could not be straightforwardly taught or learnt, but which were personal and which one possibly might be able to cultivate and practise over time. The pitch of the lectures was not unlike that one may find in Kurosawa's film *Seven Samurai*, where the master samurais early on in the movie are paraded with their individual, nearly miraculous accomplishments. Fehn is considered by many of his students to be the best teacher they ever had. In one of his last lectures before he retired, he launched the concept of "the creative lie". Whether or not the colourful and often baroque stories he told in his lectures had any counterpart in life, for many of us who studied with him, there was something cultic both about the concept of precision and about how far it was possible to take it. It was a matter of uncovering one's inner source.

Method and work

All of the projects I have described in some way take the term precision as the prevailing theme. We are among other things deeply interested in how we arrive at the dimensions in our completed drawings and in our completed buildings. One might then ask what the architect is able to contribute if constantly resorting to contextualization as a method. Is it possible to arrive at independent architectonic statements which are not merely an automatic result of interpreting site or environment? I believe it is. First and foremost, I have described methods that bring about the architectural qualities we have sought, not the works as such.

NOTES

1   The Leper's Hospital in Lasur, India, published for example in *A+U* 331, 1998.
2   The Leper's Hospital was designed with Per Christian Brynildsen in 1983–84, while we were both students at the Oslo School of Architecture. On a study trip to India in spring 1983 we were given the job quite by chance. The client wanted the project to start up immediately, and we remained there for about a year, doing the drawings while the building was being built. The building received the Aga Khan Award for Architecture in 1998.
3   We were asked by the client to manage the building work and were at the site daily, and thus continuously consulted about the work. When we were not on site, we were in a nearby cabin drawing. Up to sixty to seventy workers were active most of the time we were there. Because we had no copiers, the drawings we worked on were the only designs for the project. We set out all the buildings on site ourselves, using chalk or string, in cooperation with the local masons.
4   "Jeg driver altså med å fortelle historier som ikke kan gjenfortelles." [I occupy myself with telling stories that cannot be retold.] Dag Solstad, *16.07.41*, Oslo: Oktober, 2002, p. 146.
5   "Liasanden lay-by", *A+U* 334, 1999.
6   "Railings, Videseter waterfalls", *A+U* 334, 1999.
7   "22 Rowhouses in Ole Reistadsvei", *Jensen & Skodvin Architects: Processed Geometries 1995–2007*, Oslo: Unipax, 2007 [exhibition catalogue], p. 213.
8   "Mortensrud church", *A+U* 383, 2002.
9   "DogA, Design og Arkitektursenteret", *Forum* 1 (Sweden), 2005.
10 Sverre Fehn was a professor at the Oslo School of Architecture from 1971 until 1995. He was awarded the Pritzker Prize in 1997.

Swedish Introduction

Johan Mårtelius

With Functionalism as the Hub

Modern Swedish architecture has become famous for its pragmatic, practical, problem-focused stance. The participants in the Swedish welfare project have been able to remain relatively anonymous and subsequently architects have been bracketed with other professional groups among the ranks of "social engineers". Even the architects who attained artistic fame, such as Erik Gunnar Asplund, Sigurd Lewerentz or Peter Celsing, can be considered somewhat unforthcoming about their intentions and their theoretical reflections.

Nevertheless architecture has aroused lively debate as a social issue throughout the period. How, on the one hand, should the art of building relate to the radical modernisation, by international standards, of Sweden and, on the other, to traditions and cultural constants? Since 1901 these questions have constantly been reflected, for instance, in the architectural journals, entitled alternately *Arkitektur* and *Byggmästaren*, to which many eminent architects during the period were linked. And at least until recent decades, the majority of the most influential practitioners have played a role of some kind in the training of architects. In connection with the breakthrough of international modernism around 1930, five eminent architects contributed jointly to the cogent and widely discussed polemic *Acceptera*.[1]

In the decade before 1930 the architectural profession had been increasingly assertive about its responsibility and its artistic significance in society and public debate. In books and journals the role of the profession in the construction of society became more and more manifest, not only through their designs and plans but also through enquiries, debate and reflective texts. Architecture sought contacts with classical humanist culture and some publications discussed issues of form and history, but more frequently their subject was city planning, the provision of housing and the place of architecture in social development.

In texts and publications the architectural profession advanced its position internally as well, towards its own professionalisation. Publication of the architectural society's journal, *Byggmästaren*, began in 1922 with the humanistically minded editor Hakon Ahlberg (1891–1984), who also contributed frequently. In principle the publication was admittedly a continuation of its predecessor, *Arkitektur*, which had been issued during the previous two decades with Gunnar Asplund as editor during its final years. But in addition to a shift of publisher and its new name, *Byggmästaren* marked an official separation from the Society of Engineers. The journal now laid stress on architecture as teamwork in which different contributions had to be coordinated by the architect's shaping hand. In connection with one of the important manifestations of architecture during the decade, the great jubilee exhibition in Göteborg in 1923, Asplund gave succinct expression to prevailing attitudes: "Architectonic endeavour today, at its best, is moving towards a subordination of detail, a coordination of all the heterogeneous needs and requirements and dimensions through firm architectonic control around a central idea. It seeks organisation and character."[2]

Ragnar Östberg's renowned City Hall in Stockholm, inaugurated in 1923, and the Göteborg Exhibition of the same year both contributed to international interest in Swedish architecture. This resulted, for instance, in a sumptuous work entitled *Swedish Architecture of the Twentieth Century*, edited by Hakon Ahlberg, that was published in London in 1925. The work of twenty architects was depicted in 152 plates and in his introduction Ahlberg nominated Gunnar Asplund as the most eminent. He characterised his colleague's view of architecture thus:

> Asplund is among those who subscribe to the perhaps somewhat old fashioned faith that a clear and elegant plan is the most likely in the long run to be of practical utility. Even though the layman may feel disappointed when every incidental requirement as to detail is not immediately satisfied, the history of architecture provides many examples that it is precisely those buildings with strikingly simple and clear planning which have shown themselves in course of time to be of the greatest utility.[3]

In the summer of 1925 another major exhibition prompted more articles about architecture, the Exposition des Arts Décoratifs in Paris. In an article in *Byggmästaren* in the following year, the young architect Uno Åhrén singled out Le Corbusier's contributions for special praise but he was also inspired to write a broader manifesto for modern design in his article "Turning Points" in *Svenska Slöjdföreningens Årsskrift* in 1925. The goal was architecture that could subordinate itself undemonstratively to its purpose, "endowing practical objects with artistic form without the 'artistry' being noticed". Spatiality was to be activated by a dynamic feeling for form; architecture should manifest itself only indirectly, as a force. This standpoint could be considered the diametrical opposite of the one formulated by Asplund two years earlier. Instead of firm organising architectonic control, architecture was to take second place as a useful servant.

Towards the end of the 1920s, international modernism became more and more clearly the predominant approach in the architectural profession. Uno Åhrén became editor of *Byggmästaren* in 1929 and in the following year the shift of direction manifested itself in the major Stockholm Exhibition, for which Asplund was the chief architect. This exhibition displayed, for instance, examples of new types of dwellings designed by some of the younger architects and these, together with the large pavilions designed by Asplund, aroused public debate about architecture.[4] By this time the concept of "functionalism" had already, despite the opposition of Åhrén and several of his fellow-architects, established itself as the Swedish term for the new architecture. Both the concept and the architecture found cogent advocacy in the articles of two eminent cultural critics, Gustaf Näsström and Gotthard Johansson.[5]

In the autumn of 1931 the 200-page *Acceptera* was then published, written by the main participants in the Stockholm Exhibition. In addition to the exhibition's radical superintendent, Gregor Paulsson, five of the architects were contributors – Asplund, Wolter Gahn, Sven Markelius, Eskil Sundahl and Uno Åhrén. The book took up a wide range of themes: the transformation of cities and housing, standardisation, husbanding resources, new forms of space and urban planning. There was also reference to a radical change in the work of the architect, from creation to "organisation". The work has been regarded as the Nordic manifesto of functionalism, but it also ranges from sections that imply a radical coming to terms with the past to others that advocate a dialogue with tradition and context. Significantly, the authors act as a collective with no overall editor or signatures to the various chapters, but the most radical sections can be identified as the work of Åhrén and Markelius, the more conciliatory come from Asplund and Gahn. This may find expression in the way in which such a belligerent manifesto was launched under as defensive a slogan as "accept".

The Stockholm Exhibition and the breakthrough of functionalism around 1930 was, nevertheless, to be the point of reference in virtually all the debate or theorising about architecture during the rest of the century in Sweden. Defence, critical revision or rejection, all three positions would make their impact for a long time, even if most contributions, or at least the most interesting ones, must be ascribed to the middle category.

The exhibition's architect himself, Gunnar Asplund, is usually included among those who soon revised their 1930 standpoint. Here he expressed himself more clearly through his buildings than in his writing. He had admittedly previously been the editor of the architectural journal, but apart from comments on individual issues and buildings he contributed no articles himself. It is characteristic that both of his most substantial texts about architecture as an art form, apart from his contribution to *Acceptera*, take the form of printed lectures. His inaugural lecture as professor at the Institute of Technology in 1931 dealt with spatial perception and was a way of providing cultural-historical legitimacy to open space as an expression of the contemporary. The cultural readings of Oswald Spengler had already been presented to Swedish readers by the Finnish architect Gustav Strengell.[6] A later lecture printed in the Social-Democratic magazine *Fönstret* involved even more explicit revision of his own opinions from the 1920s.[7] Both texts reveal how the *zeitgeist* of the early 1930s made the newly appointed professor more than eager to appear to be an advocate of programmatic functionalism.

With the shifts of emphasis around 1930 it also became clear that the responsibilities of architects had shifted even further towards social planning and political concerns. This trend was augmented by the Social Democrat victory in the general election of 1932, the beginning of 44 years of uninterrupted government. In various journals linked to the political organisations and popular movements, architects at times expressed opinions on housing and planning issues, occasionally also about architecture in more general terms. Architects were involved in two popular movements in particular, the cooperative housing association HSB, founded in 1923 with the architect Sven Wallander as director, and the Cooperative Retail Society, KF, which had a number of radical architects, with Eskil Sundahl in a leading position.[8] The complicated relationship of functionalism to the social system was debated, on the one hand its links with capitalistic endeavours to rationalise, sometimes referred to as "profit functionalism", and on the other its dependence on central planning to attain its ideals.

The president of the anti-Fascist Cultural Front, founded in the mid-1930s, was Sven Markelius. In 1936 his colleague Gun Sjödin wrote a critical article in its journal about functionalism, in which she did not want to view it as a given product of industrialisation and urban culture. Functionalism was instead a response to the need to rationalise after the First World War when the "representative mentality" of the previous era had been abolished. This new idiom made "a virtue of necessity". Functionalism's dilemma could be found in the way it sought rational production, promoted by capitalism, while the social housing aspect, the creation of "new forms that match the proletarian spirit" presupposed a socialist society.[9]

Other architects, like Ragnar Östberg, took up cudgels on behalf of the historical values of architecture. Retrospection, focusing on both classical architectural periods and the older generation of Swedish architects, seemed overall to become a more prominent feature during the course of the critical 1930s. This trend found organisational support through the formation in 1936 of Svenska Arkitekters Riksförbund, SAR, with Hakon Ahlberg as its chairman.

Under the aegis of SAR, during the next few years a number of publications were initiated, not least when the decline in the amount of building during the war years allowed scope for reflection and recapitulation. This found expression, for instance, in a monograph in 1943 on Asplund who had died in 1940.[10] Hakon Ahlberg was responsible for the introductory, discursive text. He pointed to artistic synthesis as Asplund's distinctive feature and offers an image of a consistent oeuvre that transcends the changes around 1930 through links with the past.

In the same year SAR also published *Trettiotalets byggnadskonst i Sverige*, which presented a large number of buildings divided according to function. In one of the work's introductory essays, Nils Ahrbom, newly appointed to the professorship left vacant by Asplund, sounds out the prevailing situation during the war years. He describes how Sweden's lack of involvement in the war benefits the country. Practical responsibility as an alternative to artistic romanticism was also Ahrbom's thesis when a few years later he spoke as Asplund's successor about architectonic spatiality.

Throughout the 1940s social construction was influenced by Lewis Mumford, and in particular by his work *The Culture of Cities*, 1938. This was published in Swedish in 1942.[11] He found a warm adherent in Uno Åhrén, who wrote an enthusiastic review in *Byggmästaren*.[12] In the same year Åhrén himself published a pamphlet, *Arkitektur och demokrati*, devoted to the housing issue, city planning and democracy. Like Mumford, Åhrén emphasises group solidarity and a comprehensible scale as important neglected elements in city planning. Inhibiting traditional aesthetics must be replaced by a scientific and technological approach. The important tasks, Åhrén asserts with mounting emphasis, are to "study, experiment, enquire, research".[13] One fundamental principle is also that a stringently planned building does not require political dictatorship but forms part of the struggle for democracy.

The question of tradition in a more concrete sense had at the same time engendered lively discussion that mainly concerned restoration and the preservation of cultural monuments. One of the most active participants in this discussion, Erik Lundberg, an architectural historian and restorer, also helped to link the issue of cultural inheritance to the architecture of modern housing. Most influential was his major work, *Arkitekturens Formspråk*, of which the first volume of what was eventually to be ten was published in 1945.

The publication of the first volume prompted discussion for the next few years in *Byggmästaren*, where the work received an enthusiastic review and comments from the Danish artist Asger Jorn. The focus was on the sensual values of architecture, and also the spontaneous and uncalculated. "Apollonian" and "Dionysian" became the main concepts used by participants to define their positions. The debate also reflected the close contacts between the Nordic countries during the war years and the period immediately after them. Some contributions were printed, in identical or very similar versions, in two or more of the architectural journals of the Nordic countries.

The editor of the Swedish journal in 1946, Leif Reinius, explicitly represented the Dionysian standpoint. As one of the most celebrated housing architects of the day, together with his partner Sven Backström, and at the same time proficient with his pen, Reinius was, of course, highly influential in the debate. In an article in the cultural journal *Prisma* in 1948 he addresses a wider intellectual readership and expresses the desire for architecture that offers stronger experiences, colour and sensuality, "the simplicity and pulse of the primordial".

The international attention attracted by Swedish architecture also centred on the work of Backström and Reinius. Here, however, focus was not directed at the world of Dionysian experiences but the methodical planning of housing and suburbs, where Nils Ahrbom was a prominent spokesman of the Apollonian. When a group of English architecture students visited Sweden in the autumn of 1946, SAR arranged an ambitious series of lectures to present Swedish circumstances. The speakers included Nils Ahrbom, Sven Markelius, Eskil Sundahl and Sven Wallander. Their lectures, later published as a book, on the whole display great self-assurance and reveal hardly any traces of the controversy about Apollo and Dionysus. Even so they were also problem oriented and Ahrbom permitted himself the complaint that architecture in Sweden currently "lacks any clear-formed ideal".[14]

Erik Lundberg was one of several teachers who contributed during the 1950s to the humanist and intellectual ambience at the Royal Swedish Academy of Arts, where many architects took part-time courses to complete their training after graduating from the Institutes of Technology. Contact with the work of previous generations was fostered and also with other branches of art. This was the approach of its professor, Sven Ivar Lind, and the other teachers included the architects Nils Tesch and Peter Celsing, who were at times collaborators.

A freer interpretation of the modern experience of spatiality, with implicit references to the contributions of both Asplund and Ahrbom on this issue, was formulated by Peter Celsing in 1960. Like Asplund, he did so in an inaugural lecture as professor at the Institute of Technology. Celsing described collage-like encounters between the old and the new, in which spatiality was perceived as a "structure that is built up of objects of varying spatial densities" rather than enclosed or open space. Celsing's pluralistic concept affirms the ability of expressions from different ages and cultures to create a milieu that feels international in a way that differs from the "international style". At the same time Le Corbusier was still his point of departure, as in the writings of so many other architects since the 1920s.

A few years after Celsing took up his professorship, his older colleague Ahrbom finished his teaching career in 1963 and moved to the National Board of Public Building. His task there was to develop methods and norms for official building projects. He had developed his interest in built systems, harmonisation of dimensions and standardisation during his incumbency of the professorship in the 1950s and in a lecture in 1955 he had described the need to develop building elements, "the new box of bricks". He found precursors in Danish colleagues as well as in Alvar Aalto's writing about standardisation in 1941. He saw this as presaging continued emphasis on "mobility, changeability, adaptability and generality".[15] Projects should take form through combining the expertise of different professions in the building sector and Ahrbom saw the beginning of a development that was rapidly to change the conditions in which architects functioned.

He and others were to develop these premises further during the 1960s, within the National Board of Public Building, under the name of structural philosophy or structuralism. A building should be perceived not as an object but as a process from planning to demolition, a system of graded life spans. Time was architecture's fourth dimension that would materialise in the new open form. Three different levels were to be determined for the building's components, linked to social, structural and operational factors.

In the same period some young architectural practices were established that adopted and developed these tendencies. Two group practices, each with four architects, ELLT and A4, became influential settings for the active promotion of changes and systemisation in architecture. The anonymous ring of their names placed deliberate stress on both their internal team spirit and also the coordinate role of the architects in the wider context of the building process. The theoretical basis of structuralism was formulated in internal reports and studies rather than in published declarations but one exception can be found in the concise policy statement made by ELLT in 1967 and which, perhaps characteristically, was not published in any Swedish journal but in the Finnish *Arkkitehti*. One of the premises was, on the one hand, criticism of functionalism, whose "ideals for architectural expression must be abandoned". But it was implied that this new approach was, on the other hand, the most respectful attitude to functionalism, a form of upgrade to the "second era of industrialisation". The international influences that can be seen here include Reyner Banham's analysis and criticism of the first generation of modernists.[16]

The interest of architects in technological development and structuralism enhanced the forward-looking and ahistorical aspect of functionalism, but the structural ideas of the 1960s also embraced an interest for earlier popular building culture. This could involve the anonymous and typified but at the same time flexibly adaptable. Bernard Rudofsky's *Architecture without Architects* from 1964 provided international impulses but Ahrbom had already made the link in his lectures in the 1950s. His younger colleague, Professor Gunnar Henriksson, took a particular interest in the popular buildings in the region of Öland that used timber frames. More programmatic and poetic were the studies by Bengt Lindroos, who was fascinated by geometric structures, of traditional utility buildings – barns, warehouses, cattle sheds – in the Swedish countryside. These were published in an inspiring book at the end of the 1980s.[17]

When justified by circumstances, the historical references could also encourage review of the technocratic tendencies of the 1960s. The critical trends that culminated in Sweden and elsewhere during the years around 1970 translated into solicitude for urban environments, the natural environment and small-scale structures that were considered to have been sacrificed for rapid building development. The school of architecture at the Academy of Art was one milieu where such criticism flourished. It is significant that its professor, John Sjöström, was one of the four architects involved in the A4 practice, where he was responsible for its more humanist and culturally focused aspects. Together with the art historian Göran Lindahl, he developed teaching methods that concentrated on studies of earlier urban environments for sympathetic refurbishment. Later the Academy of Art also appointed Ove Hidemark, an influential teacher of restoration and the care of cultural monuments. In the mid-1970s there was widespread belief that the front line in the ideological and theoretical development of architecture lay in such issues rather than the futuristic hi-tech perspective.

One manifestation of the critical approach of the profession was the appointment in 1976 of the art historian Eva Eriksson as the new editor of *Arkitektur*, into which she introduced greater emphasis on reflective and retrospective articles. An inescapable theme during its early years was functionalism. The contributors included Lennart Holm, Director General of the National Board of Planning and Building, considered by many to be the ideologist behind the large-scale housing programmes, who attacked the critical mood of the period. He advocated what he claimed had been a knowledge-based tradition since the 1930s.[18] However, outright defence of a perceived continuity since the 1930s as the main thrust of Swedish architecture was a standpoint adopted less and less frequently. Many would rather break completely with this modernist unified approach. An alternative standpoint was to regard the post-war generation and particularly the large-scale projects of the 1960s as betraying the ideals of functionalism. The radical and popular espoused by the 1930s generation had been replaced by adaptation to production and the decisions of experts.

One attempt to formulate an alternative attracted a great deal of attention when it was published in 1978 by the young architects Stefan Alenius, Jan Angbjär and Magnus Silfverhielm, with the title "Mannerisms: Or What Can We Do With Our Functionalist Inheritance?" It took as its starting point 1930s rationalism and the current architectural crisis. The authors drew a parallel with the Italian Renaissance and its shift into mannerism. The reference to mannerism as a more sophisticated, complex and appealing variation of the Renaissance repertoire could recall Robert Venturi's influential *Complexity and Contradiction*. But the authors continued with a comparison of the way in which two Swedish architects, Harald Thafvelin and Peter Celsing, had like mannerism augmented functionalist expression in different ways. Two years later this became the theme of an exhibition that was to be followed by others on similar themes.

Among older architects generally considered to represent a critical and alternative attitude to large-scale late modernism was Ralph Erskine, born and educated in England, who during his early years in Sweden in the 1940s had declared his adherence to the Dionysian approach. With his combination of commitment to the popular and his headstrong approach to form he was later to succeed in uniting the tenor of Swedish welfarism with his international allusions in Team X. He inventively applied the regionalist concepts developed by that group to Nordic conditions in ways that would hardly have been expected from his Swedish-born colleagues. Erskine's libertarian functionalism also struck a responsive chord in the growing interest in the 1970s for global issues.

The central position still occupied by functionalism in architectural debate became clear not least in 1980, when it was time to celebrate the 50 year jubilee of the Stockholm Exhibition. A number of exhibitions were arranged in Stockholm, with both retrospective and contemporary perspectives. The anthroposophical contribution on "unfinished functionalism" was also influential with its main thesis that a more philosophically oriented modernism from the beginning of the century had been trivialised.[19] In general the anthroposophical movement enjoyed a strong position in architecture and art during this period, partly because it had a basis in theory that official architecture seemed to lack.

The 1980s were a period of criticism and self-criticism, but historical models were also analysed freely. Erik Thelaus (1919–2006), in his practice an out-and-out late modernist, published, for example, a short collection of essays in 1984 which consistently embraced a humanist and architectural-historical perspective. Their subjects could include classicists such as Asplund, Piranesi or even Vitruvius.[20] A few years later Vitruvius' classical work *De architectura* saw publication in a Swedish translation. This could be seen as the crowning moment for the classically oriented 1980s, just as the four works by Palladio betokened the culmination of the 1920s.[21]

The new directions taken in the 1990s led to new demands for hi-tech experimentation, international perspectives and American influences. In 1992 a new journal was launched, *Mama, Magasin för modern arkitektur*, by a group of young architects centred on the Berg architectural practice in Stockholm. Its editorial intentions were not as clearly formulated as those of *Magasin Tessin* twelve years earlier, but many of the contributions betrayed criticism of the interest in recent years in the traditional, regional and the classical city. In a phrasing used repeatedly, the desire was to replace "the soul of a place" with "the place of a soul".

During the 1990s and around the millennium, Swedish architecture and the formation of its ideas was the subject of a number of retrospective views. The impression that a decisive shift had taken place around 1930 survived, but attention focused not infrequently on the regional classicism of the 1920s and the regeneration of the architectural journal. A posthumous tribute to Hakon Ahlberg, editor, writer and one of the leading figures in the architectural profession for many years, was published in 1994. John Sjöström, with his extensive experience from participation in both planning on a structural philosophical basis and the academic reappraisals at the Academy of Art expressed his point of view in retrospective criticism: "For decades the role of managing a team of technologists has ended up overshadowing the artistic task of forming a milieu in which the role of technology is not to direct but to serve."[22]

The task of re-conquering the cultural heights for architecture has been the motive force in recent decades. More space has been made available in the cultural sections of the daily papers and another sign may perhaps be found in the fact that when the Architectural Museum reopened in Stockholm in 1998 in Rafael Moneo's new building, it shared the premises with the Museum of Modern Art.

The general importance of Rafael Moneo's work in Swedish architecture during the 1990s may nevertheless have been greater than the creation of a museum building. His interest in the Scandinavian, for instance through his work as a young architect in Jørn Utzon's practice, together with the cultural foundation of his theoretical stance was able to make a positive contribution to both the self-assurance and the theoretical impulses in the Swedish architectural setting. A corresponding contextual and theoretical stance can also be said to have been developed by Johan Celsing, who has had reason in several of his works to take historical settings into account. It has also resulted in some essays, for instance on Ture Ryberg, Asplund's former partner, who set the tone for the milieu in which Johan Celsing sensitively incorporated his first major building project.[23] In other articles on his own works he has found reason to refer to the sculptor Carl Milles and the architectural culture that emanated from the 1920s classicist Ivar Tengbom. As the architect responsible for rebuilding at the baroque Royal Palace of Stockholm in the 2000s, he has actively studied Tessin's palace milieu. Even though the core of Johan Celsing's reflections deal with the tectonic and structural integrity of buildings, he is still one of many examples in the perspective of the last hundred years in Sweden to show that interpretation of contexts and of the experiences of previous generations have been equally vital elements.

NOTES

1   Gunnar Asplund et al., Acceptera, Stockholm: Tiden, 1931. English translation in Lucy Creagh, Helena Kåberg and Barbara Miller Lane (eds), Modern Swedish Design: Three Founding Texts, New York: Museum of Modern Art, forthcoming, 2008.

2   Gunnar Asplund, "Bilder med randanteckningar från konstindustribyggnaderna vid Göteborgsutställningen" ["Pictures with marginal notes of art industry buildings at the Göteborg Exhibition"], Byggmästaren, 1923, p. 277.

3   Hakon Ahlberg, Swedish Architecture of the Twentieth Century, London: Benn, 1925, p. 26.

4   Eva Rudberg, The Stockholm Exhibition 1930: Modernism's Breakthrough in Swedish Architecture, Stockholm: Stockholmia, 1999.

5   Gustaf Näsström, Svensk funktionalism [Swedish Functionalism], Stockholm: Natur och Kultur, 1930; Gotthard Johansson, Funktionalismen i verkligheten [Functionalism in Reality], Stockholm: Bonniers, 1931.

6   In the book Byggnaden som konstverk [Buildings as Works of Art], Stockholm: Bonniers, 1928, and in a lecture published as "Spenglers historiefilosofi och arkitekturen" ["Spengler's philosophy of history and architecture"], Byggmästaren, 1925, pp. 186–88, 201–03.

7   Gunnar Asplund, "Arkitektur och miljö" ["Architecture and Setting"], Fönstret 29–30, 1932.

8   Hyresgästernas Sparkassebolag, Kooperativa Förbundet.

9   Kulturfront, 1936, reprinted for instance in Peter Sundborg (ed.), Svensk arkitekturkritik under hundra år, Stockholm: Byggförlaget, 1993.

10 Gunnar Asplund, arkitekt: 1885–1940, Stockholm: Tidskriften Byggmästaren, 1943; English version, Gunnar Asplund, Architect. 1885–1940, Stockholm: Tidskriften Byggmästaren, 1950.

11 Lewis Mumford, Stadskultur, Stockholm: Kooperativa Förbundets Bokförlag, 1942; with an introduction by Gregor Paulsson.

12 "Människorna och städerna" ["People and cities"], Byggmästaren 1942, pp. 265–67.

13 Uno Åhrén, Arkitektur och demokrati [Architecture and Democracy], Stockholm: Kooperativa Förbundets Bokförlag, 1942, p. 16.

14   Th. Plænge Jacobsen and Sven Silow (eds), *Ten Lectures on Swedish Architecture*, Stockholm: Tidskriften Byggmästaren, 1949.

15   Nils Ahrbom, *Arkitektur och samhälle* [*Architecture and Society*], Stockholm: Arkitektur förlag, 1983, p. 172.

16   Ahrbom has later claimed that inspiration from international developments was restricted to early examples of flexibility, such as Mies van der Rohe's houses at the Weissenhof Exhibition in 1927. On the other hand they are said to have initiated Swedish development as early as in the 1930s, in projects by Erik Friberger and Ahrbom himself, for instance. Nils Ahrbom: "Svensk structuralism" [Swedish structuralism], in Anders Ekholm *et al.*, *Utvecklingen mot strukturalism i arkitekturen* [*Developments towards Structuralism in Architecture*], Stockholm: Byggforskningsrådet, 1980, pp. 160–82.

17   Bengt Lindroos, *Ur den svenska byggnadskonstens magasin* [*From the Inventories of Swedish Building*], Stockholm: Arkitektur Förlag, 1989; with an English summary.

18   Lennart Holm, "Funktionalism är kunskap" ["Functionalism is knowledge"], *Arkitektur* 7, 1976, pp. 12–13.

19   Åke Fant (ed.), *Den ofullbordade funktionalismen* [*Unfinished Functionalism*], Stockholm: Liljevalchs, 1980.

20   Erik Thelaus, *Till arkitekturens lov. Essäer av en praktiserande arkitekt* [*In Praise of Architecture: Essays by a Practising Architect*], Stockholm: Arkitektur Förlag, 1984.

21   *Vitruvius om arkitektur, tio böcker*. Translation by Birgitta Dalgren, introduction and commentary by Johan Mårtelius, Stockholm: Byggförlaget, 1989.

22   John Sjöström, "En konstruktiv skeptiker – Hakon Ahlbergs arkitektursyn" ["A constructive sceptic"], in Eva Paulsson and Eva Rudberg (eds), *Hakon Ahlberg, Arkitekt & humanist* [*Hakon Ahlberg, Architect & Humanist*], Stockholm: Svensk Byggtjänst, 1994, p. 25.

23   Johan Celsing, "Tyre Ryberg 1888–1961", *Arkitektur* 8, 1993, pp. 42–47.

The Royal Institute of Technology Building by Sven Markelius and Uno Åhrén

1925

Uno Åhrén

Turning Points

Arts décoratifs modernes? What a surprise at first impression! An atmosphere of strange vagueness suffused this exhibition. And one soon realised that this lack of clarity was not coincidental and superficial but lay concealed more deeply in the creative will itself and its perception of ends and means.

If, to begin with, one accepted or rejected by feel alone, it was striking how everything that one immediately considered contained something that one could identify as specific in its approach, something that one would dearly like to call modern in its good sense, could, almost without exception, be classified as purely decorative. What mastery in dealing with furs! What refined taste in shoes and gloves, where luxury consists of distinct form and exquisite materials with no unnecessary embellishment! Wonderful glasses meant chiefly to be looked at. Finely bound volumes for those who prefer form to thought.

It was different where the decorative instinct was applied to objects and architecture intended for more or less practical purposes. Here one felt spontaneously at odds with virtually everything. It was not difficult to find rational grounds for this feeling: here there was far too little logical connection between purpose and form.

I remember my first impression of surprise at the lack of clarity of the overall arrangement of the exhibition and its external architecture. What a maze of buildings and items! No orderly organisation, no proud plan, no great thoughts, no living rhythm. Everything so fumbling and uncertain in its profusion. Well, it must be possible to base abstractions on coincidences and trifles. But if one decided not to regard the great event as a relative failure, in my opinion one had to go too far in the opposite direction and settle for accepting the beauty of certain individual decorative details. It would be totally misleading to ignore the fact that the bulk of the items to be found there were intended for indoor settings and with it the belief that this setting should mainly be studied and judged as a whole, as spatial art. The conception of space as architecture and setting is in fact primary in all the forms of art concerned here. But in the spatial architecture there prevailed, with a few rare exceptions, exactly the same spirit as in the architecture of exteriors. For this reason, despite the most honest intention, no closer study could alter the first depressing impression: that clarity, purity, logic were lacking. One wandered through these numerous interiors with a growing feeling that time had come to a stop. They seemed so out of touch with the age. This inane delight at allowing everything to take whatever shape one pleases, a building or a chair is not much more difficult to shape than gingerbread . . . A little more Cubist than art nouveau, and a little less seaweed . . . But not one step further towards genuine candour.

How heavy the thought of having to live in one of these rooms. The very air seems impenetrable to clear thought or healthy laughter. Forms, forms, forms . . . I experienced the same drowsy aversion that I understand must be experienced in a tropical forest, where the air is heavy with soporific scents from vegetation that only wells forth in lazy extravagance, where one plant clings to another and immensely large flowers bloom for only one night. A paradise of parasites . . . One must long for hardships in such lax exuberance of magnificent forms, where all is permitted and all is possible. For stimulating opposition. Problems.

One quite simply rebelled against it all, ready to hate all artistic concern for practical objects! Decorative form in every millimetre of our environment – how unspeakably revolting such a milieu would become in the end! Such wild longings for air, space, freedom overpowered me! My thoughts went with such gratitude to all that merely goes about its task with no concern for its appearance. Light bulbs, washbasins with hot and cold water, the crane on the wharf alongside the Seine, a normal French book. The austere forms of technology that are quite simply adapted to the work they have to do and do not give a fig for art!

The problems of form are naturally not so simple, however. Rarely does the technological govern completely. The light framework of the crane with its scoop hanging from a slender cable: that is the outcome solely of technological and economic calculations with no concern for form. But forms of this extreme kind are only displayed by a few items that are subject to stringent functional considerations. A plough, a printing press, an aeroplane. If one imagines a series of objects like these, whose practicality can be calculated absolutely, to end with the purposeless work of art, it is obvious that as the technical considerations become more manifold and lose their stringency, some free creation of form must be involved as a determining factor. And this is an emotional ingredient, it can never be anything else. The emergence of a formal idiom that is typical of the period depends on some specific feature of the feeling for form which is linked to the nature of contemporary views of life, philosophy of life.

The question then is whether there has been any deeper change in the way of viewing form on which to base a modern requirement of candour? Is it certain that modern form is anything more than a fashionable whim, slightly cleaner lines, a little less decoration? If we ignore this question, it is hopeless to try to understand the good well enough to be able to make it bear fruit and the bad well enough to avoid it.

When we require from form the logical expression of the functions of an object, what does this mean? Can perhaps this tendency be reduced to a manifestation of an intellectual sobriety that is in the process of eradicating artistic imagination and impoverishing its entire perception of form? Is all this in the end no more than a crass utilitarianism that is in actual fact hostile to all art? No, the process of transformation that feeling for form is undergoing today does not mean a loss but, on the contrary, newly gained freshness and wealth. A new kind of awareness of beauty is in the process of taking shape. Or at least the honing of a certain view of things that has previously existed diffusely. The functional itself is in the process of acquiring an aesthetic value of its own. This is the significant feature of the modern feeling for form. It finds sufficient pleasure in form when it is at work. It does not delight in the blueprint for the crane viewed in itself for its purely formal qualities. Its appearance is rather manifest in the mere external vision of the function itself, the technological rationality, the economic common sense. This is in all ways primary. The form that seems to be imposed logically by its purpose is experienced as complete; it needs no further treatment for the sake of embellishment.

Where free form creation is involved in the design of an object, we want it to endeavour to proceed directly in this functional spirit. It should render form as if it were the self-evident expression of the object's purpose and function. One can speak of the logic of feeling as an extension of the mechanical. At first sight it could be taken for granted that it is solely the outcome of technological development. That the feeling for form has, in other words, allowed itself to be beguiled by machines and now wants to turn everything into a machine. But the causes are much deeper than that. Our very attitude to life is in the process of occupying a new position. Our once overwhelmingly static perception now tends to be more dynamic. Increasingly we see the world as movement, work, change. The industrial spirit, the natural sciences, the new psychology, the new philosophy, all of these are at the same time engendering and themselves the outcome of a new world image, an alteration in our attitude to the world and to life. How could the aesthetic avoid developing in the same direction? It is always interacting fruitfully with current attitudes to life. It is endowed with a special characteristic as well as by a few factors that are becoming increasingly intensified in an overpopulated world: economic calculations, speed, intellectuality. Technology must obviously be conducted in this spirit if it wants to survive. But inevitably the feeling for form must finally focus on the constraints on its embodiment imposed by economic organisation, logical use of prevailing conditions and the rational exploitation of possibilities as well. In this way to the dynamically viewing eye everything we use will attain incontestable form like that so perfectly possessed by the purely mechanical. In its activity this new form ideal is related more to the bow and arrow than to the Parthenon and the pyramids.

But this endeavour indisputably presupposes artists with a new enthusiasm that will enable them to place their own personalities second to their works. How easy has it not been for some time to attract attention through originality – now it is a question of denying oneself. Endowing practical objects with artistic form without the "artistry" being noticed: that is the specific feature of the truly modern.

Does this mean banishing all decoration? Of course not. But what the modern feeling for form requires is a distinction between decoration and function. It finds its pleasure in the dynamics of things. But it cannot therefore deny the desire to adorn any more than fine painting or fine sculpture can, in other words the art that lacks practical justification. To stick to spatial art: what after all is a dwelling? Undeniably a small part of the world that we have separated out for ourselves and equipped for our own practical needs. But this is but one aspect of the matter. The concept of living is not unambivalent. It is also linked to irrational imagination. If where we live is a machine for the satisfaction of our practical needs, it is also at

the same time a setting that is to nourish our imagination and dreams that tran-
scend the everyday. At home both we and our descendents must, as in the past, be
able to think, converse, make music, free from all practical concerns. This is why
the natural desire to decorate our surroundings will not disappear. The purely decorative, purposeless beauty will continue to be cultivated. What may be questioned
is merely the object of the decoration.

Let us for a moment be radically theoretical. Every object that has one practical
function or another would then in its form express how it acts as simply as possible
and nothing more. The room would then mainly be a specific delimitation of space.
The aesthetic of static form would experience the space as empty and therefore be
inclined to regard the shape of the delimiting surfaces rather than the cube of air.
For a dynamic feeling for form on the other hand, the space itself possesses activity,
tension: the cube becomes primary and the walls quite simply express the energy
required to define the space. The difference in the outcome is striking. In the first
case a method that is in consequence genuinely plastic. What would be typical of it
would be the soft, richly profiled ceiling mouldings – this is called (formally) "marry-
ing" the wall and ceiling. In the second case the feeling that the space seeks to fill
the room elastically and puts tension on its surfaces. There the method will be
logical construction – what will be typical is the absence of a ceiling moulding on
the grounds that it will be perceived as pointlessly filling an angle to conceal the
interaction (genuine, structural) of the walls and ceiling. When the connoisseur of
form sees a room like this he says that it is a box (for a box is constructed of six
sides and intended to be filled with something). And he cannot understand why the
connoisseur of function can feel that a ceiling moulding is obnoxious and gives the
room the character of a cave carved into a mountain. Or why everything "fixed" to
the walls is also obnoxious to him – when it gives such a homely feeling . . .

The "decorative"? Here it has no role to play. We have made the cube to live
in, floor, ceiling and walls are to serve that purpose, that is their work. If the cube
has apparent logic, beauty, is not this work beautiful, enough for a wall?

Moreover there are the mechanical devices, for instance hygienic fittings. Here
the new feeling for form has already certainly got it right. Is there anything more to
change? (In Paris in 1925 admittedly attempts were seen in this direction, not only
one but many lavatory stools, washbasins and bathrooms that recalled days long
gone by, when it was fashionable to decorate ewers and basins with water lilies.)
Modern hygiene has continued to refine the functional; it has therefore succeeded
in attaining definitive forms that could be produced in millions of examples without
people ever tiring of them. But here, as well, the problem has been a relatively
simple one.

The reason why it is difficult for chairs, tables and beds to attain a modern
form is that people are not clear that they too are devices. Does it not seem oddly
remote from our daily needs that still today ornamental chairs are being made that
one cannot sit in comfortably? What are we to do with practical objects if we are not
their masters? How can we forgive a chair that makes our back hurt and at the same
time despise water mains that leak or a lift that gets stuck between two floors!
Because it is beautiful . . . How much the better if it had never hesitated between
the desire to be a chair and to be an imaginative work of art!

Where hygienic fittings are concerned the matter is closed. We have already made so much progress that we consider sheer logic to offer the greatest beauty. An original, personal design of these items cannot be considered anything but unnecessarily extravagant. Today when we manufacture objects of this kind we do not refrain from decoration on principle, but we simply forget to provide any. It is self-evident. But it will eventually be possible for chairs, tables, beds, light fittings to be given self-evident shapes in the same spirit. They would, in their own time, of their own accord, cease to be lumps of dough that can suitably be placed in the playful hands of an artist for their composition. Their *raison d'être* is to serve us – therefore they are still waiting for their logical form that simply says "at your service!" Anything more than that is superfluous.

And the same applies to everything that has a practical task. Decoration will disappear. But does this lead to any impoverishment of means of expression? Those who are totally convinced in one direction find it difficult to understand those with the opposite conviction. If one finds the modern trend dry and empty, the other cannot help feeling that a Baroque church is somewhat ornately dec-orated or a Rococo chair rather fussily adorned. And if by any chance both can be persuaded to admire an American grain silo, the uppermost thought of the one is of its majestic appearance, which recalls the impressive architecture of the past, whereas the other is aware of the first-rate organisation of the work that automati-cally resulted in this form. Impression and expression.

Now when functionalism is crystallising, the fine arts are doing so as well. The entire register of intermediate arts: décoratifs, appliqués, is shrinking to comprise textiles and the like, where the desire to decorate is quite naturally associated with practical purpose. The real tasks of painting and sculpture are not decorative. Instead of requiring the fine arts to "adapt" in the future to, or more accurately become embroiled in, the practical, on the contrary there will no longer be any tol-erance of such half-measures. Distinguishing between purposeful art and the pur-poseless will assist the former to do its best and liberate the latter from indentured service which, moreover, merely corrupts it. How much sounder paintings and sculptures would seem in a setting that did not itself wish to be a painting and a sculpture!

So how will things turn out if one wants to attempt to put this theoretical modernity into practice, can it offer any examples of a satisfactory reality? Yes, in extreme cases: typification driven to its utmost. Typification is a phenomenon that is most intimately related to the new age. First and foremost its grounds can be found in economic necessity. In large-scale industrialisation the methodical restric-tion of the number of models and the determination of standard forms has in certain quarters long been a fact. And one can observe how this concept is gradu-ally gaining ground in the production of more and more utility goods: behind the wide variation in form there is some rational need. What, however, actively counter-acts this trend is the competitiveness that attempts to attract buyers through the constant offer of new and original wares. In this way people find endorsement of their considerations of artistic form when they should rightly be resisted. In the end it is public taste that decides how far attempts at typification can go with any hope of success. Typification must therefore be based not only on the economics of manufacture but also the new feeling for form that is evolving. This is shown by the example of the hygienic fittings. For one must never believe that these are accepted because they are manufactured on rational principles.

This is best demonstrated by furniture production in this country. No factory has succeeded in implementing the mass production on a moderate scale of any single item. Our largest factories do not even work with series of hundreds but with dozens. The competition forces salesmen to offer unending novelty and to flatter the buyer by claiming that among the thousands of models there is some particular finesse that will match his individual artistic taste. Can one imagine anything more absurd! But if we can get the new feeling for form into our bloodstream, standardisation will become self-evident for furniture as well. We will then remind ourselves pityingly of the time when a chair was something half way between a utility item and a fine artistic composition, how we vacillated to and fro, curving one piece this way, another one that, in a thousand minor variations. Where simpler items are concerned the typical forms will be just as important for the taste of buyers as it already is for the manufacturers in their production. How salutary it would already be today if we had a million identical chairs, really good chairs, on which there was no special and original tiny details to be observed, which did not perturb you with the idea that they had some relationship to "art furniture". How pointless our current connoisseurship of curlicues is! In the end, is not all this one great self-deception?

However, life modifies theory a little even in the most straightforward cases. And even if a chair is a device, it should hardly present itself in the same dutifully serviceable tone as, for instance, a razor. Its form must offer some pleasure, the good-humoured mien that makes it a pleasant companion in a room. This applies in particular if it is intended for the home, where we want to be able to live with as much liberty and few constraints as possible. But not even offices need, after all, search for tedium. The golden rule that could be formulated is: be consistent, be consistent – do not be too consistent!

This circumstance can be seen even more clearly when we move up the scale towards a higher class in quality and price and consequently a lower degree of standardisation, to pure luxury production, which works with unique versions of everything. The irrational element, of which a hint is concealed in what we demand of a normal chair when we require it to offer some form of pleasure, becomes increasingly powerful. But it is completely in the modern spirit that luxury primarily involves the materials: the obvious form, perhaps a little more detailed but still logical, executed in noble and costly materials. However, here the decorative nature is finally so overwhelming that function is lost from view. Ultimately there is of course nothing to stop a luxury cupboard or a small luxury table from being treated simply as a gem. And a hanging mirror, after all, almost invites the application of playful imagination. It belongs to the category of trifles that admittedly have a purpose but whose purpose is of the amiable kind, if I can put it so, that offers itself as the basis for the desire to decorate.

Even so there is something seductive in the slogan: "Death to decoration!" Because this is correct, up to a point. Decoration as a means of rehabilitating a form that would otherwise appear defunct or as cosmetic concealment of something unresolved has had its day. It is quite different with decoration that either emphasises the qualities of the form or of the material or quite simply uses the object to anchor a free imaginative vision.

In the first case the object itself is organised by the decoration. Its task is to cultivate the very form, to allow it to harmonise with the tone of cultural human intercourse we want our immediate environment to be imbued with. This is, after all, really a purposeful logic that is as good as any other. Accordingly its means will be minute and unremarked. This is the significance, for instance, of a small moulding about which it is as easy to say theoretically: it is not required for the object's sincerity! as it is to say: it is required if the object wishes to be sincere in a pleasant way!

In the second case the decoration applies itself to the object. Here as well decoration is not the most appropriate epithet. It applies mainly to the stylistically enjoined standard compositions with which every architectural era has equipped itself. What is characteristic of the new feeling for form is the tendency to abandon the stylistic kind of schematic decoration for the singular, imaginative, much more autonomous work of art that is covered by the concept of embellishment. The difference between function and decoration in one and the same object leads on the one hand to total artistic dedication to its purpose and on the other to complete liberation from it (with of course account being taken of reasonable adaptation to the object). The consequences of this are quite important. The concept of embellishment includes wealth, not necessarily in terms of materials but almost certainly in terms of wealth of imagination and the artistic capacity for suggestiveness. But here in Sweden we have experienced the elevation of simplicity as a gospel. What a misleading half-truth! Neglect of the ornamental element may pose a risk for the entire modern trend. This is at the moment an observation of particular significance for some sections of Swedish applied art to which I hope to return in another article.

But to return to rooms: here too theory has to concede a little. The desire may, in fact, arise to want to deprive a room of its expression of firm closure as a cell in a building. This is just what one does when the walls are papered with an outdoor pattern. If this does not at the same time offer an illusion of an outdoor trellis or the like with air around and above it, at least it loosens up the surfaces a little and denies them some of their tangible density. The need to deprive a room of its cell-like nature, or delight in doing so, is hardly likely to disappear and therefore neither is the means to enable it. However, what is going to vanish, because from the point of view of the new feeling for form it must appear paradoxical, is the kind of decoration that in a "stylised" dilution of itself betokens respect for the surface of the wall. A wall with a surface that one wants to retain is in itself enough – if one wants to turn it into a picture, then all right! But something half-way between a picture and a wall is a mongrel. I would like to demonstrate the difference by comparing Hilding Linnqvist's decoration of a corridor at the Royal Institute of Technology with his painting for the vestibule of the Skandia cinema. In the one case the constraints of an impossible decorative dogma have resulted in a tedious mediaeval-looking imitation, which is merely redundant and trivialises the architecture. In the other we have a painting full of immediate life and natural beauty – it is worn like a jewel which the architecture has donned to enter into the appropriate festive mood together with its beloved (the audience).

It is roughly like this that I believe one can sketch the trends in the new utilitarian art. As often happens with phenomena that emanate from the spirit of the age, they are emerging simultaneously in different quarters. Specific events at the exhibition demonstrated with all the clarity that could be desired that the conception of the modern in Stockholm, Copenhagen, Paris, Vienna, Prague are one and the same in essence. Let us take a look.

First and foremost, one thing pervades all forms of artistic form in all ages, regardless of their specific features. It always involves disciplining a natural material, organisation of the unwieldy material, the human desire to make an impression on it. The impotent and inartistic fails to conceal nature, which can still be seen, intact in its ponderous brooding silence. It is distressing to have to admit it but a large part of this exhibition, at least most of the architecture, both exteriors and interiors, belonged irretrievably to the inartistic category. Is this not what contributed most to the air of gloom? Every pretentious display of incapacity is enervating and wearisome to behold.

But even faced with the interiors of good artistic standards one usually remained relatively unmoved. Beautiful perhaps, but so little that was up-to-date, so remote from our own era! One walked around pleading and begging for something irresistibly alluring, liberating, some trace of art that demonstrates its living concern by speaking directly to us in its own unmistakeable way, by appearing to us as an instantaneously living and manifest formulation of something that we have felt move within us more or less distinctly.

It is so little and, however, so much that is needed – control! One often points out a car with smooth, precise bodywork: look at modern beauty! This is more often than not totally correct, but there are also cars whose forms lapse into snobbery and which no longer meet the mark! What is typical of the latter is that they normally make a lot of noise. But it is definitely not a genuinely modern feeling to drive around with a full-throated roar from the exhaust when it is possible to travel silently. It was exactly the same with the way art was encountered here, it was driving around with a full-throated roar, striking an attitude, smug.

The genre that carries on composing rooms and furniture in this way, devoid of all common logic, is merely interesting as a curiosity. I shall not therefore spend a great deal of time on it.

Holland must then be given the doubtful honour of being mentioned first. My impression has been that this is a nation with a fairly sober merchant's attitude to the world that focuses on practical reality. No trace of this could be seen here, but it may perhaps have been the lust for publicity that deceived itself by forcing originality to extremes. One Dutch interior made a favourable impression by the straightforward manner of its assured composition. But even so it would serve just as well to exemplify the spirit I have opposed.

An overwhelming number of the French productions belonged to the same category. Paul Follot's smoking room displayed by Le Bon Marché shows its average character. Here we find almost all that is modern which we would like to reject. This room is a veritable cavern, it has no distinct spatial form, no structure. Nothing is allowed to be what it really is. Everything is carefully "composed" with something else so that the overall effect is one of sloppiness. The walls and furniture are clothed in a similar material and the same stylistic details are repeated not only on the furniture but on the walls and ceiling as well. However, if one looked at the more luxurious exhibits, nothing changed, as could have been expected, for the better. Jacques-Emile Ruhlman was the important name. An incredible number of panegyrics were written about him in the summer of 1925. In my opinion he is nothing but a fairly unprincipled artist who uses details with a certain sweetness of a preciously feminine variety. His large salon could at least have been a fine room, but the whole thing was botched by the profuse wilderness of decorations, which, to crown it all, were of the most banal kind. As a rule the French interiors behaved with all the affectation of a *nouveau riche* lady of somewhat dubious character: "Now that I can afford so much jewellery (here = ideas) why should I not display it for all to see. . . ." But this merely demonstrates the triviality of the person behind it all. One decided exception was a dining-room by René Lalique, impressive in its clarity. It had many of the qualities suggested by the word salon – lofty space, a specific emptiness that is merely waiting to be filled by people, albeit in this case particularly refined people, perhaps somewhat too cultivated.

Among simpler things there were a few creditable but relatively incomplete attempts at candour by Jean Burkhalter and Pierre Chareau.

A motley mixture of tentative, although fundamentally uncertain, wills! Auguste Perret (exhibition theatre): a reliable constructively, manly uprightness, who is without doubt the fixed point in the new French architecture and should play a healthy role for its modern development. The grand staircase in the Grand Palais by Charles Letrosne: a whiff of freedom and breadth of traditional French architectural exteriors, although no more than that. The hall of the ambassador's apartment by Robert Mallet-Stevens or the tourist office in the same building: a clarity, an uncluttered combination that is indisputably moving in the right direction – not, alas, fully convincingly, however, when one has had occasion to note how easily the architect relapses into the superficial "modern" aeroplane manner without any functional content.

For me the real highpoint of the exhibition, indeed the only display of any awareness of the new age, was the building arranged by the journal *L'Esprit Nouveau*. Its architects, Le Corbusier and Pierre Jeanneret, are French, but their work has a modern, supranational character. The way in which they work is the direct opposite of decorative composition. Instead of starting with the making of the room and how it is to be furnished based on a more or less vague personal feeling for the kinds of forms that may suit us, they explore modern housing needs and their underlying conditions in depth. From the solutions to purely practical economic, organisational, hygienic and structural concerns the architectonic project finally crystallises, down to rooms and furniture. It goes without saying that this art focuses entirely on regular mass-production. I cannot go into the major features of the impending project in any more detail. (I recommend the study of Le Corbusier's work *Vers une Architecture* and *Urbanisme*, Les Editions G. Crès et Cie, 21 Rue Hautefeuille, Paris). In brief, a section with a type of suburban terraced "immeuble-villas" (freehold maisonettes), in which the main element consisted of two very large and high spaces designed to enable the combination of all possible domestic needs within them, one treated as a garden with one façade entirely open, the other as an everyday room with one large window. Behind them the necessary smaller spaces are arranged in two storeys. What is of greatest interest to us here is that the solution is completely in the modern spirit, above all in its radical distinction between function and embellishment. Here we ran no risk of tramping into an artistic composition whose delicate balance could perhaps merely be marred by our presence. Here there was space to allow freedom of movement, serious discussion or jocularity, here there was as much light and fresh air as one could want, open walls on which to hang works of art, free floor-space in which to group furniture in any way desired.

In comparison with this, it is less important that certain details in this project can well be discussed. The method of replacing dividing walls mainly with low divisions of moveable cupboards, in other words to combine virtually everything in one single room, probably has a number of drawbacks, at least for a nation with a somewhat less social predisposition than the French. But even in Sweden there are grounds for asking whether the number of rooms does not play an unjustifiably important role in public awareness, whether one large, airy dayroom with its freedom to furnish in various groups for different purposes offers a natural solution to modern inclinations. It was also comparatively unimportant that the furnishing turned out to be unsatisfactory, far too theoretically arranged. This illustrated what I touched on above, the danger of neglecting the minor necessity of some additional treatment for the sake of cultivation. In the midst of our delight in what is new we must ensure that we retain our humanity intact. It is somewhat ominous if, like these architects, we elevate technical apparatus to the status and dignity of ornamental objects. Strictly speaking it is not much more appropriate to place chemist's crucibles and the like as ornaments than it was previously to embellish the technical with decorations.

The Austrian exhibition was interesting in its mixture of good, bad and half-good. Among the bad I include, to begin with, Peter Behren's exotic, musty imaginative conservatory. One could speak of a modern romanticism: the conquest of distance and the romance of the great contexts, radio, communications, the universal dominance of human thought and technology. But this sick work contained nothing of this kind.

Josef Hoffman is a pioneer, a reformer. This is an ungrateful task that demands more effort than its results offer evidence of and in the end perhaps is merely judged half-good. Compare him with similar artists and works in Sweden. Hoffman's weakness is apparent, apart from the cheap Wiener Werkstatte work he offers in the form of silver objects and light fittings, mainly in his furniture. The woman's bedroom, on the whole respectable in character, is appreciably impaired by the heavy and unmotivated, formalist treatment of the furniture. One lacks the resilient, economical organisation required by the modern feeling for form.

The good is represented by a newer school, with Oskar Strnad, Oskar Bwlach, Josef Frank, Oswald Haerdtl as the leading names. At the moment it is probably impossible to find anywhere else in Europe a relatively extensive production that more than theirs realises the healthiest and most viable in the spirit of modernity.

Their buildings merit the study of Swedish architects. But even in the form of their interior details and furnishings they unite extraordinary mastery of means with a freshness, a resilience and a practical liveability that we far too rarely attain in Sweden. But they do not seek virtuosity in their work, which was probably why they were allocated so little space. Strnad's organ room, garden room and individual items of furniture are enough at any rate to confirm the conviction that the adoption of this direction in the utilitarian arts in Austria bodes well for the future.

Denmark. It is probably a mistake to consider that in recent years Danish architecture has set a pattern through its aspirations to modernity, in the best meaning of the term. There is far too much emphasis on form for this to be the case. Not that it can be accused of creating compositions in the air, on the contrary it works resolutely from the fundamental but nevertheless with form as its far too overrated target. This takes firm hold of clarity and order as a purely external feature. In consequence the clarity degenerates far too easily into the embodiment of architectural theory, order far too easily becomes rigid symmetry and petrified consistency. Therefore it easily ends up in sterile neo-classicism as well. Both the shortcomings and the merits are clearly reflected in the interiors on display. Extraordinarily skilfully proportioned and with volumes and masses balanced against each other – an art that displays masterful command of the primary formal qualities, cubes and rhythms. But something was missing, something that is also a "thing" and requires its particular candour: the human being, the not merely rational but also somewhat irrational human being! Even so the Danish psyche longs for cosiness! I am in no way pleading for the picturesque petit bourgeois. The general trend in Danish architecture cannot be valued too highly. However, it is merely not enough on its own.

The feeling of life could best be found in Kay Fisker's study, which offered a relaxed place to work at its large, tranquil desk and for reading in its comfortable leather armchairs. The wall decoration, by Axel Salto, possessed a gentle bloom and modest beauty that if it had been continued all around the room would have offered the kind of calm found in a monastery garden. Here it was spoilt somewhat by the large figurative scenes, which demanded artistic merit that was wanting. Proof of the truth of my words about the decorative treatment of walls.

Kaj Gottlob's dining room possessed a similar superior spatial impact and mastery of the formal devices. But that is not enough – standing before it one can only express the hope that Danish architecture and interior art will also involve itself more in the inner dynamics of life so that its practical development is healthy and spirited.

Sweden at last! At the moment we have no rabid experimentalists to be compared with Le Corbusier or Strnad. But the lack of obvious audacity is balanced by a mature awareness of the realities. It is obvious that Sweden derives immense strength from the way in which its impulses to renewal never lose contact with what is practically useful for the average cultivated individual. One gets the impression that we are neither ahead of nor behind our age – we are at one with it.

This means that even the most radically new is coloured by real life, so that it can be accepted by every unprejudiced individual. Asplund's studio (*Svenska Slöjdföreningens Tidskrift* 1925, p. 112) was, I dare to assert, one of the most consummately modern items in the entire exhibition. Did it shock? On the contrary, the beauty of this room and its furnishings seemed completely manifest. Here everyone came to a stop with a sigh of relief, weary and exasperated after the bewildering orgy of forms. What dignified calm, what restrained and nevertheless sumptuous art. What a fortunate balance between the rational and the irrational, matter-of-factness and imagination. True utilitarian art, at the service of humanity. I have, however, one reservation about the decoration of the leather upholstery of the tables and chairs. All ornamentation apart from the painting on the wall, the sculpture on the bookshelf and the relief on the tiled stove felt redundant. Here there was genuine delight in the room itself, in the furniture itself. And in the lamp! This is a detail worth noticing. It was certainly no coincidence that a similar lamp could be seen in one other exhibit, in Kay Fisker's room.

"Artistic form impressed on practical things without drawing attention to the artistry" – that is where the secret lies.

Consider Asplund's chair, it shows what the new feeling for form is capable of at its best. You need not wonder whether this is a chair, in other words a device for sitting on. It has the obviousness of a machine. Here nothing has been added for its own sake, no form leaps forward to greet us. And indeed what could be added? Nobody gives lectures on art about a chair like this, one accepts it, views it with delight – and then sits down.

Carl Malmsten's living room (*Svenska Slöjdföreningens Tidskrift* 1925, p. 111) displays the specific shade of utility, the specific treatment of surfaces and edges that offers the hand that touches them the pleasant feeling of comfort with which their creator has the gift of endowing his works. This strength is balanced by a weakness. If you regard Asplund's room as exemplary in the relationship between rational and irrational, Malmsten on the other hand has too little of the intellectual-architectonic stance that the Danes on their part cultivate to excess. Among some of his later works, like the long table depicted on page 149 in *L'Art Décoratif Moderne en Suède*, one can see that he is beginning to appreciate clear logical form. But weakness is still evident, in the structure of his cupboards, for instance, in the treatment of the cube and in particular the supports, which often detract from his consummate feeling for material and his marquetry.

There are some circumstances that should be taken into account in judging the Paris exhibition and which to some extent could serve to ameliorate the unprepossessing impression.

First and foremost, French spatial art, which in terms of quantity predominated at the exhibition, is still obviously at a stage that has already been left behind in most countries in Europe. It seems to have achieved nothing worth mention since it experienced the art nouveau movement. Comparison with an exhibition taking place at the same time at Musée Galiera of "Les renouvateurs" from 1890–1910 confirmed this. Liberating oneself from tradition is one thing, creating something sensible and new is another. It may well be the French predilection for decoration that makes it so difficult to adopt modern trends. At any rate the difficulty for the applied arts in France to find some healthy line of development consists largely of its failure to focus primarily on the mass production for large numbers of buyers that is of such practical importance and not to limit themselves to *objet d'art* for a few wealthy individuals. France has no movement with a programme like that of the Swedish Arts and Crafts Association.

But in other respects did the exhibition enjoy the conditions to enable a sound presentation of the best in the applied arts? Hardly. The understandable need of the exhibitors to show as much as possible of their technical expertise and artistic inventiveness favoured the unique luxury articles at the expense of ordinary household wares. To a certain extent, Sweden was an exception from this rule.

The overall impression remains that future art historians will hardly ascribe any significance to Paris 1925 apart from its final demonstration to the world of the necessity of altering production to fit in with the renewal of the feeling for form during the transition to a new era. And that is no mean feat, even though it does not correspond precisely to the intention.

Stockholm Exhibition Restaurant by Erik Gunnar Asplund

1931

Erik Gunnar Asplund

Our Architectonic Perception of Space

It is not, perhaps, unnatural for an architect, alongside his normal activities with their continuous study of detailed facts and specifications, occasionally to attempt some form of survey, even though it may be of a somewhat sweeping nature. I am venturing an appraisal of our architectonic perception of space, even though I am fully aware of both the difficulty of presenting this perception as concisely and clearly as could be desired as well as the impossibility of dealing with it exhaustively in any way.

The concept of space comprises not merely the space offered by the rooms in which we live and in our public buildings. It includes spatiality in general, in squares, streets, "cityscapes" and not only there but also in the spatiality of all the objects that surround us.

Initially I would like to refer to a philosopher's observations on my subject. In *Der Untergang des Abendlandes* Oswald Spengler has dealt with architectonic perception of space among the various expressions of culture in the past.[1] He claims that the spectacle of world history is enacted in a series of cultures that grow, flourish, wither and die. Each has its own means of expression, its own distinctive, characteristic view of the world. For every culture all manifestations of its existence are a symbolic expression of a "cultural soul".

If one attempts to plumb the depths of a cultural soul as far as possible, one arrives at the primordial symbol on which it is based and which can be discerned in all its creations by those with an eye for internal coherence. This primordial symbol, which never manifests itself in visible form, affects the feeling for form of every individual belonging to the culture and ordains the style of every embodiment of its existence. Spengler claims that "it is inherent in the form of a state, the religious myths and cults, the ethical ideals, the forms of painting and music and poetry, the fundamental nations of each science". Spengler considers that the primordial symbols for the different cultures can be found in their perceptions of space.

He distinguishes eight different cultures and analyses four in somewhat more detail.

Egyptian culture was characterised by its passionate adherence to the past and solicitude for that which is to come, for which the pyramids and mummies and use of the most permanent building materials such as porphyry and diorite are eloquent symbols. In Egyptian culture space was seen as a direction, a path, best illustrated according to Spengler by the temples with their unending, narrowing, majestic routes between rows of sphinxes, through pillared chambers, courtyards and passages towards the goal.

Classical culture focuses only on the positive and real, the material, tangible and immanent. "The whole world-feeling of the matured classical world led it to see mathematics only as the theory of relations of magnitude, dimension and form between bodies." Classical mathematics consisted of stereometry. The Greeks did not view space as space but as a delimited body. The enclosed, outward-facing mass of a Doric temple and, perhaps, even more the brilliant marble figure in the sun with its magnificent physicality are clear symbols of classical culture.

Arabic or Byzantine culture viewed the world, according to Spengler, as a hole or cavern, irradiated by supernatural light. While the Greeks perceived the extension of space as a body and emphasised the enclosed *corpus* of a building, Arab culture stressed the enclosed built *space*. In Arab culture the counterpart of the Greek temple with its external colonnades is the basilica with its internal colonnades – Spengler says that a basilica is a Greek temple that has been turned inside out like a glove.

Western culture, which according to Spengler suddenly emerged in the eleventh century and is now facing its decline, is characterised in his work in a number of ways. While classical morality is a morality of "posture", Western morality is one of "deeds". Classical mathematics used physical numbers, in Western thought numbers are relationships. Classical architecture is an architecture of the body and delimitation and is by nature static. Western architecture is an architecture of the soul, the spirit, force, and is dynamic by nature. Like Arab architecture its starting point is the interior, but it links the inner with the outer and perceives the internal and the external as one single space. The primordial symbol of Western culture is infinite space.

Spengler offers brilliant evidence for his belief that infinite space predominates in our culture: he sees it in our modern mathematics with its theories of functions, imaginary numbers, the infinite series; in our music which springs from the awareness of infinity; in our art, which perhaps Spengler is the first to label "functional".

Undoubtedly our Western architecture was also in its first, *Gothic*, period, a clear expression of this perception of space. The Gothic is the first form assumed by dissolved space. It does not seek to delimit space from the world around it but to open out to it instead.

The structure itself dissolves the dividing walls between external and internal, it removes classical corporeality by channelling weight through compression lines, enclosed within slender pillars or through counterpoise; it also removes the Arab-Byzantine enclosure by placing expanses of glass between the supporting frame, which had previously been unknown and only become common again in our time.

In actual fact Gothic dwelling houses and their long galleries with windows have, through the half-timbered buildings that succeeded them, provided the prototypical form for the modern frame structure buildings with their horizontal rows of windows.

We can perhaps find the clearest expression of the new Gothic perception of space through comparisons with our mental images of a classical temple, such as the Parthenon in Athens, which is purely external and in which no interior can be found; an Arab-Byzantine temple such as St Sophia in Constantinople, which is an enclosed interior; and a Gothic temple such as Sainte-Chapelle in Paris, which may not perhaps open out to the earth, verdure and the life around it but, on the other hand, to the light of the sky.

While the Gothic turns to the heavens, Renaissance and Baroque rooms turned to the earth itself – the difference in focus could well characterise the culture of the two eras.

To sum up, traditional Western architecture combined to some extent both exterior and interior into one structuring form. Its loggias, porticos and terraces allowed rooms to merge into gardens or parks and the combined building and park into, if not infinite space, then at least long and wide perspectives.

Perception of space extended, therefore – the concept of the vista, which is so closely related to the idea of infinite space, was deliberately incorporated into the form of the structure. Open spaces, squares and streets, became ends in themselves for urban planners and the primary intention of the city building ordinances that for a few centuries regulated the mediaeval town centres was to create large, impressive squares that assumed the character of unroofed anterooms for the churches or palaces whose pompous magnificence was to be asserted. Everything else, which on the whole merely provided housing, was permitted to survive in its old, extremely congested and unhealthy form.

Squares were composed as enclosed, rhythmically accented spaces and as a result the *squares determined what was built*, their façades decreed what form buildings should take, whether they would fit in or not.

The actual perception of space of the Baroque citizen involved therefore many extraordinary juxtapositions of magnificent façades, decorated with colonnades, porticos, blind niches and so on and often extremely simple and primitive buildings which, for the sake of the impressive palaces, were deprived of light and air, and became crooked, maimed or disfigured, which were in fact mere ancillaries.

Popes and princes, however, needed the trappings of magnificence as back-drops for their processions and celebrations, to impress the populace and offer the spectacle they required. In actual fact Baroque squares and rooms are often no more than stage sets on which popes and princes and their courts performed. All of these squares and rooms with their scenically arranged perspectives, their stair-cases, their incredibly fluent massiveness, also strongly resembled the theatrical sets that are so characteristic of Italy during the same period.

The argument that infinite space is our Western signature is correct, as far as the Baroque is concerned, in that it linked, if not always visibly at least in our awareness, interior space with the square or park outside and perhaps also in the way that it did not, as in Greece and Byzantium, differentiate between the treat-ment of internal and external space but allowed architectural interiors to be as external as the exteriors themselves.

But otherwise the Renaissance and the Baroque, and to an even greater extent imitations of these styles, closed off their spaces to the plebeian world outside. They enclosed space with delimiting walls that were extremely firmly accentuated frequently with a forceful array of architectural detail or paintwork that appeared to be, and was permitted no other guise, solid, excluding masonry. Here, floors, walls and ceilings were an end in themselves, the destination of our gaze, that *should* attract attention.

Before we move on to our own era we should remember that the perception of space that emerged after the Baroque period, with the simpler scales adopted in the eighteenth and nineteenth centuries forming a kind of architectonic "comme il faut", takes us even further from Spengler's theory. Its signature was to close off the squares and block the streets that lead from it; treat the street as a room and allow it to dictate what is to be built; treat the enclosed space as a completed unit, closed off from the surrounding world.

But a far-reaching change in our architectonic perception of space has occurred in the last few decades. We are well on the way to showing finally that the Spenglerian thesis about infinite space being the primordial symbol of Western culture points, at least where architecture is concerned, in the right direction. However, it is by no means the practitioners of architecture that have acquired a new idea, a new architectonic direction, adopted because the old one was threadbare and no longer provided inspiration. No individual profession, not even architects like us, enjoys a position that allows it to reverse developments, but the new human circumstances, the new social, economic and technological circumstances impel, whether we like it or not, our professional perceptions to take a new course.

A general upheaval took place in society in the latter half of the nineteenth century. So let us review what happened then (all the things that a lecturer dealing with the subject of modern architecture or industrial art always has to repeat).

What mainly happened was the population of Europe rose between the years 1800 and 1900 from 187 million to 400 million, that is more than doubled. What happened was that industry developed to an enormous extent so that it could both meet old needs and create new ones.

The expansion of the population and of industry led to extraordinary conglomerations of people, so that towns grew at a rate that made it impossible to formulate the problems of these large new urban areas, let alone solve them.

The old town plans, that were spacious and sound for their populations and the two- or three-storey houses they were intended for, had now, with the same narrow streets and very cramped courtyards, to allow for buildings of six, seven or eight storeys and with three to four times as many inhabitants.

The cities were crammed full of dwellings along narrow, sunless streets, their deep courtyards full of children and clutter of all kinds, while "culture" did what it wanted to on monumental squares with statues or fountains at their centres. During the nineteenth century democracy also marched up with its demands for better and healthier dwellings, a place in the sun for the populace and a general rise in their social standards.

The incredible development of communications within countries and between populations predisposed them to demand more openness, freedom in their rooms and neighbourhoods. Our living rooms began to feel too cramped. And the quantity of local traffic expanded enormously, filling our old streets totally, cluttering up the monumental squares and robbing them of their nobility. And all of these were factors that when they had become strong enough inevitably ruptured the fabric of our old towns.

But that was not enough, they also led to some extent to a new mentality that in architecture and the field of urban planning destroyed our conceptions and led us to a general reappraisal which I think emerges most clearly in the issue I am dealing with today, our perception of architectonic space.

I shall attempt to illustrate our, that is our era's, perception of space from a few different aspects.

It is probably generally believed that architectonic values are almost exclusively linked to shapes, surfaces and relationships that have some degree of extension in space. In other words, that it is the floor, walls and roof, the façades of a building, the lines of a bridge, that is the spatial values, that are decisive in this respect.

Does this mean, however, disregard of the values that can be perceived with senses other than sight? Has there not been, for instance, some degree of neglect of the architecture of hearing? Good acoustics, effective sound insulation, offer aesthetic values as well? Or smell? Fresh air and the scent of plants also offer aesthetic values.

And above all, alongside the spatial values do we not have to pose utility values, the functional values that are not merely of practical but also of aesthetic importance? What works well and requires the least amount of effort offers a feeling of well-being, comfort, that is just as valuable as beauty that pleases our eye. A chair, for instance, that is attractive but unpleasant to sit on is also aesthetically unsatisfactory as using it leads to discomfort.

There can be no doubt that functional values characterised a great deal of architecture in the past, but it has to be admitted that the eighteenth and nineteenth centuries far too often disregarded them, with their undue emphasis on formal spatial values, "the home as a work of art", "buildings as works of art", "the city as a work of art".

It is probably the case that our perception of architectonic space has changed to such an extent that the supremacy of architectonic spatiality has been displaced in favour of other values.

The relationship of this altered perception of space to what went before is the same as that of Western morality to Classical morality according to Spengler, that is of deed and posture. It attaches more weight to deeds-life than to posture-art, at least to the extent that lives, purpose, working methods more directly provide the starting point for architectonic creation.

We could perhaps – although admittedly crudely schematically – express this by saying that there is one architecture that primarily aims for good spatial effect and another that aims primarily for sound and pleasant utility and that we believe our own era is evolving towards this second belief.

The second observation on our architectonic perception of space affects the embodiment of space itself and here we encounter what may more than anything else distinguish our modern art of urban planning and architecture from the past.

The architectonic signature of our era is the dissolution of architectonic space. Urban planners and architects have devoted a great deal of effort and expertise to maintaining our old spatial ideals in spite of all the incredible pressures in the form of the unimaginable growth of the populations of our cities, social upheavals and the explosive expansion of traffic. On the basis of our old ideals we have made attempts to admit more light to our apartment blocks, ease the circulation of traffic and we have to admit that some improvements have been made.

But it has also become apparent that we cannot satisfy the needs in our cities and in our housing if we adhere to our earlier architectonic perception of space, to the enclosed squares and streets, to enclosed space in any form. Under the pressure of reality, all over the world people are beginning to reject this perception as it prevents the satisfaction of the genuine needs and instead they are beginning to turn to the *principle of dissolved space*, a principle that is natural for our actual circumstances today and behind which we feel we can also glimpse new architectonic values.

From this perspective architectonic space does not therefore attempt to enclose itself as an architecturally determined and independent unit but opens out, more or less firmly, to the sun, the countryside and human life and movement.

Le Corbusier: lecture notes

Le Corbusier is a pioneer, a theoretician, who has clarified our concepts. His theses are *build in the open air and the green city.*

Not primarily residential suburbs but urban areas with population densities as large as those of today's cities, organised for modern traffic and the supply of necessities and all modern conveniences. At the same time one great park. He wants to kill the enemy – the "street-corridor", the prehistoric street, the quadrilateral town plans of the past. In a perspective drawing he scrawls "Ciel" across the sky.

He and all the rest of us want to gain as much light, air and sunshine as possible. He aims to enable people to use 100 per cent of the total area for movement and relaxation (in one project he considers that he has won 120 per cent of the area as free space!).

He warns us about the illusion of movement and freedom offered by radiating roads and enclosed squares.

Place Vendôme, Paris

Here Le Corbusier warns us against monumental squares that only have a value in themselves. We must all share his opinion – Place Vendôme is magnificent and beautiful but we no longer build like this.

A magnificent idea of Louis XIV, who wanted a setting for his statue; a brilliant affair for the consortium that constructed the square and erected the free-standing façades of sandstone behind which the purchasers of the sites were allowed to build; a series of charming apartments for the Parisian élite.

But pay attention as well to the glaring contrast with those who live behind them and their scant access to air or light.

Place de l'Etoile, Paris

If enclosed, monumental squares are nothing for us, nor is the kind of city that is *only* intended for traffic, human needs must also be taken into account.

Haussman's concept of spatiality involved only channels for traffic, the walls of these channels were turned into buildings as best they could. *What was left between the streets was used for buildings*, distorted, dark, unhealthy buildings of the kind we find everywhere in our cities today.

Plan Voisin

This is what it has been like. *The architect* with his often somewhat one-sided formal perception of spatiality has designed beautiful, monumental, enclosed squares and streets, impressive city settings. The *traffic engineer* with a totally opposed but also one-sided perception of spatiality has intervened either with mild medical remedies or the use of sharp-edged surgery to carve out room for the traffic. In both cases the buildings are treated more or less brutally.

But what is the real state of things – are not buildings the most important aspect of a city? Is not a city a collection of buildings rather than a collection of streets and squares? We must assert that the buildings are what cities are created for; streets are merely ways of getting to the buildings.

To attain something of general benefit a clear analysis is required, first and foremost of the requirements of buildings but also those of streets so that a synthesis can be produced. The solution must at the same time resolve problems from every point of view. The principle of open space seems to do so.

Le Corbusier's familiar "Plan Voisin" for a part of Paris displays a practical solution that, if not complete in itself, indicates the direction to be taken. Much greater population density, much more openness. Organised clarity for traffic, scope for housing to develop according to its own needs, areas for recreation. Almost the entire area is covered with trees, shrubs or grass.

Perception of space – dissolved space, almost landscape, cultivated landscape. "The age of machines" according to some, "le nouveau lyrisme" in Le Corbusier's words.

The easiest way for us to understand the Voisin plan is to imagine Östermalm in Stockholm as a park running from Djurgårdsbron to Stureplan and in it a few high-rise buildings with room for everyone living in the area today. Would we not enjoy this openness instead of the narrow, isolated enclosure of our current streets? But note well that this is not a proposal but an equation with far too many imponderables. After all, we no longer endure the Baroque despotic power that would be needed to implement a plan of this kind.

If Corbusier's radical plan is at the moment impossible in practice, it has nevertheless been incredibly illuminating and influential for all modern urban planning. The actual perception of space it involves is not tied to the current dimensions and shapes of streets, squares or buildings but makes free use of *built volumes and open areas*, it builds upwards to leave large open areas, in every case it concentrates the open areas. Its principle: large open areas, small built-up areas.

Siedlung Dürrenberg

The concept of the space, in its normal meaning, has disappeared in reality from our modern urban plans. Open areas merge with each other, the distinctive contrast between narrow streets and open squares that was typical of our old cities has gone.

Nor do we want to perceive our cities as if they were motifs for picture postcards. We do not stand still at some well chosen point to enjoy their rhythm and colours but we consider how they live and function.

Our cityscapes do not become apparent until we move around in them and survey their entire nature, shape and meaning. *Life, the very idea of movement, has become part of our perception of space.*

Terraced houses, Basle

I said that the contrast between streets and squares had gone. Indeed, the concept of the square is beginning to disappear.

So, will there no longer be any contrasts in modern spatial planning? Definitely, in the contrast between soft vegetation (which is now included as an essential component) and the cool simplicity of the architecture. The contrast between movement and repose, because if movement becomes more intensive, repose will be more absolute. The contrast as well between entire areas of parkland – low buildings – and high-rise buildings.

The modern architectonic perception of space will therefore not be of the schematic kind that reduces all to the same level, that kills personality, but one that offers scope for individual lives.

A city block around 1920

Consider our old enclosed hotchpotch of tenements or our fairly reasonable, interconnected but enclosed courtyards that have something "institutional" about them in relation to the newer forms of planning.

Magdeburg

Enclosure has turned into space.

Angora radio station

I have been talking about the dissolution of architectonic space and the open city areas. But our modern perception of space contains something else as well – and this is the third observation on the subject. It also applies to the spatial values of the buildings and the objects themselves.

I would not say that our perception indicates dissolution of the building volume in the same sense as for urban areas, as a building must always have a certain delimited physical mass, but it does indicate relaxation of the volume, removal of its material weight, massiveness, intensification of structural expression – as we can learn in principle from a beautiful piece of engineering, the radio station at Angora, as well as from the Gothic.

Le Corbusier: Pessac

The modern perception of spatiality also, according to Spengler's hypothesis about infinite space, continues the path characterised by the Gothic and the Baroque, that is the linking of exterior and interior. It does not want to regard the external as one delimited space and the interior as another, there is a more intensive link than before, made possible by our modern technologies, less static volumetric forms, where exterior and interior are built, as it were, in connection with each other.

The interior opens out and in this way expands; its walls are not the object of our gaze, not ends in themselves, to some extent, like the exterior, the interior shifts from being a room to being space.

In our modern conception of space there is a fourth point of view. We do not want to perceive a space as something that is too constant, unvarying. It includes movement, variability, adaptation to different circumstances and different people.

Openness should not prevent closure. We must be able to cover the windows that offer spatiality to allow closure and the seclusion that we sometimes require.

Japanese interior

The variability of spatiality is included in our modern conception just as absolute closure (which finds expression in the saying "My home is my castle") belongs to a time that is long past.

Someone has described this conceptual difference by saying that buildings used to have eternal values but are now articles of consumption. Although an exaggeration, this contains some kernel of truth.

The dissolution of space and its variability clearly indicates a fundamental change in our basic perceptions; in the West we are perhaps approaching the Japanese idea of a building as a not too solid, heavy and long-lasting object. We are perhaps finding ways to vary our rooms, as has long been the Japanese practice, from season to season, from tenant to tenant according to their needs. As the Japanese do by removing entire walls to allow circulation of air during the summer.

The dissolution of space and its variability, decomposition of the building volume, the close interconnection of exterior and interior, all seem to me to display an architectonic perception of spatiality that is close to Spengler's primordial symbol: infinite space.

Before I finish I would like to add a few remarks.

What I have said is not at all new, and many of the observations I have made have already been made forcibly at my department at the Royal Institute of Technology. But I have placed this new perception of space in perhaps intensely polemic opposition to an earlier one to enable me to express these opinions more clearly.

I have also used the term "dissolution of space". Dissolution has an unpleasant ring, rather like decay. Is that what it means? No, it is merely the dissolution of architectonic and rather narrow and petrified forms in connection with a change of the nature of our lives and our society itself. It is not degeneration but regeneration.

I am myself convinced of this, as it appears to me that there is an agreement, a unity in all these ideas that are bound to our modern perception of space, urban planning and the objects that surround us – in the conception of the open city, lack of spatial delimitation, the demands for light, air and mobility, the shift of our interest from the architectonic wall as the destination of the life enacted before it and from the shapes of rooms as ends in themselves to their impact.

Spengler, our philosophical companion, says that the primordial symbol of a culture, its fundamental concept, is reflected by and dictates the forms in which it finds expression. It seems to me that the same basic view that emerges in our modern architectonic perception of space also sustains many other areas of our contemporary culture.

NOTE

1   See Alf Ahlberg, *Västerlandets Undergång. Oswald Spenglers filosofi: framställning och kritik*; Olle Holmberg's essay on Spengler; Gustaf Strengell, "De stora arkitekturernas uppkomst enligt Spengler".

Östergötland County Museum by Nils Ahrbom and Helge Zimdal

1945

Nils Ahrbom

Spatial Design: Philosophy or Architecture?

I

Currently the debate about architectural theory is fairly multifaceted. The clear, straightforward path that seemed to have been discovered in the 1930s has divided into perplexing and winding tracks, some of which still lead forward while others indisputably take us backwards or round in circles. On the one hand the demand for rationalisation, standardisation, industrialisation is louder than ever; on the other side we find that notions about the forms of architectonic expression, the nature of architecture and its innermost values are tentative and uncertain. In this respect the current debate about issues of form in *Byggmästaren* is significant.

Attempts are now beginning to patch up the link with tradition, architectonic continuity, which in some quarters was considered to have been fairly ruthlessly terminated by functionalism. Architectonic style is tentatively seeking for tried and tested elements and writing and research about architectural history is booming. Every year new works appear about the history and theory of architecture that deal with familiar matters from new points of view and with direct address to our own age. Sometimes their authors view architectural idiom as the creation of types based on structural and decorative criteria (Erik Lundberg: *Arkitekturens form-språk*), sometimes as the outcome of ways of living and social structure (Rudolf Broby-Johansen: *Hverdagskunst – verdenskunst*). The Baroque and the nineteenth century, neither of which were particularly favoured fifteen years ago, have been exposed to daylight and related to our own age relatively brilliantly – Baroque for instance by Nils Erik Wickberg's studies in *Arkitekten* and *Finsk Tidskrift*, the nineteenth century through Giedion's publication of *Space, Time and Architecture* and the studies of the nineteenth-century perceptions of form by Gregor Paulsson and his colleagues, which will be the contents of a somewhat delayed volume commemorating the centenary of the Swedish Arts and Crafts Association. Henrik Cornell and Oscar Reutersvärd have also made contributions to our knowledge of this fairly sombre, in architectural terms, century.

The hesitancy and uncertainty about the idiom of modern architecture and the lively contemporaneous interest in the historical continuity of form could be perceived as a reaction to the dogmas of functionalism, but one can also see it as a search for a tradition. It is not until efforts to realise the new become inordinate that youth appreciates the necessity of following Goethe's wise advice: "What from your father's heritage is lent, earn it anew, to really possess it!" The

standardisation and typification of buildings offers a more realistic way of deliberately and actively seeking to form a tradition that matches our current methods of
production. When these two tracks, which undeniably lead in the right direction,
once again unite, then perhaps the path ahead will again be straightforward for
some short distance.

If architecture, to use a definition by Hakon Ahlberg, is the materialised
expression of the culture of a people and an age, then like society it is subject to a
development that, even though it appears to take place in leaps, is nevertheless
based on given historical and material circumstances. Architecture that is, in the
true sense, alive can therefore never entirely lack traditions. Sigurd Erixon said on
one occasion:

> New creations are admittedly normally the work of one individual but usually merely as one link
> in a long chain. An innovation will have no significance apart from the part it plays in the life of
> an individual or a family, unless it is capable of creating a tradition, which means the same as
> saying that it spreads and survives or is *typified* in terms of time and place.

Therefore clarification of the links between our own age and the eras closest to it is
particularly meaningful.

The Baroque and its shift into Rococo and so on are normally regarded as the
final manifestation of a long, uninterrupted tradition of form. The nineteenth
century was, despite its stylistic masquerade, a period without an *architectonic* tradition, when developments were pioneered instead by engineers. For the first time
the art of engineering could act independently of architecture and engineers took
the lead. Architecture became nothing more than embellishment of the structure.
Given this background, it seems fairly natural that the architects grew tired of
playing the role of the decorator and wanted instead to become engineers. Functionalism was one sign that the architects had found their way out of the labyrinth
of styles back into reality, but that was not in itself enough to provide the basis for
a tradition that was capable of development. Functionalism meant, among other
things, that architecture accepted the technological advances of preceding periods.
The reaction against functionalism can, to adopt a benevolent view, be seen as an
attempt to incorporate irrational values into the tradition as well.

*The essential task for architecture is and always has been spatial design, the
definition and creation of space for human life.* This proposition is fundamental for
the rest of my argument. *How* spatiality is defined in this context is of subordinate
importance. The architectonic design of spatiality can provide one starting point for
this study and a suitable way of limiting the enormous subject of architectural
idiom. It is a limitation that means that for the moment one may disregard all the
other factors of a material, intellectual, political, sociological and technological
kind that together make architecture the "materialised expression of a culture". It
also enables concentration on certain unchangeable architectonic values that can
be studied independently and in their context in tradition. At a time when architecture is faced with enormous tasks and when architecture, not long woken from its
century of slumber, somnolently views a world of technological and social chaos, a
study of this kind may well be justified.

II

It is not only architectural historians that are attempting through their assiduous research to support developments and link it firmly to tradition, but the philosophers have also contributed their mite, both the professionals and those in other disciplines with philosophical leanings. Here I shall refer to one of them, Oswald Spengler and his pessimistic metaphysics of history, without deciding to which group he should be assigned.[1]

As is well known, in his attempts in *Untergang des Abendlandes* to systematise all the disparate expressions of culture in world history he also dealt with the architectonic concept of spatiality in past ages. He found that the primordial symbols of the different cultures lay in their spatial concepts: the *Egyptians* viewed spatiality as a direction, a path, the *Greeks* perceived spatiality not as spatiality but as a delimited body, the *Arab and Byzantine culture* stressed spatial enclosure, holes or caves and *Western culture*, which according to Spengler emerged around AD 1000 and is now facing its decline, has infinite spatiality as its primordial symbol, which has been construed by later interpreters to be the same as dissolved spatiality. It has been claimed that dissolved spatiality has become the architectonic "signum" of our age,[2] a view that I am unable to share. Applied consistently it would involve denial of spatial design as the most important task for the architect and therefore for architecture itself as one of the factors that shapes culture. Dissolved spatiality is a pure negation and a symbol of a culture in dissolution. This may at the moment appear to be a fairly strong reason for accepting Spengler's pessimism, but I do not believe that the modern notions of spatiality provide any support for this point of view.

The examples used by Spengler to support his theses are mainly taken from the architecture of palaces and religious monuments. To a large extent the task of architecture consisted in many eras of creating these buildings, which were the focus of architectural ambitions. This is hardly the case any longer. The spatial conceptions they express cannot therefore always be reproduced directly in the most important building tasks we face today.

The conclusions one can draw from the spatial conceptions of cult buildings also seem to me to provide an inadequate basis for a judgement of the spatial symbol of an entire culture. They can offer varying impressions in the search for the eternal that characterises all advanced cults, but this also means that they share certain features and this makes it difficult to differentiate between them. There are, for example, many points of contact between Arabic and Baroque architecture as there are between the axial systems of the Egyptians and the Baroque. Nor would it be totally inappropriate to describe air-raid shelters, bunkers or underground factories as the spatial symbols of our age, akin more to the Arabian enclosures than dissolved spatiality.

If we consider profane architecture it should become fairly difficult to go on distinguishing any spatial symbols that are characteristic of different cultures. Here there is manifestly a continuous emergence of typical forms through the ages. In urban architecture one can point to the similar conception of open squares in Greek and medieval cities, two cultures that according to Spengler should have diametrically opposing conceptions of spatiality. One could also wonder why Greek and Western cultural symbols should be so totally different when Western civilisation is based to such an extent on its "classical inheritance". It seem simpler to me, on the whole, on the basis of the structural possibilities, access to material, ways of living, climate and forms of government, all of which form the foundation of a culture, to find similarities and points of contact in their conceptions of spatiality than differences.

If, therefore, I strongly doubt the tenability of Spengler's theories in general, a suitable starting point for continued argument may be provided by referring for a moment to his thesis that infinite spatiality is the primordial symbol of our culture. Here I consider it important to regard infinite and dissolved spatiality as two separate concepts.

Let us take two examples – a Gothic and late-Baroque church interior, both from cultures based on pronounced cults. They can each be described as being the expression of the desire for infinity, materialised within the bounds of what was structurally possible, but they cannot, as it has been claimed, be called dissolved spatiality.

Scholars dispute about whether the Gothic cathedrals are the outcome of a conscious endeavour to shape spatiality in a specific way, which forced new construction methods into being, or if the buildings evolved naturally because of technical developments. This seems to me as fruitful a discussion as the one about chickens and eggs. The spatiality was the symbol of a cult that did not consider life on earth to have any value in its own right but merely as preparation for the life to come. It represents the transcendental in medieval society and is in this way radically different from profane spaces created in the same period. But it does not symbolise these higher values through dissolution of the spatiality into the external world – not even towards heaven – but by attempting to render both heaven and hell visible with architectural and sculptural forms of expression. If Gothic ecclesiastical interiors are to be regarded as examples of infinite spatiality, then infinity is expressed by the architecture itself as abstract art and within the limits of the building's own confining walls. The large windows do not serve to establish contact between the space and the exterior world. They were filled with stained glass, which provided a fantastic and illusory illumination that instead of offering a connection to the external world emphasised separateness more immaterially but no less completely than the thick walls of Romanesque architecture.

As my second example I have chosen a late-Baroque church, Vierzehnheiligen by Balthasar Neumann, completed in 1772, the time when the first cotton spinning machines were constructed in Birmingham and Manchester. The clearly marked distinctions of Gothic, Renaissance and early Baroque church interiors between their different elements, the porch or entrance, nave, aisles and chancel or between the separate structural sections are totally eliminated here. The ground plan is based on intersecting circles and ellipses. In a cruciform church of this kind the centre of the cross is normally crowned by a dome. The spatial determination provided by this feature is lacking here and is instead replaced by the point of intersection of the four differently shaped vaults above the nave, chancel and two arms of the cross. All the spatial elements work together to create one mighty impression of movement. Using a modern cliché one could describe it as one single dynamic milieu. In this way this volume has a much closer relationship to modern conceptions of spatiality than the Gothic church interior. And in the same way, according to Spengler it can be said to exemplify infinite space. But no more than in the Gothic interior is this through dissolution of spatiality but through the interplay of all its elements to form one single, mighty whole. The various architectonic elements interact with each other and are woven into each other with as much artistry as the various themes in a fugue by Bach. The unity is attained by the interaction of highly refined architectonic and artistic elements and an equally advanced mastery of building techniques. The ribs of the vaulting form three-dimensional curves, which must have been worked out with the help of integral calculus.

In this example of late Baroque architecture one can therefore determine a partially new creation of spatiality that has been achieved through purely architectonic and structural devices – not through dissolution but through interaction. In this example the construction imposes spatial forms far less than Gothic architecture does. It is not the interaction between supporting and supported elements that gives this spatiality its characteristics, but a loftier architectonic intention that has taken advantage of the construction. One can without disparagement label Gothic as constructivist, but this spatiality cannot be described in the same terms.

I want to take another example of Baroque spatial conception before I proceed with my polemic against dissolved spatiality as the primordial symbol of Western culture – its palaces and gardens. Both express a markedly ceremonial form of living and both interact to form an indissoluble unit. The link between the building and the garden is emphasised more than ever before, but this interaction takes place without annulling spatial form. Both the building and the garden are constructed of more or less interacting but independent spatial creations. The perspective from the garden towards infinity is not one that I can perceive as a feature that dissolves spatiality but I would rather view it as a symbol of the ruler's hunger for absolute power. In other words, it is an expression of the insatiable desire for expansion of the despot – a cult symbol linked to a social and political system. The entire society is focused through a strictly axial system towards the ruler's palace – power extends from him throughout the world.

Seen like this, Baroque architectonic symbols have experienced a Renaissance during the twentieth century. In democratic societies they have for the same reason been regarded with hostility and the Baroque has been a culture that was despised. Recently it has been possible to discern changes in this respect. For the study of spatial design the Baroque is also of specific significance for our era, because it denotes the final stage of a long organic development that was cut short by industrialisation. The social symbols of Baroque architecture on the other hand do not betoken a society of free individuals and so can only interest us from the point of view of history. While the way in which Baroque spatial complexes created settings that are important for spatial design, whether in individual buildings or in city plans, their manifestation of princely power is bound up with the special circumstances of the period.

Before going any further, I would also like to touch briefly on Japanese houses, which have also been cited as examples of the architecture of dissolved spatiality. If you look at the floor plan of a typical Japanese dwelling you will hardly get the impression of spatial dissolution. The floor plans are admittedly open, but the individual rooms are clearly marked one by one in the sizes determined by the fixed size of a mat. Because of the climate the buildings are easy to air thoroughly and the structural system this requires therefore enables the creation of open links between the different rooms in a dwelling and its natural surroundings. But the surroundings the Japanese house opens on to are merely a small piece of stylised nature – the Japanese garden – an outdoor space that is carefully isolated by high walls or dense fences. The rooms can either be divided from each other or united with each other or with the garden to enable an interacting milieu. In this way the plan is flexible, a feature it shares with modern buildings constructed of load-bearing frames. But this flexibility does not at all mean the dissolution of spatiality. Each room retains its autonomy and its clear delimitations, even though its walls are made of paper.

I have already mentioned that because of the French Revolution and industrialisation the architectonic tradition was cut short. Developments could no longer, except for certain brilliant exceptions, be studied in the works of architects but were pioneered by engineers and to some extent by master gardeners, and the direction they took was determined by the emergence of new materials and structures – cast iron, wrought iron, glass and reinforced concrete. This is the period of the industrial revolution and the era of great world exhibitions, and these two phenomena were also linked in the structural advances. Frame construction was already being used for warehouses and factories in the early years of the nineteenth century and the enormous halls at the world exhibitions, in which the latest mechanical constructions were displayed for the admiration of their astounded contemporaries, were themselves masterpieces of bold constructivism. Spatial dimensions were increased enormously because of the vast spans that the new materials enabled and because of new requirements, and glass was incorporated in previously unknown quantities to provide lighting for the large interiors. In comparison with buildings of solid masonry these spaces acquired a totally new character, but they were still distinctly demarcated static rooms partitioned into structural sections. The trappings of architectural decoration disappeared and were replaced by structural expression. The constructions formed enclosed spaces in the same way, in principle, as the Gothic cathedrals, but the materials were different and so were the characteristics of their spatiality.

These exhibition halls and other creations by engineers during the period of decadence for architecture have justifiably been regarded as the forerunners of a new architecture. They have demonstrated the possibilities of the new materials and the intrinsic value of straightforward structures, but there is nothing new about the spatiality of these buildings and they should rather be regarded as a development of the Gothic structures of cathedrals and half-timbered houses. Only the coming of reinforced concrete created possibilities of developing the experience of spatiality.

However the myth of dissolved spatiality has found staunch support in these buildings. It was espoused by the architects and incorporated together with constructivism in functionalism. Its further development can perhaps best be studied in town plans.

I do not believe that one can consider nineteenth-century town plans to have been based on any generally cherished philosophical conception of the symbolic import of spatiality. We who have the benefit of Spengler's guidance could perhaps perceive the enclosed spaces that are so characteristic of these plans, even though they should, according to his system, be open ones, as symbols of a culture that was building for profit and the ruthless exploitation of power. And it was the social shortcomings that the new architecture opposed with its battle cry of sun, light and air. The plans for the new high-rise and tower blocks were drawn up on the basis of careful calculations of hours of daylight and the angles of the sun's rays. They are the product of purely rational considerations and in the best of cases also of a change in social attitudes. From a philosophical point of view they undeniably constitute a complete dissolution of enclosed spatiality, sometimes so radically that it is no longer possible to talk of the creation of any spatiality at all. But the reaction to these plans soon came. It came from the people who were meant to live in them and who found no comfort in their windy thoroughfares between rows of identical buildings.

It was also discovered to be uneconomic to use the free areas only as corridors. Instead of three parallel high-rise blocks they were arranged in the form of a U around an interior enclosure. It is no more than normal economic planning to attempt to reduce the areas used for communication to a minimum and try to create as many useable spaces as possible. And at no extra cost sunny play areas protected from the wind could be provided as well. But one requirement for this kind of planning is narrow apartment blocks with the apartments traversing the entire building. And now the art of town planning is once again very much a matter of creating spatiality. Intimacy and enclosure is sought. Once again streets are very different from mere open areas.

Wickberg once made the witty comment that the "amoeba" is the rocaille of functionalism. But developments are rapid and today ornamentation consists not of amoebae but of hexagons. They can be found in all modern Swedish architecture from city plans to hall windows. Perhaps they betoken an aspiration to create more distinct and enclosed spaces. In that case I believe they can be viewed with some degree of sympathy, although rather reservedly. As mere decoration they are paltry and deficient. One must also watch carefully to ensure that intimacy and the creation of spatiality in city plans does not collude too obediently with land speculation so that our interest in the creation of human environments and massing buildings does not lead us back to city plans with the density of the nineteenth century. After all the amoeba of functionalism, unlike the rest of the species, had a backbone of strong social ambitions. Hexagons have hard shells but often reveal a dreadful degree of spinelessness.

In American town plans the creation of spatiality has traditionally always played a major role, even in plans that as a whole involve something entirely new in the sphere of town planning, as in the case of Radburn, for instance. This plan is based on groupings around restricted courtyards. In modern town planning groupings play a dominant role and they find formal expression in the creation of more or

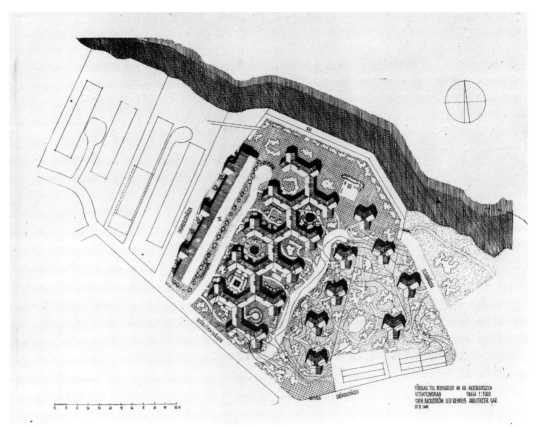

City Plan for the Akterspegeln Neighbourhood by Sven Backström and Leif Reinius

less marked spaces around certain centres. In his book *The City*, Saarinen has compared the organic city with a healthy cellular community and the city of slums with
a cellular community overwhelmed by disease. This biological parallel can also be
applied to spatial design.

We have seen how the creation of spatiality has again become part of town
planning. It has represented the human factor. Engineering is a purely rational art
and functionalism attempted to be so as well. This led to the dissolution of spatiality. Not the infinite spatiality that many wanted to perceive in this concept but the
negation of spatiality – no spatiality at all. In this way we have abandoned architecture, whose task is to create spaces for people – rooms of different types and with
different characteristics according to their functions. One can with justice criticise
applications of functionalism for their negligence of spatial design. Dissolution of
spatiality became a template for all sorts of buildings. Daylight was sought at any
cost and priority given to vistas. Naturally a view has great value in itself but it has
often been arranged at the expense of a building's more important features. Views
have ended up playing far too important a role for speculative builders.

A room that is entirely open to the outside world is in its basic form a loggia or a portico, a form of spatiality that has been used in every era to supplement an enclosed space or to link it with the surrounding world. Many of the spatial creations of functionalism can be seen to derive from the archetype of the loggia. A building consisting only of loggias is not appropriate for our climate. Therefore the functionalist form of spatiality has turned out to be unable to meet human needs.

III

In all planning the rhythm created by various forms and sizes of spatiality is important. The artistic value of a plan depends to a large extent on its rhythm. The plan for a hotel with rooms of equal size on each side of a corridor lacks rhythm to all extents and purposes. The plan for a dwelling by Frank Lloyd Wright, for instance, possesses a great deal of rhythm. The rhythm of a plan depends on the size of the rooms, their height and illumination. It can be enhanced by giving rooms of different sizes different heights, by leaving some rooms with an enclosed character while others open freely out on to the environment. A rhythm of this kind can be found in all architecture. In its most primitive form in the contrast between the hall and its outside portico in the megaron or a loggia house. In the interaction, in other words, between Spengler's two forms of spatiality, the enclosed and the open. Or in an atrium house in the link between the enclosed apartment and the open courtyard. It therefore seems to be so pointless and misleading to talk about the spatial symbols of certain cultures. Architecture has always made use of various kinds of spatiality, and artistic expression depends on the interaction of spaces with different characteristics.

A plan can be made up of a series of spaces of various types grouped rhythmically, each room separate in itself with its own character and its own uses. This is often the case with the plans for houses in the Anglo-Saxon world. It can also take the form of an interacting milieu in which the various spatialities are directly linked to each other – a suite of rooms in a Baroque palace – or merge into each other with no definite boundaries. Without wishing to succumb to any form of systematisation, I would like to describe this approach, which has become a typical feature of modern architecture, as a continuation of the Baroque traditions from "Vierzehnheiligen".

Le Corbusier offers a good example of the way in which modern plans create spatial milieus. He permits the interaction of the entire interior of a building. The enclosure of the separate spatialities is nullified and the entire plan creates a large dynamic setting in which the necessary differentiations are attained with a minimum of fixed structures. The spatial rhythm is emphatic, at times dramatic. The structure no longer creates spatialities. External walls are freed of their supports, as are the dividing walls. Construction is merely a means to attain the cohesion and unity of the plan. It is not an end in itself and attracts no attention. Reinforced concrete has opened up the possibility of creating spatialities that are not determined by the structure. The constructive possibilities of reinforced concrete are so enormous that if mastered correctly they offer complete liberty for the creation of spatiality in the same way that advanced vaulting techniques did during the Baroque. It is a perfect instrument for purely architectural and artistic creation.

Even in Le Corbusier's most dissolved spatial creations there is a pronounced awareness of spaces and their boundaries with the outside world. In his houses in Pessac-Bordeaux and in Villa Savoye the enclosing walls and ceiling of the room are extended to delimit outdoor spatialities. His roof terrace in Paris is a stringently cohesive spatial composition. The residential areas in his town plans are never lacklustre collections of high-rise blocks with no open spaces protected from the wind. Clearly defined volumes are, by and large, one of Le Corbusier's characteristic features, as for all modern architecture, whose conception of form can be traced back to Cubism. Cubism abandoned perspective as a means of rendering an object visible, depicting it instead from the interior and exterior as well as from different sides. This way of seeing has been fundamental for the means of expression of modern architecture in its search for interaction between interior and exterior, for its conception of spatiality. That this does not mean dissolution will be revealed by even the most cursory study of Le Corbusier, for one. Cubism, which has had such an impact on the way we see and experience things, is one of the more recent phenomena in Western art that refutes Spengler most firmly.

Nor is the coherence of a spatiality or a building with nature necessarily a function of the area of glass or of the proximity of its floor to the ground. This link, mastered with such sovereignty by the Baroque, is also a question of spatial composition and volumes. One of the winners in a competition for a house and garden some time ago made the following comment on this point:

> however I would maintain that the main hall, the living room, situated at the end of the house with windows facing in three directions, is a room that offers more intensive contact with the surrounding garden and the countryside than a room in any other position, however large its perspective windows may be.

The high thresholds that are used so often in all the houses built in Sweden, often have a disastrous impact on the link between house and garden when they rise abruptly half or a whole storey above the ground. But a Japanese house, with a floor structure raised high above the earth does not lose this link. Perhaps this is because the house rests on plinths so that the ground can be seen vanishing under it, so that it becomes an object sited in the garden. It may be due to the fine distinctions of light and shade as the house merges into the garden and the numerous details, for both form and function, that unite the exterior with the interior. It is with purely architectonic devices like these that Le Corbusier also creates the cohesion between his firmly delimited spatial volumes and their natural surroundings.

Spengler's "infinite space" is not, in my opinion, dissolved spatiality but spatiality that is designed freely within itself. Openness outwards is in this context of secondary importance. It would be more correct to describe an enclosed cell, spatiality isolated within itself, or space defined by structural determinations as *static spatiality*, provided that the visual impression made by the structure is static, while the Baroque conception of spatiality and our freely created milieux, which include both spatiality and the natural surroundings, could be called *dynamic spatiality*. Flexible plans become dynamic over the years as the room divisions can be changed from time to time. This kind of mechanical mobility in the planning has nothing to do with the nature of the spaces that are altered.

IV

Finally I would like to offer some brief analyses of some of Gunnar Asplund's spatial creations based on the opinions expressed here on spatial design.

Forest Chapel, 1918–20

The interaction of a totally enclosed and an entirely open space as in a megaron. The portico offers a subtle transition between the enclosed room and its surroundings. In an old medieval church, where one enters the shadowy interior directly from the sunlight outside, this contrast can at times be too powerful.

Stockholm City Library, 1920–28

Both in form and treatment a firmly enclosed space that provides room for books and invites the visitor to pore over them.

Stockholm Exhibition, 1930

The Stockholm Exhibition had a programme that focused on social issues in the housing exhibition as well as architectural liberation from the forms of preceding eras. The architecture itself was festive occasional architecture. The exhibition offered a marketplace and a daylight fireworks show, as the loggia was the appropriate form of spatiality for both the display of wares and recreation.

National Institute of Bacteriology, 1933–37 and Göteborg Law Courts, 1934–37

The central hall is a space that is delimited from the outside world which because of its position in the plan offers links to the various rooms in the building.

The Courthouse in Göteborg does not offer dissolved spatiality. On the contrary it is a concentration of all the important spaces in the building, which have been composed to form a clear, lavish and varying milieu. The atrium and the firmly enclosed courtyard are not two spatialities but one. In its details this spatial design is highly constructivist.

Skövde Crematorium, 1938

The section of this building that lies above the ground contains only one room – the committal ceremony room. Both the exterior and the interior possess an extremely enclosed character.

Woodland Crematorium 1935–40

This plan is an example of interaction between spatialities with different character-istics and values: the enclosed chapel, the intimate waiting rooms with windows opening out on to the small walled gardens, the open vestibules, the sweeping, open landscape edged by the dark strip of trees. The constructivism of Göteborg Law Courts has disappeared. The enclosed and open rooms interact consummately to create a feeling of eternity.

NOTES

1   A critical study of Spengler and music that is not without interest in this context can be found in the collection of essays by Moses Pergament, *Nya vandring med Fru Musica*, 1944.
2   Erik Gunnar Asplund, "Our Architectonic Perception of Space".

The Stjärnhus by Sven Backström and Leif Reinius

1948

Leif Reinius

Architectural Experiments

In the late winter it is fun to go out during the day to stamp on the thin ice that forms at night on all the puddles. A wonderful shattering noise and sunrays reflected like the bow of a violin. Or so one thought when one was younger. On slopes small streams begin to flow. Helping Nature. The more streams the better. New rapids and waterfalls. Happy and content, home one came with wet boots. Springtime duty had been done and the waters set free. Perhaps there was a feeling of helping spring on her way – winter's bonds unbound.

It is fun to help the sun to release the little dams of ice, open up the sources so that streams can flow to water the banks and life can return. Life engendered by sunshine and water.

It is so parched and frozen in all the areas that offer life and human happiness. As frozen as one is oneself. We long, our longings tear us apart, for a deep context, for the warm heart of life, for happiness and the joys of spring.

The artist is the one who opens up the sources of life. He mediates. Constant truth sayer and reaper. Constant opponent of all that has petrified and frozen, in constant revolt against all the enemies and oppressors of mankind. Indeed the more heartfelt the love and warmth he communicates, the more he sets in motion and the greater the flow of happiness we feel when at last we experience it. He is the intermediary that tries to take us as close to the sources and roots of life as possible. To the depths of clarity and mystery.

Fundamentally all forms of art are linked, are different aspects and expressions of one and the same thing, just as everything in the universe is linked. One can learn as much about architecture by looking at a living face or listening to live music as by studying buildings.

Architecture is a primary need of life, as necessary as food and clothing. It is a constant attendant through life and continually shapes our environment.

The architect seeks (or should seek) to develop and cultivate architecture, endow it with life and turn it into art (just as we should with food and clothing). He wants (or should want) to create a setting that enhances people's lives. Provide stimulation, excitement, pleasure. At some rare moments he also succeeds in enrapturing us and making us happy.

Of all forms of artistic expression, architecture is the one that is most fettered, fettered by social, economic, technical and bureaucratic conditions. These conditions form part of his material. But they also help to inhibit and have to be overcome if a building is to have any chance of being a living work of art. In cultural development architecture, because of its inherent inertia, is the last to make an impact. It is so easy for it to become bogged down in predetermined paths, to freeze and petrify, never live up to what is meant by art. Of all forms of art it is the most subject to habitual thinking and the dogma of orthodoxy. It is dreadfully easy for it to become frozen melodies or merely dry gravel.

It is by no means easy either to allow the springs to flow undammed and create freely and without restraint, when a building project has to plough through a fantastically labyrinthine and complex bureaucratic system and is at the same time subject to the stormy gusts of the desires of disparate parties. Cherished nature is so easily trampled underfoot by thick-skinned heavyweights in the continual struggle for power between "the great ones". Usually the whole thing goes no further than more or less skilful routine architecture, at best "tasteful and restrained". Two awfully vapid adjectives often used by Swedish art critics, which mean more or less the same as sterile, half-hearted, uninteresting and impersonal and, at the same time, well-groomed, polished and well-bred. In other words sufficiently inoffensive to be worth a pat on the shoulder.

There is also a strict and perhaps unconscious dogmatism about form. In Sweden a building should have a certain appearance, preferably resembling an oblong box or a combination of them (the dream is a coffin). Some claim that this is a traditional form derived from our ancient timber buildings, others that it is inherited from Greece. The recipe: first take your form (looking roughly like a box of chocolates) and bake the house in it. One lives calmly imprisoned by the convention of form. The guards make spiteful assaults on anyone who tries to break out. As soon as a new independent form takes root and emerges from the context of life, we hear jovial catcalls from the prison guards: "Pathological, perverse, schizophrenic!" The trailblazer is arrested by the state police. "He was led away at dawn."

Petrification causes petrification. This is a partially justified complaint that is heard about most of our new housing developments all over Sweden. They are cautiously impersonal, timorous, monotonous, anxiously pallid, dirty grey or dirty beige and without any touch of bold or rhythmic interaction or rivalry with nature. Far too easily engendered, their buildings stamped out to a pattern. Neutered and with no feeling, "tasteful and restrained" or tasteless (it hardly matters which). Dead is dead. There they stand like the outcome of an enormous impersonal bureaucratic apparatus in which architecture and the architect form a very subordinate element. Small, small circles on the upmost surface of the ice.

The ice really needs to be trampled to pieces. An attempt that the architect will have to make. Otherwise people will believe that sources no longer exist. Admittedly it will soon be frozen over. The struggle will never end against the hamstrung methods, habits of thought, that endow buildings with a system of conventional forms, that match society's grey prisons. "Bake me a cake . . ." Instead of getting to the bottom of the problem, experiencing it and allowed the building to germinate, acquire its own form, from within, however unusual and shocking. The free method. The more difficult instead of the mere routine. The pleasurable rather than the stricter one. With no style rather than stylistic constraints. The natural as opposed to the artificial. And this does not mean any new naturalism or photographs of nature.

But all that grows needs time. And this is where our so-called modern age thwarts the old practices of our art in demanding the completion of commissions in an incredibly short time. This favours the routine use of patterns. A feverish illness, a nervous disorder. Urgency that will not allow the crop to ripen, the foetus to become a person or a building to live. Closer examination almost always reveals that this urgency is also artificial, the outcome of nonchalance or ignorance. Instead of organic working methods today we have conferences and meetings, a monstrous and deadening method that spells the death of art.

In its search for truth a free method of working, or artistic creation that probes deeply, is closely related to scientific research (totally distinct superficially but with fundamental links) and gathers its wisdom from all of nature's sources.

The main object of the study is mankind. Seeking as deeply as possible to understand ourselves. Human studies, with psychology and physiology, should be the main subject at schools of architecture. We Swedes are said to lack interest in people and psychological insight. At least they are suppressed by the overwhelmingly technological and economic approach in our society and our schools. The impoverished dullness that prevails is also based on this deficiency – the lack of interest in people and fear of being philanthropic. Fear of the deriding taunts of cowards.

In spite of everything, our society kills off the spontaneity and healthy receptiveness of children. In the end we lose the natural physical desire for the sources of simple, primary pleasures, like bright, saturated, clear, unadulterated colours, for instance, and sensually rounded forms and shift instead to anxious, well-bred pallor and wooden boxes. Architects working on public buildings are offered a palette of infinite variations of the same deadly dirty grey to help them with their choice of colours. This is typical of the spirit of timidity and disdain. No wonder one is drawn again to the simplicity and pulse of the primordial, seeking it under all the accreted layers, all the pallid, veiling untruths. One longs for the essence of colour and variety of life and for organic and yielding primordial form. One must regain a healthy, tactile feeling for materials and their relationship to different degrees of warmth. (Timber is warm, stone is cold. Pitch and red paint look good on a timber building in the snow, and so on.) The instinctive feeling that society kills off with its erroneous values. How many children are butchered with lukewarm benevolent incomprehension?

His profession brings the architect into contact with every deeply human problem. The ideal free method of working attempts to give architecture the same liberty and supple accommodation to natural laws as nature has. A long, difficult and fundamentally utopian task. But so what?

Healthy artistic impulses must come all the time to make life rich and vital. Like the contractions of the heart that impel blood throughout our bodies. Without impulses life comes to a stop. Health wanes, layer on layer of prejudice rapidly cover the primordial source and soon it has frozen, reaction prevails and triumphs with its habits of thought and lack of feelings.

Hard-hearted incomprehension is the best murder weapon known to mankind and society. Calmly and callously we organise, systematise and catalogue. But there is no feeling for the human. With calm clarity we argue about the effectiveness of lethal new weapons (to improve the world). We perhaps exclaim over the potential death of so many beloved children. Bold aviators are trained to bomb with precision and escape close-up vision of their butchery. And even more refined and cultivated are our rockets and now finally the atomic bomb and bacteria. Heartless callous cruelty is almost certainly the same today as it was during the Stone Age. We accept activities that threaten life with the same fatalistic calm as cattle blindly led to slaughter. Through the centuries the concept of goodness has emerged in our discussions sporadically only to vanish again. Just now it hardly exists at all. Either Apollo or Dionysus, or both of them together, but not the third, which is the most valuable and, more to the point, is found in all great art, the art that penetrates furthest: comprehension, goodness, love. The art that submits entirely to the jeering and booing of the Pharisees (aesthetes) and is finally crucified. Love is always an ingredient where art is concerned. The more a building is engendered in love, the better. The more an artist gives of himself – abandons himself to his work – the greater its truth and sincerity.

The functionalism of the 1930s had a deep and true ideology. It was humane – democratic. But its forms, although superficially new, were just as constrained as before. It was a new dogma of form. Coldly intellectual even though it was embraced with almost religious fanaticism. The building, the work of art, lay concealed behind mathematical and geometric formulae. Now and again one can hear

Own Summer Cottage by Erik Gunnar Asplund

the occasional sentimentalist complain that style vanished so quickly and we ended up in our current nondescript era. But the human content survives with greater vigour and probes into the depths. Form has not yet been liberated and revived. But it seeks out what sprouts organically.

We are moving towards architecture without style. We are attempting to crush the dogma of the straight lines, right angle and level surface. Buildings must not be restricted by any kind of formal system at all but should be shaped as integral parts of their surroundings and society. And this setting – this society – must be a living context.

Kulturhuset on Sergels Torg by Peter Celsing

1960

Peter Celsing

About Space

Let us begin by considering Piero della Francesca's famous painting of the *Flagellation of Christ*. In this work we see how the space is well defined; della Francesca was known as one of the first who took great pains to render perspective. Christ is located at the back of the physical space. But at the same time there is a metaphysical space in this work that separates and surrounds the three men in the foreground. It is marked furthermore by their gazes, which are lost in the distance as if the three men could see beyond the window of the imaginary walls that surround them.

I have described these physical and metaphysical spaces as opposites. One could just as easily contrast the measurable quantitative room with immeasurable qualitative space. It is a question of how the architect sees, how he understands space, and in which space he wants to belong that is of ultimate importance for problem solving.

In the following I will try to illuminate the way of seeing a structure that is built up of objects of varying spatial densities. Our understanding of a nebula is dependent on the different concentrations of the stars and their light strength, their literal brilliance. In the same way one can understand the surrounding environment, the cityscape, an interior, or the artwork as a force field that exists under these various objects' influences and their rays.

To exemplify this modern spatial experience we can take a trip to Skeppsholmen's old naval environment. When we climb the embanked roadway towards barrack number two, we have a strong spatial impression. We experience a continuous series of sensory impressions, as the buildings' position seems to change in relation to our movement. The freestanding, simple structures create a mutual connection that brings about a spatial experience as tangible as if we were to move within a set of encircling walls. We find ourselves subject to a force field, a metaphysical space.

Through the apparent movements of the building we seem to feel ourselves inside a giant mobile, a sculpture of Alexander Calder, with the cross on Skeppsholmen church as the fixed point around which the mobile turns. And we recall that Calder said that the conception of form underlying his work rests on the universe's own principle with isolated bodies of varying size and density floating in space, some resting and others in peculiar movement, some tight-close together and others at an enormous distance.

We enter into the Modern Museum. We now leave one structure and enter a new one. How well the Museum fits us and the art it contains, these large undivided floor surfaces, where we freely place our symbols, paintings and drawings.

The generously sized floor space reminds us that in today's residences and offices space is the greatest luxury. Therefore these great halls present themselves as so appealing. Because at the same time as they answer our contemporary need for space, they satisfy even our desire to furnish spaces with objects of high enough quality. Our almost cult-like interest in everyday objects, in their functional and formal aesthetic qualities can be said to reflect a need to compensate the environment for what is often missing in the limitations of architectonic space.

It is that freedom from limitations that abounds in *Catalan Landscape*, the painting by Joan Miro – another structure – where objects and symbols are freely spread out on the canvas, and form a poetic landscape.

The definition of art as vitality comes easily to mind. Refer to artists such as Picasso, Matta, Mathieu, or Jackson Pollock and one can almost say their works are examples of energy transformed into object and the space of each work is defined by its radiance as a separate unit.

Within the Modern Museum there is no oppressive physical space limitation that draws us away from the art object's own force field. The roof's wire armature, electric fittings and metal duct work, create a structure with such low density that the light steadily filters down and the feeling of freedom which is inspired by the large expanses is accentuated further.

Our free movement across the floor has its complement in the light roof construction that wanders overhead. The large open space that offers the freedom to change, and movement, provides the essential character in the room. The architectonic space limitations' task in this situation is to facilitate and emphasize the manifestation of freedom. The Modern Museum is a space furnished with expressions for modern spirits limited by the object's force field.

To a room's metaphysical contents memories and associations are contributed. In the Modern Museum one is easily reminded of the large Le Corbusier exhibition of 1958. How Le Corbusier, the pioneer, with the Ville Verte project already in 1922, with his apartment skyscrapers grouped together with a large space in between, showed the possibilities of the free cityscape, and inspired the whole world's city builders to follow. The Villa Savoye with its isolated geometric forms freely collected in a cubic shell, like the blocks in a box of building blocks. The church in Ronchamp where the ceiling and walls became free objects with shapes like fluttering sails. They meet and capture some of the outer space outside. The space is almost furnished with drops of light, while the façades become the object's backside with material of varying density.

The governmental buildings in Chandigarh are nearly surreal in their scattered layout, as if it would correlate with the high plateau's thin mountain air. What structural organization!

Le Corbusier loved clean shape and the remarkable thing is that we find it even in his paintings of everyday common things, such as the glass and bottles from his purist period. Architecture, says Le Corbusier is "the masterly, correct and magnificent play of masses brought together in light".

The play between masses in light . . . When we leave the museum we look between the masts of the full-rigged ship "af Chapman" – in itself a space where the concept of space created out of objects and masses is felt very strongly. We see

Stockholm laid out: Skeppsbron, the Royal Palace, Parliament, banks, the Opera. Here the buildings are not shells in the same way as when the Modern Museum's space limiting units were seen from inside. They are clearly separated and clearly limited in the physical space.

But at the same time they are also tokens, symbols, embodied institutions, and by virtue of this dignity they form together a poetic landscape like Miro's painting of the Catalan landscape. These classical forms under a Nordic sky reveal a desire to participate in a common world culture.

This is what the revealing façade tells us. The façade is the meeting between outside and inside. It can be a solid wall of great density, or a structure of considerable thinness wherein the walls' tasks are clearly distinguished by room boundaries, climate zones, and by constructive elements. The façade shows our activities, our organization, our attitude towards the environment, our ethical and aesthetic judgments and needs.

The façade reveals where we want to feel at home, whether in a common world culture or in a regional culture zone. Or if we conceive of the world as a room, we all want to share under the same conditions or a narrower room limited to the community, the nation and so on. One can talk about an international architecture without meaning a certain architectural style. Therefore, when in the following I refer to international architecture, it is not implying a certain architectural style, but an architecture that corresponds with and expresses an international approach to life.

The form language of international architecture may not be completely suitable to all places on the earth. But, after all, it is a theoretical possibility that when faced with regional segregation, one can imagine preferring an internationalist solution even though it is less advantageous from a functional and economic viewpoint. The UNESCO Building in Paris should be able to illustrate this. Its open attitude has meant that even the sunscreen has become glass – and to no effect. Miro has painted on the wall in the foreground.

Were not earlier architectural epochs international, ever since Roman times? And, were not, for example, the classical motifs in earlier Swedish architecture the expression of a desire, to prove that even in the provinces of no man's land it was possible to feel like one belonged to the continental cultural community?

The prophet of international understanding in architecture is Le Corbusier. In his writings he prophesied, explained, formulated. Every house he has designed has widened the possibilities of the world's architectonic expression. His work moves us all. With the clarity of a scientific discovery it influences and transforms our worldview.

For Le Corbusier man's place in nature – as the master of nature – is clear. Often he places houses on pillars and by that he also lifts human creation's crown above the surrounding nature. Here we see the Cloister in Lyon, that clearly illustrates that there is an organizing spirit that has worked, that sorts, that thinks structurally, rather than just about building construction. He gives the organization a visual expression, a *gestalt*, without the dry dogmatism.

Le Corbusier sees "the spirit that intervenes in nature" as an organizing spirit. One can add that whichever solution the architect appropriates it is his job and his way from his understanding to give his impressions a structural organization, to create order and context.

If Le Corbusier stands out as a representative of the type of person who sees nature as a given, an inherent right, Frank Lloyd Wright can be understood as the person who preserves the tradition from the American settlers for whom adaptability to the character of the surroundings is natural. In his houses we see how well he supports and seems to explain the landscape's character.

We find ourselves in a similar situation as a settler. To place societies, to group, orient and build our houses according to the climate and topographic conditions is an urgent project in the same way as our road builders find themselves compelled to accept the fact that traffic must go on the left side of the road.

We must proceed to an organized building process dependent on local conditions of both psychological and physical nature. We must complement our research, increase our knowledge about weather and wind, light and air, and about our own way of reacting to many different sorts of life situations.

We must answer the question why we allow windows to run around the façades of our houses without respect to north, south, east or west, the way the light falls and the actual positioning of the window – maybe under the inspiration of Mies van der Rohe who said "we refuse to recognize the problems of form, but only problems of building".

Then we may possibly come to a place where, finally, our streets are ventilated without being windy, our houses are kept warm economically, our roofs covered with snow racks, our windows draft free, with a row of geraniums along the window sills instead of big black holes set against the arctic winter night.

But if acceptance of local conditions cannot be driven to its conclusion, then the ultimate consequence would be that home construction like other industries, like the military supreme command and the jet plane hangar will go underground, thereby securing itself with adequate protection against the elements, with adequate warmth and humidity.

Under the circumstances humanity is facing today, when space opens itself up, it seems important to belong to a general human cultural community, even if it means that one has to place oneself above the limitations that local issues would seem to dictate.

The architect faces a conflict: whether to choose between the international lifestyle or regional appropriateness. The question is whether these obligatory choices do not make architecture into an art? The choice forces the architect to evaluate and specify function, to choose consciously the most appropriate solution. In the most successful cases the conflict creates the kind of charge from which a "work of art" is born.

Architecture is not a mechanical satisfaction of human needs. Therefore the public, open life in the UN's workrooms is not balanced by a dark meditation room with a block of iron ore which through its density produces a radiation which invites us to something like the heathen's worship, an insult to convinced members of any religion.

A similar disregard, this time pointed towards ancestral beliefs occasionally meets us in the still-continuing restoration of our churches. To select a building epoch purely on aesthetic principles and take away the contributions of all other periods is both repulsive and naïve.

It is particularly naïve to believe that the environment can be fixed forever, that our surroundings will not adapt to ethical and aesthetic sets of values different from our own.

The tendency to renounce all claims to one's heritage is repulsive. Within the church's metaphysical structure, an integral part of native home, is where our interests and our attitudes are laid out.

In a similar fashion, we cannot look at our houses as finished objects, completed on the day of moving in. The environment is something that will be in constant change under the influence of diverse living habits and work needs. The long building history of Skeppsholmen and its ongoing stimulating changes have taught us that to the extent that the architect in his organization of the structure creates many-sided and versatile possibilities to satisfy varying needs, he also contributes to creating environments for freedom.

Ski and Fishing Hotel by Ralph Erskine

1963

Ralph Erskine

The Challenge of the High Latitudes

I am not an expert on architecture for northern regions because I do not think there can be such a thing as an architect-expert at all. What I have to say, therefore, is based on experience accumulated working in a northern situation over a relatively long period of time. The conclusions I have arrived at were mainly formulated as a guide for my own practice, and are therefore not necessarily the right ones for someone else to use. However, it is very important, I feel, that we in Scandinavia, you here in Canada, and the people who live in Alaska, Siberia and Russia, get together and exchange research findings and experiences.

Architecture is whole and indivisible. The climate and technical aspects of the north must always be evaluated against the background of the human situation. The predominant interest can only be the people – in my particular case the people who live in the high latitudes: the arctic, the sub-arctic and the high and desolate mountain regions. This part of the world, although it has been inhabited since historical times, has hardly been studied at all.

As an architect, one sooner or later realizes that all one has learned, all one has grown up with, and all one has seen in central and southern Europe somehow does not fit the northern situation. One may be tempted to ignore the specific characteristics of this region altogether, thereby avoiding a lot of problems, but in doing so one is not facing reality. The practice of true architecture – the architecture of reality – requires that we face the problems squarely.

The first impulse that led me to start thinking about climate was the fact that upon close analysis, many buildings did not seem to meet the requirements of the northern latitudes. When dealing with a specific situation, such as this one, part of one's interest becomes scientific in nature, namely to find the extreme situation, that is the test-tube condition in which the stresses are so great that they become easily measurable, and apply the results to areas where conditions are not as severe. The achievements in Sweden are largely of a technical nature and have been made by technicians, real technicians, not amateur technicians such as we architects are. They have solved the heating and insulation problems. These however, are merely technical solutions.

In Sweden, primary industries which are expanding rapidly in the north have great difficulty in both attracting and retaining necessary personnel for a sufficiently long period to utilize fully their specialized knowledge, and to establish communities of a permanent and balanced character. In our expanding economy we can no longer rely solely on the arctic enthusiast or the native people. It is very difficult to run a modern industry efficiently with people who are constantly on the move. Stable communities are an absolute necessity.

While many men may, for a time, enjoy the high pay, quick advancement, extensive responsibilities and the open-air life which the north offers, and while children show no great difficulty in acclimatizing themselves to the snow and the cold, many other men and most women miss the contact with relatives and the amenities of more southern towns – the shops, entertainment, the well-developed school system, and so on. The frontier offers few advantages for women, who are often as lonely as golf widows. Sooner or later these women reject the insufficiency and the claustrophobia of the frontier community and draw their husband and families out.

To find the melody of the sub-arctic life, which will provide the amenities as well as the emotional and spiritual satisfaction within the specific conditions of this region, is the only way to avoid the nostalgic longing which adds to the natural stresses created by the climate and the isolation. In Sweden this melancholy is known as Lapp-illness. It is not an illness which is felt by the Lapps, but a mental state which, especially in the old days before radio and television, was very prevalent and led to alcoholism, insanity and suicide.

An international group of doctors engaged in a detailed study of the north found, among other things, that there is nothing unnatural or harmful about life in very cold regions. People can live well; they do not even require special food, other than heavy food if they are doing heavy work. What they need most of all is sufficient clothing. The doctors established (contrary to traditional belief) that viruses and bacteria are not killed by the cold. The northerner is therefore susceptible to all the diseases of the southerner, as illustrated by the Eskimo who, when he came into contact with the white man, contracted all his diseases. It was found too that the typical mental illnesses of the north, which lead to alcoholism, suicide and murder, are caused, to a large extent, by the environment. It is clear therefore, that this question of environment must concern not only the sociologists and the engineers, but the architect-planners as well.

I propose to start by defining the arctic, and especially the sub-arctic situation; then to show what the aim of the designer in the north should be, and finally to explain the synthesis resulting from the careful analysis of the sub-arctic problems with which I myself have been concerned over the past ten to fifteen years.

I think we all agree that, in architecture, our main interest must be the people, and since architecture can be said to be the art of forming a framework for human associations, we are especially interested in groups of people. These groups may range in size from a couple without children to very large communities.

The Lapp represents much of the wisdom which we must learn if we want to know what the north really is. He, or the Eskimo, know far more about it, or did know, until we broke down their culture. He is much better adapted to life in the northern regions than most Europeans can ever hope to be. The trappers and prospectors who penetrated the north in recent times assimilated certain habits of the native people but relied mainly on the traditions of their southern homelands. As a result they failed to create a truly indigenous culture.

In the landscape itself it is apparent that we are not dealing with a political or ethnic region, but with a region that is defined in terms of climate, terrain or vegetation. All too often we think of the northern regions as being the continually cold part of the world. This is only partially true, in fact there is tremendous contrast between the very cold, relatively dark winters, and the relatively warm, bright summers. This great difference between summer and winter is one of the most important characteristics of the north.

The climate is not as violent as people usually imagine. As soon as the Baltic Sea and the lakes freeze over, there is little daily variation in the overall seasonal temperature, except in certain coastal areas where the sea does not freeze up. At the Arctic Circle the temperature ranges from a summer high of 30 degrees Celsius to a winter low of about minus 50 degrees Celsius. There is little wind, and the precipitation is low. If the climate were warmer, and if the water could drain away, the tundra would be a desert. And of course, the further north you go above the Arctic Circle, the longer become the periods of total darkness and total sunshine.

The sub-arctic zone is part of the polar region and stretches from the polar sea southward, well past the tree line. It consists mainly of the flat, bleak, treeless tundra, held frozen during nine months of the year by ground frost. In the south it changes into the coniferous forest of the cold temperate zone. In May, the ground begins to thaw and plants start their short summer of flowering and growth. Clouds of insects fill the air and numberless birds move up from the south. The tundra becomes a landscape of lakes and ponds, each one formed by the snow water of many seasons, unable to drain away due to the frozen ground underneath. In the forest regions limited cultivation is possible. By September the days are shortening rapidly and the frost again takes control. The snow does not always follow immediately and there may be a long and dark autumn before the sterile cold period sets in. These characteristics of the environment impart to the region an ever-changing beauty and govern human life completely.

In winter, all human activities, except the most necessary, take place indoors. One leaves the shelter only for work or for outdoor recreation. In the spring one can move into outdoor areas, provided they are well protected from the wind. The sun can be relatively warm, but the air is cold and the slightest air movement causes discomfort. In the short summer, the people desert their winter dwellings and the towns and move out into the country to enjoy the beautiful landscape which surrounds them. In the fall one is again forced back into the protected outdoor spaces, and in winter into the interior of the shelter.

The Scandinavian people definitely change character between summer and winter. In Stockholm, on the first day of spring after the long, dark, cold winter, when the sun begins warming your skin, you can see hundreds of people sitting on the steps of the Stockholm Concert Hall, their faces turned toward the sun. This is true sun worship and is based on a very real experience.

It becomes obvious that the different aspects of the situation which affect human beings will affect the buildings and the towns which we are called upon to design for them. The first and foremost of these factors is the temperature differential between the interior and exterior of a building. It may fluctuate as much as 60 degrees Celsius. This cannot be ignored or treated lightly. Any physicist will tell you that the most efficient shelter should have a central heating core and that a maximum volume should be enclosed by a minimum surface. The economist will tell you the same thing because, in our cold climate, the outer walls of a building are much more expensive than the inner partitions. The problems of the skin of the shelter therefore are of tremendous importance.

A sphere would obviously be the geometric form to enclose the maximum volume with the minimum surface; but it would be unreasonable to use it as a building form, since it has minimum contact with the ground warmth. Although the air temperature varies enormously between summer and winter the ground temperature in Sweden usually remains a constant seven degrees above freezing, except at the surface where frost occurs. With a snow cover however, the frost will not penetrate the ground very deeply. It seems logical, then, to use the ground as a means of insulation, unless you happen to live in Greenland or somewhere else where the ground is frozen solid to a great depth.

A highly articulated building form is therefore much less appropriate than a compact one. The engineers, scientists and economists somehow knew this instinctively and told me so all along. I became quite frustrated by their statements until I finally began to understand the logic of physics.

A house which we designed for an engineer who is intensely interested both in technology and in art, is an essay based on the scientific analysis of the climactic determinants. I was talking to this man one day about the matter of enclosure and he became extremely interested. As a result we built this very unusual shelter, a half dome sunk into the ground for protection. The windows have to be a certain distance above ground level so that the snow will not drift over them in the winter. In front of the house there is a protected terrace (which we call the spring and

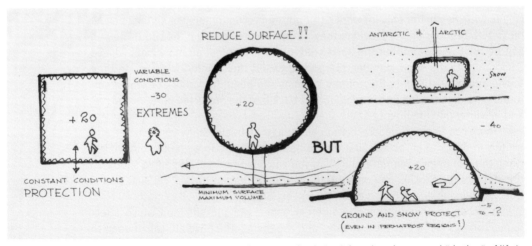

Villa Engström near Stockholm, a study in "sub-arctic" architecture. The design is based on the seasonal "rhythm" of life in the north – the completely protected winter cell, the surrounding semi-protected spaces for spring and fall and beyond this a free summer life with nature.

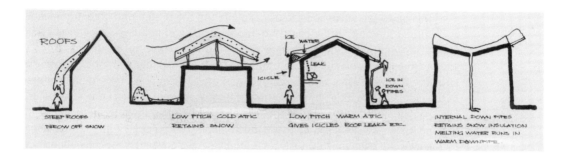

autumn room) where the sun comes in, but where you are protected from air move-ment. The real pleasure of spring and early summer is experienced when you can open the door and leave it open. You step outside and look at the water and the green slopes; you sit in this spring room or any other place where you can find pro-tection from even the slightest wind. As the summer advances you move to the more and more exposed terraces until you finally leave in your boat for the islands. In winter you skate and ski on the slopes surrounding the house.

Inside the shell there is great freedom in the arrangement of spaces. The number and sizes of windows were restricted for technical, financial and aesthetic reasons. I believe that large window openings are not essential because during the winter the snow is an admirable reflector, and in the summer there is almost con-tinuous sunlight. In locating the windows I tried to provide a maximum variety of views, since during the long winter, most of the time is spent indoors.

Insofar as the entrance to the house is concerned, I feel that in our motorized society the entrance for the car should perhaps be more important than that for the pedestrians. Logically you should be able to drive your car right into your building. You should not have to put on heavy clothes to get from your house to your car. (This I had to do everywhere in Winnipeg and when the wind blew I felt quite uncomfortable.)

Prefabrication is now generally accepted as the most appropriate construction technique in Sweden. Our client-engineer owned a factory that produced cranes and other structural steel equipment. The skin of the house was fabricated in his factory in flat sections. A small crane was mounted on the chimney core, and the panels were lifted into place, bent and then welded together to form this simple shelter. One of the important factors involved in the design of this house is the concept of the skin with relatively small openings. In a way it is a negation of every-thing that modern architecture stands for today. The tendency, in the western world has been to break down the traditional barriers between exterior and interior and create a continuity of space from the inside to the outside.

Snow has always been used for protection and insulation in northern coun-tries. Vegetation seeks protection under the snow. The Russians, for instance, have developed apple trees which grow horizontally, close to the ground and are thus protected by the snow cover in winter. Some birds and mammals, such as bears, dig themselves into the snow.

This snow factor we consciously exploited in the design of a hotel for a small township in the north of Sweden. We had the choice of building a nice little glass tower, showing how clever we were (or rather how clever our heating engineers were in keeping us warm in spite of the most difficult conditions); or of building a structure that would live with the climate and the surroundings, take full advantage of the insulating qualities of snow, and be less dependent on mechanical services. I was very tempted at first to use the former approach, but then decided against it. For one thing, the client did not have much money, and though it might have been technically and economically feasible to build a glass tower, it would have been out of place. I felt it would be better to conform to the character of the region, to build into the ground and to let the snow help insulate the building.

The large roof has two functions: to protect the building and to act as a practice ski slope, which is something the client wanted us to provide near the hotel, since the good ski slopes are a little distance away. I also attempted to use snow sculpturally, by inducing it to drift at specific points. In certain places the snow will drift right on to the roof; elsewhere little slopes will form where children may play. I have to confess, however, that scientifically speaking, a few more centimetres of insulation in the roof would have provided just as good, if not better, insulation than the snow cover.

The building is built of wood both because of its economy and its appropriateness in this climate. It is painted in extremely bright colours, with emphasis on the warm hues, to provide the desirable intense colour experience in this generally white and grey region. Also, we felt that this hotel was not a big and serious building; rather a wooden toy for the people from the city. Construction is simple; the whole of the building is built of sawn wood, chosen not primarily for aesthetic reasons, but for economic ones. With the logs right there on the site and by using a circular saw (which meant that it could not be cut very precisely), we were able to build the hotel for about half the cost of another hotel of similar size, located not too far off, where stone, steel and the whole gamut of modern techniques were used.

Another important consideration in cold climates is structural separation. It seems wrong to me to use structural or architectural elements on the exterior of a building which increase the passage of heat from the interior to the exterior. Take for example a balcony. The usual method is to extend the interior floor slab to the exterior. This creates a very complicated insulation problem at the point where the balcony penetrates the building. It is, of course, technically possible to cope with this problem but it seems to me to demand more effort than the situation warrants. I have wondered, therefore, if it would not be possible to separate the balcony completely so that the skin of the building and its insulation are unbroken. In one apartment house in Vaxjo we decided to hang the balconies from the roof and fasten them to the façade with small metal clips.

As you know, in winter most materials contract considerably and in summer the reverse. These stresses are transmitted from interior to exterior and vice versa. Cracks develop in the materials and along the joints, and, when water penetrates, frost damage results. It seems, therefore, advisable to separate the exterior from

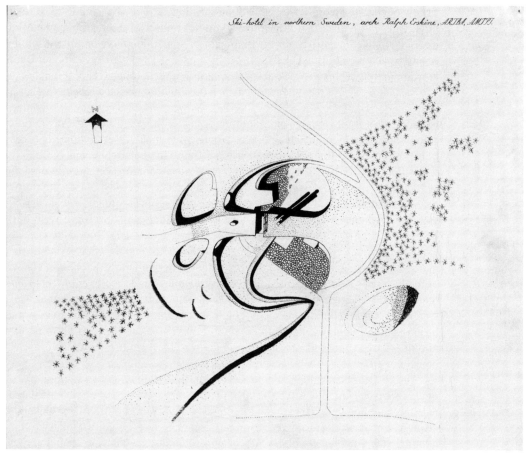

Ski and Fishing Hotel near Borga, northern Sweden, plan

the interior elements as much as possible. Any unnecessary projections and corners on the external envelope should be avoided, as they are potential trouble spots. Following this line of reasoning you will arrive at a very simple building form that has no shadow lines.

In the design of another apartment block I started off by using that old cliché, the piloti, to articulate the building above a dramatic rock formation. Le Corbusier says that to see the underside of a building is very important because this transforms the building from a wall into a volume. Fair enough, but you know beforehand that the engineer will tell you this piloti idea is nonsense; that not only will you have to insulate the underside of your building, but the roof of your basement as well. Since this was public housing, the authorities told me right away that the idea was ridiculous and that it would be much more economical and therefore better to eliminate those two layers of insulation and enclose the open ground floor, thus providing one full floor of enclosed space at practically no extra cost. This sort of situation is often very irritating and you immediately say that these people obviously do not have a clue about aesthetics. But when you think about it for a while you realize that it is *you* who did not understand the problem and that you overstressed aesthetics to the detriment of something more important. During the 1930s architects preached functionalism as the saving philosophy, and now they are getting it thrown back at them. Many architects today feel that functionalism has not really filled the need. I believe it has but that we have misinterpreted it.

Prefabrication is obviously very appropriate in the far north because of the long cold period. It is more logical and less expensive to make things indoors in a controlled atmosphere than outdoors. Having all the elements ready you can quickly assemble them on the site at any time. I visited a construction site in Winnipeg where they were excavating and building under a cover of vinyl plastic supported on a light wood frame. I have been preaching such a procedure in Sweden without getting anywhere, so I am going to take a few pictures to show the people back home how you do this sort of thing in Canada.

Coming back to this matter of heat transfer, you all know what an air-cooled motor cycle engine looks like. To dissipate heat generated more quickly the surface of the engine is enlarged in the form of fins. It would be foolish to apply this same principle to buildings in an extremely cold climate. In winter you notice that every exterior corner in a building is a point of frost concentration. In old buildings which have plastered interiors, hoarfrost forms in every corner and around the windows. In order to overcome this problem I have gone so far as to use rounded corners in one of our projects.

In the Canadian prairie climate I feel that the cold winters and hot summers demand exactly the same type of architecture: an architecture of well-insulated, compact building forms, where the interiors are designed as efficiently as possible, since interior space is expensive. And since cooling is even more expensive than heating, the summer condition too seems to indicate that you should reduce window sizes and lower the ceiling heights. In other words, if you live in a cold climate, do not look to the temperate zones for inspiration. Look instead at the hot-dry regions where, just as in Sweden, thick, heavily insulated walls and relatively small window openings are used.

Let us now turn our attention to the problems of the community. I believe that we all agree that the structure of the community is more important than individual buildings and that we must concern ourselves with the way a building relates to other buildings, to the street and the landscape.

In our rigorous climate it seems logical that several community functions should be grouped together, sheltered under a common roof. Bees seem to know all about physics: they build maximum living space enveloped by a minimum amount of surface, within which they have intricate circulation and zoning systems. I wonder, therefore, if it would not be a good idea to take a lesson from the bees and to bring functions of similar nature into direct and intimate contact with one another. This is very possible, especially in the central part of a city. In fact, the whole town could become one single, complex building. Residential areas, schools, hospitals, ateliers and so on, could be related to each other on an upper level. At the street level, and continuing into the interior of this very large structure

Lulea Shopping (Community) Centre, north Sweden. An extensive speculation in the social, technical and aesthetic consequences of the sub-arctic situation. During a number of years of use it has shown itself to meet the human and social needs of the community.

(where one would have a large amount of inexpensive, warm space) could be located all the other human activities: commercial, recreational, religious, cultural and so on.

In the old towns, the market square was not only an architectural open space; it was the main shop, the department store. In the town centre of Lulea, we used the medieval concept of the market square, where all sorts of social, commercial and official functions can take place, not in the open, but under cover. Before this centre was built, the main shopping street of Lulea was cold, windy and bleak, with no sunlight during several weeks in winter.

In the very beginning, when I talked with the client about the possibility of creating a covered centre, where in a warm semi-tropical climate, people could move about freely in winter time, he said: "A wonderful idea: 'Honolulu of the North'!" I managed to get him to realize that this would only be a pale imitation of the real Honolulu, and asked if it would not be better to conceive of it as a warm northern centre and build it of concrete, use granite gravel from the river as the exposed aggregate and timber from the forest. In other words make it a fine native building so that one day in Honolulu they would want to build a "Lulea shopping centre of the South!" Well, the idea was accepted and the building was built.

In this centre we have grouped all the facilities under one roof – hotel, cinema, shops, clubrooms, administration offices, library, restaurants, service areas, public spaces and so on. The internal space is rather complicated, but in a small town where people return again and again to the same building, variety of visual experience is essential.

The enclosed town square is used for a great variety of public and social functions: dances on Saturday nights, Salvation Army religious services, art exhibitions and chamber music concerts. All these activities, and many more, take place here in a warm and protected atmosphere. Obviously in a building such as this, one would not, I imagine, use more glass than absolutely necessary to provide daylight and vistas, except in certain specific locations. We proposed large sliding windows, which would have permitted certain areas to be opened completely to the exterior. Unfortunately this suggestion was not accepted by the client.

Of course, the problem of enclosing these various functions under one envelope could have been solved, for instance, by putting a big plastic dome over the whole centre of the town. But this, to me, seems basically wrong, because it would not take into consideration the summer and spring-winter, the periods when it is nice to be outside. I have been told that this kind of hermetically sealed environment on the DEW line has not had very good results. The people there apparently have almost no contact with the exterior. All they do is read books and look at movies from the south, and this, eventually, will lead to melancholy. This type of totally enclosed environment is probably inevitable in the Antarctic, where there is no desire at all to move about outside.

But in our situation, I would at all times offer alternate external and internal paths of circulation, and would make the external paths at least as beautiful as the internal ones, and somewhat shorter, so as to encourage the people to move outdoors. The choice offered seems to me to be very important, because I am quite sure that architects and planners cannot, or should not, dictate the way of life. This is not their job. Their job is to form a framework within which many good ways of life may be possible.

Sunlight in the north demands two things: in winter you do not want the low winter sun casting shadows on buildings. Low buildings therefore have to be placed in front of large ones. In summer, however, sun-protection from the midnight sun is desirable.

In the light of these specific winter and summer considerations, the problem of the window, as I mentioned earlier, is quite important. I have been working on the design of a variable window. In its present experimental form the window shutter can close any portion of the opening; it can be moved out of the way completely; it can be fixed in a horizontal position above the opening so as to form a shade (the underside would be painted white to increase the amount of reflected light into the interior), and when the house is not occupied, or during the light summer nights, it can close the opening completely.

In another house we designed, the sunlight is picked up from a different direction by reflectors located on the roof. In the north, where it is logical to build compact buildings which tend to become rather deep and thick, it becomes quite difficult to light the central area properly, but nowadays you can treat the roof like an elevation and put windows there. In other words, if I stretch my hand, I can grasp the horizontal rays of the sun and bend them down into the centre of the house. An ordinary window would only throw a little patch of light on an interior wall, whereas these reflectors on the roof flood the interior with warm, reflected light.

Some of the most fascinating experiences in the north are the wide views. These are very important to people and have to be considered very seriously, especially in mining towns, where men spend their working hours underground, or in towns within the arctic circle. It is a fantastically exhilarating experience, after having been cooped up inside your shelter during the long, dark winter, to open the door on the first day of spring and make contact with the surrounding landscape stretching into the far distance.

The psychological aspect of the northern region is rather complex. On the positive side are the seasonal contrasts, an invigorating climate, unspoiled nature, abundant space, scope for initiative and outdoor recreation. On the negative side are the long periods of darkness, winter storms, midnight sun, mosquitoes, lack of amenities and isolation.

The northern communities must free themselves from the prevalent colonial attitude and develop their own culture, based on their way of life. They should, because of their isolation be made more attractive than their equivalents in the warmer and more densely populated regions.

To make these towns comfortable to live in, they would have to have well lighted and heated (or at least wind protected) paths of circulation; plazas and gardens which could be covered in winter and opened during the short warm summer. They should be planned in such a way as to encourage human contact, allowing at the same time personal freedom and privacy. Even more so than elsewhere, building design should be based on technical rationalisation and standardization, inasmuch as building costs will be very high. Yet any such standardization must offer a maximum of human choices, whether rational or irrational, and we should strive to de-emphasize the exceptional circumstances in order to lessen the feeling of isolation.

IBM Conference Centre by ELLT

1967

ELLT

Working Principles

Definition

The tasks of architecture can be divided into specific and general ones.

By specific tasks we mean, for instance, planning buildings whose function is so static that it can be analysed to provide a basis for design.

By general tasks we mean buildings that are based on a general structure, for instance a frame that can be adapted to changing functions. It may be that the function of a structure is not defined from the beginning or that the functions may alter several times during its lifespan.

Specific tasks

Up until now we have mainly worked with specific tasks. In these cases the way we work does not differ from the norm: we analyse the task to identify a synthesis in the form of a strong and viable theme and we then attempt to implement this concept consistently in all its aspects as both a functional and architectonic whole.

What we consider to be the benefit of group work in this kind of method is the intensive exchange of ideas that can be attained through discussion at the same level.

The way we organise our work is characterised by joint commitment to those aspects of the work in which issues of principle or the main features of the concept are dealt with, while implementation takes place under the personal superintendence of one of the four of us as "principal" and another as "second in command".

Our joint discussions offer both a basis for our analyses through the hypotheses that emerge and also the next phase in the concept or theme that then provides the framework in which the personal creative contributions can be made.

General tasks

In our opinion it is clear today that in the future the task of the architect will predominantly involve work with the general tasks. The industrialisation of the building process will continue despite fluctuations in the economy. We consider this hypothesis to be likely in view of:

1   accelerating urbanisation;
2   human endeavours to attain the same or better material results with less manual labour.

We have been experiencing an era of profound industrialisation for about the last 100 years and now we are at the beginning of the second era of industrialisation, which involves the rationalisation of organisation and administration. Our familiar working patterns will dissolve. New forms will be established at an increasing pace. It will be of the utmost economic importance for our society to erect buildings that permit rapid and continual ongoing alteration of their functional content.

Architectural expression

The functionalist ideals of architectural expression must be abandoned – in which architecture is expression, the symbol of *one* well analysed function. The new expression has to be found in the way in which a building forms a general frame for its continuously changing functional content. (The concept of building will, in most cases, mean something that consists of more than one building, that is it refers rather to urban planning.)

Architectural tension is created by the contrast between the long-lasting general structure and its highly varied, impermanent content.

The need for general rules

The urbanisation process will continue with growing human needs of increased interchanges with each other. The important task will be to focus the major urban planning processes on providing an environment that is as well adapted to human life as possible. To deal with a process like this what are needed are:

1   general regulations to coordinate the dimensions of all urban planning, including the buildings;
2   general quality standards that lay down the degree of functional adaptability (flexibility) required of the separate sections of a building, which physiological and which psychological demands are to be made.

The functional service life of a building's elements

Some of the elements that compose a building will be general and not dependent on the functions it serves, others, however, will be determined by function. Elements will have differing life spans. It is functionally and economically important for elements with different life spans not to be included in each other but, on the other hand, rather easy to assemble and dismantle. It should be simple to replace elements with short functional life spans with new functionally adapted elements.

Awareness of these factors must be included in the economic assessment of a building. That is clear when comparing tables for the allocation of costs for an office block. The major annual capital costs are borne by the elements with short depreciation periods. The frame is less significant. From an economic point of view it should be regarded as a general platform that provides the possibility of replacing elements with shorter functional life spans. Even though such tables should not be taken to offer absolute costs but seen rather as an example, the tendency is obvious: groups of building elements with different depreciation periods should be kept separate and the major task of the frame is to offer a general platform for additions to and replacement of its functionally adapted elements. It must also be possible to develop these elements systematically and industrialise them.

The architect's future task

What then will the future tasks of architects be and how should they be organised to make the best of their work?

We believe that the building process outlined above will demand:

1   The development of general regulations to coordinate dimensions. The regulations will allow variations for different types of buildings.
2   The development of a method for laying down various quality requirements.
3   The development of different building systems that meet the regulations on dimensions and quality standards. The systems can include frames, installations or spatial divisions.
4   Urban planning or framework planning using general regulations and with awareness of developed systems.
5   The functional furnishing of frames using the general regulations and with awareness of developed systems.

In every aspect of this process the architect will have an important role to play. Drawing up the general requirements that will apply to all buildings is just as important as creating a system of dividing walls and ceilings that is as functionally effective and as aesthetically pleasing as possible.

It is just as important to direct the urban planning process towards well functioning organisms with strong environmental values in long-lasting squares and streets, as to design purpose-built solutions that give appropriate expression to a specific function with the expressiveness, commercial impact and so on required.

The organisation of architectural practices

We believe that undertaking these tasks will make it more important for architectural practices to merge to form groups with several equally qualified members. We believe that the more mechanical work of producing drawings will decline in parallel with the development of ready-made systems or that they will develop as specific tasks within each practice. The tasks will become larger, greater quality will be required in the actual organisation of the work.

Raising the quality of the main organisation of the task involves demanding greater knowledge in all the areas of practice outlined above coupled with the necessity to keep abreast in every sector. No sector can develop without awareness of the others. An effective system for documentation, filing and transferring know-how to each other will be required so that tasks can continually be undertaken in the best way possible.

We, ourselves, have felt a powerful need to be involved in and shape the new industrialisation process that we consider to be inescapable. We have therefore together with another architectural practice, A4, established a joint service office that will manage our joint knowledge bank and disciplines that have been developed for cost-control and so on.

Artistic quality

One can ask whether organisation of this kind will make artistic expression impossible. We do not believe it will. Our belief is that access to the necessary knowledge will not hinder but will, on the contrary, provide a platform for the development of living, architectonic artistry.

Admittedly not all architects can have developed the same artistic sensibility or the same talent to empathise with human problems. Insofar as an architect has these qualities, we believe that they will make themselves felt and function as guidelines for an organisation like ours.

We do not believe in a hierarchy with someone who has to know everything at its apex neither in society nor in an architectural practice. That period is over. We believe in the organisation of society and of architectural practices in the spirit of democracy, so that several can, with their different skills and shared standards of quality, work together to offer as good a solution as possible to the task they have been given.

Toscansks Landskap

Stefan Alenius 77/78

Sketch by Stefan Alenius

1978

Stefan Alenius, Jan Angbjär and Magnus Silfverhielm

Mannerisms: Or What Can We Do With Our Functionalist Inheritance?

What does a building represent?

Architecture expresses its society. That there is *some* connection between a society and its architecture is probably something most of us can agree with. It is more difficult to agree on *what* the link looks like.

When a society changes substantially, so does the expression in its architecture. This is a proposition that we naturally add to the previous one so that it then gives us the conditions that enable meaningful study of architectural expression.

All the signs suggest that we are facing a crisis that seems to embrace several important areas of society. How does architecture *express* this?

Our functionalist inheritance

What then is our aesthetic point of departure? Well for most of us our functionalist inheritance still provides the basis for our aesthetic judgements and endeavours. "Inheritance" because we have generally not ourselves been involved in forming functionalism but have experienced it as a given truth in our everyday lives and in our education.

Moreover the meaning of "functionalism" for us today is certainly not exactly the same as it was for those that created it, so that "inheritance" can be a suitable caveat. With these reservations let us now try to characterise this functionalist inheritance by seeing how it has developed.

The functionalist approach can be described in very simple terms as follows: "A building, constructed using simple and rational building techniques, should meet the user's reasonable needs of space and hygiene." With a clear concept like this of the task of building, the radical functionalist architects took an optimistic view of the industrial adaptation of building processes to respond to the rapidly expanding building needs of society. How broad, long, tall or large a building was to be could be determined simply by study of the dimensions and movements of the individual users. Architecture became science.

It is this scientific attitude that together with the desire for industrial adaptation can be seen in the functionalist style. "Funkis" is the architectonic expression of the new, healthier society's optimistic belief in the power of its own development.

The appearance of functionalist expression is familiar to us. In very simple terms we could say that a funkis building represents a rational shell around the empirically computed spatial needs of a healthy and rational human being. This finds expression in quadrilaterals, straight lines, box shapes and genuine materials composed and arranged so that the building is stripped bare of all meaning but "light source", "protection from the rain", "hole in the wall" and "structural component".

Funkis lays claim to be an international style as well. The fundamental, simple needs of light, air, hygiene and a reasonable amount of space do not change significantly from one place to another. The functionalists eagerly studied the dimensions and needs of *individuals*. For this reason we usually find in early functionalism dimensions and sizes that are adapted to and easily understood by individuals: the scale is human. Subsequent developments were to offer major changes.

Let our next stop be thirty years later. The expansive development of society now means that the buildings are generally much greater in size. This is the age of large buildings. Concepts and words like construction systems, building units, flexibility, generalisability and optimal supply systems are key terms. Under the influence of the social sciences, buildings are viewed as structures and their users are now *groups* of individuals. The sound economic theory of large-scale production demands numerous machines and large construction companies. And, with some irony, we could say of the product that more and more buildings resemble each other, irrespective of their circumstances, on equally levelled sites.

What does the aesthetic expression look like? Well in principle the elements of functionalist form – squares, lines and boxes – are still valid, but they are often incorporated into some kind of overall form. The framework or the supply system is visible and it *structures* the functionalist battery of forms.

The technical or non-figurative expression that derives from functionalism acquires a further tinge of scientific anonymity when the structures declare their readiness to house any functional content at all without affecting their external appearance. Buildings represent merely anonymous structures to be used for any purpose at all.

As it is often the structure that gives these buildings their architectonic expression, they lose what we referred to previously as the human scale. The fundamental principle of functionalism is magnified at every level, along with the explosive development of society.

Architecture reflects its society. In the mirror we now see ungovernable belief in progress with its unrestrained consumption of disposable items and constantly expanding car ownership. The ceaselessly varying social activities move in and out of massive built machines that are open to the differing needs and inclinations of every group.

And then today arrived. The crisis at most levels of society that we are discussing today has of course developed slowly into what it has become. Not until now has it seemed possible for growing environmental destruction, energy crises, stiffening political oppositions and other phenomena to make any fundamental impact on the capitalistic faith in progress. Crisis is a good description, as in this situation there hardly seems to be any obvious or simple alternative courses of action. Even the good "socialist alternative" is undergoing changes so that it can cope with the new reality and in areas where a new ecological social model is being sketched there is no obvious cogent alternative that we can adopt immediately either.

In comparison with such grave perspectives our subject, architectural expression, must naturally be considered highly peripheral, but if architecture is to reflect its society then there is still some interest in considering how an incipient crisis of this kind is revealed in architecture. What are we doing with our functionalist background in this new situation?

The clearest evidence in our case in Sweden of future adaptations or the need for different architectonic expression is the period of nostalgic country cottage romanticism that has flourished, and still does. The mullions, bay windows, garden benches and pre-fabricated idylls conceal of course needs that differ from those that profiteering capitalism believes it is meeting with all its products.

Other tendencies to change in architecture derive from the technical aspect of the crisis, the energy crisis. We have already seen several interesting energy-saving building techniques, particularly for private homes. These have been easy to devise as a kind of functionalism.

Is "post-functionalism" of this kind the architectural expression that our new social situation is going to demand? Let us introduce a historical parallel. In the evolution of Italian Renaissance architecture into mannerism we can intuitively discern a *structural resemblance* to our own development from functionalism to where we stand today.

The Italian Renaissance

The cradle of the capitalist social system can be found in the city states of fifteenth-century Italy and it was this new expansive force that was eventually to demand expression in the revival of the classical secular style. God's supreme power over human beings was questioned during the Renaissance. Families of merchants acquired enormous fortunes and power. Finally, like the popes, these new secular rulers assumed the role of God's representatives on earth.

This new society sought its architectonic expression in classical, pagan patterns. With their reminders of earlier Italian eminence, the dormant architectural styles of classical Rome could serve to express a new incipient period of grandeur. The classical idiom has never been abandoned entirely in Italy and Gothic expressions of religious community did not suit this new materialistic power. Let us illustrate this with a few examples!

The early Renaissance urban palaces in Florence are axial, symmetrical and fundamentally cubic in organisation but are nevertheless imbued with a lightness of touch in their details. In the façades, the blocks are considerably divided in the classical rustic order from solid to slender.

Somewhat later the grave, substantial Roman urban palaces adopt the entire spectrum of classical architectural elements: plinths, pilaster orders and entablatures. Familiar elements from classical buildings are logically arranged in a static, harmonious structural concept. The aesthetic pattern is therefore given and its continued development was merely towards greater weight and gravity.

The ideals and styles of the Renaissance are spread to the rest of Europe. In Rome, architecture attains full maturity in the High Renaissance buildings of Bramantes and Raphael. Expression is now more forceful, at times bombastic and at times severe, but the harmonious order of the façades remains the same. Bearing elements and what they support are arranged logically to form a static balance. The volume of buildings is composed of mathematically determined forms such as hemispheres and cubes, which correspond to squares and circles in floor plans and in façades. Equilateral symmetry and balance is the architectural aim. Familiarity with the classical patterns is now so great that they are easily plagiarised when the creative imagination of a master is lacking.

The secular nobles of the Renaissance succeed each other on the papal throne. In the Vatican State's own church, Renaissance concepts should attain their most forceful expression. With the enormous dimensions envisaged by Bramante, St Peter's was obviously going to offer an experience of infinite might. Utmost magnificence and harmony is attained by simply magnifying the familiar pattern.

St Peter's never became a completely High Renaissance building but even so today we can see how it portrays the naïve optimism of the Renaissance. We can agree with the comment of Ehrenswärd when he visited Rome that St Peter's has never succeeded in making the impression of being as big as it actually is.

After a long period of optimistic progress, Italian society faces a crisis. The Reformation is a revolt against the lack of religious content in papal power. The Catholic church redoubles its efforts and the Counter Reformation begins with the Jesuit order, inquisition, censorship and stricter rules of conduct. The licentious and depraved social life that flourished without restraint during the Renaissance is relegated to courtyards and alleyways. At the same time, everyday life during the new crisis displays elements of the strictest asceticism and the most vulgar pornography.

The social crisis is accompanied by a change in architectural expression. Architects like Peruzzi, Romano, Michelangelo, Palladio, Vasari and Vingola turn this new expression into the style we call *mannerism*.

We are familiar with mannerism in painting. In it Tintoretto, Correggio and Bronzino abandon the harmony of the High Renaissance for deliberately inharmonious, unbalanced expression, sometimes perversely emotional, sometimes self-effacingly disciplined.

In this crisis there is no clear path to take. The artists seek their own individual ways out of their shared Renaissance background. Mannerism never becomes a coherent style to match the Renaissance. Here, however, are some architectural examples!

Michelangelo's Laurentian Library in Florence shows us something new where the links between the rooms and their different proportions are concerned. The ideal High Renaissance room was symmetric in composition and indicated neither movement nor direction. A sequence of rooms consisted merely of additional ideal rooms of the same type.

In the Laurentian Library the two rooms interact so that the very shape of the manifestly high and narrow vestibule compels the visitor up the stairway to the corridor-like reading room of which it forms the plinth. There the movement is converted into an equally compelling "forward".

The floor space of the vestibule is taken up entirely by the staircase that cascades from the reading room. The forceful tension in the sequentiality of the rooms (up-forwards) is further enhanced by the sudden and surprising way in which it is first viewed. This is from the side as we enter through a modest entrance in the plinth of the vestibule.

The same tension can be seen in the structure of the walls of the vestibule. Its muscular and surprisingly numerous pillars could be expected to support a great weight but turn out to bear almost nothing. In the same way, the sturdy corbels in the plinth section have no static role to play in the function of the walls. The forms used by the High Renaissance in a logical, harmonious sequence of supporting and supported elements are combined by Michelangelo to form an illogical, disharmonious clash of forces. Each element braces itself but encounters no resistance and in this way no totality can be engendered.

In the Palazzo Massimi in Rome by Baldassare Peruzzi we find another form of mannerism. Here we are not dealing with Michelangelo's vaunting gravity and disharmonious tension but rather the connoisseur's bent for the exquisite. This small private palace already displays its idiosyncratically "illicit" composition in the street façade. The entire façade is slightly curved in a way that the Renaissance would have found impossible. Here what would have been massive in a High Renaissance palace is instead light and slender. There are no classical patterns for the order of the façade – composed freely and, for the Renaissance, illogically. The entrance lies deep inside a loggia on the ground floor that lacks the usual rustic distinction from the floors above.

The ground plan of the entire building complex is asymmetrically composed. One side of the entry arch provides access to the courtyard. This only has arcades on two facing sides. Again we find interest in imposed movement and direction in a way that is alien to the inert compositions of the Renaissance. The courtyard contains classical sculptures and at one end a sensuous fountain. On one side the main staircase leads to a high, wide open loggia on the upper floor, where the sparing use of plastic ornamentation is supplemented by painted patterns and illusory landscapes and architectural details. Everything is imbued by voluptuous refinement. Only those who are complete masters of the Renaissance aesthetic rules of play can offend against them so exquisitely.

And then to Giacomo Vignola. In him we see even more clearly the mannerist interest in movement and spatial direction. In his little church of St Andrea in Via Flaminia the squares and circles of Renaissance floor plans have been stretched into rectangles and ovals.

In his delightful Villa Giulia the courtyards are united in an axially arranged succession of garden views. Through openings at the end of one courtyard the next appears and in this way the visitor is led through the entire sequence.

Originally Michelangelo was commissioned to design Il Gésu, Rome's Jesuit church, and its mediaeval features are probably something that Vignola inherited from him. The new religious interest in mannerist Italy led several architects to seek inspiration in mediaeval ecclesiastic architecture. For many years Michelangelo wanted to endow the dome of St Peter's with a Gothically inspired elevation. In Il Gésu we can see how the interior expresses the religiously sublime rather than the material, secular order that the Renaissance invokes. Its floor plan has a direct mediaeval origin. The use of light enhances the compelling motion towards the altar as the discreet illumination of the nave is almost extinguished before we encounter the intense light that streams from the dome.

Here we are a long way from the simple materiality of Renaissance society. We have seen how mannerist architects confront and stretch their Renaissance backgrounds in search of expression that will harmonise with the social changes. A clear, straightforward development has encountered crisis. The tension forces material rationality and religious emotions into the same architectural garb.

Harald Thafvelin

Now we return to our own age and our current situation. How are we dealing with our crisis and our functionalist backgrounds to make the architectural garb fit? In our Swedish context we feel that the following examples are interesting.

Harald Thafvelin's church and parish offices at Vårby Gård is a remarkable and in many ways surprising building. From outside the building complex seems to be composed of two units. In the surroundings the parish offices appear as a large, simple urban façade in which the smaller volume of the church building is protectively concealed. Seen from the cliffs and landscape on the other side the complex appears to be more rugged and composed of smaller elements. The urban appearance and the natural appearance intersect dramatically and create in the parish building a volume that is composed, from a functionalist point of view, "illogically". The materials, the bricklaying, roof shape and size distinguish the volume of the church interior from the parish offices but even so they are combined in a remarkable manner to form a unit: at variance but coherent.

Rainwater is drained from the church in an explicit and complicated manner whereas it is arranged with technical efficiency from the parish offices. On the side facing the cliffs, the solid, foundation plinth is plainly engineered and the soil falls away irregularly from its level surface. The plinth beneath the façade facing the surrounding buildings is its opposite, following the soil irresolutely and resting on it.

These and other formal oppositions at different levels in the composition permit interpretation at virtually a verbal level. The opposing pairs are rarely of a purely black and white nature, in other words contrasts that balance, but rather they create different kinds of dissonances. This and the way in which elements are permitted to cut across one another contribute to an overall experience that is highly reminiscent of the disharmonious, tense emotional qualities of some of our Italian examples.

Details of the façade provide other examples. The firmly sculptured plinth that signals its function in very much the same way as in the palace in Stockholm is pierced in a patently illogical way by cellar windows. The large façade of the parish offices towards the urban surroundings is surmounted by a cornice with a remarkable staircase pattern that casts doubt on the way in which it is obviously supported by the walls below it. The porch in front of the entrance contains a peculiar opposition between material and expression of form. A similar relationship can be found in the brickwork of the church walls, where the traditional weight of a brick wall is questioned by the "timberlike" appearance produced by contrasting horizontally laid stone.

The interiors offer this tense interplay of oppositions even more clearly. Their different elements are contrasted with each other at different levels of significance in what is often a provocative manner that tempts us to try to interpret the significance of their relationships.

The interior of the church is shaped freely with no clear correspondences to the external form. The ceiling consists of a series of strict timber vault shapes that recall mediaeval ecclesiastical models and the spiritual elevation to which they aspire. A number of very sturdy columns rise from the floor and their muscular, bulging shapes suggest a roof of enormous weight. However, they are merely linked to the ceiling by thin iron structures which are virtually concealed behind the almost banal motif used in cartoons to symbolise emerging force. Where the spiritual and material worlds encounter each other, sparks are struck in a tense motif that is never allowed to fade harmoniously.

The illumination of the church interior comprises another but smaller motif on the same theme. At its centre, where the congregation sits, light glows from carbon-filament lighting in gently formed brass fittings whereas along the sides ordinary naked light bulbs on long, rigid arms rather invoke movement or spatial orientation. This functionalist way of allotting atmospheric values in their form and positioning is, however, composed so provocatively that one immediately looks for the significance that underlies the objects. And again we seem to be able to discern a variation on the theme of "spiritual versus material", "nature versus technology" or some similar pair of opposites.

Opposites like this, different variations on the same theme, can be found everywhere, from the overall context to the detail solutions. They are, however, hardly arranged in mutual harmony but they cut across the spatiality, above and through each other and sometimes, in formal terms, give rise to dissonances. In this way the building appeals to both the emotionality and rationality of visitors so that they will experience the theme, the meaning of the entire structure. The meanings of the individual pairs of opposites are not truly self-evident. We have offered only suggested interpretations. What is important, however, is that they invite interpretation. Tracing the process of meaning becomes a search and a test of both the emotions and the intellect.

The building demands something of those that use it to disclose its inherent function as a "church". In our attempted interpretations keywords like dissonance and tension have seemed to be necessary.

In the parish offices the theme seems to be dealt with less solemnly, almost with palpable resolution. In an enormous act of will the building is divided into two colour halves, so that all the rooms on one side are bright red and on the other all equally bright blue. The line dividing red from blue forms a diagonal through the building at the same position as the drastic diagonal division in its external form. Here there is an obvious reference to a functionalist background, but functionalists would certainly describe it as grotesque or formalist. This remarkable diagonal of colour reflects neither technical nor spatial function and what it contributes to finding one's way around the building is far too little to justify the vehemence of its execution. Where green and red would provide a harmonious balance, we find blue against red in a form of skewed opposition, a dissonance. And this offers a keynote for a whole series of similar lesser oppositions that are allowed to cut across the major diagonal division everywhere. The major theme permeates each minor variation. Let us give some examples!

The crystal chandelier over a dining table and ordinary office lamps over school desks are allowed to coexist in the same room in a stylistic mix that would be impossible in any formal aesthetic. Calm conversation and day-to-day actual work are equally part of parish routine but they also have to permeate and influence each other.

Another example. In one room there are two concrete elements with the same shape. One is used as an ordinary load bearing beam while the other merely shades a lamp.

Thafvelin repeatedly uses the methods we have tried to exemplify here to impose on ordinary simple building and furnishing elements meaning that differ from those we conventionally use. Some concluding examples may provide further demonstration. In several places there are sparse painted patterns. These offer just the additional visual impact needed for a whole wall with its doors and other fittings to suddenly appear to be a large, playful pattern. The concepts of "door" and "pattern square" jostle for position in the same object. Correspondingly a bundle of ordinary, visible wires on a wall can, because there are too many of them, appear to form part of a large, decorative wall painting. Or as in the remarkable sensuous and religiously suggestive altar, where the stone floor is sucked into the wooden support by means of a painted stone pattern that also has the peculiar lightness of a textile.

In a newspaper article Ulf Hård af Segerstad has described the structure as a "building in protest". The spontaneous experience of protest, topsy-turviness and chaos allows itself, however, after a while to be registered as an alternative to what it is protesting against.

Anyone who walks into this structure wearing a lumber jacket, jeans, moon boots, skiwear, an Indian patterned sweater, Palestine scarf or some other form of everyday wear will not look out of place. In fact we are faced with materials, colours and objects that also surround us in our everyday lives: Mexican tiles, fluorescent light fixtures, house bricks, ordinary windows, Spanish vaulting, bright colours, ordinary furniture, council house cornices, blue mood lighting in brass fittings, classroom lighting, pictures in gold frames or eighteenth-century chairs. The array of objects, colours and materials will not, as it were, bother someone who is not wearing a tie. This is not an aesthetically arranged "shade by shade" setting but rather one that at first glance is reminiscent of a mixture of shapes from department stores, pizzerias and affluent residential districts. Briefly, the building has been constructed with our ordinary day-to-day objects as its building blocks whereas its language, its meaning, can be found in the interpretations of the way in which the objects have been put together.

In a setting like this, those who use it can buy new furniture, paint their own pictures, refurnish, put in new doors or get other lighting and so contribute to or change the interpretation process without destroying the aesthetic order. The form the structure takes now rather urges its users to make their own changes, test things for themselves to explore and improvise around the generous theme the building provides.

Peter Celsing

Our other example, Peter Celsing, uses the functionalist background in a different way.

If Harald Thafvelin takes handfuls of "everyday bits and pieces" and melds them into a challenging bizarre narrative on the meaning of a building, then Peter Celsing is someone who with refined tenaciousness endeavours to attain the ideal solution to the problem.

Let us characterise his method like this: at this unique spot in the world there is only one optimal solution for any conceived building project. Note the two-fold implication of this wording. The building is to express what is unique about the location and at the same time serve its purpose. Moreover, the best solution for Peter Celsing is always a simple form that, seemingly at least, makes the task of building and planning a simple one. It is easy to formulate the solution at every level to offer mastery, an overview and refinement.

The totality provided by an immediately experienced form is fundamental to Celsing's architecture. As we have seen, no such totality can be found in Thafvelin. In the Vårby Gård complex the total experience is an intellectual, laboriously organised series of separate experiences. Where Peter Celsing severs the Gordian knot by supplying solutions to all the problems encountered in what appears to be a self-evident finished form – Thafvelin's building is instead a manifestation of the multifaceted problem itself.

A globe can be any size at all without alteration of its form. Irrespective of the actual size of their contents, externally Celsing's buildings are always simple geometric volumes. He consistently applies the functionalist experience that a building need not look like a "building".

With this relationship between absolute form and actual size he succeeds in providing an explicit, simple shape for every complex building project. The method used to form the church in Vällingby is the same as for the far more extensive Sergels Torg project.

Thus far the similarities with a generally classicist tradition are striking, both in terms of the "good" form and a manifest lack of "human" adaptation in dimensions and size.

How then does he select the "good" design? Let us describe it like this. The walls of Kulturhuset in Stockholm set a resolute stop to a long-standing dispute in the history of building in Stockholm. From now on there will be no extension of Sveavägen to the palace. To make room for a new orientation, the building walls project like a chisel into the Brunkeberg ridge and now, at last, like retaining walls perpetuate the difference in levels at the site. And behold! From the wall spouts water like a curtain of glass in front of the concrete! Slightly angled, the wall stands firm against the old city structures that now, freshly apparelled, press against it.

Perhaps the Sergels Torg case is unusually explicit, but in many of Celsing's recent projects there are a similar series of local motifs that firmly anchor the good design in the uniqueness of the situations themselves. Form can be interpreted with the help of its context at several levels apart from the purely functionalist. In this way Celsing succeeds in the basic approach of augmenting his projects with a kind of "taste" that enhances what the buildings can normally offer themselves.

The expression of sophisticated refinement imbues the smallest details in the buildings. With their powerful, irreproachable external forms as frames, both exterior and interior details and entire interiors can be designed with eclectic liberty. Celsing's keen artistic desire for formal, aesthetic order still knits it all together into a "style" that transcends pure eclecticism.

Even inspiration from the East can happily assume a Swedish guise. Inside the shell, rooms are given the space they need often with unconventional but always geometrically simple contours. These often punctuate or are askew to the external outlines. Each room expresses something more than its actual function. In a Celsing bath you not only wash yourself but "perform your ablutions".

Celsing shows constant interest in the quality of surfaces. In his search for the precise form, externally and internally, surfaces can be cross-hatched, striped or patterned in various ways or wrenched into precise corners to ensure that they align. When oblique angles and pointed corners are justifiable, they are readily employed.

This aspiration for refined precision makes every building a completed composition. In this way, for instance, every individual whose uniform city suit does not match the polished interiors of the Bank of Sweden stands out against the building's aesthetic order.

Mannerism

On the basis of our argument we would like to assert the following.

Thafvelin and Celsing use their functionalist background in their architecture in the same way as the mannerist architects used their Renaissance backgrounds.

The functionalist concept must have seemed appealingly self-evident to the society of its day with its inherent readiness for action. It was a simple answer to the question of how to get to grips with the building needs of a rapidly expanding society.

The idiom of the Renaissance must have appeared to be a given form of expression for the focus of newly created expansive commercial capitalism on the material world. The classical pagan ideals of beauty with their mathematically determined logical harmony lay waiting to be brought to light.

Then comes a crisis in the optimism about development in both cases. And then in both cases art and architecture is deprived of self-evident, socially coherent expression. Each architect seeks his own path through the old, now refashioned, parameters of form to attain new, elevated expressive values in harmony with altered social conditions. Disharmony, dissonance and tension or sophistication, over-explicitness and refinement can be viewed as architectural keywords – in both cases.

History, like the history of art, is full of crises, stylistic shifts and transitions. Other periods of "mannerism", with roughly the same meaning as we have used, can also be found. But we would like to maintain that the Italian example is the one that has greater relevance than any other with regard to the development of architectural expression. We have selected Thafvelin and Celsing as examples to try to demonstrate this. Outside Sweden there are so many other similar examples that we venture to declare that *much of the innovative architecture of today displays a mannerist relationship to the fundamentally* functionalist *architecture that preceded it.*

What are we doing with our functionalist inheritance?

Architecture expresses its society. Is the manneristic expression we have attempted to describe what we can generally expect in tomorrow's buildings? Or are the works of Thafvelin and Celsing merely examples of introverted artistic individualism with no particular basis in society?

Alienation resulting partly from a monotonous environment which offers users no articulated opportunity to identify and no intellectual or physical stimuli is of course unfortunate. Regrettably, we have to admit that to a large extent this is what further development of functionalism has led to. The different architecture of Thafvelin and Celsing involves reaction *against* development of this kind and *for* firm emphasis on the distinctiveness and local setting of every building. The major advances that resulted from the functionalist view of the task of architecture, cannot, however, be relinquished. Nor is that what is suggested here. On the contrary, in both Thafvelin and Celsing we see a desire to supplement the fundamental "functionalist" needs architecture is to fulfil with additional and more complex ones.

Human beings are complex, this is what our life is like and architecture should be the same! But the complex offers scope for the opposite. Disharmony and dissonance are also part of our everyday lives – not least today. This is what our life is like and architecture should be the same and the approach we have described indeed enables possibilities of expressing precisely this. But is our age, our society, in any deeper sense manneristic or is this merely a matter of a few artists who are bored with a worn-out idiom?

Millesgården by Johan Celsing

2007

Johan Celsing

The Robust, the Sincere

The robust

Buildings should be built to last. What is still typical today, despite all the new technology, is after all that architecture is a genuinely unwieldy, slow medium that requires
major resources for its creation. For this reason the robust is important if architecture is
to be taken seriously and contribute to the development of a sustainable community.

The robust is an alternative to the architecture that is mainly based on visual
features. The really significant qualities of a building are complex and not always
visually accessible. They quite simply demand a different commitment, or even
presence, if they are to be judged.

The robust should not be interpreted to mean something crudely hewn and
therefore sturdy through its brute strength. Instead it is intended to engender
durable and multifaceted architecture. There are many factors that make architecture relevant in the long term and appearance is only one of them. Robust architecture affirms the context of a project in the broadest sense. Its physical,
concrete surroundings are one aspect of this. Other aspects are the technical conditions that apply to the project, its financing, its social context, its history or
current or expected social role. Robust architecture aims to determine the state in
which all the circumstances can be scrupulously taken into account and synthesised in the form of a building. When one or more of these circumstances change,
the building will continue to be relevant, but now superimposed with its own
historical overlay.

Sigurd Lewerentz's works provoke thought in this context as they focus on the
essential, the poetic, advanced experiments, but not as visually challenging buildings that demand the attention of those who are not really affected by them. On the
other hand, those called upon to use them find them more interesting than most
other buildings.

Another aspect of the robust, but different, is how the building may be combined
with other buildings, or perhaps even rebuilt. In this respect robustness denotes how
clearly, or as it were self-evidently, the building manifests itself. Here we could
describe the robust as the cut-off point where functional requirements have been fulfilled and where the design acquires an almost generic character. This can also be
expressed by saying that it is also open for other forms of use. This is easier said than
done. There are many examples of buildings with a contrivedly archaic appearance
and even more whose appearance is merely the sum of all their functions.

The robust need not necessarily refer to the material circumstances of a building but can just as easily concern how they function in their context. The Austrian architect Hermann Czech has presented arguments claiming that architecture is *background* and should only speak when it is spoken to. This should not be taken to mean humility or false modesty but rather the expression of seriousness. The starting point is, of course, Adolf Loos's observations about façades and also garments in the modern city. Loos claimed that the correct degree of unassertiveness in both garments and façades was a form of collective agreement in cities. The deliberate unassertiveness of exteriors offered, in his opinion, protection and was a prerequisite for the private inner sphere and its individuality of expression. I consider that Czech's argument from the 1980s is just as relevant today when some architecture seems to focus on arbitrary issues such as branding and design strategies for the commercial world. The projects completed by Czech, primarily in Vienna, are themselves eloquent proof that robust architecture takes no single stylistic form. One point of departure for Czech's creations appears to have been aversion to ready-made style. Instead he endeavours to find numerous reasons for each form and consequently functional trifles can easily be combined with special solutions when these are required. If Czech can be viewed as an architectural philosopher and hyper-functionalist, he also calmly gave new life to Viennese café culture. With his contemporary adaptations of furniture by Thonet in light interiors of our time, Czech once again renewed this culture in the 1990s in the MAK Café in Vienna's Museum für Angewandte Kunst. Inspiring examples of how architecture that retains focus on the contemporary can transform and develop existing architecture on a large scale can also be found in Otto Wagner in Vienna in the early twentieth century. Even more breathtaking transformations were undertaken in Chicago at roughly the same time. The classical rules of architecture were adapted on a new metropolitan scale without vanishing in the process. One example of such a change can be found in the architecture of Louis Sullivan, who replaced the earlier contributions of craftsmen to buildings with industrially produced ceramic elements with oriental features that were arranged, like the pixelated images of today, along the surfaces of façades.

The robust need not endure or be built to last. Shigero Ban's emergency dwellings of paper reels and Lacaton & Vassal's many low-budget projects are excellent examples of this. The robust need not result in buildings that are compact and visually subdued. In a series of buildings during recent decades the Norwegian architects Jan Olav Jensen and Børre Skodvin have created environments with a highly complex array of materials but nevertheless very convincing results.

Resisting the seemingly radical and visually determined architecture opens up other possibilities of linking today's buildings to those of earlier periods as well as what should be one of the most important tasks for our age: looking after what already exists and in the name of sustainability developing and augmenting it. One example of a worthwhile task in Sweden concerns the massive renovation of the housing erected on the outskirts of our cities in the 1960s and 1970s. Developing, augmenting and revitalising these major concentrations is an important and demanding task that should not be entrusted to anyone who would have preferred rather that the buildings of this entire era had never been erected. In actual fact these areas possess a scale, organisation and structure that, on the whole, make infill and revitalisation quite reasonable. Unlike housing from the 1980s, for instance, which was from its conception intended to have visual appeal, with all this means in terms of dodgy planning, adornment and pitched roofs, one can view the projects of the 1960s and 1970s as having been inspired by the ambition (unfortunately far too tight-fistedly) to produce the largest possible number of apartments given the limited resources and time available. We should not, in my opinion, approach the task of enhancing these environments, as is done in many quarters, by adding a few storeys, covering their trivial façades with fashionable layers of coloured glass and then crowning their once flat roofs with more contemporary vaulting or other trimmings. Instead of such clichés we should make robust additions in the form of infill and extensions where they have genuine and not cosmetic importance. We should pay the same careful respect to these arte-facts that may seem strange to us as to individuals we do not know, and allow the design of what we add to be determined by the existing environments and the lives of their inhabitants and not by the dictates of current styles that will soon be just as obsolete as the environments they were meant to renew.

Endeavouring with empathy to understand how additions can be made to what already exists should be an important issue of our time. Melding the old with the new without attempting to make distinctions for their own sake. Additions need not lack wilfulness. What is important is that the wilfulness is not all that the archi-tecture can offer. Manipulating existing buildings, or even creating links to them, physically or architectonically, raises the issue of tradition. Gustav Mahler is reputed to have commented on this subject: "Tradition is not the worship of ashes, but the preservation of fire."

One architectonic theorist who is inspiring where the robust is concerned is the Austrian Josef Frank (1885–1968), who lived and worked in Sweden from the 1930s onwards. Frank could be described as the link between Adolf Loos and Hermann Czech. In his *Accidentism* from 1958, he asserts that the settings that please us have arisen by chance and that we should therefore shape our surround-ings as if they had arisen in the same way. Frank, who was anything but a romantic, does not of course mean that we should imitate earlier buildings. His standpoint can be seen as a rejection of the "uniformity [that] has not risen for practical reasons but as a result of an ideology – an ideology that is not even our own". Without underrating the importance of the design of individual buildings, Frank claimed that the most important problem for architecture today was town planning. He continues: "What variety offers us is character rather than generalised beauty. A theatre does not have to look like a factory, any more than a bank has to resemble a bakery." In his ironic and sarcastic text he goes on to say:

> The idea of "elevating" everything to the level of art is of course highly seductive. But let us not forget one thing: even if we cannot define what a work of art is, one of its essential attributes is that it is unchanging and serves no purpose other than to be looked at. In this sense, it imposes demands on people, and I do not believe that one can, in the long run, feel completely comfort-able in an environment consisting only of objects that impose such demands.

The attitudes cited here have been one obvious inspiration for the varied tasks I have undertaken in my practice. In 1997 Bonniers, Sweden's most important media

Bonniers Konsthall

group, invited entries to a competition for an art gallery and offices next to its head office in Stockholm. The result of the competition, the newly erected Bonnier building with an art gallery on the ground floor is intended through its volume and its linkage with the curvature of the street outside to merge with the disposition and scale of the surrounding built fabric. Simultaneously and by contrast, its exterior of glass and steel singles it out as a distinct institution alongside the brickwork complex by Ivar and Anders Tengbom from the end of the 1940s. Inside the gallery all of the enclosures, large and small, wedge-shaped closets or narrow corridors, are viewed as potential exhibition rooms, with the ceilings of the same height, the same materials and illumination. The equivilation of the interior spaces means that all the rooms in the building can be used in varying constellations. The rooms in the art gallery are elementary, flexible and hopefully playfully inviting in character. Very large sliding walls (11 by 4.2 metres) can be parked manually in enclosures in the walls or form part of the variable exhibition arrangements. The gallery's transparent façades to the surrounding streets and waterways are motivated by the desire not to isolate the exhibitions behind closed external walls but instead to display art in contact with, and also against, the background of the surrounding city.

The addition to the Museum of Sketches in Lund's mediaeval town centre is the first stage of a major expansion. The museum was established to exhibit a study collection for students at Lund University in the 1930s and is housed in a number of buildings of varying age. Its first gallery occupies what used to be a gymnasium built at the end of the nineteenth century. The exhibitions and collections in this gallery have gradually expanded to overflow into neighbouring buildings and in 1958 and 1984 these were supplemented by the erection of new buildings. The most recent addition is a compact extension and its interior serves to link each section of the museum to form a route that takes you through the entire exhibition area. The siting of the extension creates an outdoor exhibition area, a courtyard, at the centre of the museum. The new compact extension will also provide a plinth for the next phase of the expansion. It is linked to the large exhibition hall built in 1958. This section of the museum is made of concrete cast *in situ* using moulds of timber. The exterior of the extension is constructed of very large pre-cast concrete elements and the joints and grooves between them form an integral aspect of the design of the façade. Some of the elements contain windows and a few smaller details which reveal for those who perceive it that the industrially manufactured elements are also delicately chiselled-out building stones. In the interior, the galleries in the extension for temporary exhibitions echo the informal atmosphere in the study collections on show in the rest of the museum. Daylight is admitted by clerestories which are supplemented in some positions by recessed windows into which visitors may withdraw from the galleries to survey their surroundings. The flooring is of solid lye-treated pine.

The harbour building in the port of Skanör is intended with its volume to provide a distinct, well-ordered structure for its motley harbour setting. It has recessed verandas facing the sea, a tower for the lifeguard, newsstand, and restaurant and is surmounted by a roof terrace so that it becomes a multi-purpose building, almost like the casino of old-fashioned bathing resorts. The building methods with timber columns, laminated wooden beams and joists of solid timber relate the unfamiliar new erection to the wooden sheds, smokehouses, dockyard machinery and bathing huts that surround it. The uniformity of the material and the repetitiveness are intended to provide an explicit frame for the constant comings and goings in the restaurant and bar. Further reasons can be found in the reality that in Swedish architecture today architects often play a marginal role in the detailed planning process which requires great clarity in the proposals that are submitted.

The sincere

The sincere may seem to be an unarchitectonic aspect of building. Nevertheless it is indispensable if one considers that buildings should primarily serve those that use them. If the robust is an essential quality if buildings are to survive and become part of the structure of a community, then sincerity concerns another side of what is built. When the robust is not far from concepts such as organisation and logic, I consider that what characterises sincerity in buildings involves wilfulness, audacity, playfulness or even something as unusual in architecture as the naïve.

These qualities may be both unassuming and subtle but as a rule they provide a work with presence or warmth and can even invite some form of dialogue. For most people buildings are something they occupy or pass through but they are not

Model of Skanör Harbour Building

generally interested in the architecture as such. For occasional individuals who have the time and interest or who have quite simply become aware of their environ- ment a building can, however, offer a wealth of possibilities and significances and provide a genuine voyage of discovery.

The sincere does not demand attention. It is quite simply part of the care with which the building has been designed.

Playfulness knows no age
Describing the architect Nicodemus Tessin the younger (1654–1728) in terms of sin- cerity may seem to be a breathtaking anachronism. After all, he more than anyone else shaped the monuments and rituals of Swedish autocracy following models from Rome and the court of Louis XIV in Paris.

The palace in Stockholm is undoubtedly Tessin's masterpiece. For many it is an austere, almost impregnable building and its design is based, in part, on the Palazzo Farnese in Rome. It cannot be denied that the building is furnished with all the pomp and an architectonic setting that fits its purpose. In this context I would like to point out something that I consider raises it well above the expected solem- nity to become instead the building's most unanticipated and vibrant spatial arrangement.

I am thinking of the two ceremonial staircases that are placed on each side of the east–west axis of the palace and which provide access to all of its royal apart- ments. In their contemporary baroque magnificence the staircases provide all the splendour that can be demanded. Tessin himself proudly described, in the spirit of Alberti, how the staircases with their eighty columns and half-columns were of gen- uinely royal majesty. At the same time they are so ingeniously designed that even though they occupy the entire breadth of the building of about 15 metres they also easily open into the apartments of the central building and their guardrooms. In

Stairway in the Stockholm Palace by Nicodemus Tessin the younger

practice the staircases form generous extensions of the royal apartments and have been particularly useful for major festivities. In other words it is clear that they provide all the magnificence, functionality and festiveness that can be required. But what they have in addition to this can be described as follows.

The staircases are, despite their enormous size, discreetly incorporated into the palace. From outside there is no indication in the façades of where these asymmetrically sited stairways are placed. From within, however, the staircases offer spectacular views with the dramatic play of light between the eastern and western façades. The ascent from the ground floor is actually spiral and involves crossing landings of various sizes, and neither the subject ascending to visit royalty nor those standing above to receive him can survey the course of his ascent. Instead of being magnificent the stairs are alluring rather, complex in their tortuous and diagonally illuminated rising motion. There is poignancy in their manifest lack of the predictable majesty that is so often the outcome of the rituals of kingship.

If elsewhere the palace is endowed with perceptible processional routes and symmetries, this major spatial complex is a sensual departure from the rule. For Tessin, working in the second half of the seventeenth century, his profession was not stamped with the desire for individual originality that prevails today. In describing these staircases as his own invention he confirms, however, that he relied on his own imaginative faculties rather than base his palaces in the spirit of the age on "the most excellent examples" he had come across during his studies in Paris and Rome.

Another example if not of sincerity at least of wilfulness can again be found in the palace in a staircase situated in the same eastern section. In this case it is quite a minor feature of the building that must have had particular significance for Tessin. This is not an invention but certainly a copy of the circular staircase in the Palazzo Barberini in Rome designed by Borromini. This lovingly incorporated caprice seems to have had some specific significance. This staircase also evades the building's symmetrical design and, in contrast to its subordinate role in the plans, it is still a spectacular and memorable space in which the stairs spiral upwards around an open centre (required functionally as a water-lift). The staircase is unexpectedly magnificent in relation to its subordinate role in the building and the contrast creates the effect of surprise and captivates the visitor with the magic of its architecture.

Being able in this way to enrich the predetermined order while the function remains unimpaired is the idea behind what is referred to here as the sincere.

Another more contemporary example of architecture with great sincerity and wilfulness is Örebro's great civic hall from 1965. Its architects were the brothers Erik and Tore Ahlsén. This large and somewhat Palazzo-like edifice is a genuine

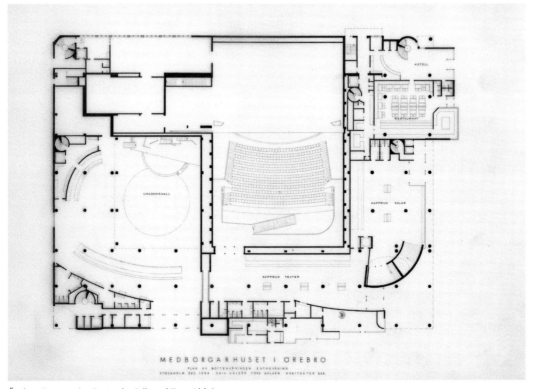

Örebro Community Centre by Erik and Tore Ahlsén

complex with a theatre, conference facilities, a dance-floor, offices, hotel and restaurants. The exterior of the building is typical of its day and only partly hints at the richness of its contents. The frame and structure is rational although complicated by the stage and auditorium of the theatre. This rational structure contains, or once contained, a number of spaces that were arranged wilfully. One of these is the free-form dance-floor in the centre of the otherwise orthogonally structured floor plan. Together with other almost organically shaped stairways and niches these spaces with their curvatures provide the building with an opulence and a sense of solicitude that can primarily be experienced by those who are inside it. The building displays further wilful features to the occupants of the offices in the upper storeys that extend above the theatre's auditorium along the façades around the courtyard. High up in the middle of this large building in the centre of the city, among its high-rises, complex green, rolling countryside can be seen. The shape of the yard surmounting the auditorium of the theatre and its stage reflects their differing heights and takes the form of a gently undulating, grass-covered landscape. This advanced courtyard design can be seen as an expression that seems to herald all sorts of contemporary projects, in the subordinate role it plays in the exterior design of the building it is, on the other hand, unusual and provides food for thought. And to round off the story, it is said that during the first few summers there were sheep grazing on these urban slopes . . .

The supreme virtue

As I write this it strikes me that Nicodemus Tessin and the sincere may not be as incompatible as they may at first seem. In Tessin's project for the palace in Stockholm there are drawings showing what form the Hall of State was to take (carried out by Carl Hårleman, 1698–1752). A longitudinal drawing illustrates how the walls were to be provided with inscriptions. The texts are by Cicero in Latin and have recently been translated into Swedish. The first maxim reads: "The supreme virtue of kings is clemency."[1]

NOTE

1   A quotation from Cicero's *De Officiis*, "Nihil laudabilius nihil magno et praeclaro viro dignius placabilitate et clementia" taken from "Om moralen i Nicodemus Tessin d.y.s byggnadskonst – Några tolkningsalternativ", an unpublished manuscript by Bo Vahlne, Stockholm, 2005.

Epilogue

Wilfried Wang

Between Arrangement *and Subtle Rebellion*

The Creator created paper for drawing on. Everything else is, at least for my part, to misuse paper.[1]

Alvar Aalto's thought summarizes a cultural stance taken by numerous architects, probably widely shared by Nordic architects even today. For Aalto and his Nordic colleagues, buildings embody ideas. Buildings speak for themselves. Buildings speak about the culture in which they have been created. A building is worth a hundred thousand words. Laypeople often find it easier to immediately grasp the significance of a building than many architectural critics, some of whom, it is unfortunately true to say, cannot even read plans.

Some architects hardly published any writings, notably Sigurd Lewerentz. The few words left from his oeuvre are competition mottos that read like philosophical entreaties (for example for the Uppsala Cathedral competition entry the motto was "Reflexion") or the name chosen for his ironmongery company "Idesta" (a common Swedish practice of adapting Latin words for company names), meaning, "it is". The ironmongery is what it is, the name refers to this ontological state, how much more laconic can both the product and the name be. Therefore, why write if what you want to say can be built?

The thoughts on architecture as documented in these selected writings do not stand for the totality of buildings constructed over the last century in the Nordic countries; they do not represent the reality that can be seen there today. Instead, they express the desires and hopes of a group of exceptional architects, who sought to influence the course of production as well as the cultural discourse by their pleas and polemics. Some of these thoughts stand for the dominant discourse; the majority of these texts, however, represent the minuscule group of architects, whose work is much admired today, but who had very little influence on the actual development of building culture throughout their own countries as well as in the Nordic countries as a whole. To state this is a bitter truth, but it is a truth seen through the eyes of history.

From the safe vantage point of hindsight then, the selected texts by architects from the Nordic countries can be characterized as a spectrum of thought and senti-ment encapsulating the complete transformation of a previously agrarian to a post-industrialized landscape and society. These writings range from the lacklustre admission that industrialization would inevitably command all aspects of life to the mere logical, but not emotionally embraced, conclusion that continental European ideas on modern architecture, as specifically summarized by Le Corbusier, were incontrovertible, at least at that moment. To be sure, there were also alternative positions to this embrace of modernism; in these texts we find shades of dissent and voices of subtle rebellion.

However, it is also obvious to state that these fine shades of dissent had little chance to be embraced by a wider audience of architects and planners that had nothing more powerful in their sight than the wholesale replacement of poor and unhealthy inner-city housing, often erected by speculators. The new environment would give rise to a new human being; that was the seemingly unchallengeable credo of the interwar years.[2]

With the flood of images of examples spreading across Europe and the USA, the machine aesthetic coerced some architects into an attitude of *arrangement*, that is to say, grinning and bearing it, and others into a posture of subtle rebellion. Few words summarize this ambiguous attitude towards modernity as well as the title of the manifesto-like publication on the occasion of the 1930 Exhibition in Stockholm: *Acceptera*.[3]

It is as if, and this with the benefit of hindsight, many writings of the interwar period were written with the unexpressed passiveness of fatalism: somehow, the Swedish, Norwegian, Finnish and Danish societies would have to pass through the developmental stages, regardless of their side-effects, in order to reach a purified state of existence: the radiating, white utopia of modern times. It was to be an advanced state of civilization that would promise high levels of quality in architecture and quotidian objects and these in large and affordable numbers. The Nordic countries would no longer be left behind in their agrarian ignorance, but advance to equal the continental European and, indeed, the North American standards of blissful material and cultural surfeit.

The ideas and images published alongside the slogans in the 1930 publication *Acceptera* were similar in contents and purpose to those found across continental European treatises of the early twentieth century. Whether *L'Art et la Société*,[4] *Ins Leere gesprochen*,[5] *Vers une Architecture*,[6] *ABC – Beiträge zum Bauen*,[7] *das neue frankfurt*,[8] *Kritisk Revy*,[9] *ReD (Revue Devetsilu)*,[10] *Russland Europa Amerika*,[11] the plea by Erik Gunnar Asplund and his colleagues to "accept the reality before us – only in this way do we have a chance to master it"[12] echoed the entreating pathos of their predecessors.

Whereas Adolf Loos did not believe that his words and deeds would find a receptive audience (hence his title *Ins Leere gesprochen*, or in English "on deaf ears"), nine years later, people in the Nordic countries were more insistent in their plea for the recognition of reality as the true context in which to set the architectural discourse. By this time, however, the logic of industrialization had already begun to emancipate itself from the cultural strictures of high architecture. A few decades later, industrialization was to become the Saturn that would devour its own children.

Mass housing on the one hand, the sure font of social-democratic policies, and the incessant development of bourgeois houses, the late Palladian, now Corbusian ideal of nuclear-family life in the "countryside" – the euphemism for the suburbs, turned into a sociological disaster. The cultural void that opened as a result of the ubiquitous onslaught of industrialization was already, if one-sidedly, attacked by Oswald Spengler's influential, foreboding book *The Decline of the West* of 1918.[13] Two years later it was potently summarized by William Butler Yeats' poem "The Second Coming":

> Things fall apart; the centre cannot hold;
> Mere anarchy is loosed upon the world,
> The blood-dimmed tide is loosed, and everywhere
> The ceremony of innocence is drowned
> The best lack all conviction, while the worst
> Are full of passionate intensity . . .[14]

The best architects, to paraphrase Yeats, could not convince the majority, while the busybodies perfected technocratic modernism. This paraphrase may not accord with the dominant historiographic reception of Le Corbusier and others, however, if all architectural and urbanistic criticisms, even those of the hallowed Le Corbusier are taken into account, and given the benefit of hindsight once again, there is some legitimacy in paraphrasing Yeats thus. Hindsight has been mentioned a number of times in this context: it is because formalist-modernist rearguard actions have been fought ever since the critique of modernism had become popularized by Robert Venturi and Aldo Rossi in 1966.[15] The criticism of *Modern Times*[16] is of course as old as modernism itself.

Lewis Mumford's *Technics and Civilization* of 1934 sees the state of civilization in balance: he provides dire warnings of the excesses of overbearing mechanization but also combines this with the hope of assimilating the power of the machine so as to enable civilization and technology to develop together towards a more organic and more profoundly human state.[17]

No such hope was given ten years later by Max Horkheimer and Theodor W. Adorno in their essays under the title *Dialectic of the Enlightenment*.[18] They only saw the dark cloud that the resultants of the Enlightenment cast over humanity. Nils Erik Wickberg formulated technology's fall from grace thus:

> The pride which people take, and the explicit belief they have in the unlimited potential of the human intellect, primarily manifested in the triumphs of technology, is beginning to turn into dissatisfaction and fear here in Europe and even in America, since there is now evidence both of how human existence is threatened by mechanization and how, when man gets hold of the instrument of force, it may lead to his own destruction and that of the civilization that he has created.[19]

Wickberg formulated a counterposition to Le Corbusier's "machine for living in": "The home is the last defence against the mechanization of life",[20] the home and its personal contents, as Josef Frank had also contested, was the realm of personal sentiment, a quality that modernist architectural design, with its exclusive emphasis on the quantifiable, was unable to adequately capture. Thus separated from personal desires and aspirations, within functionally segregated modernist culture, isolated aesthetic experiences became easy prey for the aestheticization of politics, now in the guises of the modernist *panem et circenses*.

Thus, similar to Mumford's argument that global war was the logical outcome of uncontrollable (mechanical) forces,[21] Horkheimer and Adorno considered, amongst other issues, the public's mass deception to be the outcome of a perverted cultural industry: the context of this mass deception was the bleak urbanism and grim mass architecture that inevitably forced the public into diversionary entertainment. Horkheimer and Adorno paint this picture right at the beginning of their essay on "Culture Industry": "The palpable unity of macrocosm and microcosm demonstrates to the individual the model of its culture: the false identity of the general as well as the particular."[22] Knut Knutsen said from a holistic point of view some seventeen years later:

> The architecture of the future must create a counterbalance against the monotony of machines. The human being must undergo an apprenticeship in nature. Only people who have studied nature will command machines in such a way that they serve society at large, harmoniously placed in the whole. Only people like that will be protected against the ruinous effects of mass production and against the "mass unemployment" that leisure time is turning out to be.[23]

Commentators from within architecture such as Sigfried Giedion, however, come to the same calculated optimistic conclusion as Mumford. In his post-World War II book *Mechanization Takes Command*,[24] Giedion argues for a dynamic equilibrium between civilization and the environment, the latter being otherwise threatened by an uncontrolled process of mechanization. In the same year of 1948, and along similar lines taken by Spengler, now specifically on issues of art and architecture of the nineteenth and twentieth centuries, Hans Sedlmayr came to a more negative assessment of modernism's effect on civilization,[25] which might best be summarized by Francisco Goya's title of his renowned engraving of 1799 "When reason dreams, monsters are born".

Josef Frank, the Austrian émigré to Sweden, underscored the irrational aspect of rationalization. His refined irony, echoed at the same time by Poul Henningsen's essay on "Tradition and Modernism", offers an immanent criticism of an out-of-control modernity:

> Every day new forms are offered as sacrifices to the machine. As the machine is nothing else but a tool that can do everything, there is no single shape that was invented for it. But with a frightened considerateness for the beloved creature, full of respect not to overwork it in any way, elements such as the straight line, function, simplicity and uniformity are taught with the ulterior motive . . . to return to the same antiquities via the back door. Consider asking one of our modern arts and craftsmen to design the modern shoe. He will have at once grasped the functional shape for the machine. He will take two tubes, the one vertical, the other horizontal. A single shoe for everyone. For the left and for the right foot. Whoever does not fit into them, let him pad them out![26]

Two years earlier, Uno Åhrén had warned in a similar vein:

> In the midst of our delight in what is new we must ensure that we retain our humanity intact. It is somewhat ominous if, like these architects [Åhrén is referring to Le Corbusier] we elevate technical apparatus to the status and dignity of ornamental objects. Strictly speaking it is not so much more appropriate to place chemist's crucibles and the like as ornaments than it was previously to embellish the technical with decorations.[27]

In this critical review of the 1925 Parisian exhibition "Arts décoratifs modernes" Åhrén refers to Asplund's contribution and summarizes the attitude thus: "'Artistic form impressed on practical things without drawing attention to the artistry' – that is where the secret lies."[28] Its "fortunate balance between the rational and irrational, matter-of-factness and imagination" was a credo that inspired numerous "silent" architects.

Modernism, none the less, retained its hypnotic power over most architects up to the late twentieth century, and the dominant attitude amongst the building industry in the Nordic countries was not to be overruled by the odd substantive and critical architects, most of whom are represented here. The positions outlined in these dissenting texts cannot, alas, be taken as representative of the dominant attitudes of Nordic building culture, they stand as minority reports on failed attempts to civilize the technocratic monster. As we review the state of the built environment across the Nordic countries today, this is what we have to recognize: a reality that Asplund and his colleagues would shudder to confront.

All those architects favouring the pre-eminence of function over cultural form, technology over craft, pre-fabrication over small construction companies, flexibility and indeterminacy over generosity, dispassionate professionalism over personal responsibility and so forth can be readily identified in the texts. It is probably not even fair to blame any of these for the current state of the built environment or that of the profession, for most of the time architects would like to consider themselves to be at the forefront of change, only to find out that they are commentators of *tempi passati*.

However, before industrialization, before rationalization, before the Enlightenment even, a greater and more enduring force has been at play, and one that can be linked directly to the instrumental aspect of architecture: the process of autonomization.[29]

If the thesis is correct, that western civilization has over the millennia undergone a process of autonomization, particularly visible in the built environment, then the rationalization and mechanization of all aspects of life, formal abstraction and social alienation are amongst the logical, if not teleological, results.

What is this process of autonomization? It is one in which civilization becomes independent from its context, from nature, from climate, from time, from history, from location and from culture. It is a process that extends to groups within societies; they become autonomous from one another, as do individuals from society as a whole. If there is a justification in referring to the teleology in this process, then it is only for the simple reason that the process of autonomization appears unstoppable, irreversible. Its comprehensiveness affects all segments of civilization, every individual and all interfaces of a natural and artificial kind. It is as if there were an inherent goal to achieve complete freedom of choice over where and when, under which circumstances and for which duration a human activity may or may not take place.[30]

It is in a thankless existence that architecture, not just in the Nordic countries, finds itself today. The process of specialization, of continued division of labour, of increasing losses of spheres of activity for architects,[31] the continued refinement of building tasks, the proliferation of social institutions, the expansion of physical infrastructure and the constant search for marketability and identifiability through formal inventions continue to be the issues on which the process of autonomization still exerts pressure.

Seen in this context, many of the subtle rebellious positions held here by Nordic architects can only be considered quixotic. For those architects, who fully agree with the role of modern architecture as being that of a professional executor or service provider for the needs and requirements by "the client", for whom the building industry standards are unassailable truths, whose formal consequences are unquestioningly enshrined in modernist rationalistic aesthetics, and for whom the word "art" only elicits a raised eyebrow, the text by ELLT of 1967 with the title "Working Principles" will be their manifesto.

The realm of the rational, once established, rules until its final logical, if bitter, conclusion.[32] What began with the call for the acceptance of reality, for the need to be the master of industrialization and mechanization, has turned into a blueprint for corporate and corporatist "culture" (if the term "culture" deserves to be used in this context at all); both forms of professional service distancing themselves from the expressive and identity creating aspects of form while ensuring the lubricated turning of the great wheels of faceless committees.

Within the shades of these corporatist committees, architects would pathetically seek a *raison d'être* for their practice, and thus for themselves. The slogans emerging within the corporatist "culture" were "design as scientific research",[33] "democratic participation",[34] and "structuralist order".[35] None or all of these issues would save architecture from oblivion, for, first, architectural design has always been pursued as its own specific form of research, on this matter, there is little that distinguishes the various scientific or artistic forms of search and research; second, buildings have always – at least until functionalism – been flexible; and third, democratic participation is fine as long as the roles and skills of the participants are openly acknowledged (there is no reason why architects should abrogate their expertise in the context of participatory processes simply for fear of appearing knowledgeable and therefore potentially authoritative).

On the issue of large projects, Arne Jacobsen and Christian Norberg-Schulz would fight against the loss of confidence that politicians began to have *vis-à-vis* commissioning architects to design large complexes such as neighbourhoods or entire new towns. Jacobsen's and Norberg-Schulz's own texts,[36] however, also go some way to explain why politicians mistrusted architects and architectural theoreticians. Norberg-Schulz's explicit criticism of urban sprawl and his attempt to define morphological parameters can, from today's vantage point, only be described as rudimentary. The essay abounds with generalities such as "human scale", wishful thoughts such as "that settlements should be relatively concentrated" and the desirability of neighbourhoods having their own "definite character", without giving a definition for either the morphology of density or character.

It is in the nature of subtle minds that phenomena are judged with precision and gradation. The shades of opposition to the overwhelming chorus for modernism were fragmented, timely and numerous. The quotation from the Danish caricaturist Robert Storm Petersen selected by Knutsen to begin his essay "People in Focus" aptly characterizes this state of affairs: "One thing we agree on – something must be done. But what must be done, we will probably not agree on."

Post-World War II positions in the Nordic countries were equally still under the hegemonic impression of modernism. Peter Celsing, in his inaugural lecture on the transformed conception of space over the course of time at the Royal Institute of Technology in 1960,[37] ventured freely between the fields of art and between different periods, presumably to the amazed shock of some of the audience. Celsing was well informed on contemporary art. He was widely travelled and thus saw many commonly received opinions from other points of view. Ultimately for Celsing "architecture is not a mechanical satisfaction of human needs", but one that values both the collective memory of a society as well as the psychological needs of the individual as contexts within which an architectural design has to arrive at a dignified solution. For Celsing, wherever possible, the architectural design should result from the regional culture, society and climate. Celsing's built work paralleled the written world of Aldo Rossi; the Nordic architect was little publicized, the Italian rose to fame with his eclectic, post-modernist rationalism. While Celsing's architecture sought inclusiveness of human occupation and culture, Rossi's later buildings were three-dimensional images, ideally void of occupation like the haunting paintings by de Chirico.

Knutsen was even more emphatic on this issue. To him, architecture should on the one hand be built for people, not systems, while on the other hand it should respect, and if possible emphasize, the existing landscape, and maybe even form a new landscape. Architects, according to Knutsen, should "have to take into consideration nature and economize with the resources of the world so that things of value are not unnecessarily wasted".[38] Knutsen stressed the temporal and spatial continuity that new buildings should respect:

> We have to stop using architecture as an expression of the thoughts and ideas of the times. New materials should not create new design just like that. The architecture is not there for the sake of the material and should not serve the ideas of the times. It is there for the sake of the unchanging person.[39]

Knutsen's essay of 1961 is one of the most urgent of all texts here for the intensity that it musters. In continental Europe, only one other architect formulated such a position with equal radicality: Hermann Czech. In 1971 Czech wrote: "Architecture is not life. Architecture is background. Everything else is *not* architecture."[40]

Along the same lines, Wenche Selmer's terse note on "Tradition and Distinctiveness" of 1978 reiterates once more the insistence on earnest modesty as Uno Åhrén had outlined over fifty years earlier. In discussing the notion of "adaptation", by which is meant the integration of an architectural design with its context, Selmer suggests that "a subdued form of expression growing out of honesty and sensitivity is not to be disdained".[41] In their thoughts, Knutsen and Selmer urged their colleagues to share these approaches. Both felt responsible for the whole.

Juhani Pallasmaa's thoughts are focused on architecture itself.[42] Were one only to read this text one would suspect that there might have been something untoward prior to its formation. Hardly any comments are passed on the grand themes of the modernist era; all is concentrated on the notion of continuity with culture and architecture's history. The font of knowledge is not constituted by function, programme, new materials, constructional processes, sun, light and air, but by nature, society and the individual's experience.

Novelty for the sake of itself, architecture as spectacle, is the subject of Pallasmaa's attack, itself reminiscent of the early modernists' attack on clamouring historicist architecture of the late nineteenth century. The thrust of his interest, however, is far from the establishment of a new style, of a synthetic recipe for the making of architecture, but the elevation of the roles of time, location, memory and experience through which both the collective as well as the individual should find its specificity again.

From Peter Celsing to Pallasmaa, the subtle rebellion has grown to a fully-fledged alternative position to modernism. The search for styles has disappeared; the urgency for the larger whole to be considered before designing has been brought to the fore. Nature, landscape, the existing built context, distant and close history, culture – broad and specific, resources, climate, collective and individual desires and memories, the personal inspiration of the architect, imagination, are all subjects of the broader context in which those alternative voices would have us work as architects. What can be unearthed in the nooks of early twentieth-century writings has surfaced to the visible discourse. These voices have not reached the degree of dominance of the early modernists, for that they are too distinct and varied. Perhaps it is time to relinquish the desire to synchronize the actions of individuals and to have confidence in the ability of each architect to discern the necessary things that need to be done.

Perhaps – no, surely – the reader of these essays will weave another texture and, perhaps, on further reflection and writing, or even building, a contribution to a change in course will take place; this time, without the empty promises, cold rationalism and excessive hubris: "Artistic form impressed on practical things without drawing attention to the artistry."

NOTES

1   Alvar Aalto, "Instead of an Article" in *Arkkhitehti*, 1958; republished in Göran Schildt (ed.), *Sketches: Alvar Aalto*, Cambridge MA: MIT Press, 1978, p. 160.

2   See for instance the much publicized housing projects in Germany: Berlin under the guidance of Martin Wagner from 1925–35, Frankfurt am Main under the leadership of Ernst May from 1925–30, and Karlsruhe-Dammerstock, first phase 1928–29.

3   Gunnar Asplund *et al.*, *Acceptera*, Stockholm: Tiden, 1931. English translation in Lucy Creagh, Helena Kåberg and Barbara Miller Lane (eds), *Modern Swedish Design: Founding Texts*, New York: Museum of Modern Art, forthcoming, 2008.

4   Hendrik Petrus Berlage, Brussels: Èditons Tekhné, 1914.

5   Adolf Loos, Paris: Éditions Crès, 1921.

6   Le Corbusier, Paris: Éditions Crès, 1923.

7   Editors Emil Roth, Hans Schmidt and Mart Stam, Basel: Thalwil, 1924–28.

8   Editor Joseph Gantner, Frankfurt am Main: die neue stadt, 1926–33.

9   Editor Poul Henningsen, Copenhagen 1926–28.

10 Editors Jaroslav Seifert, Karel Teige, Prague: Odeon, 1927–31.

11 Erich Mendelsohn, Berlin: Rudolf Mosse Buchverlag, 1929.

12 Asplund et al., *Acceptera*; reprint, Ärlöv: Berlings, 1980, p. 198.

13 Oswald Spengler, *The Decline of the West*, original German title *Der Untergang des Abendlandes: Umrisse einer Morphologie der Weltgeschichte*, first published Munich: C.H. Beck Verlag, 1918. Nils Ahrbohm's essay "Spatial design: Philosophy or Architecture?" touches on this "missing link" between tradition and functionalism.

14 William Butler Yeats, "The Second Coming", *The Dial; a Semi-monthly Journal of Literary Criticism, Discussion and Information* 69, Nov. 1920, p. 466.

15 Robert Venturi, *Complexity and Contradiction in Architecture*, New York: The Museum of Modern Art Press, 1966; and Aldo Rossi: *L'architettura della città*, Padua: Marsilio, 1966.

16 The celebrated early popular critique of industrialization and rationalization by Charlie Chaplin's film created between 1933–36 (United Artists) marks a high point in the widespread awareness in industrializing societies.

17 Lewis Mumford, *Technics and Civilization*, New York: Harcourt, Brace & World, Inc., 1934, p. 363.

18 Max Horkheimer and Theodor Wiesengrund Adorno, "Dialektik der Aufklärung" in *Philosophische Fragmente*, New York: Social Studies Association, Inc., 1944, first English trans. as *Dialectic of the Enlightenment*, New York: Herder & Herder, 1972.

19 Nils Erik Wickberg, *Försök över Arkitektur*, Helsinki: Söderström & Co, 1963, pp. 12–13.

20 Nils Erik Wickberg, "Thoughts on Architecture".

21 Mumford, *Technics and Civilization*, pp. 307–11.

22 Horkheimer and Adorno, "Dialektik der Aufklärung", Frankfurt am Main: Fischer Verlag, 1969, p. 108.

23 Knut Knutsen, "People in Focus".

24 Sigfried Giedion, *Mechanization takes Command: A Contribution to Anonymous History*, New York: Oxford University Press, 1948.

25 Hans Sedlmayr, *Verlust der Mitte: Die bildende Kunst des 19. und 20. Jahrhunderts als Bild der Zeit*, Salzburg: Müller Verlag, 1948, trans. into English as *Art In Crisis: The Lost Center*, Chicago, IL: H. Regnery Co., 1958.

26 Josef Frank, "Der Gschnas fürs G'müt und der Gschnas als Problem" in *Bau und Wohnung*, Weissenhofsiedlung Stuttgart: Stuttgart, 1927, pp. 56–57; trans. in 9H 3, London: 9H Publications, 1982, p. 6. Considering the content of Frank's criticism, this was a direct attack on the conceptual premise of those modern architects who had enslaved themselves to the logic of industry.

27 Uno Åhrén, "Turning Points".

28 Åhrén, "Turning Points".

29 See the "Introductory Essay" by the author in *World Architecture: A Critical Mosaic 1900–2000, Vol. 3 Northern Europe, Central Europe, Western Europe*, Beijing: China Architecture & Building Press, Springer, 2000, pp.xvii–xxix.

30 Take the development of the theatre for instance. During Greek antiquity the theatre was ideally embedded in adapted natural topography; the Romans sought freedom from suitable natural sites and constructed freestanding theatres for which they now invented façades. Vela protected the audience from sunshine; evaporative cooling, even perfumes were used to increase the audience's comfort. During the Renaissance artificial lighting became a topic of innovation; artificial ventilation was perfected during the early nineteenth century; the black box was the penultimate state of the modern theatre in the late twentieth century until directors decided that performances in disused factories allowed them the greatest liberty in their theatrical productions: away with bourgeois architecture! Away even with black boxes whose aesthetic pretends freedom, but in the end only restricts in a costly way! Architecture, once the handmaiden of progress for this building type, at the end of the twentieth century, found itself thanklessly eliminated from this task.

31 Interior, furniture and lighting designers, services engineers, environmental control engineers, structural engineers, façade engineers, landscape architects, project managers, contract managers, site managers, clerk of works, building permit consultants, conservation consultants, public relations agents et al.

32 PLAN, "Our Agenda". Besides the critique of the "humanists/culturalists" of the excesses of the

new international movement, there were the fundamentalist moderns as exemplified by the programme of the Association of Socialist Architects in Norway. Their critique of Le Corbusier follows
in the wake of Karel Teige's 1929 attack on Le Corbusier's Mundaneum project, accusing Le Corbusier of becoming formalist. Teige and Hannes Meyer were close friends; PLAN's attitude towards
the creative aspects of architecture was equally nihilistic as those of Hannes Meyer. In 1933, PLAN
believes that "the idiom of form itself is no longer what is primary. The design of buildings
emerges, conversely, as an end result of competent, professional work in the service of housing
design."

33   Leif Reinius, "Architectural Experiments" and PAGON, "CIAM".
34   Tegnestuen Vandkunsten, "It Can Be Done!"
35   Kjell Lund, "Structuralistic Architecture".
36   Arne Jacobsen, "Contemporary Form and Design" and Christian Norberg-Schulz, "Order and
     Variation in the Environment".
37   Peter Celsing, "About Space".
38   Knutsen, "People in Focus".
39   Knutsen, "People in Focus"
40   Hermann Czech, "Nur keine Panik", in *Zur Abwechslung*, Vienna, Löcker & Wögenstein, 1978, p. 67
41   Selmer, " Tradition and Distinctiveness".
42   Juhani Pallasmaa, "Space, Place, Memory and Imagination".

Text sources

The texts are published by courtesy of the authors (or the authors' descendents) and the previous publishers.

All translations by Pete Avondoglio, Tim Challman, Layla Dawson, David Jones, Dan Marmorstein, Nicholas Mayow and Margo Øhrn are copyright © Routledge, 2008.

Alvar Aalto (1898–1976), "Research for Reconstruction. Rehousing research in Finland", *Journal of the Royal Institute of British Architects*, 17 March 1941, pp. 78–83. Publisher: RIBA Journal, www.ribajournal.com.

Nils Ahrbom (1905–97), "Rumgestaltning – Filosofi eller Arkitektur" (1945), *Byggmästaren* 5, 1946, pp. 73–80, translated by David Jones. Publisher: The Swedish Review of Architecture.

Uno Åhrén (1897–1977), "Brytningar", *Svenska Slöjdföreningens Årsskrift 1925*, 1925, pp. 7–36, translated by David Jones.

Stefan Alenius (1944–), Jan Angbjär (1940–) and Magnus Silfverhielm (1945–), "Manerismer eller vad gör vi med vårt funktionalistiska arv", *Arkitektur* 5, 1978, pp. 3–11, translated by David Jones. Publisher: The Swedish Review of Architecture.

Erik Gunnar Asplund (1885–1940), "Vår Arkitektoniska Rumsuppfattning", *Byggmästaren*, 1931, pp. 203–10, translated by David Jones. Publisher: The Swedish Review of Architecture.

Aulis Blomstedt (1906–79), "Arkkitehtonisen muodon ongelma", *Arkkitehti* (*The Finnish Architectural Review*) 12, 1958, pp. 200–202, translated by Nicholas Mayow.

Johan Celsing (1955–), "The Robust, the Sincere", previously unpublished, translated by David Jones.

Peter Celsing (1920–74), "Om rummet" (1960), in A.-M. Ericsson *et al.*: *Peter Celsing. En bok om en arkitekt och hans verk*, Stockholm, Arkitekturmuseet and Liber Forlag, 1980, pp. 118–23, translated by Kerstin Beyer Lajuzan. Publisher: The Swedish Museum of Architecture.

Johan Ellefsen (1895–1969), "Hvad er tidsmessig arkitektur?", *Byggekunst*, November 1927, pp. 161–70, translated by Tim Challman.

ELLT (Alf Engström, Gunnar Landberg, Bengt Larsson and Alvar Törneman), "Arbetsprinciper", *Arkkitehti* (*The Finnish Architectural Review*) 5, 1967, pp. 4–7, translated by David Jones.

Ralph Erskine (1914–2005), "The Challenge of the High Latitudes" (1963), *Royal Architectural Institute of Canada Journal* (January, 1964) pp. 33–41. Publisher: The Royal Architectural Institute of Canada.

Kay Fisker (1893–1965), "Funktionalismens Moral", *A5* 4, 1947, pp. 7–14, republished as "The Moral of Functionalism", *Magazine of Art* 2, 1950, pp. 62–67.

Poul Henningsen (1894–1967), "Tradition og Modernisme", *Kritisk Revy* 3, 1927, pp. 30–46, translated by Pete Avondoglio.

Arne Jacobsen (1902–71), "Über Form und Gestaltung in der Gegenwart" (speech on the occasion of his accepting the Fritz Schumacher Prize, 6 December 1963), previously unpublished, translated by Layla Dawson.

Jan Olav Jensen (1959–), "Affinity", previously unpublished, translated by Margo Øhrn.

Knut Knutsen (1903–69), "Mennesket i Sentrum", *Byggekunst* 4, 1961, pp. 129–31, translated by Margo Øhrn.

Markku Komonen (1945–), "Rakentamisen tekniikka ja taide", *Arkkitehti (The Finnish Architectural Review)* 4, 1995, pp. 92–93, translated by Nicholas Mayow.

Osmo Lappo (1927–), "The Need for Flexibility – A problem of modern architecture" (1967), *Arkkitehti (The Finnish Architectural Review)* 1, 1968, pp. 17–19.

Henning Larsen (1925–), "Danish Architecture" in *Politiken*, 24 November 1987, translated by Pete Avondoglio.

Kjell Lund (1927–), "Strukturalistisk Arkitektur – fanget eller fri?", *Byggekunst* 2, 1983, pp. 66; translated on behalf of Kjell Lund, republished as "Structuralistic Architecture. Strapped or Free?", *Le Carré Bleu* 3, 1984, pp. 45–46.

Boje Lundgaard (1943–2004), "Byggeteknikkens Krise", *Arkitekten* 12, 1992, pp. 334–42, translated by Dan Marmorstein.

Kirmo Mikkola (1934–86), "Architecture: Its ideals and reality", *Arkkitehti (The Finnish Architectural Review)* 8, 1974, pp. 53–54.

Christian Norberg-Schulz (1926–2000), "Orden og Variasjon i Omgivelsene", *Byggekunst* 2, 1966, pp. 45–52, translated by Margo Øhrn.

PAGON (Arne Korsmo, Carl Corwin, Robert C. Esdaile, Sverre Fehn, Geir Grung, P.A.M. Mellbye, Håkon Mjelva, Christian Norberg-Schulz, Erik Rolfsen, Odd Østbye and Jørn Utzon), "CIAM", *Byggekunst* 6–7, 1952, pp. 93, 108–12, translated by Tim Challman.

Juhani Pallasmaa (1936–), "Space, Place, Memory and Imagination. The temporal dimension of existential space" (based on lecture given at the University of California, 9 March 2007), previously unpublished.

Reima Pietilä (1923–93), "Arkkitehtuuri ja teknokulttuurin maailma" (1973), *Arkkitehti (The Finnish Architectural Review)* 1, 1974, pp. 66–67, translated by Nicholas Mayow.

PLAN (Association of Socialist Architects), "Vårt Program" in Carsten Boysen (1906–96) *et al.* (eds), *PLAN* 1, February 1933, pp. 1–8, translated by Tim Challman.

Steen Eiler Rasmussen (1898–1990), "De første oplevelser", in *Om at Opleve Arkitektur* (1957), republished in *Experiencing Architecture*, 2nd edn, pp. 9–34, © 1959 Massachusetts Institute of Technology, by permission of The MIT Press.

Leif Reinius (1907–95), "Arkitekturförsök", *Prisma*, 1948, pp. 62–66, translated by David Jones.

Eliel Saarinen (1873–1950), "Address of Eliel Saarinen", *The Octagon. A journal of the A.I.A.*, April 1931, pp. 6–13. Publisher: The American Institute of Architects, 1735 New York Avenue, NW, Washington, DC 20007.

Wenche Selmer (1920–98), "Tradisjon og Egenart", *Fortidsvern* 4, 1978, pp. 20–22, translated by Margo Øhrn. Publisher: Fortidsminneforeningen (The Society for the Preservation of Norwegian Ancient Monuments).

Erik Christian Sørensen (1922–), "On Form" and "In Space", *Arkitekten*, 1957, pp. 161–72, 201–203.

Jørn Utzon (1918–), "Platforms and Plateaus. Ideas of a Danish Architect", *Zodiac* 10, 1962, pp. 114–17.

Tegnestuen Vandkunsten (Sven Algren, Tony Andersen, Jens Thomas Arnfred, Michael Sten Johnsen, Hans Jørgen Kløvedal and Steffen Kragh), "Det ka' la' sig gøre!", *Arkitekten* 11, 1974, pp. 217–31, translated by Pete Avondoglio.

Håkon Vigsnæs (1962–), "Er eneboligen interessant sett fra utsiden av hekken?", *Byggekunst* 8, 2004, pp. 16–20, translated by Margo Øhrn.

Nils Erik Wickberg (1909–2002), "Tankar om Arkitektur", *Finsk Tidskrift* 2, 1943, pp. 79–91; republished as "Thoughts on Architecture" in *Abacus* 3, Helsinki: Museum of Finnish Architecture, 1983, pp. 143–58.

The texts have been edited for clarity and length.

Andersen's essay was translated by Pete Avondoglio, Harlang's essay by Dan Marmorstein, Mårtelius's essay by David Jones, Tostrup's essay by Margo Øhrn and Vartola's essay by Nicholas Mayow.

The editor would like to thank Christoffer Harlang, Esa Laaksonen, Johan Mårtelius, Elisabeth Tostrup and Anni Vartola for contributing to the selection of texts.

Illustration sources

Page x, rendering and permission by Steven Holl Architects.

Page xi, photo and permission by Paul Warchol Photography Inc.

Pages 18 and 34, permission by Danish National Art Library, Architectural Drawings Collection.

Page 40, photo and permission by Jens Frederiksen.

Page 50, photo and permission by Finn Christoffersen.

Page 62, permission by Government Printing Office Collection, State Library of New South Wales.

Page 66, photo and permission by Strüwing.

Page 72, permission by Tegnestuen Vandkunsten.

Page 86, photo by Richard Bryant, permission by Henning Larsen Architects.

Page 92, permission by Lundgaard & Tranberg Architects.

Pages 116, 138 and 160, owner of the pictures: Museum of Finnish Architecture.

Page 126, photo by Kari Hakli, Alvar Aalto Museum, permission by Kari Hakli.

Page 131, permission by Alvar Aalto Foundation.

Pages 148, 174, 176 and 180, photos by Pietinen, owner of the pictures: Museum of Finnish Architecture.

Pages 154 and 181, photos by Simo Rista, owner of the pictures: Museum of Finnish Architecture.

Page 158, © Ezra Stoller/IPNSTOCK.

Pages 162 and 179, photos by Martti I. Jaatinen, owner of the pictures: Museum of Finnish Architecture.

Page 170, photo by Karno Mikkola, owner of the picture: Museum of Finnish Architecture.

Page 173, photo by Heikki Havas, owner of the picture: Museum of Finnish Architecture.

Page 175, photo by Heinrich Heidersberger, Alvar Aalto Museum, permission by Alvar Aalto Foundation.

Page 178, photo by Pertti Ingervo, owner of the picture: Museum of Finnish Architecture.

Page 182, photo by Jussi Tiainen, permission by Heikkinen-Komonen Architects.

Page 188, photo by Rauno Träskelin, permission by Juhani Pallasmaa.

Page 195, photo and permission by Suomen Ilmakuva Oy.

Page 196, photo and permission by Paula Patterson.

Page 199, "Frau am Fenster" by Caspar David Friedrich, © Bildarchiv Preußischer Kulturbesitz, 2007; Nationalgalerie, Staatliche Museen zu Berlin, Photo: Jörg P. Anders.

Pages 214, 272 and 286, photos by Jiri Havran, permission by The National Museum of Art, Architecture and Design, Architectural Collections, Norway.

Page 226, permission by Magnus Boysen.

Page 238, photo by Guillemot, permission by The National Museum of Art, Architecture and Design, Architectural Collections, Norway.

Page 243, permission by The National Museum of Art, Architecture and Design, Architectural Collections, Norway.

Page 248, photo and permission by Are Carlsen.

Page 254, photo by Christian Norberg-Schulz, permission by Anna Maria Norberg-Schulz.

Page 268, photo by Frode Larsen, permission by Gaidaros Forlag. Previously published in Elisabeth Tostrup, *Norwegian Wood*, New York: Princeton Architectural Press, 2006, p. 78.

Pages 276, 278, 279, 280 and 281, photos and permission by Nils Petter Dale.

Pages 288, 289, 291, 293 and 294, photos by Jan Olav Jensen, permission by Jensen & Skodvin Architects.

Pages 310, 334, 360 and 372, photos by Okänd, permission by The Swedish Museum of Architecture.

Page 324, photo by C.G. Rosenberg, permission by The Swedish Museum of Architecture.

Pages 342, 364, 365, 367 and 398, permission by The Swedish Museum of Architecture.

Page 348, photo by Yngve Andersson, permission by The Swedish Museum of Architecture.

Pages 352 and 369, photos by Sune Sundahl, permission by The Swedish Museum of Architecture.

Page 354, photo by Max Plunger, permission by The Swedish Museum of Architecture.

Page 378, permission by Stefan Alenius.

Page 390, photo by Fabio Galli, permission by Johan Celsing.

Page 394, photo by Zoltan Gavai, permission by Johan Celsing.

Page 396, photo by Sven Etzler, permission by Johan Celsing.

Page 397, photo and permission by Fabio Galli.

Index